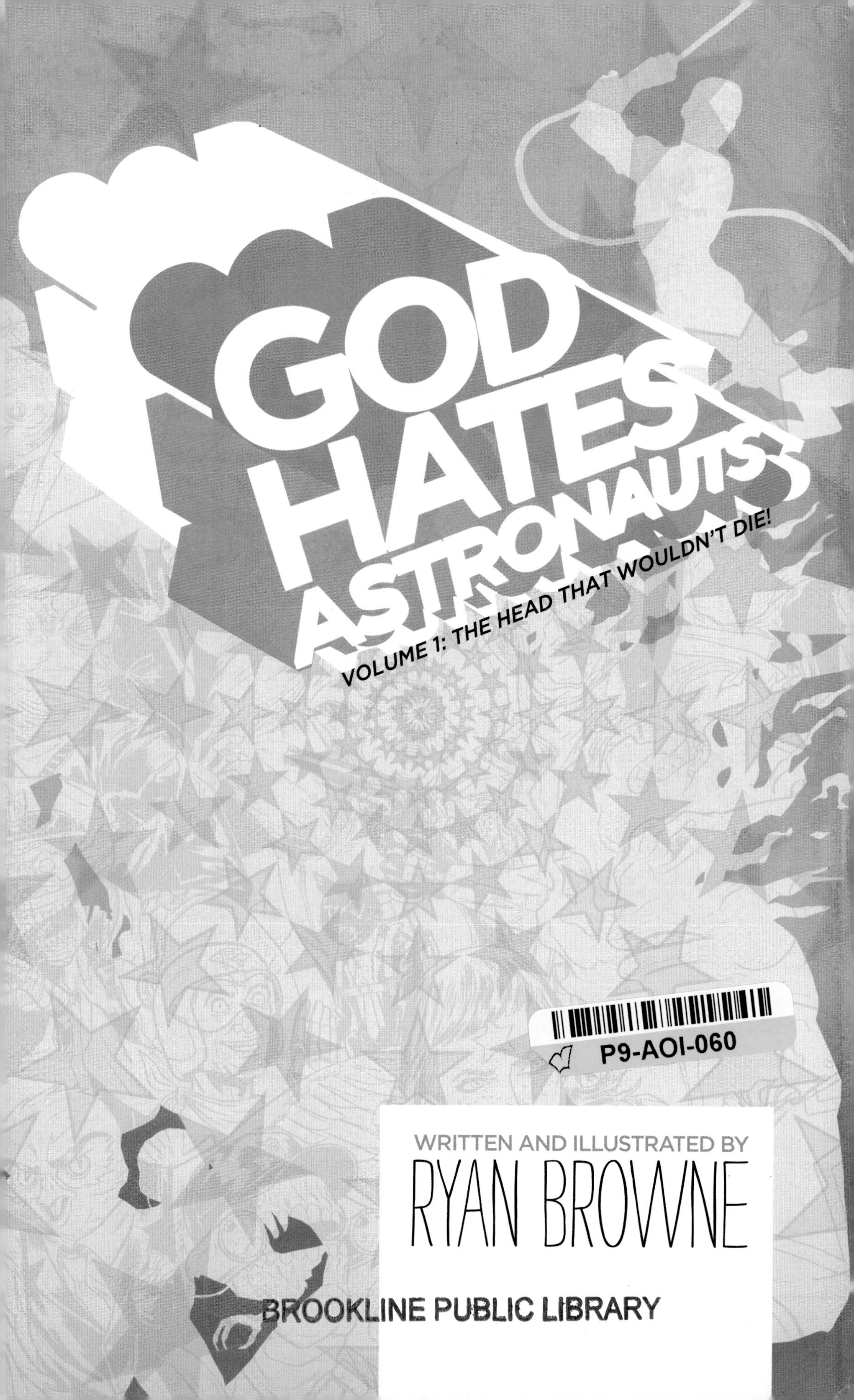
GOD HATES ASTRONAUTS
VOLUME 1: THE HEAD THAT WOULDN'T DIE!
WRITTEN AND ILLUSTRATED BY
RYAN BROWNE

INTRODUCTION!!!

I met Ryan Browne a few years ago at the Chicago Comic-Con (A.K.A. Wizard World) where he was showing the first issue of God Hates Astronauts around. Here's the email I sent him about it:

"God LOVES Astronauts!!!

Holy shitballs! That book is fucking bonkers! Admiral Tiger Eating a Cheeseburger is the new black.

We met at the Chicago Comic-Con a couple of weeks ago. I'm the guy that drew Officer Downe... your buddy who writes Transformers or something was there.

Please do me and the universe a favor and get yourself addicted to those pills that truckers take so they never need to sleep. Only with you pulling a 168-hour workweek will I ever get enough of this crazy nonsense.

I think you said that you drew the first issue three years ago. If you make me wait three years for the next issue I will peel the skin off your face so you'll be too ashamed to go out in public... and you'll have no choice but to draw comics all day long. (Peeling your skin off somehow made me win the lottery so I could pay your rent. Try it with your neighbor's kids!)

-CHRIS"

We got to be pretty fast friends after that. I spread the news about God Hates Astronauts, I invited him to a weekly drink and draw, I got him a seat at a local comic store's sold-out 24-Hour Comic Day, and I got him invited to a secret comic pro message board where he met most of the artists who drew the amazing short origin stories at the back of the book. If it sounds like I'm taking credit for his hard work, GOOD! I need all the help I can get! When this book makes him a kabillion dollars, I need each and every one of you to make him feel guilty for banning me from his platinum swimming pool. Urine is sterile, goddamnit!

But before we start spending the money that Ryan so richly deserves, let's do a little expectation management. God Hates Astronauts is not the best comic you'll ever read. Nor is it the funniest, most exciting, or the best drawn. But despite having absolutely nothing to do with any deity's distaste for space travel, it is absolutely the GodHatesAstronauts-iest.

That might be a little wonkily tautological (look it up, it's a good one), but I stand by it. I've spent the last two years drawing Batman comics that aren't perceived as being particularly Batmanny. And I dunno about you, but I thought the ending of that last James Bond movie was downright Three Amigish. You're not going to have that problem here. This book is a creation unto itself. Suis generis. The sort of thing you'd like if you like that sort of thing.

None of which is to say that this comic is a work of high art or meaningful in any way. This trash is as inane as it gets. Low brow? No brow! A real gold-plated, kernel-packed turd. Hell, if there were any justice in the world, God Hates Astronauts would be printed on soiled condoms. How's THAT for a stretch goal?

Anyhow. It's pretty good, I like it a lot, and I think you will too.

...

I WAS LYING BEFORE, BY THE WAY. GOD HATES ASTRONAUTS IS THE BEST COMIC YOU'LL EVER READ.

CHRIS BURNHAM
CHICAGO, ILLINOIS
JANUARY, 2013

SUGGESTED VOICE TALENT
(IN ORDER OF APPEARANCE)

STAR FIGHTER: *JOHN C. REILLY*
STARRIOR: *MAGGIE GYLLENHAAL*
THE ANTI-MUGGER: *BURT REYNOLDS*
THE IMPOSSIBLE: *FAST FOOD SPEAKER*
CRAYMOK: *RIP TORN*
JOHN L. SULLIVAN: *HIMSELF*
DR. PROFESSOR: *DEAN STOCKWELL*
TEXAS TOM: *WALTON GOGGINS*
BLUE GRASS: *A COW*
MONTEL WILLIAMS: *MONTEL WILLIAMS*
THE BEAR HIGH WIZARD: *THE BEAR WHO PLAYED CHEWBACCA*

PAUL BLORT: *SIR LAURENCE OLIVIER*
OWL CAPONE: *AL CAPONE*
OWLVIN: *SKEET ULRICH*
OWL WITH CROSSBOW: *JEFF BRIDGES*
STAR GRASS: *JOHN C. REILLY DOING A COW IMPRESSION*
ADMIRAL TIGER EATING A CHEESEBURGER: *ROBERT DENIRO*
MR. CRABTREE: *DWAYNE "THE ROCK" JOHNSON*
ZOMBIE JOHN L. SULLIVAN: *MUMM-RA*
HOBBS: *REGINALD VELJOHNSON*
MONKEY ALAN: *MCKENZIE CROOK*
RAWHIDE THE SEAHORSE: *BILL LAIMBEER*
HARRYET WINSLOW: *JO MARIE PAYTON*
KARUHL/GNARLED WINSLOW: *WENDELL PIERCE*
REED SPACER: *CRISPIN GLOVER AS GEORGE MCFLY*
CRAZY TRAIN: *DAME JUDI DENCH*

THAT LITTLE DUDE ON THE COVER OF ISSUE 3: *THE "TOASTY" GUY*
PANDOR: *HARRY DEAN STANTON*
KING TIGER EATING A CHEESEBURGER: *JAMES EARL JONES*
JUDGE BUFFALO WILLIAM: *JEFFREY JONES*
MUMMY BAILIFF: *LARRY MILLER*
WALTER SKULLMEN: *JESSIE "THE BODY" VENTURA*
SIMON THE CAT LAWYER: *MICHAEL CERA*
HUGH MANATEE: *SAM MACMURRAY*
STAR BEARS: *WINSTON CHURCHILL*
SIR HIPPOTHESIS: *JOHN CLEESE*
THE ASTRONAUT CENTAURS: *JOHN HALL & DARYL OATES*
RUPERT: *BRAD PITT*
SUPER SULLIVAN: *SUPER SHREDDER*

Uhhh so this is in no way any sort of celebrity endorsement and no actual
celebrities have anything to do with this book... it's just supposed to be funny.

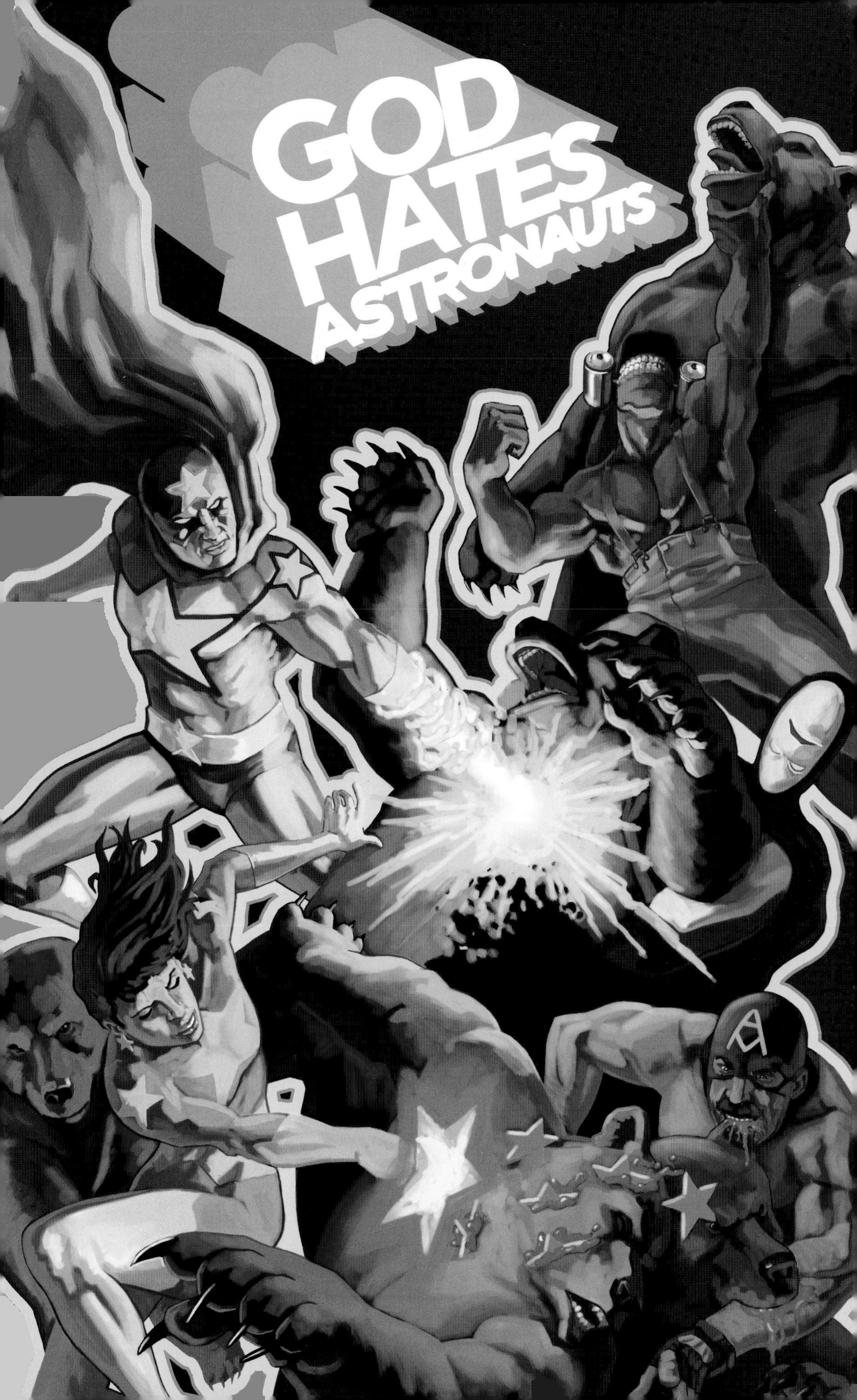
GOD
HATES
ASTRONAUTS

BOSTON MASSACHUSETTS

THE GYM OF JOHN L. SULLIVAN, WORLD HEAVYWEIGHT CHAMP 1882-1892.

PUGILIST EXTRAORDINAIRE.

TOTAL DICK.

DEATH TO THE WEAK! SHOW NO MERCY!

DESTROY ALL OPPOSITION LESS YE' BE DESTROYED!

THOSE WHOM COUNTED OUT THE GREAT JOHN L. SULLIVAN WILL BE MADE TO PAY!

CHUT!

FLAK!

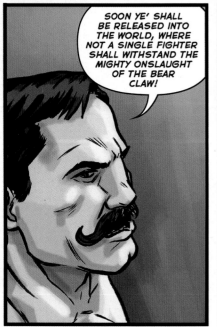

SOON YE' SHALL BE RELEASED INTO THE WORLD, WHERE NOT A SINGLE FIGHTER SHALL WITHSTAND THE MIGHTY ONSLAUGHT OF THE BEAR CLAW!

WITH ALL OF MY ENEMIES DEFEATED, I SHALL RECLAIM THE WORLD HEAVY WEIGHT TITLE!

HONEY WILL FLOW LIKE WATER, AND SALMON WILL LEAP INTO YOUR JAWS!

WE SHALL LIVE AS KINGS! THERE IS NO ONE ALIVE WHO CAN POSSIBLY STOP MY DESTI--

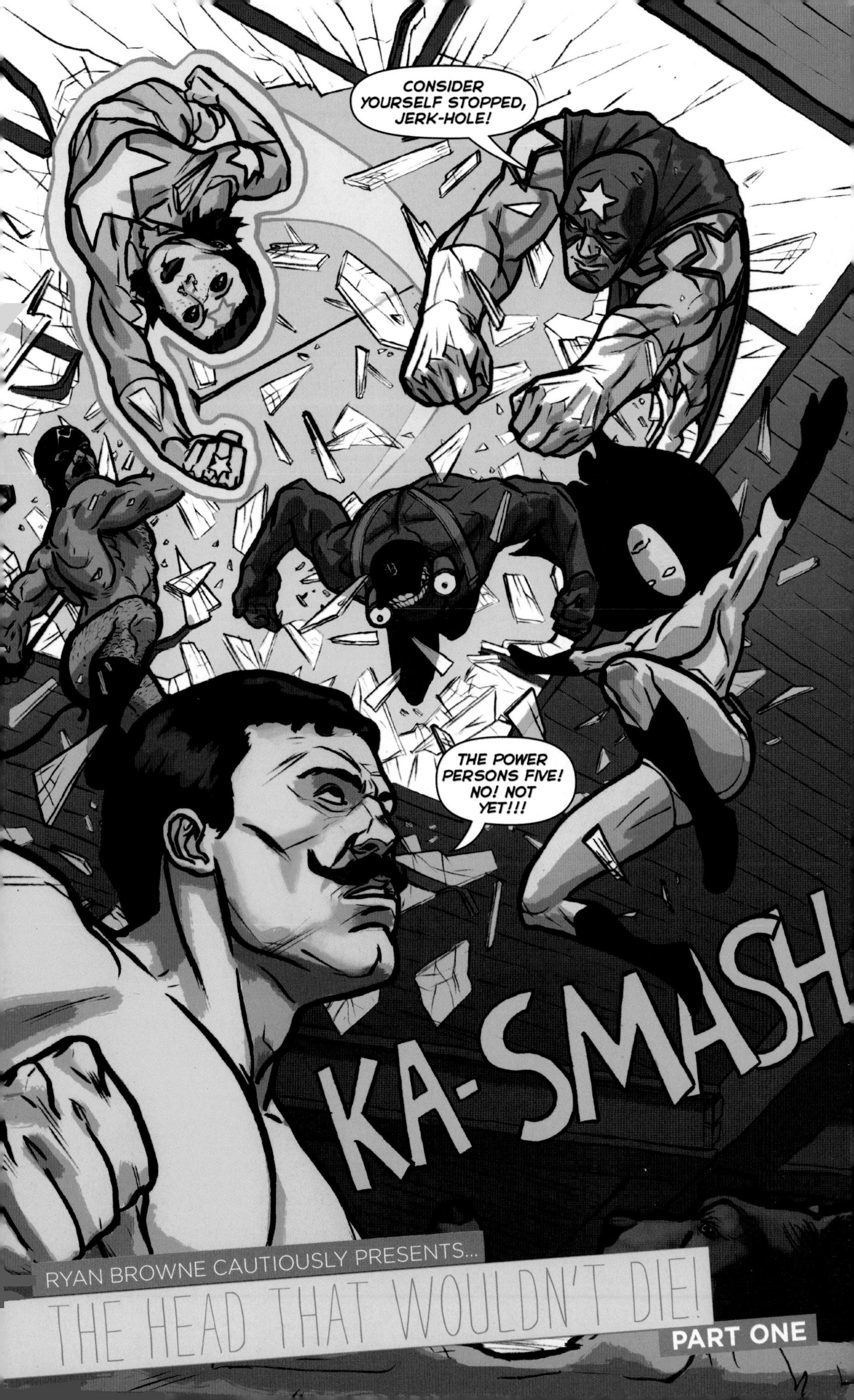
CONSIDER YOURSELF STOPPED, JERK-HOLE!
THE POWER PERSONS FIVE! NO! NOT YET!!!
KA-SMASH
RYAN BROWNE CAUTIOUSLY PRESENTS...
THE HEAD THAT WOULDN'T DIE!
PART ONE

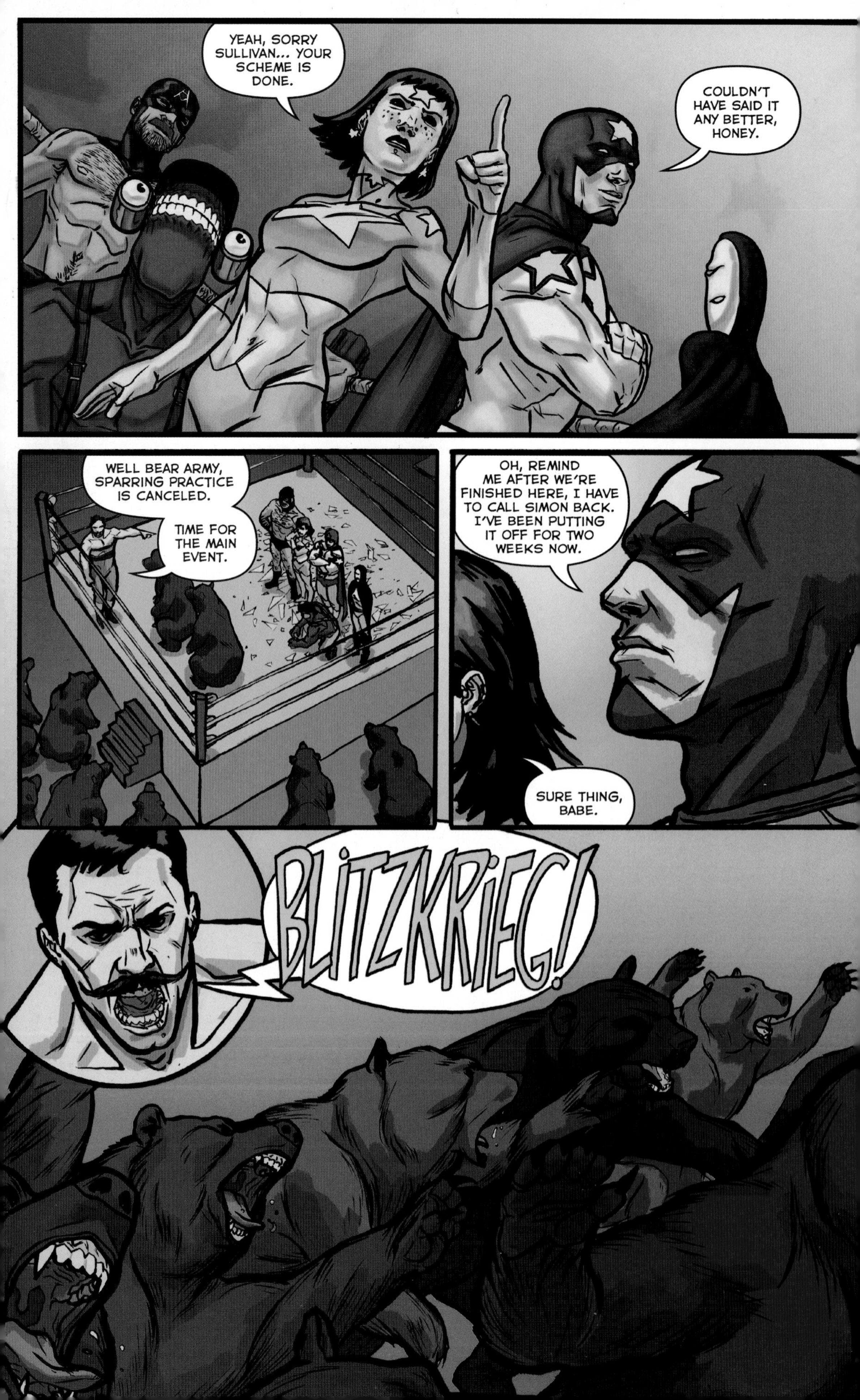
YEAH, SORRY SULLIVAN... YOUR SCHEME IS DONE.
COULDN'T HAVE SAID IT ANY BETTER, HONEY.
WELL BEAR ARMY, SPARRING PRACTICE IS CANCELED.
TIME FOR THE MAIN EVENT.
OH, REMIND ME AFTER WE'RE FINISHED HERE, I HAVE TO CALL SIMON BACK. I'VE BEEN PUTTING IT OFF FOR TWO WEEKS NOW.
SURE THING, BABE.
BLITZKRIEG!

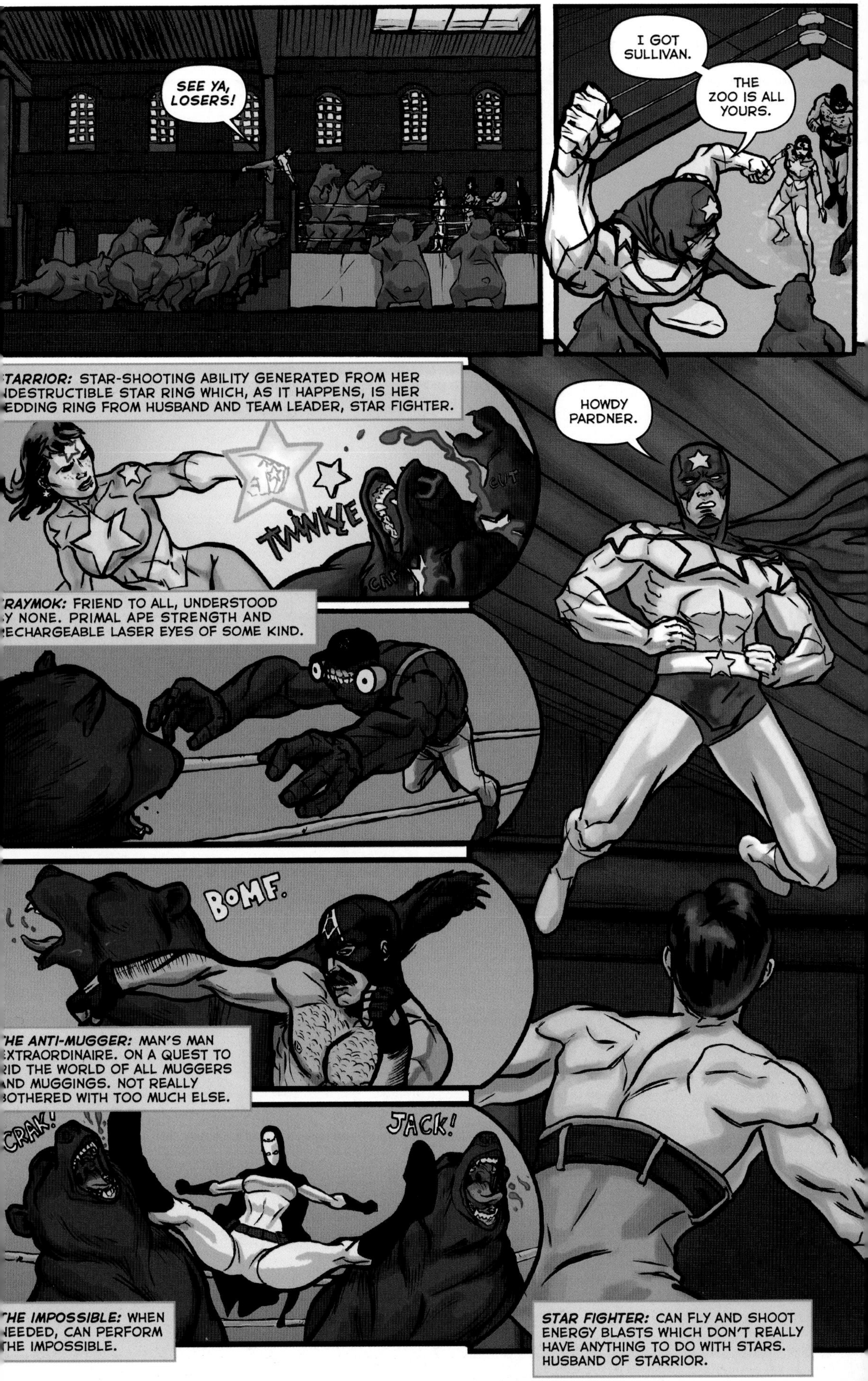
SEE YA, LOSERS!
I GOT SULLIVAN.
THE ZOO IS ALL YOURS.
TARRIOR: STAR-SHOOTING ABILITY GENERATED FROM HER NDESTRUCTIBLE STAR RING WHICH, AS IT HAPPENS, IS HER EDDING RING FROM HUSBAND AND TEAM LEADER, STAR FIGHTER.
TWINKLE
HOWDY PARDNER.
RAYMOK: FRIEND TO ALL, UNDERSTOOD Y NONE. PRIMAL APE STRENGTH AND ECHARGEABLE LASER EYES OF SOME KIND.
BOMF.
THE ANTI-MUGGER: MAN'S MAN EXTRAORDINAIRE. ON A QUEST TO RID THE WORLD OF ALL MUGGERS ND MUGGINGS. NOT REALLY BOTHERED WITH TOO MUCH ELSE.
CRAK!
JACK!
THE IMPOSSIBLE: WHEN NEEDED, CAN PERFORM THE IMPOSSIBLE.
STAR FIGHTER: CAN FLY AND SHOOT ENERGY BLASTS WHICH DON'T REALLY HAVE ANYTHING TO DO WITH STARS. HUSBAND OF STARRIOR.

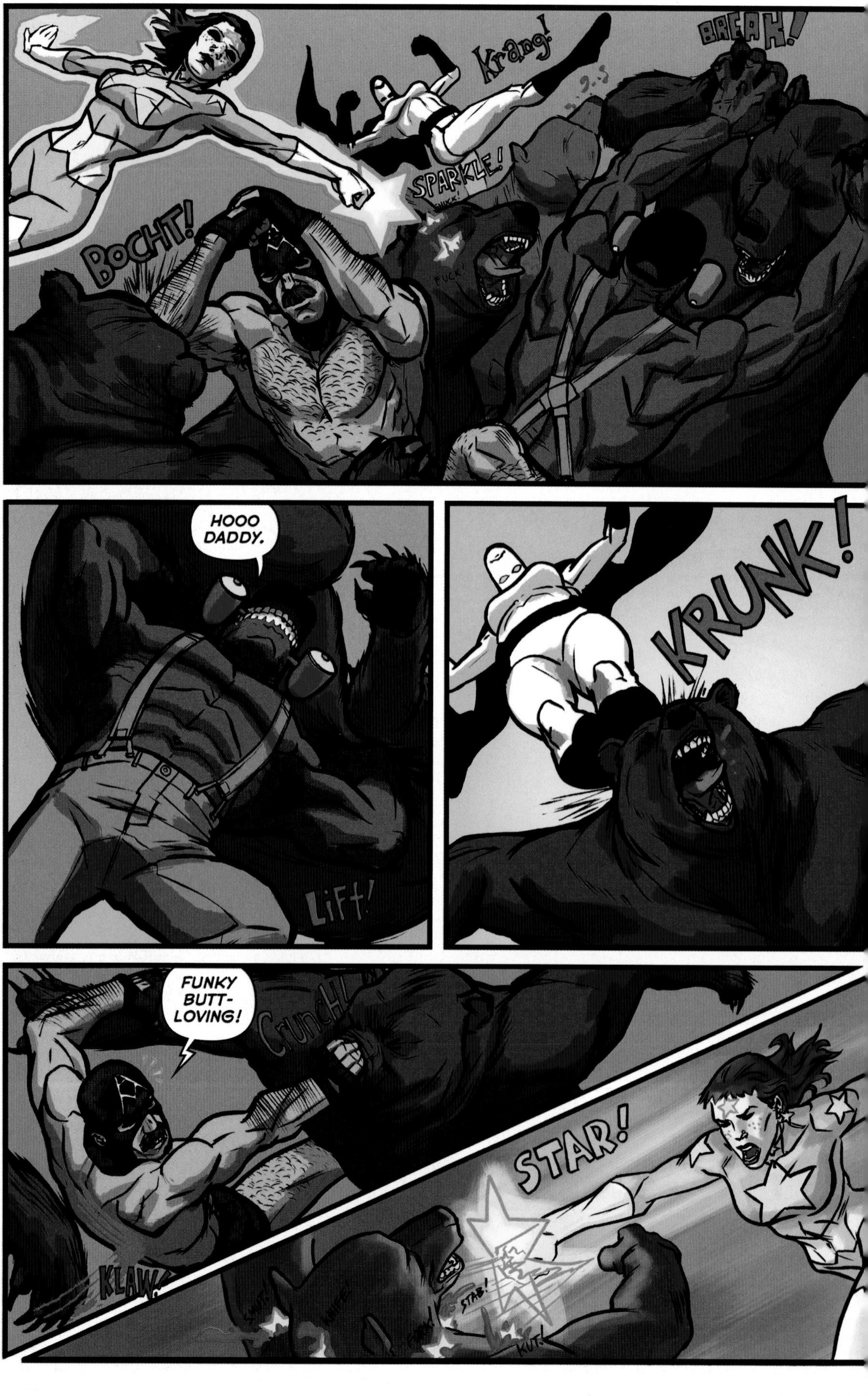
Krang!
BREAK!
SPARKLE!
BOCHT!
HOOO DADDY.
KRUNK!
LIFT!
FUNKY BUTT-LOVING!
CRUNCH!
STAR!
KLAW!
STAB!
KUT!

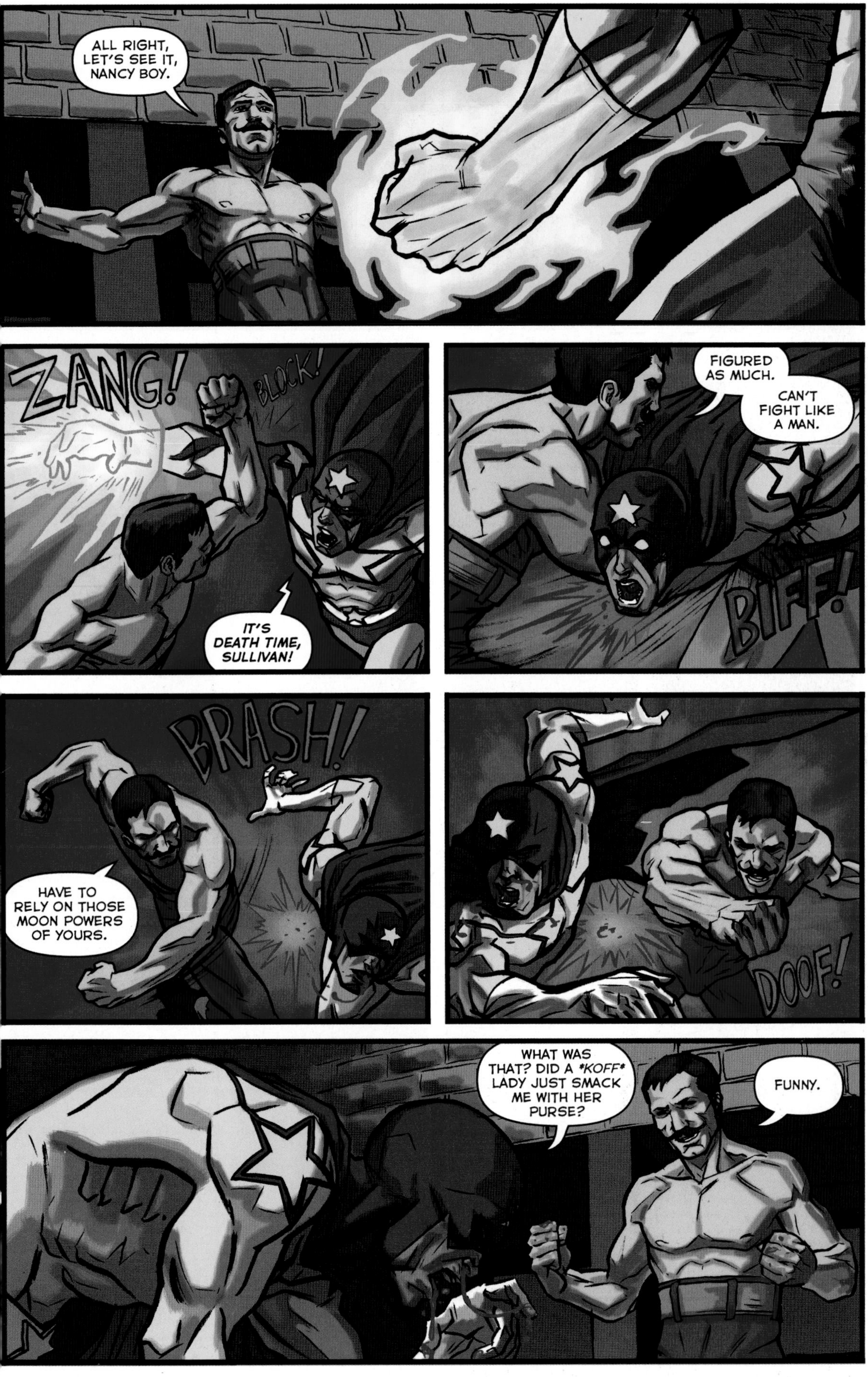
ALL RIGHT, LET'S SEE IT, NANCY BOY.
ZANG!
BLOCK!
IT'S DEATH TIME, SULLIVAN!
FIGURED AS MUCH.
CAN'T FIGHT LIKE A MAN.
BIFF!
BRASH!
HAVE TO RELY ON THOSE MOON POWERS OF YOURS.
DOOF!
WHAT WAS THAT? DID A *KOFF* LADY JUST SMACK ME WITH HER PURSE?
FUNNY.

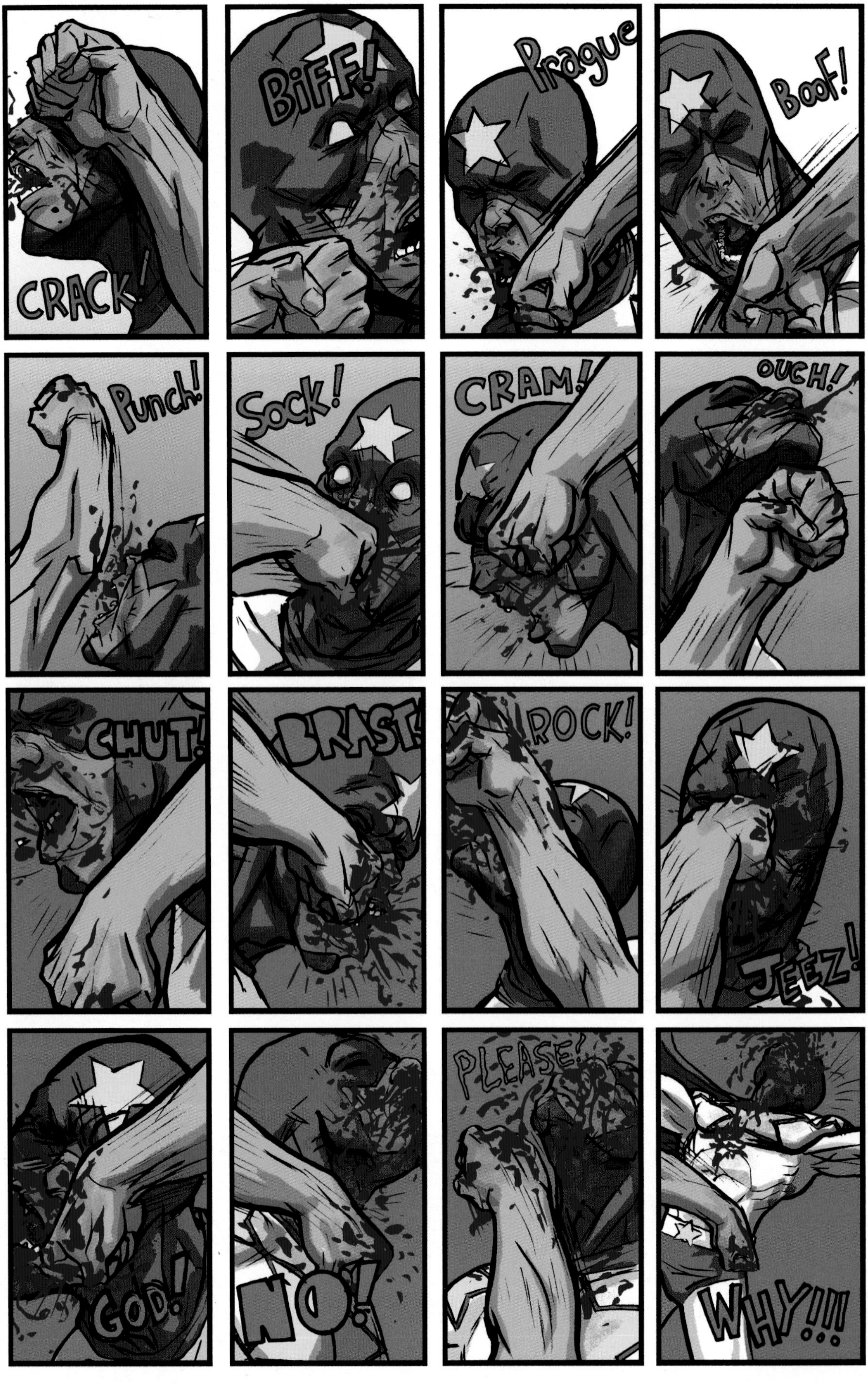
CRACK!
BIFF!
Prague
Boof!
Punch!
Sock!
CRAM!
OUCH!
CHUT!
BRAST
ROCK!
JEEZ!
GOD!
NO!
PLEASE!
WHY!!!

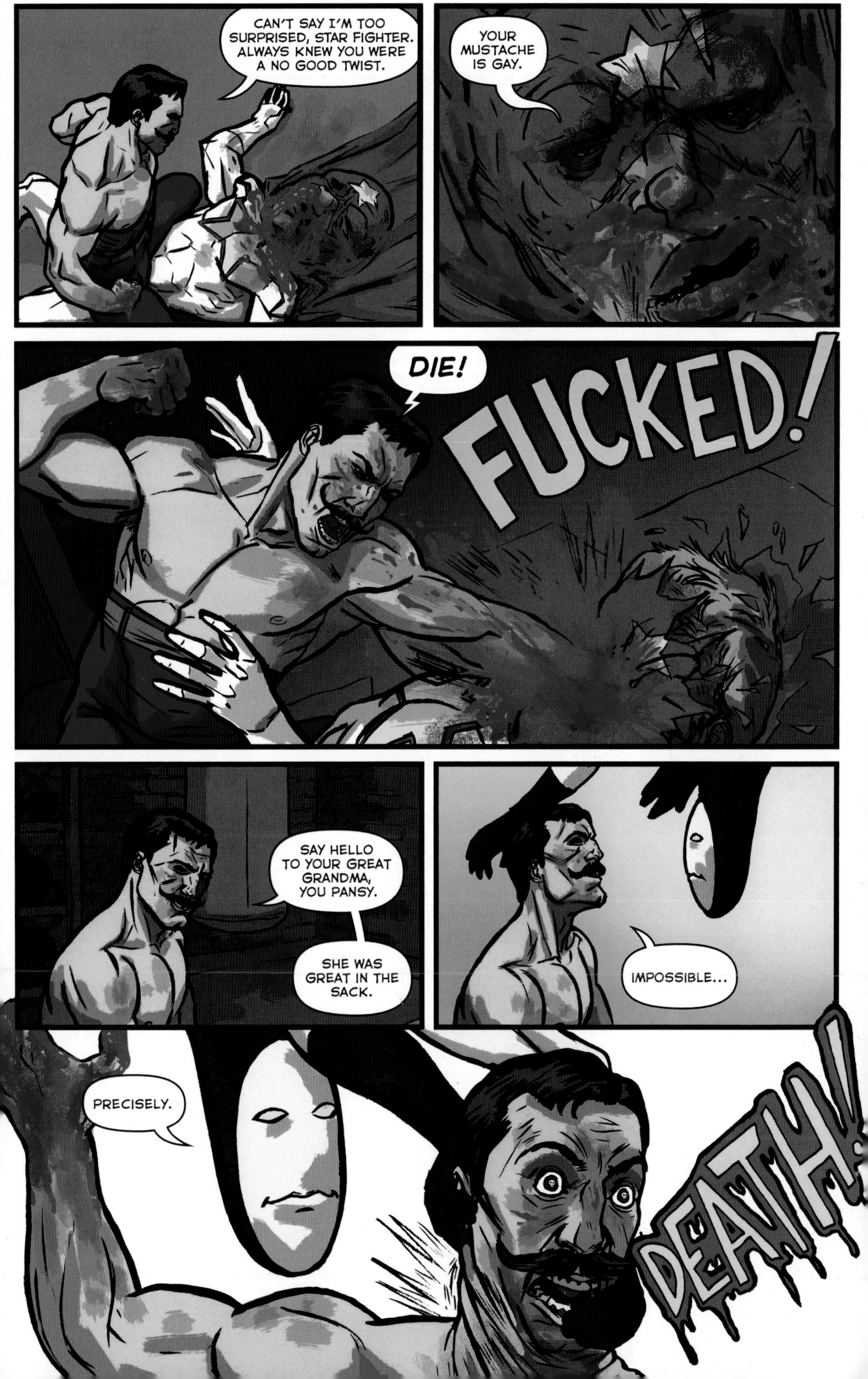
CAN'T SAY I'M TOO SURPRISED, STAR FIGHTER. ALWAYS KNEW YOU WERE A NO GOOD TWIST.
YOUR MUSTACHE IS GAY.
DIE!
FUCKED!
SAY HELLO TO YOUR GREAT GRANDMA, YOU PANSY.
SHE WAS GREAT IN THE SACK.
IMPOSSIBLE...
PRECISELY.
DEATH!

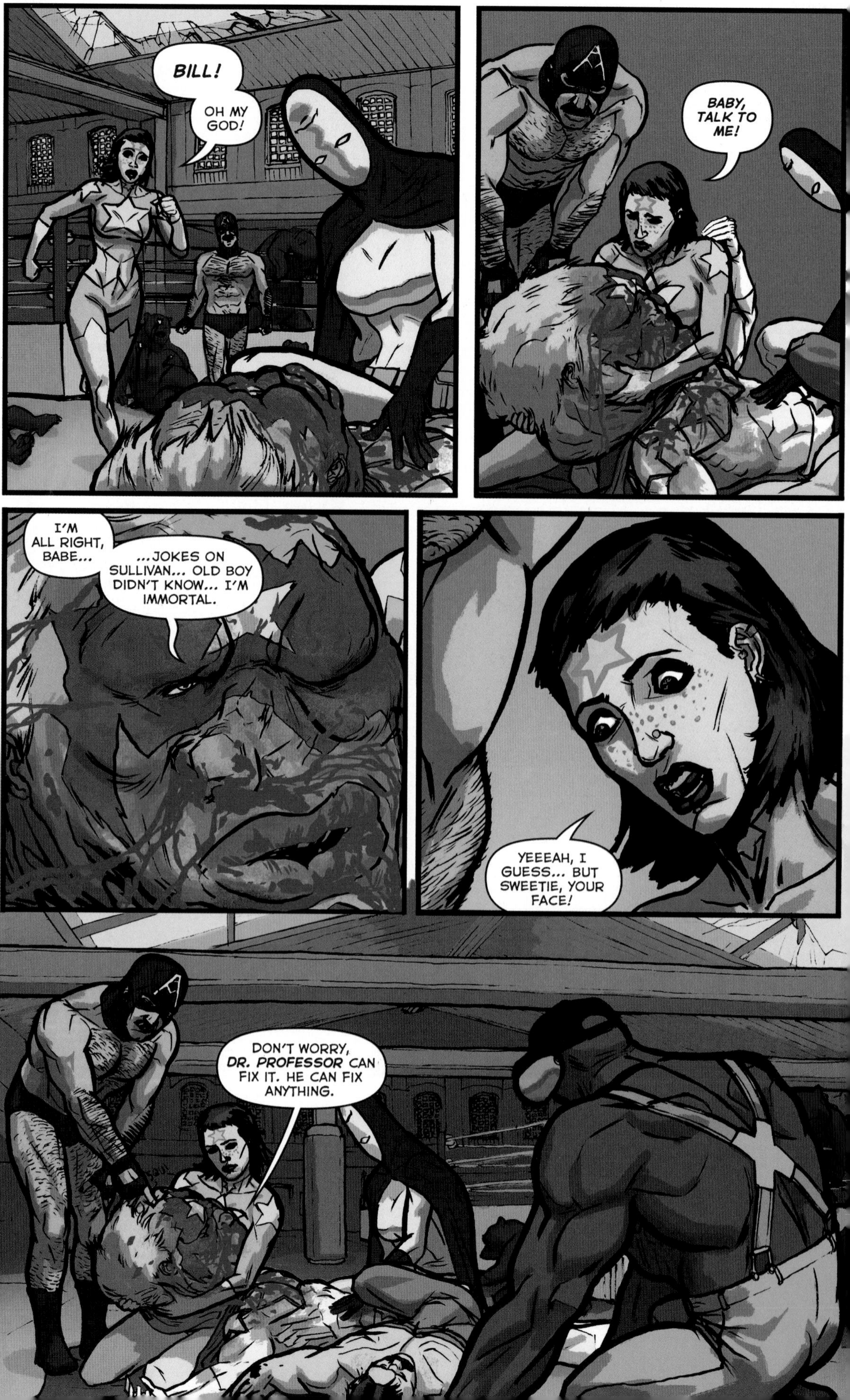
BILL!
OH MY GOD!
BABY, TALK TO ME!
I'M ALL RIGHT, BABE...
...JOKES ON SULLIVAN... OLD BOY DIDN'T KNOW... I'M IMMORTAL.
YEEEAH, I GUESS... BUT SWEETIE, YOUR FACE!
DON'T WORRY, DR. PROFESSOR CAN FIX IT. HE CAN FIX ANYTHING.

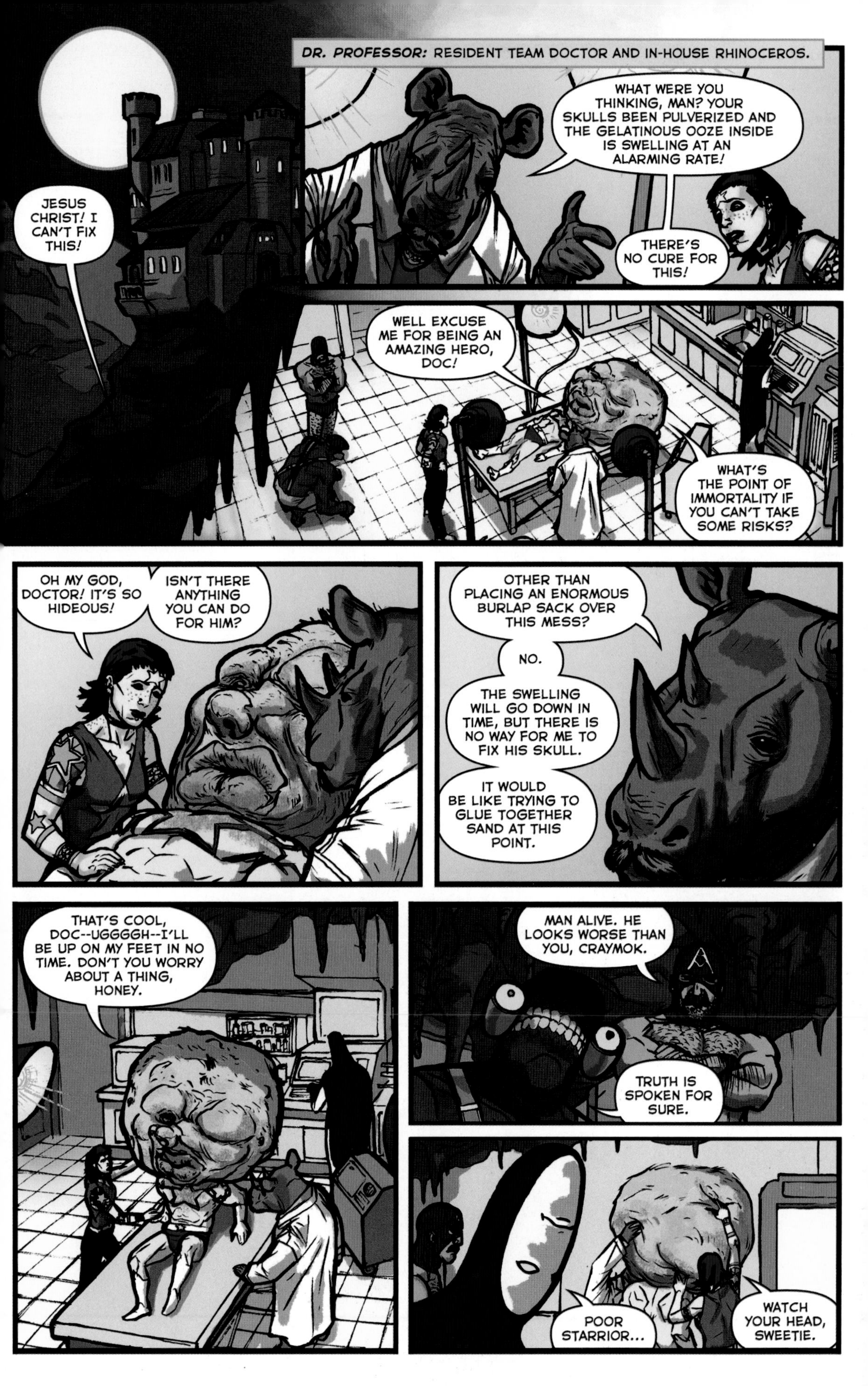
DR. PROFESSOR: RESIDENT TEAM DOCTOR AND IN-HOUSE RHINOCEROS.
JESUS CHRIST! I CAN'T FIX THIS!
WHAT WERE YOU THINKING, MAN? YOUR SKULLS BEEN PULVERIZED AND THE GELATINOUS OOZE INSIDE IS SWELLING AT AN ALARMING RATE!
THERE'S NO CURE FOR THIS!
WELL EXCUSE ME FOR BEING AN AMAZING HERO, DOC!
WHAT'S THE POINT OF IMMORTALITY IF YOU CAN'T TAKE SOME RISKS?
OH MY GOD, DOCTOR! IT'S SO HIDEOUS!
ISN'T THERE ANYTHING YOU CAN DO FOR HIM?
OTHER THAN PLACING AN ENORMOUS BURLAP SACK OVER THIS MESS?
NO.
THE SWELLING WILL GO DOWN IN TIME, BUT THERE IS NO WAY FOR ME TO FIX HIS SKULL.
IT WOULD BE LIKE TRYING TO GLUE TOGETHER SAND AT THIS POINT.
THAT'S COOL, DOC--UGGGGH--I'LL BE UP ON MY FEET IN NO TIME. DON'T YOU WORRY ABOUT A THING, HONEY.
MAN ALIVE. HE LOOKS WORSE THAN YOU, CRAYMOK.
TRUTH IS SPOKEN FOR SURE.
POOR STARRIOR...
WATCH YOUR HEAD, SWEETIE.

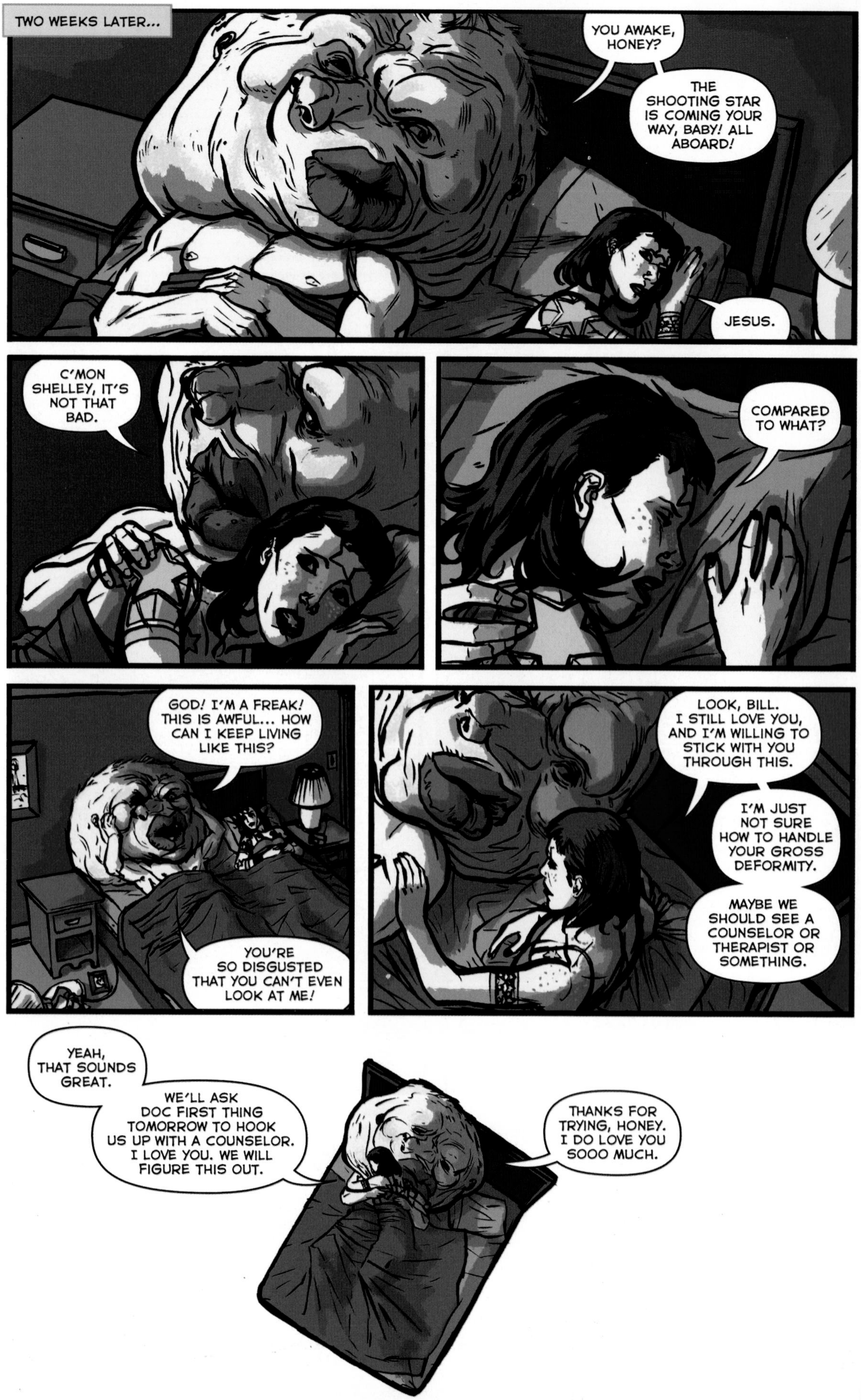
TWO WEEKS LATER...
YOU AWAKE, HONEY?
THE SHOOTING STAR IS COMING YOUR WAY, BABY! ALL ABOARD!
JESUS.
C'MON SHELLEY, IT'S NOT THAT BAD.
COMPARED TO WHAT?
GOD! I'M A FREAK! THIS IS AWFUL... HOW CAN I KEEP LIVING LIKE THIS?
YOU'RE SO DISGUSTED THAT YOU CAN'T EVEN LOOK AT ME!
LOOK, BILL. I STILL LOVE YOU, AND I'M WILLING TO STICK WITH YOU THROUGH THIS.
I'M JUST NOT SURE HOW TO HANDLE YOUR GROSS DEFORMITY.
MAYBE WE SHOULD SEE A COUNSELOR OR THERAPIST OR SOMETHING.
YEAH, THAT SOUNDS GREAT.
WE'LL ASK DOC FIRST THING TOMORROW TO HOOK US UP WITH A COUNSELOR. I LOVE YOU. WE WILL FIGURE THIS OUT.
THANKS FOR TRYING, HONEY. I DO LOVE YOU SOOO MUCH.

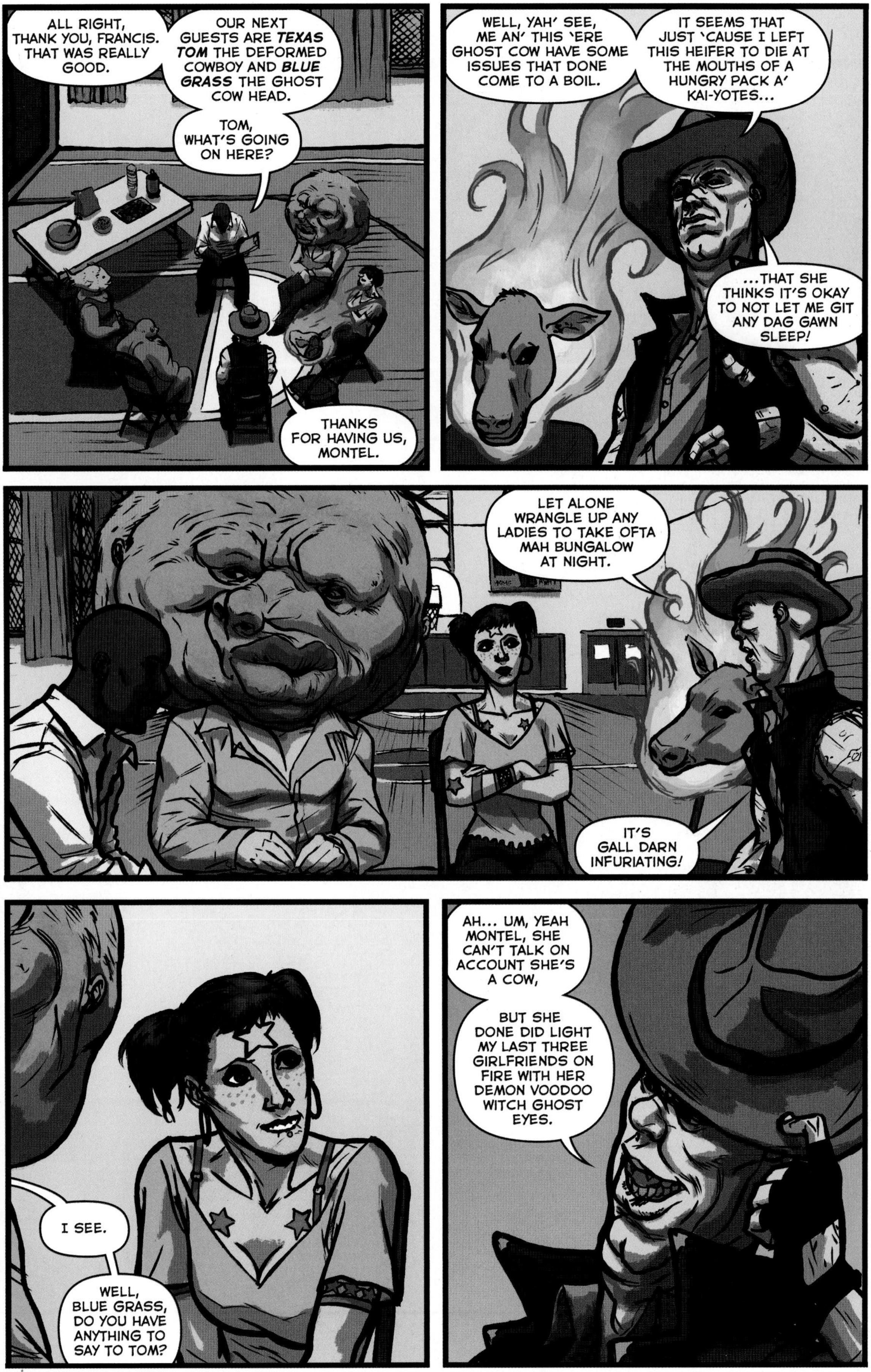
ALL RIGHT, THANK YOU, FRANCIS. THAT WAS REALLY GOOD.
OUR NEXT GUESTS ARE TEXAS TOM THE DEFORMED COWBOY AND BLUE GRASS THE GHOST COW HEAD.
TOM, WHAT'S GOING ON HERE?
THANKS FOR HAVING US, MONTEL.
WELL, YAH' SEE, ME AN' THIS 'ERE GHOST COW HAVE SOME ISSUES THAT DONE COME TO A BOIL.
IT SEEMS THAT JUST 'CAUSE I LEFT THIS HEIFER TO DIE AT THE MOUTHS OF A HUNGRY PACK A' KAI-YOTES...
...THAT SHE THINKS IT'S OKAY TO NOT LET ME GIT ANY DAG GAWN SLEEP!
LET ALONE WRANGLE UP ANY LADIES TO TAKE OFTA MAH BUNGALOW AT NIGHT.
IT'S GALL DARN INFURIATING!
I SEE.
WELL, BLUE GRASS, DO YOU HAVE ANYTHING TO SAY TO TOM?
AH... UM, YEAH MONTEL, SHE CAN'T TALK ON ACCOUNT SHE'S A COW,
BUT SHE DONE DID LIGHT MY LAST THREE GIRLFRIENDS ON FIRE WITH HER DEMON VOODOO WITCH GHOST EYES.

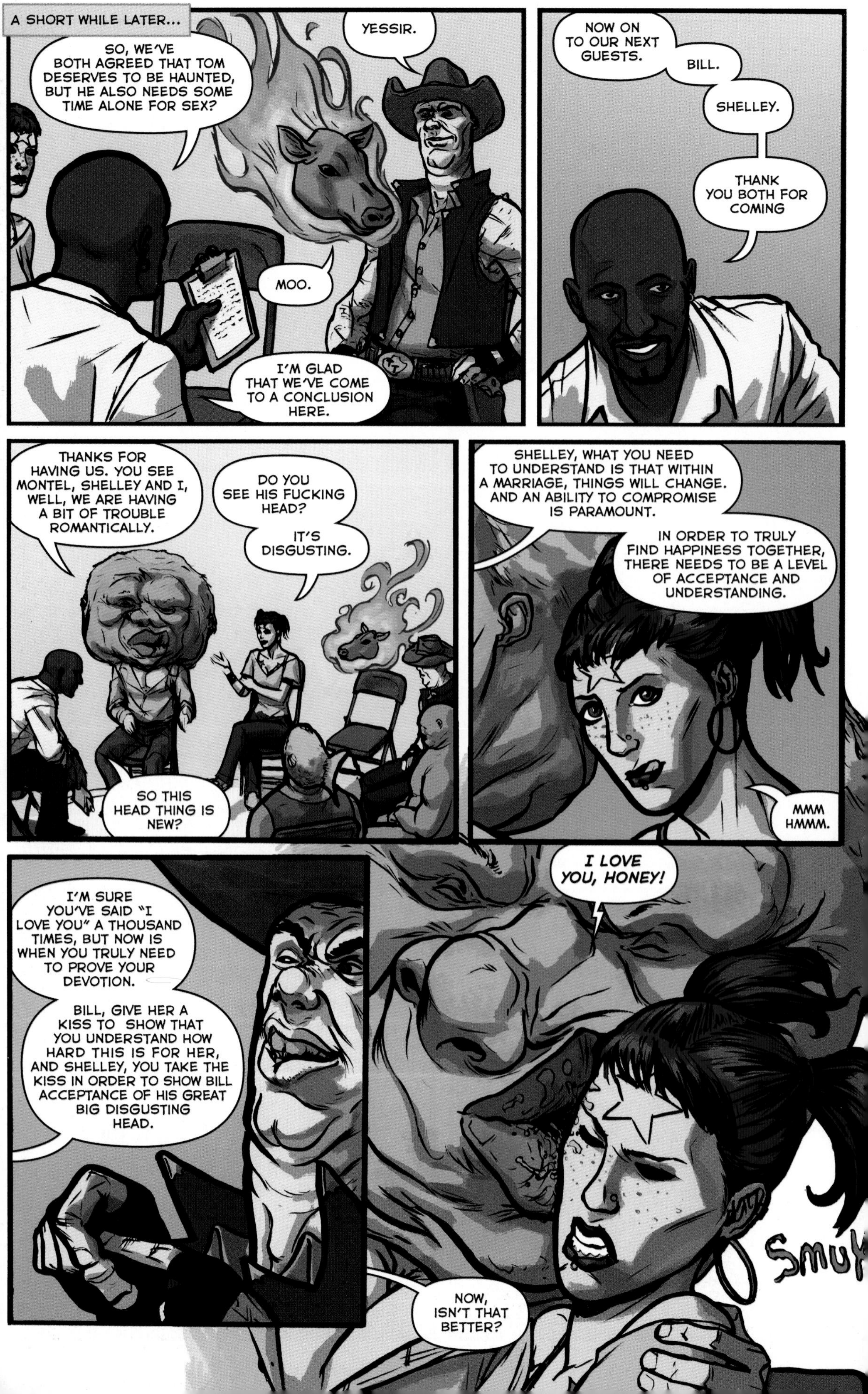
A SHORT WHILE LATER...
SO, WE'VE BOTH AGREED THAT TOM DESERVES TO BE HAUNTED, BUT HE ALSO NEEDS SOME TIME ALONE FOR SEX?
YESSIR.
MOO.
I'M GLAD THAT WE'VE COME TO A CONCLUSION HERE.
NOW ON TO OUR NEXT GUESTS.
BILL.
SHELLEY.
THANK YOU BOTH FOR COMING
THANKS FOR HAVING US. YOU SEE MONTEL, SHELLEY AND I, WELL, WE ARE HAVING A BIT OF TROUBLE ROMANTICALLY.
DO YOU SEE HIS FUCKING HEAD?
IT'S DISGUSTING.
SO THIS HEAD THING IS NEW?
SHELLEY, WHAT YOU NEED TO UNDERSTAND IS THAT WITHIN A MARRIAGE, THINGS WILL CHANGE. AND AN ABILITY TO COMPROMISE IS PARAMOUNT.
IN ORDER TO TRULY FIND HAPPINESS TOGETHER, THERE NEEDS TO BE A LEVEL OF ACCEPTANCE AND UNDERSTANDING.
MMM HMMM.
I'M SURE YOU'VE SAID "I LOVE YOU" A THOUSAND TIMES, BUT NOW IS WHEN YOU TRULY NEED TO PROVE YOUR DEVOTION.
BILL, GIVE HER A KISS TO SHOW THAT YOU UNDERSTAND HOW HARD THIS IS FOR HER, AND SHELLEY, YOU TAKE THE KISS IN ORDER TO SHOW BILL ACCEPTANCE OF HIS GREAT BIG DISGUSTING HEAD.
I LOVE YOU, HONEY!
NOW, ISN'T THAT BETTER?

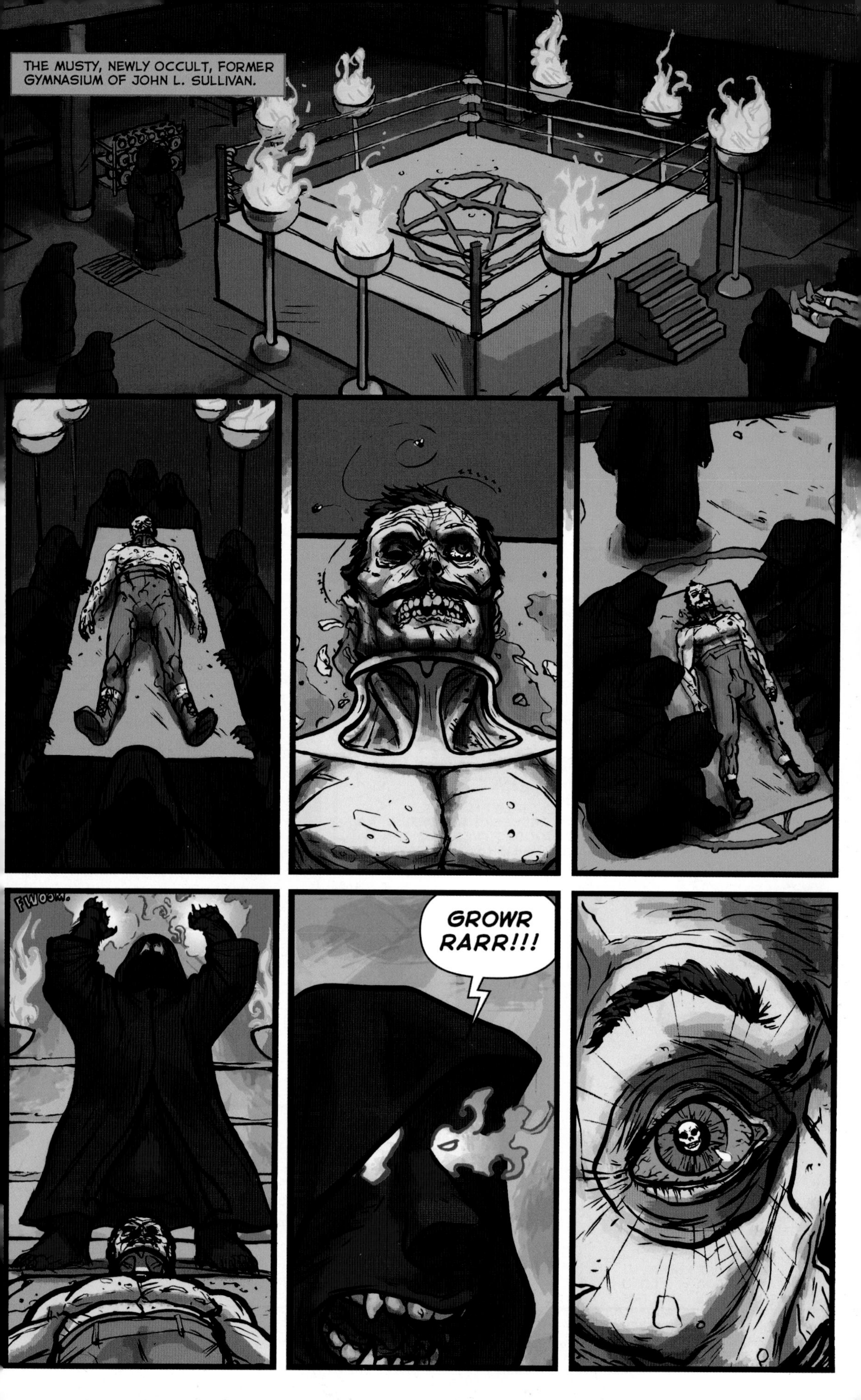
THE MUSTY, NEWLY OCCULT, FORMER GYMNASIUM OF JOHN L. SULLIVAN.
FWOOM.
GROWR RARR!!!

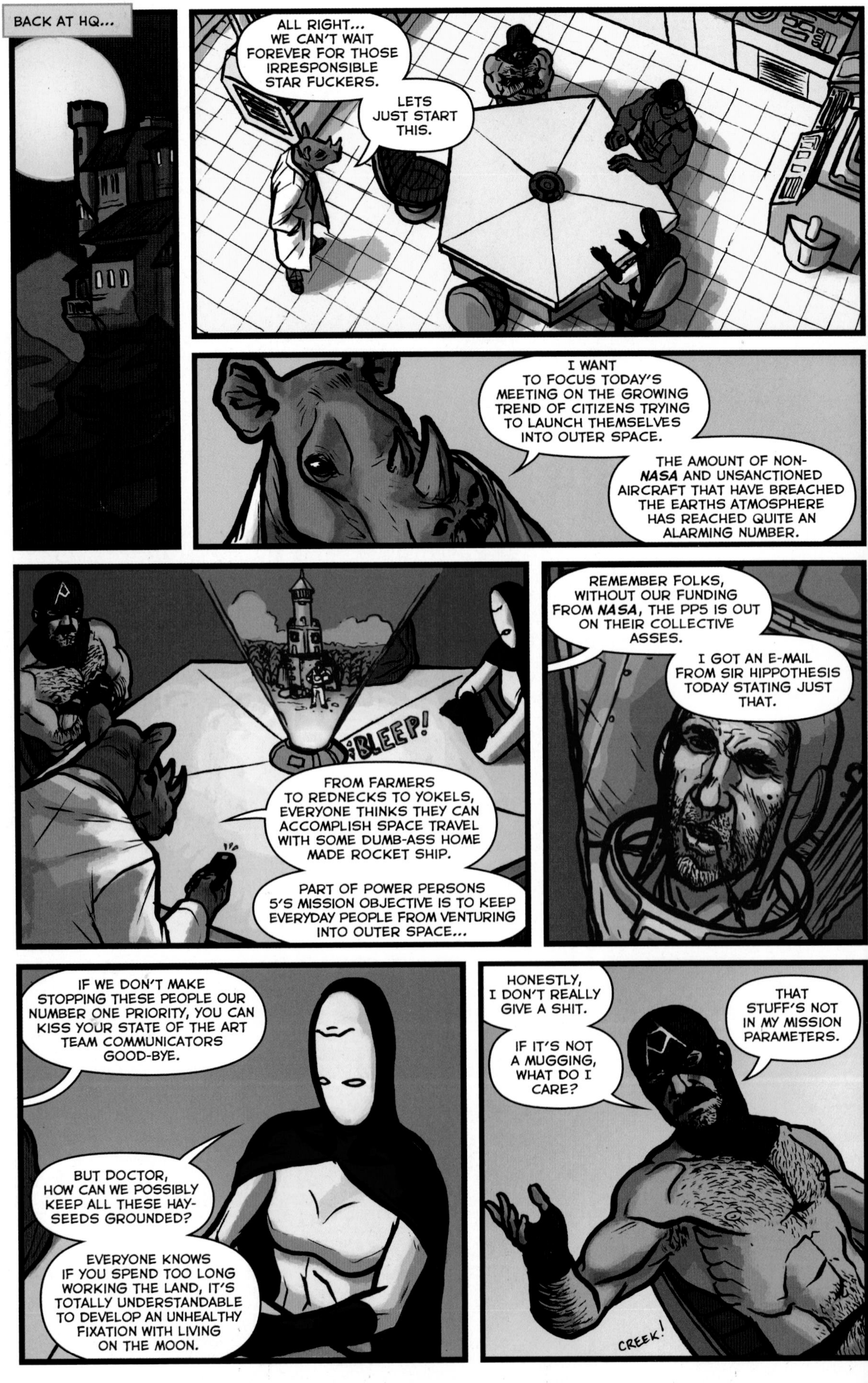
BACK AT HQ...
ALL RIGHT... WE CAN'T WAIT FOREVER FOR THOSE IRRESPONSIBLE STAR FUCKERS.
LETS JUST START THIS.
I WANT TO FOCUS TODAY'S MEETING ON THE GROWING TREND OF CITIZENS TRYING TO LAUNCH THEMSELVES INTO OUTER SPACE.
THE AMOUNT OF NON-NASA AND UNSANCTIONED AIRCRAFT THAT HAVE BREACHED THE EARTHS ATMOSPHERE HAS REACHED QUITE AN ALARMING NUMBER.
BLEEP!
FROM FARMERS TO REDNECKS TO YOKELS, EVERYONE THINKS THEY CAN ACCOMPLISH SPACE TRAVEL WITH SOME DUMB-ASS HOME MADE ROCKET SHIP.
PART OF POWER PERSONS 5'S MISSION OBJECTIVE IS TO KEEP EVERYDAY PEOPLE FROM VENTURING INTO OUTER SPACE...
REMEMBER FOLKS, WITHOUT OUR FUNDING FROM NASA, THE PP5 IS OUT ON THEIR COLLECTIVE ASSES.
I GOT AN E-MAIL FROM SIR HIPPOTHESIS TODAY STATING JUST THAT.
IF WE DON'T MAKE STOPPING THESE PEOPLE OUR NUMBER ONE PRIORITY, YOU CAN KISS YOUR STATE OF THE ART TEAM COMMUNICATORS GOOD-BYE.
BUT DOCTOR, HOW CAN WE POSSIBLY KEEP ALL THESE HAY-SEEDS GROUNDED?
EVERYONE KNOWS IF YOU SPEND TOO LONG WORKING THE LAND, IT'S TOTALLY UNDERSTANDABLE TO DEVELOP AN UNHEALTHY FIXATION WITH LIVING ON THE MOON.
HONESTLY, I DON'T REALLY GIVE A SHIT.
IF IT'S NOT A MUGGING, WHAT DO I CARE?
THAT STUFF'S NOT IN MY MISSION PARAMETERS.
CREEK!

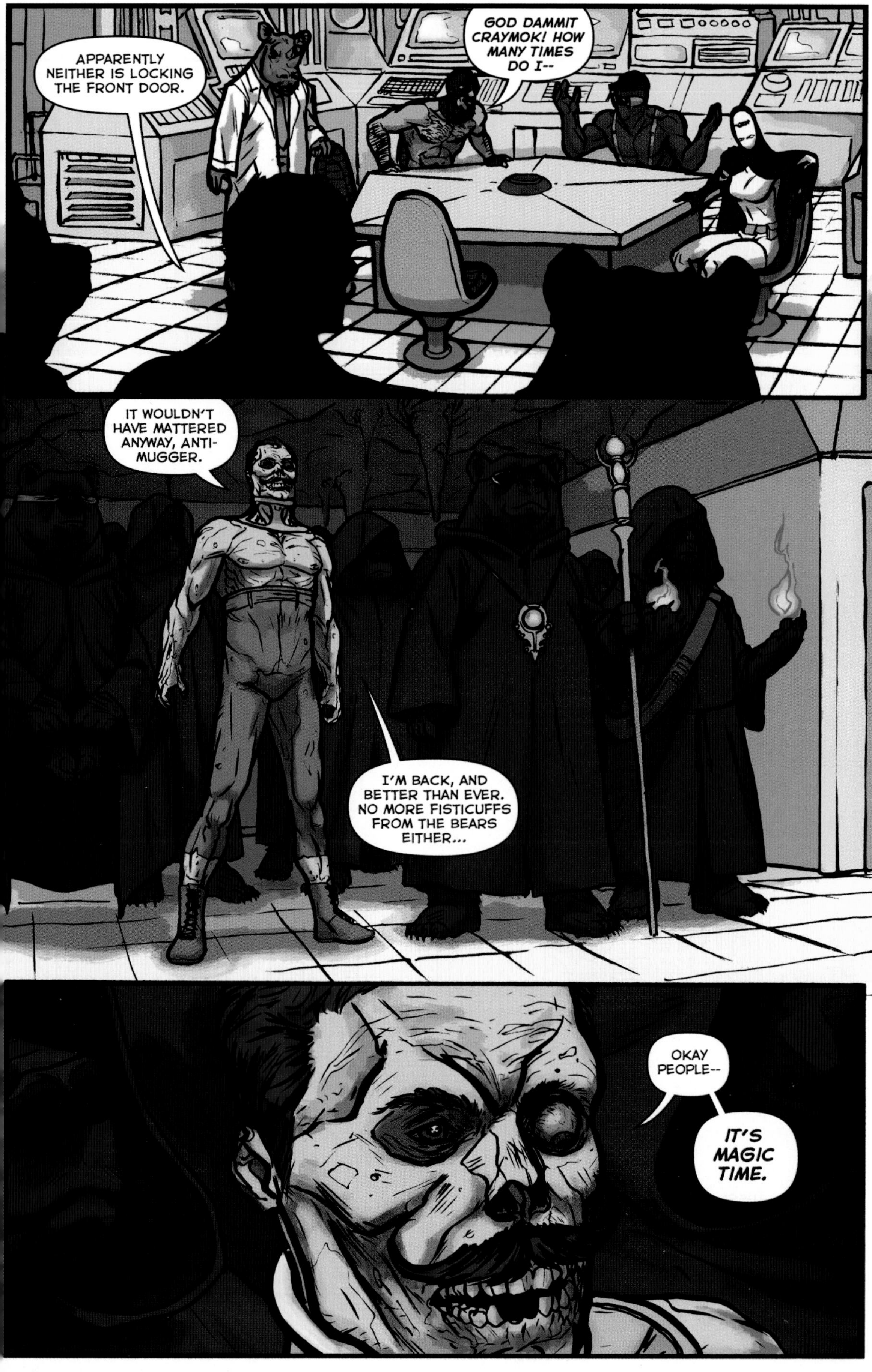
APPARENTLY NEITHER IS LOCKING THE FRONT DOOR.
GOD DAMMIT CRAYMOK! HOW MANY TIMES DO I--
IT WOULDN'T HAVE MATTERED ANYWAY, ANTI-MUGGER.
I'M BACK, AND BETTER THAN EVER. NO MORE FISTICUFFS FROM THE BEARS EITHER...
OKAY PEOPLE--
IT'S MAGIC TIME.

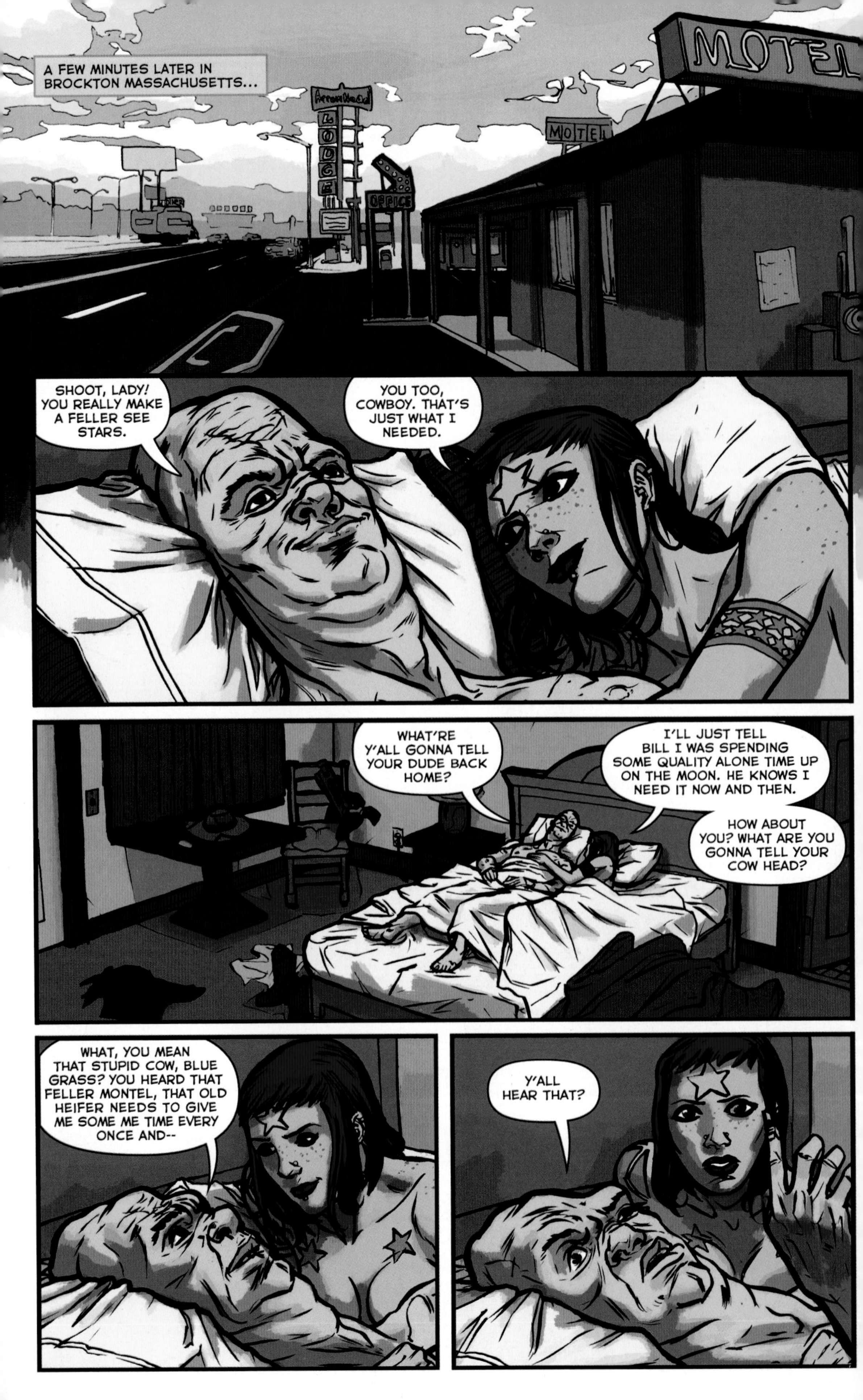
A FEW MINUTES LATER IN BROCKTON MASSACHUSETTS...
MOTEL
MOTEL
OFFICE
LODGE
SHOOT, LADY! YOU REALLY MAKE A FELLER SEE STARS.
YOU TOO, COWBOY. THAT'S JUST WHAT I NEEDED.
WHAT'RE Y'ALL GONNA TELL YOUR DUDE BACK HOME?
I'LL JUST TELL BILL I WAS SPENDING SOME QUALITY ALONE TIME UP ON THE MOON. HE KNOWS I NEED IT NOW AND THEN.
HOW ABOUT YOU? WHAT ARE YOU GONNA TELL YOUR COW HEAD?
WHAT, YOU MEAN THAT STUPID COW, BLUE GRASS? YOU HEARD THAT FELLER MONTEL, THAT OLD HEIFER NEEDS TO GIVE ME SOME ME TIME EVERY ONCE AND--
Y'ALL HEAR THAT?

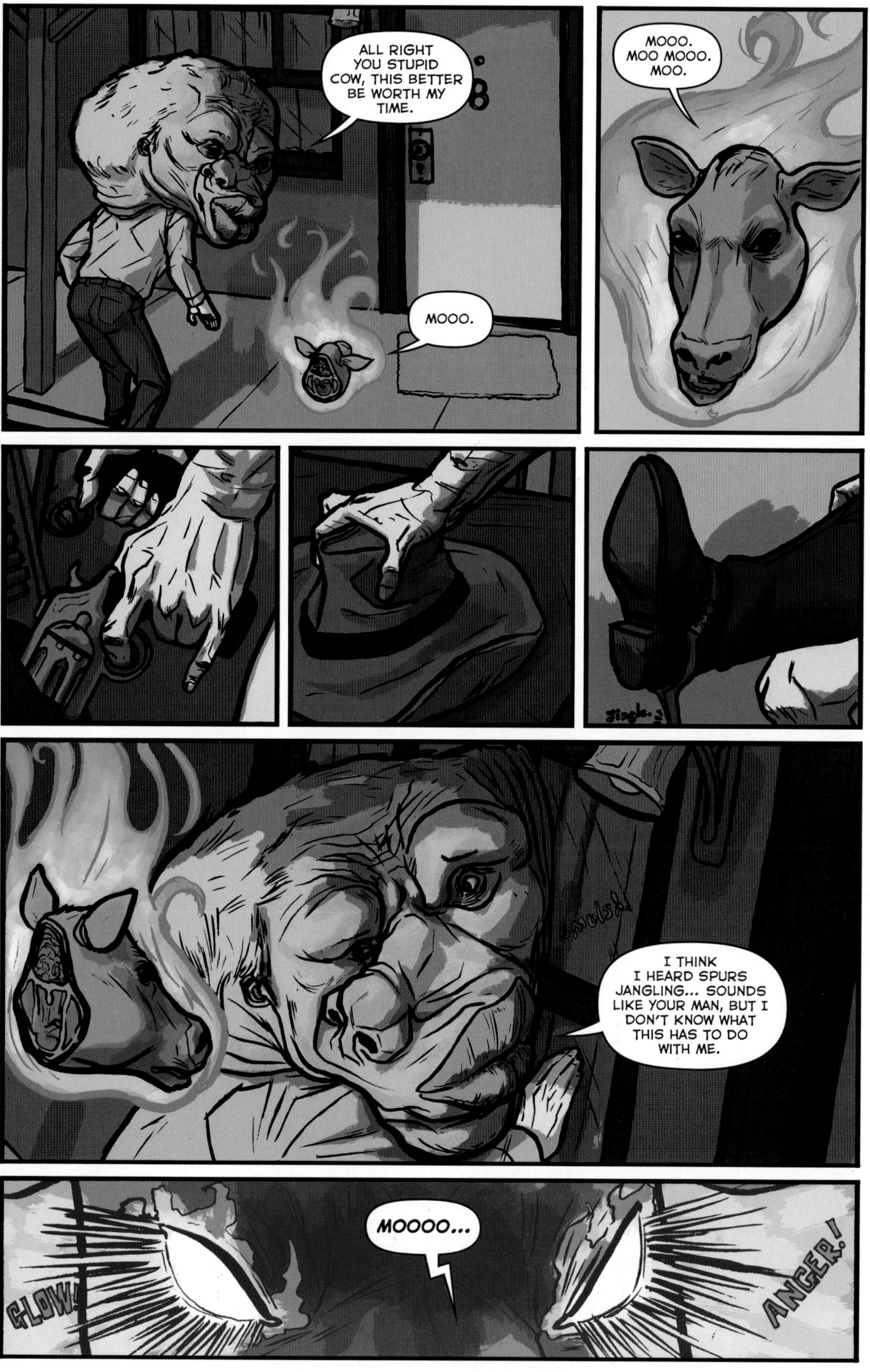
ALL RIGHT YOU STUPID COW, THIS BETTER BE WORTH MY TIME.
MOOO.
MOOO. MOO MOOO. MOO.
jingle.
I THINK I HEARD SPURS JANGLING... SOUNDS LIKE YOUR MAN, BUT I DON'T KNOW WHAT THIS HAS TO DO WITH ME.
MOOOO...
GLOW!
ANGER!

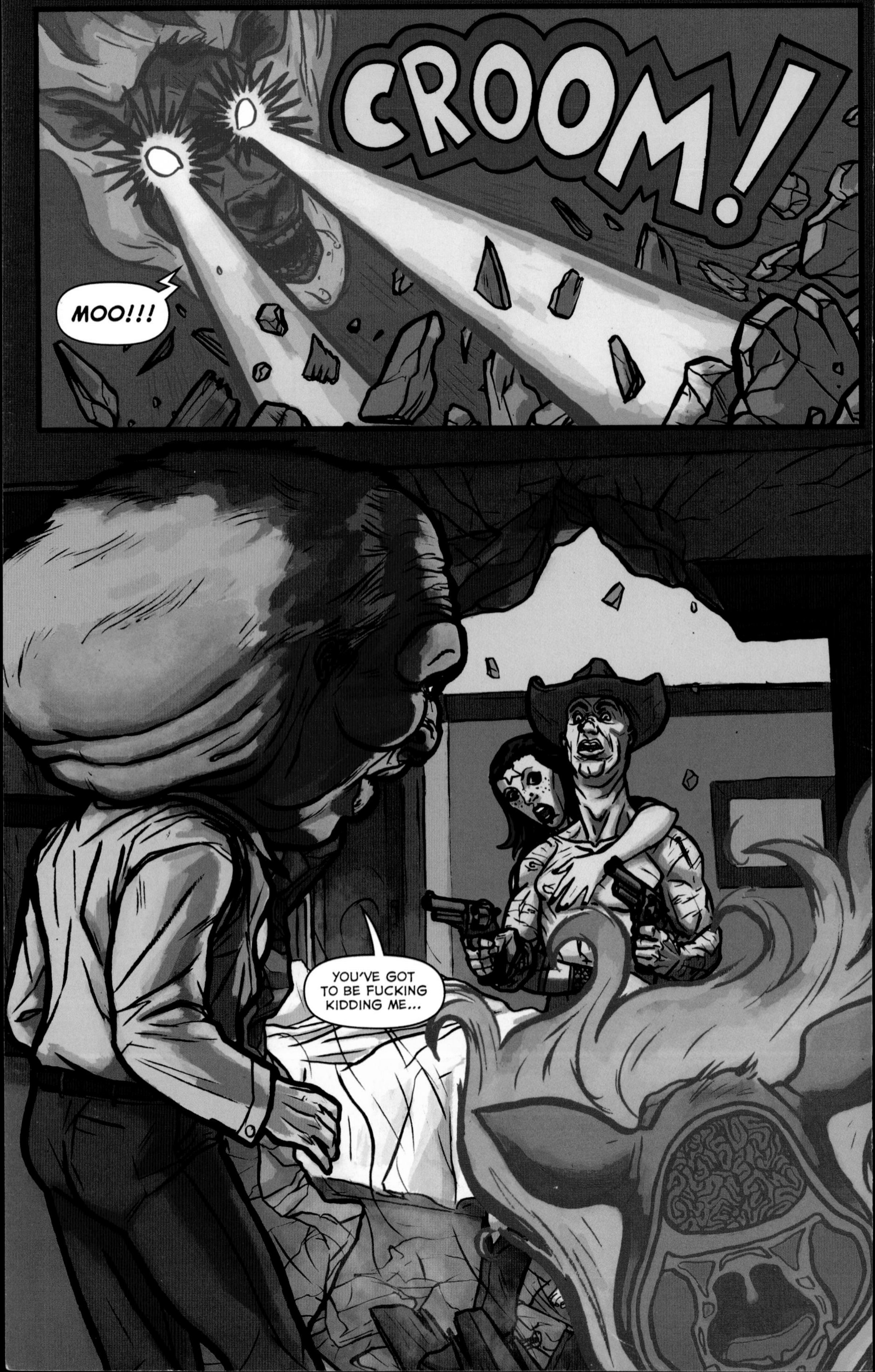
CROOM!
MOO!!!
YOU'VE GOT TO BE FUCKING KIDDING ME...

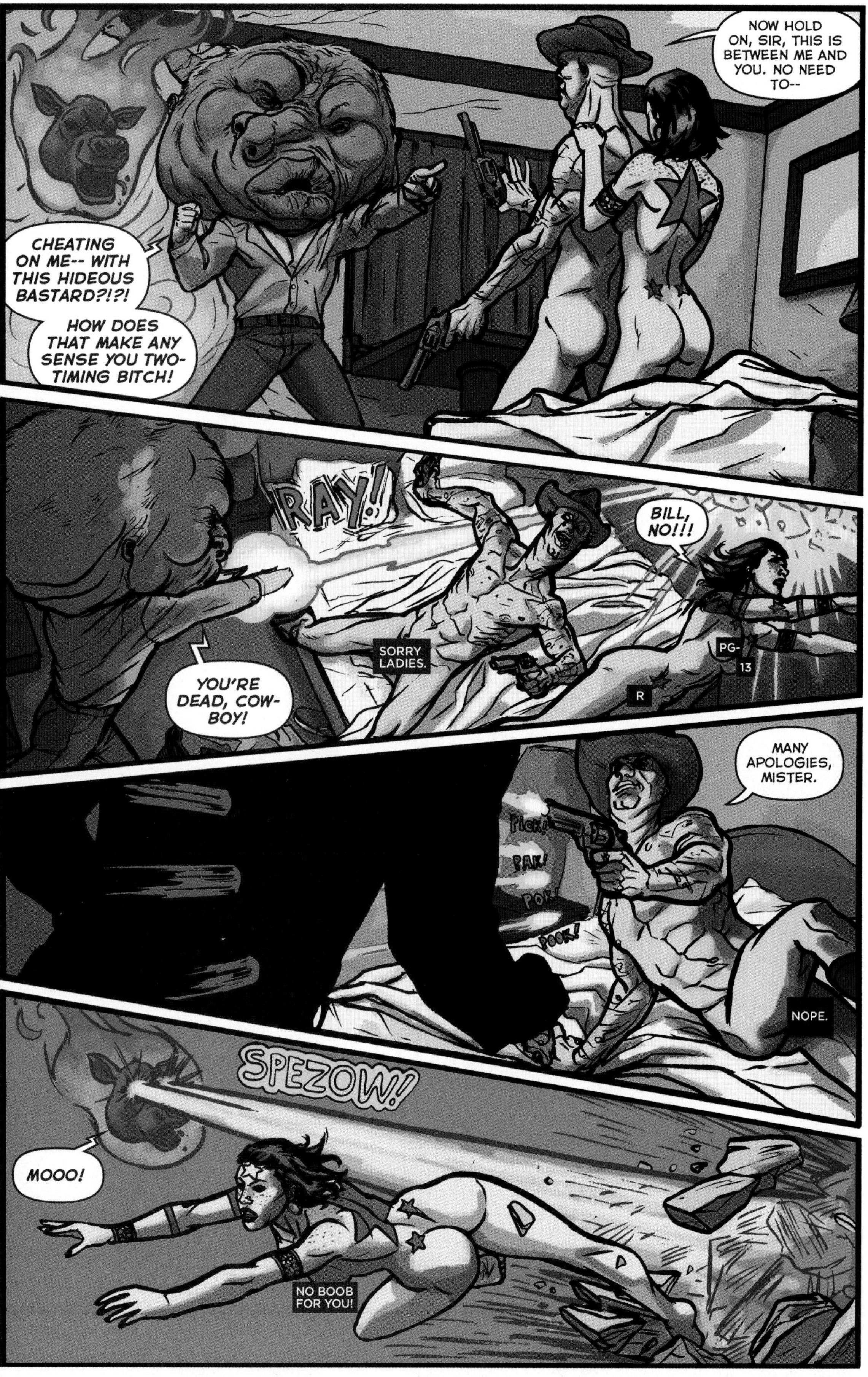

NOW HOLD ON, SIR, THIS IS BETWEEN ME AND YOU. NO NEED TO--
CHEATING ON ME-- WITH THIS HIDEOUS BASTARD?!?!
HOW DOES THAT MAKE ANY SENSE YOU TWO-TIMING BITCH!
RAY!
BILL, NO!!!
SORRY LADIES.
PG-13
R
YOU'RE DEAD, COW-BOY!
MANY APOLOGIES, MISTER.
PICK!
PAK!
POK!
BOOK!
NOPE.
SPEZOW!
MOOO!
NO BOOB FOR YOU!

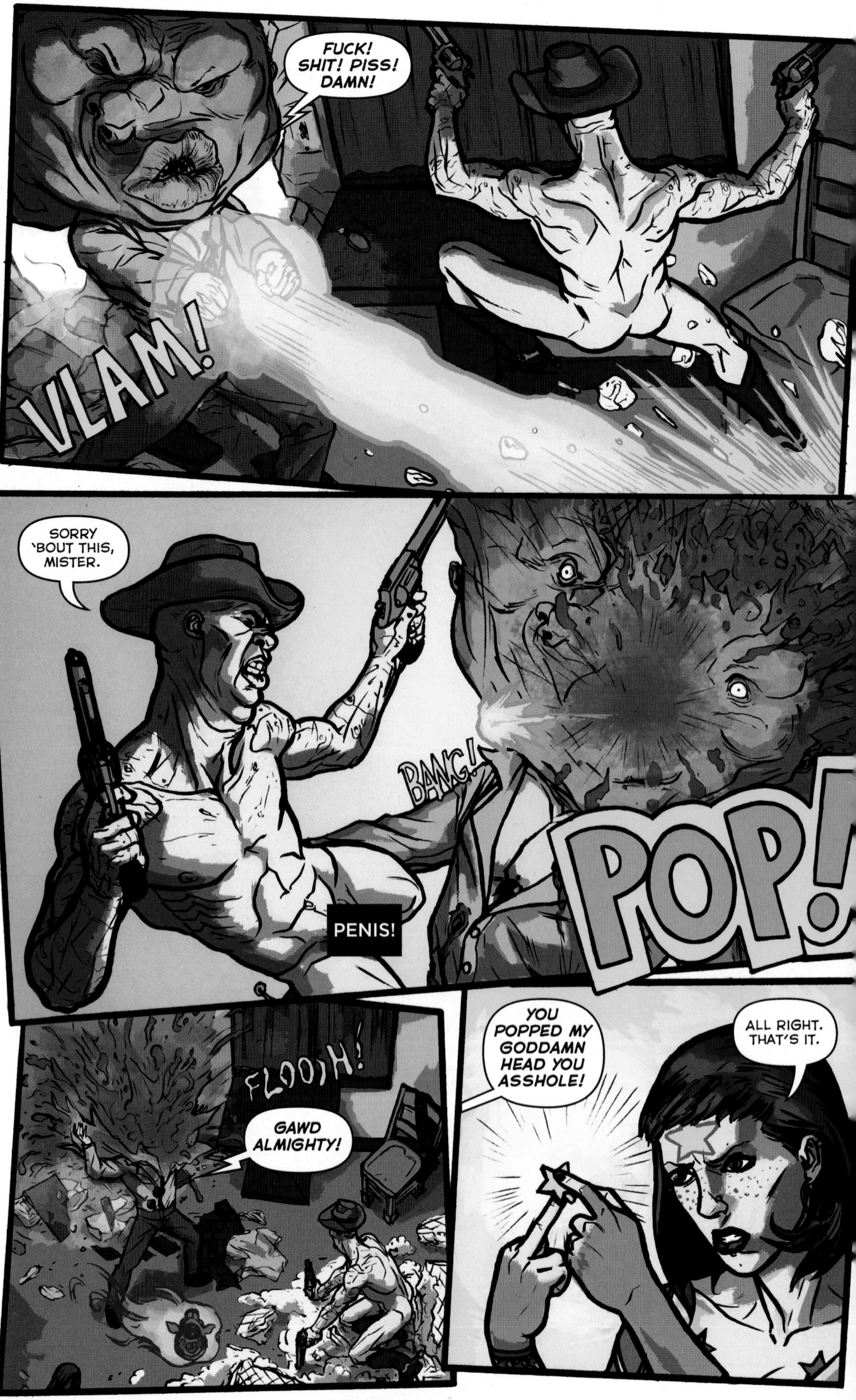
FUCK! SHIT! PISS! DAMN!
VLAM!
SORRY 'BOUT THIS, MISTER.
BANG!
PENIS!
POP!
FLOOSH!
GAWD ALMIGHTY!
YOU POPPED MY GODDAMN HEAD YOU ASSHOLE!
ALL RIGHT. THAT'S IT.

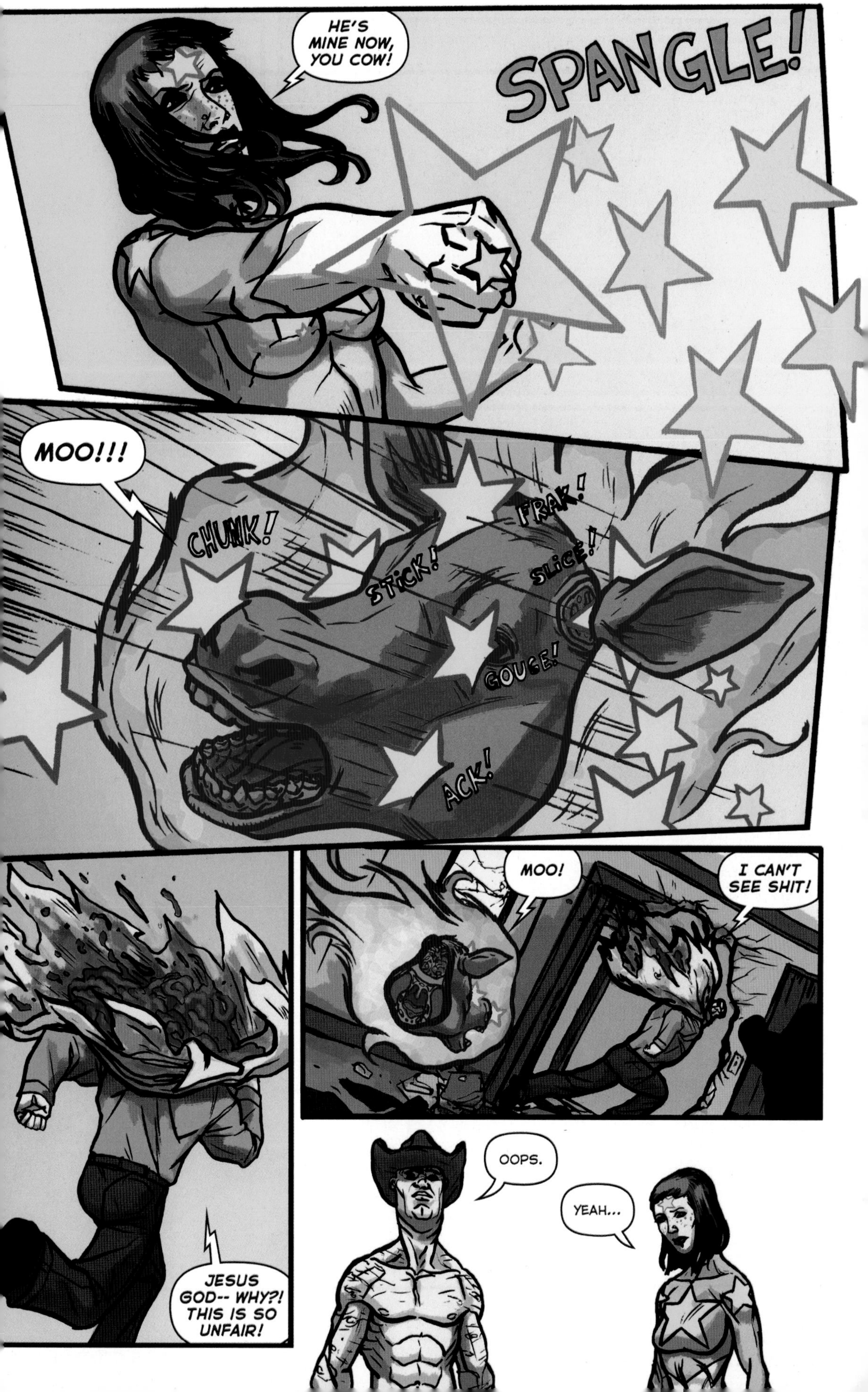
HE'S MINE NOW, YOU COW!
SPANGLE!
MOO!!!
CHUNK!
FRAK!
STICK!
SLICE!
GOUGE!
ACK!
JESUS GOD-- WHY?! THIS IS SO UNFAIR!
MOO!
I CAN'T SEE SHIT!
OOPS.
YEAH...

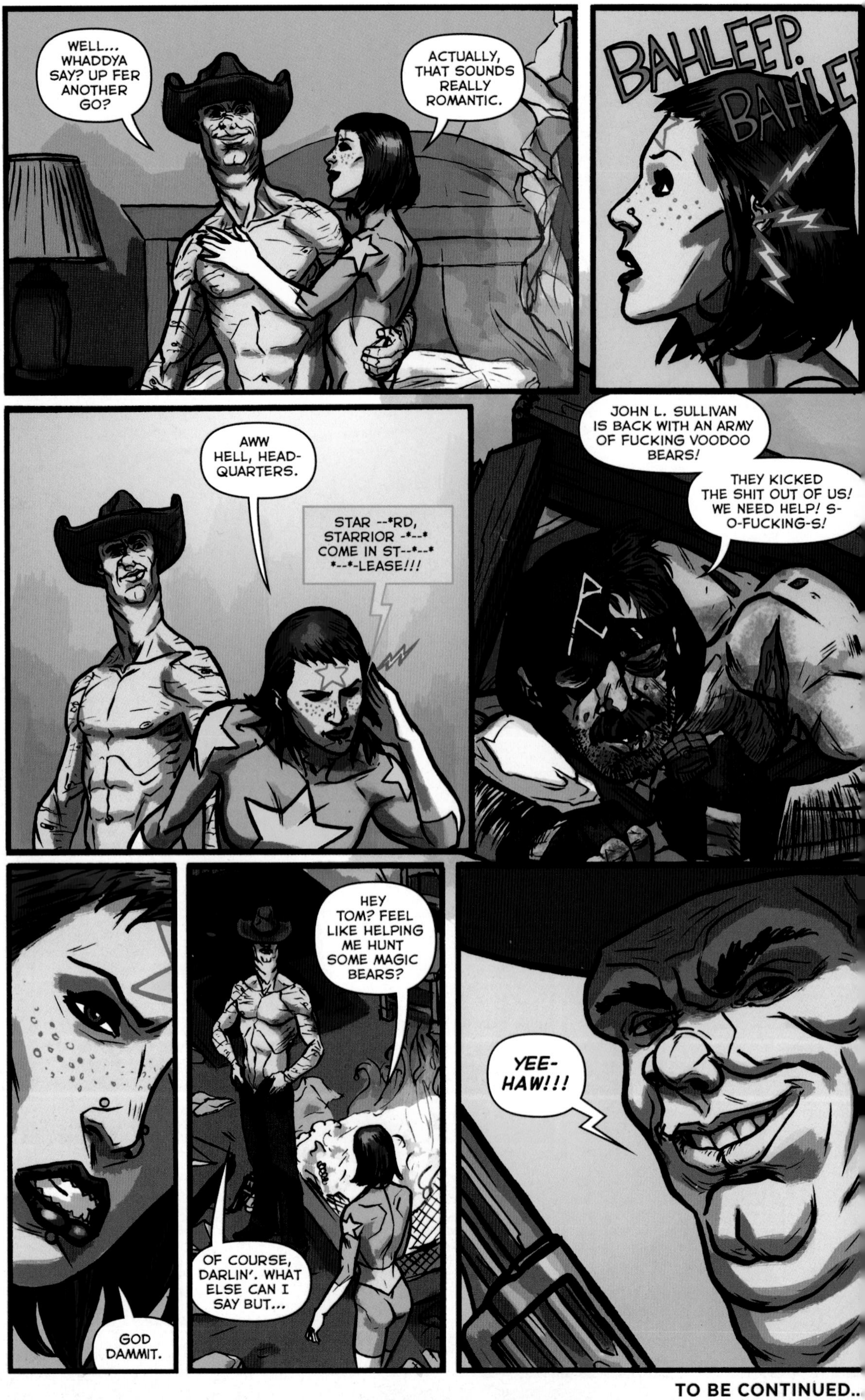
WELL... WHADDYA SAY? UP FER ANOTHER GO?
ACTUALLY, THAT SOUNDS REALLY ROMANTIC.
BAHLEEP. BAHLE
AWW HELL, HEAD-QUARTERS.
STAR --*RD, STARRIOR -*--* COME IN ST--*--* *--*-LEASE!!!
JOHN L. SULLIVAN IS BACK WITH AN ARMY OF FUCKING VOODOO BEARS!
THEY KICKED THE SHIT OUT OF US! WE NEED HELP! S-O-FUCKING-S!
GOD DAMMIT.
HEY TOM? FEEL LIKE HELPING ME HUNT SOME MAGIC BEARS?
OF COURSE, DARLIN'. WHAT ELSE CAN I SAY BUT...
YEE-HAW!!!

TO BE CONTINUED...

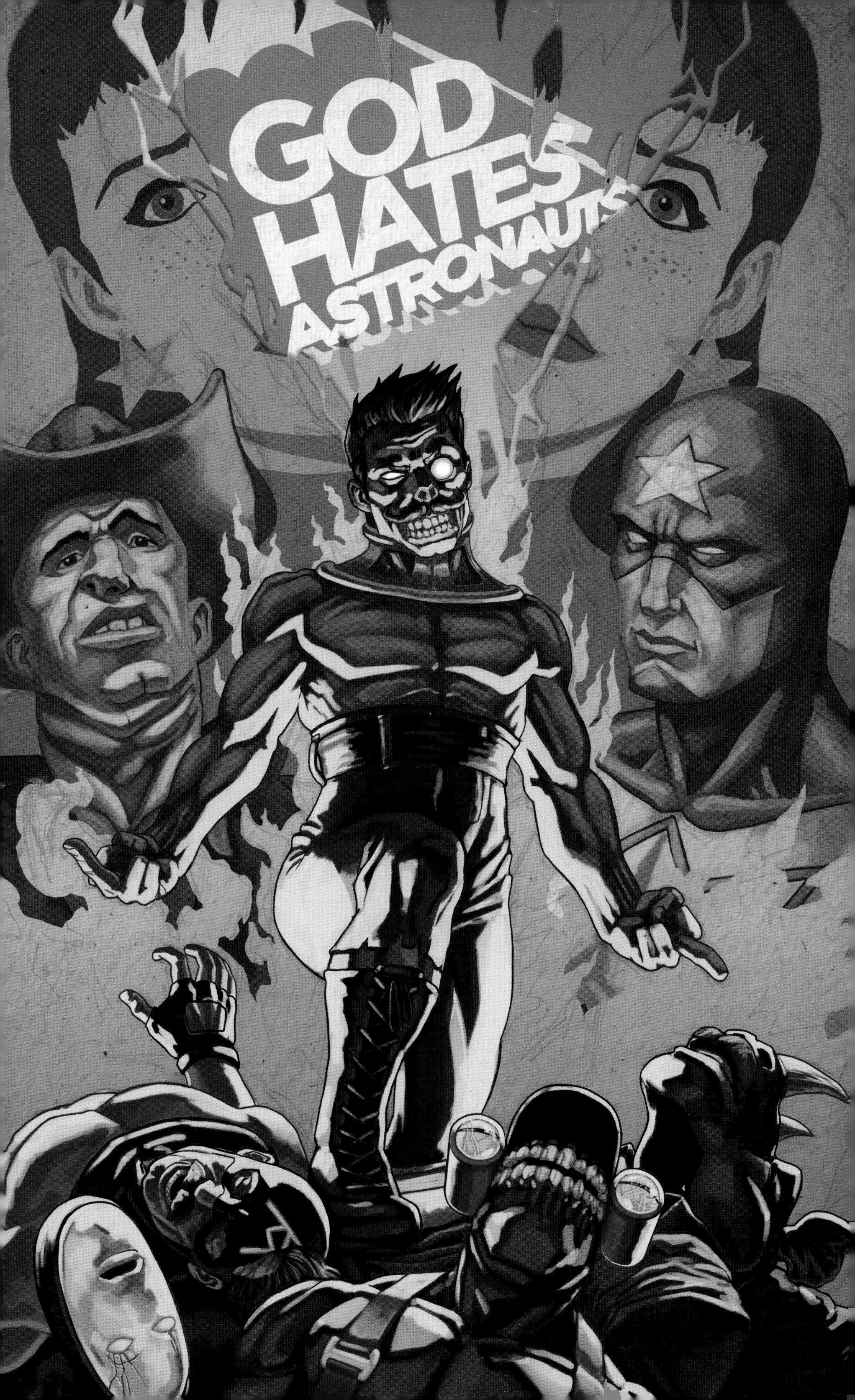
GOD
HATES
ASTRONAUTS

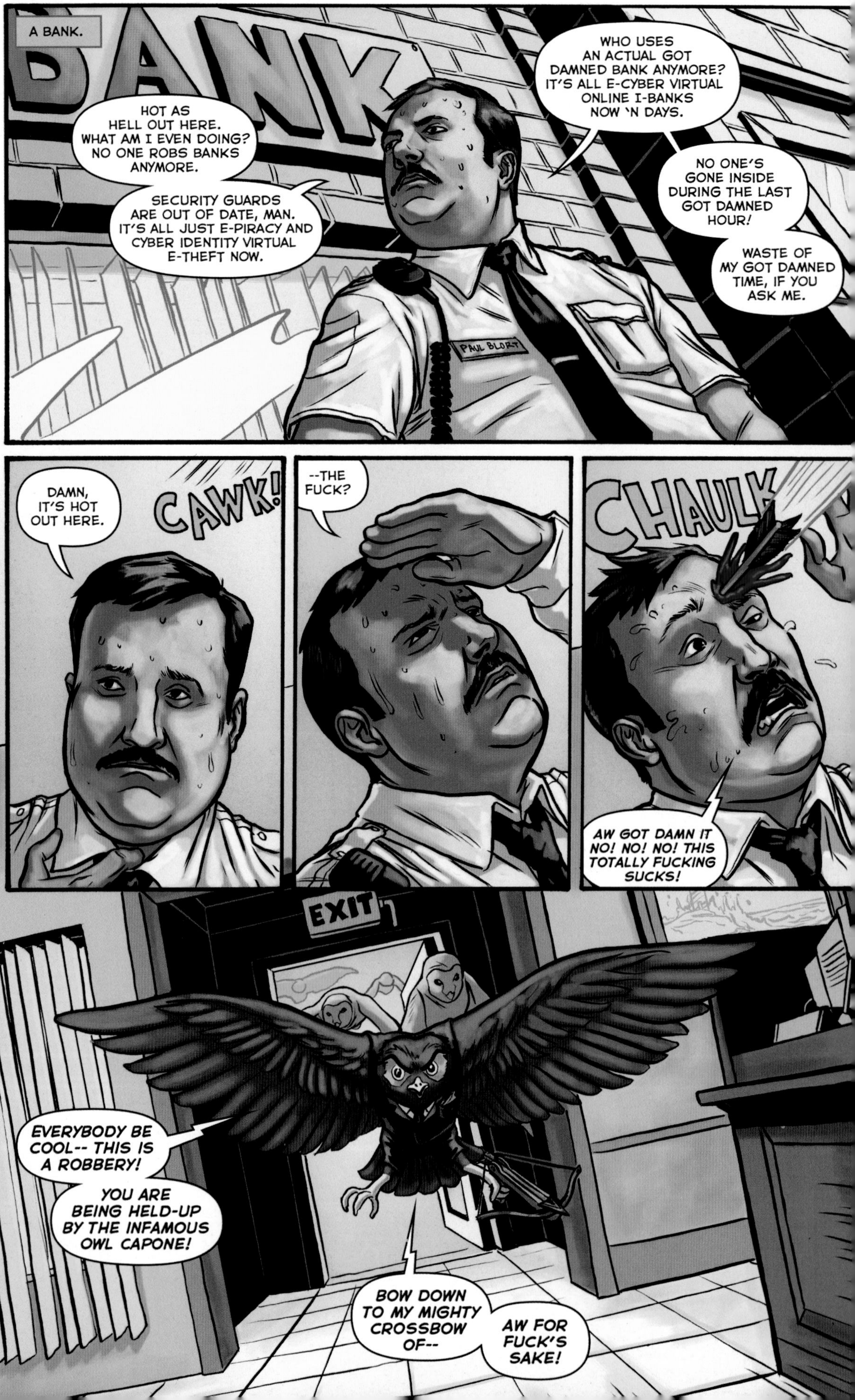
A BANK.
HOT AS HELL OUT HERE. WHAT AM I EVEN DOING? NO ONE ROBS BANKS ANYMORE.
SECURITY GUARDS ARE OUT OF DATE, MAN. IT'S ALL JUST E-PIRACY AND CYBER IDENTITY VIRTUAL E-THEFT NOW.
WHO USES AN ACTUAL GOT DAMNED BANK ANYMORE? IT'S ALL E-CYBER VIRTUAL ONLINE I-BANKS NOW 'N DAYS.
NO ONE'S GONE INSIDE DURING THE LAST GOT DAMNED HOUR!
WASTE OF MY GOT DAMNED TIME, IF YOU ASK ME.
PAUL BLORT
DAMN, IT'S HOT OUT HERE.
CAWK!
--THE FUCK?
CHAULK
AW GOT DAMN IT NO! NO! NO! THIS TOTALLY FUCKING SUCKS!
EXIT
EVERYBODY BE COOL-- THIS IS A ROBBERY!
YOU ARE BEING HELD-UP BY THE INFAMOUS OWL CAPONE!
BOW DOWN TO MY MIGHTY CROSSBOW OF--
AW FOR FUCK'S SAKE!

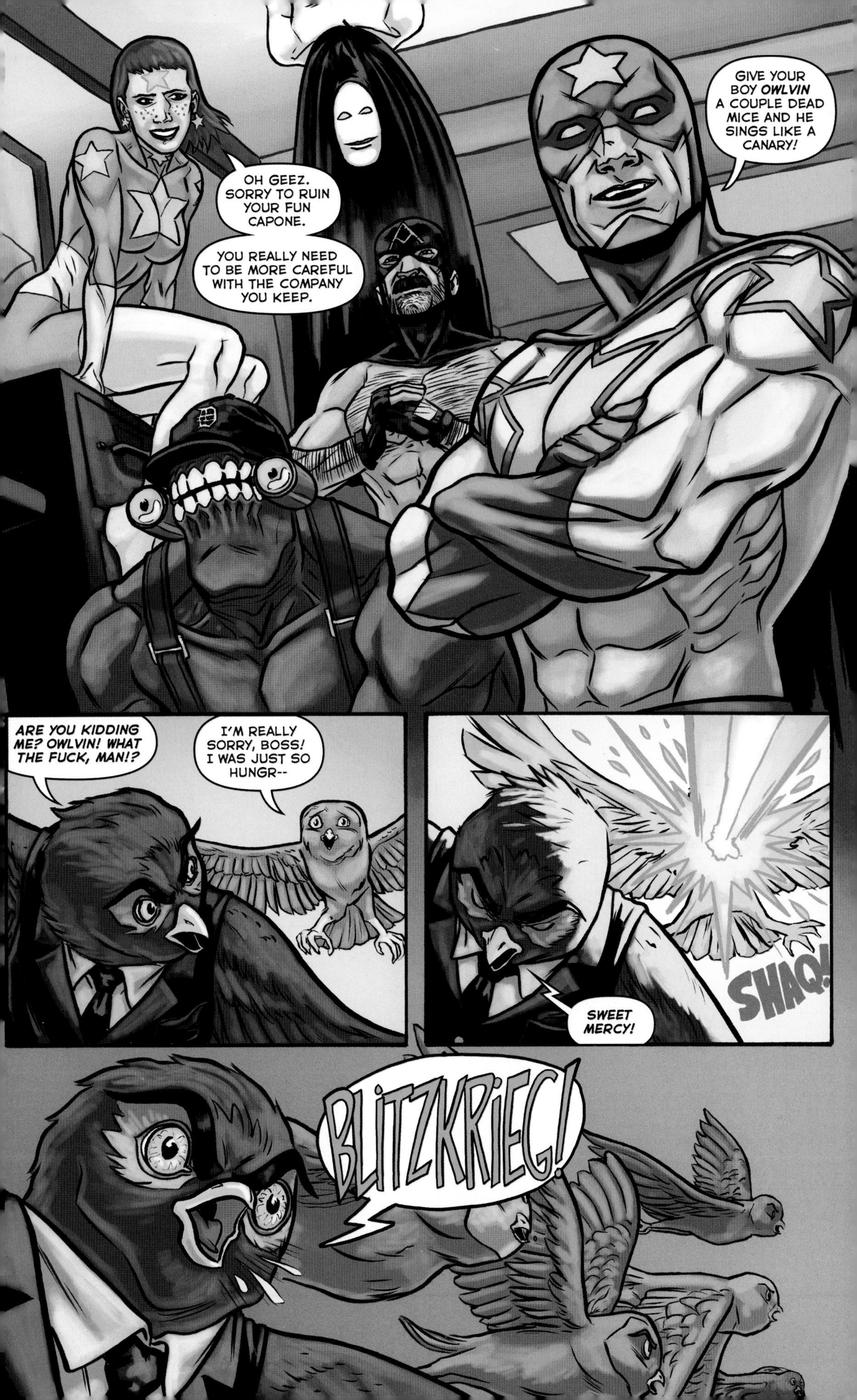
GIVE YOUR BOY OWLVIN A COUPLE DEAD MICE AND HE SINGS LIKE A CANARY!
OH GEEZ. SORRY TO RUIN YOUR FUN CAPONE.
YOU REALLY NEED TO BE MORE CAREFUL WITH THE COMPANY YOU KEEP.
ARE YOU KIDDING ME? OWLVIN! WHAT THE FUCK, MAN!?
I'M REALLY SORRY, BOSS! I WAS JUST SO HUNGR--
SHAQ!
SWEET MERCY!
BLITZKRIEG!

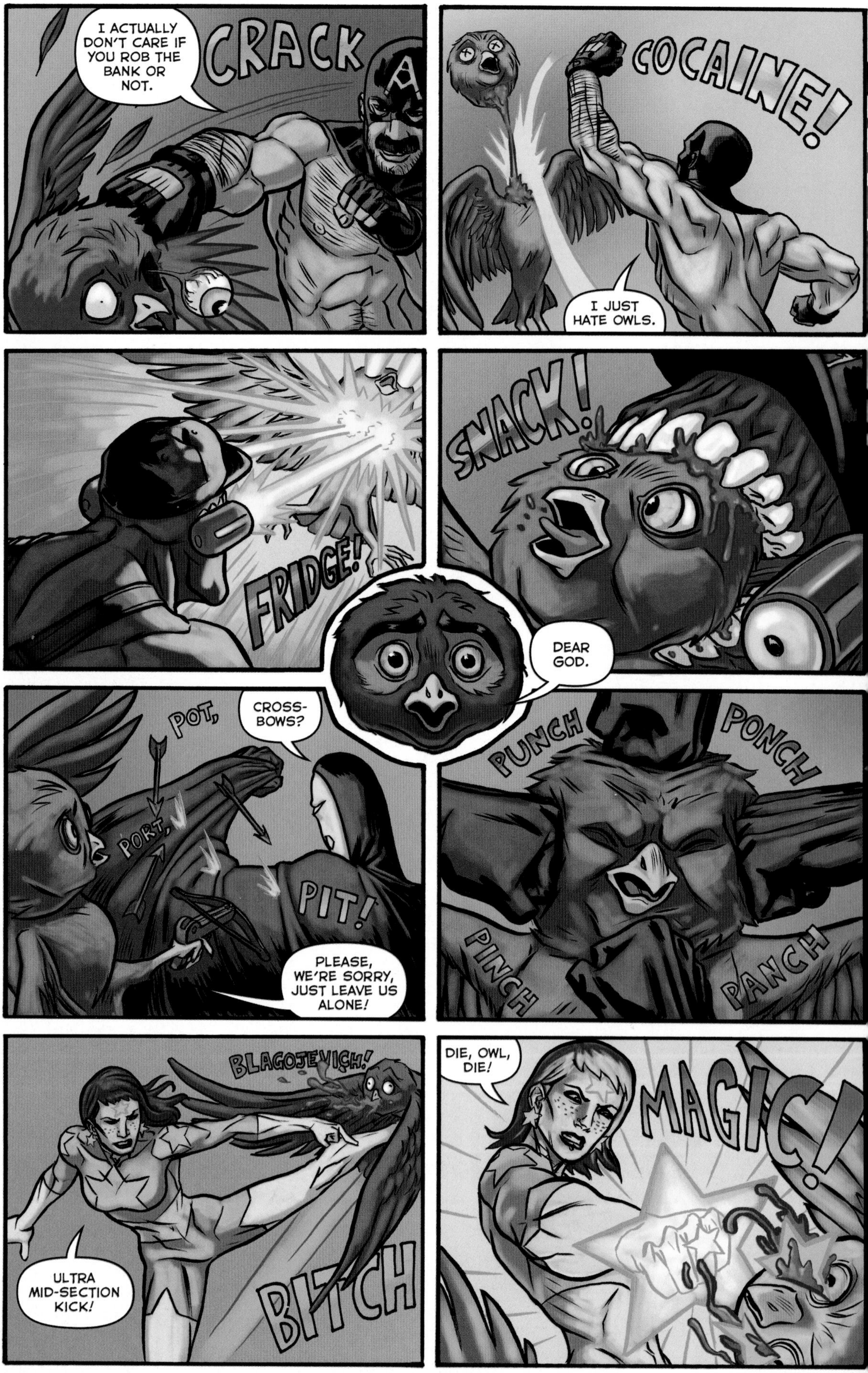
I ACTUALLY DON'T CARE IF YOU ROB THE BANK OR NOT.
CRACK
COCAINE!
I JUST HATE OWLS.
FRIDGE!
SNACK!
DEAR GOD.
POT,
PORT,
PIT!
CROSS-BOWS?
PLEASE, WE'RE SORRY, JUST LEAVE US ALONE!
PUNCH
PONCH
PINCH
PANCH
BLAGOJEVICH!
ULTRA MID-SECTION KICK!
BITCH
DIE, OWL, DIE!
MAGIC!

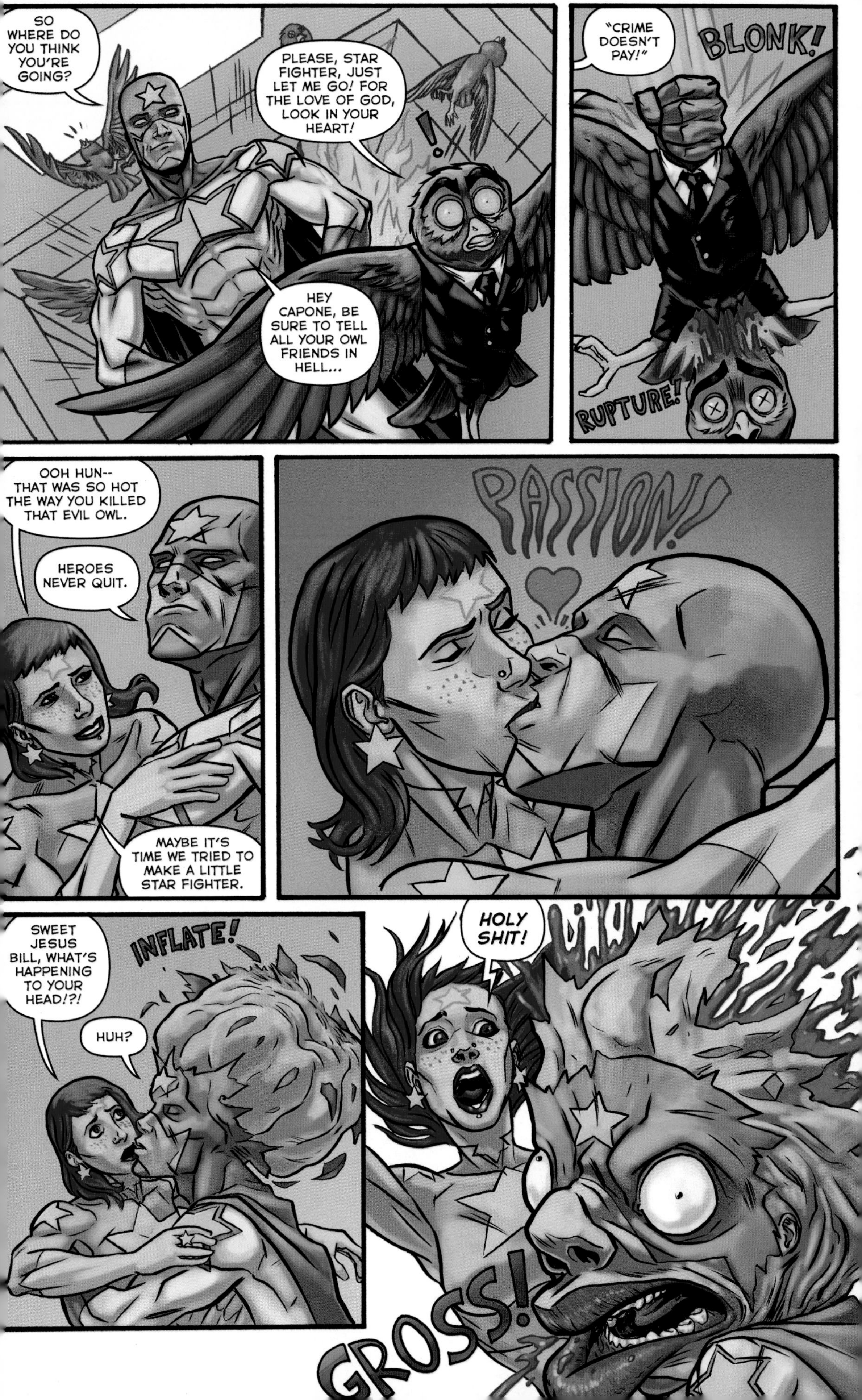
SO WHERE DO YOU THINK YOU'RE GOING?
PLEASE, STAR FIGHTER, JUST LET ME GO! FOR THE LOVE OF GOD, LOOK IN YOUR HEART!
!
HEY CAPONE, BE SURE TO TELL ALL YOUR OWL FRIENDS IN HELL...
"CRIME DOESN'T PAY!"
BLONK!
RUPTURE!
OOH HUN-- THAT WAS SO HOT THE WAY YOU KILLED THAT EVIL OWL.
HEROES NEVER QUIT.
MAYBE IT'S TIME WE TRIED TO MAKE A LITTLE STAR FIGHTER.
PASSION!
SWEET JESUS BILL, WHAT'S HAPPENING TO YOUR HEAD!?!
INFLATE!
HUH?
HOLY SHIT!
GROSS!

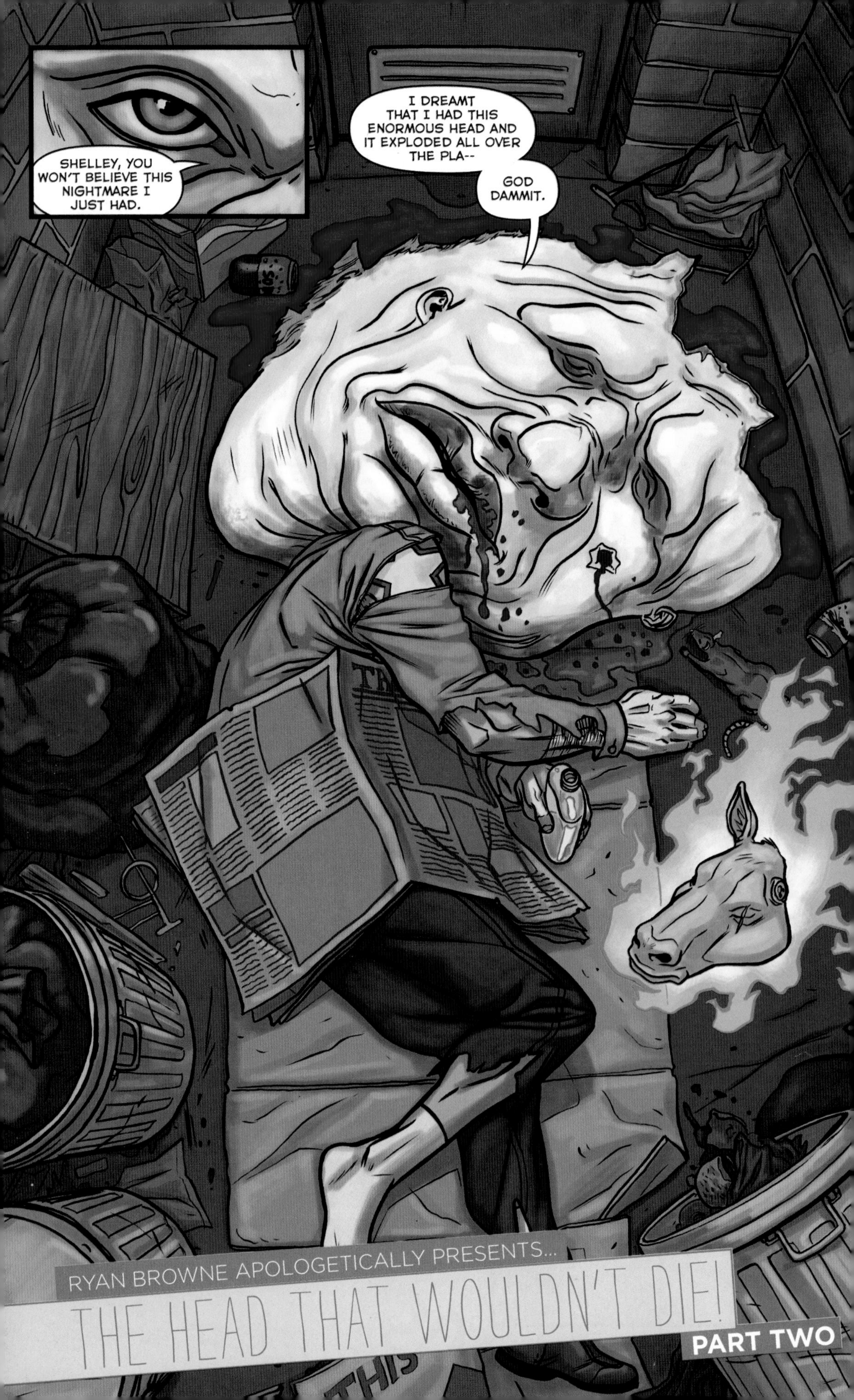
SHELLEY, YOU WON'T BELIEVE THIS NIGHTMARE I JUST HAD.
I DREAMT THAT I HAD THIS ENORMOUS HEAD AND IT EXPLODED ALL OVER THE PLA--
GOD DAMMIT.
RYAN BROWNE APOLOGETICALLY PRESENTS...
THE HEAD THAT WOULDN'T DIE!
PART TWO

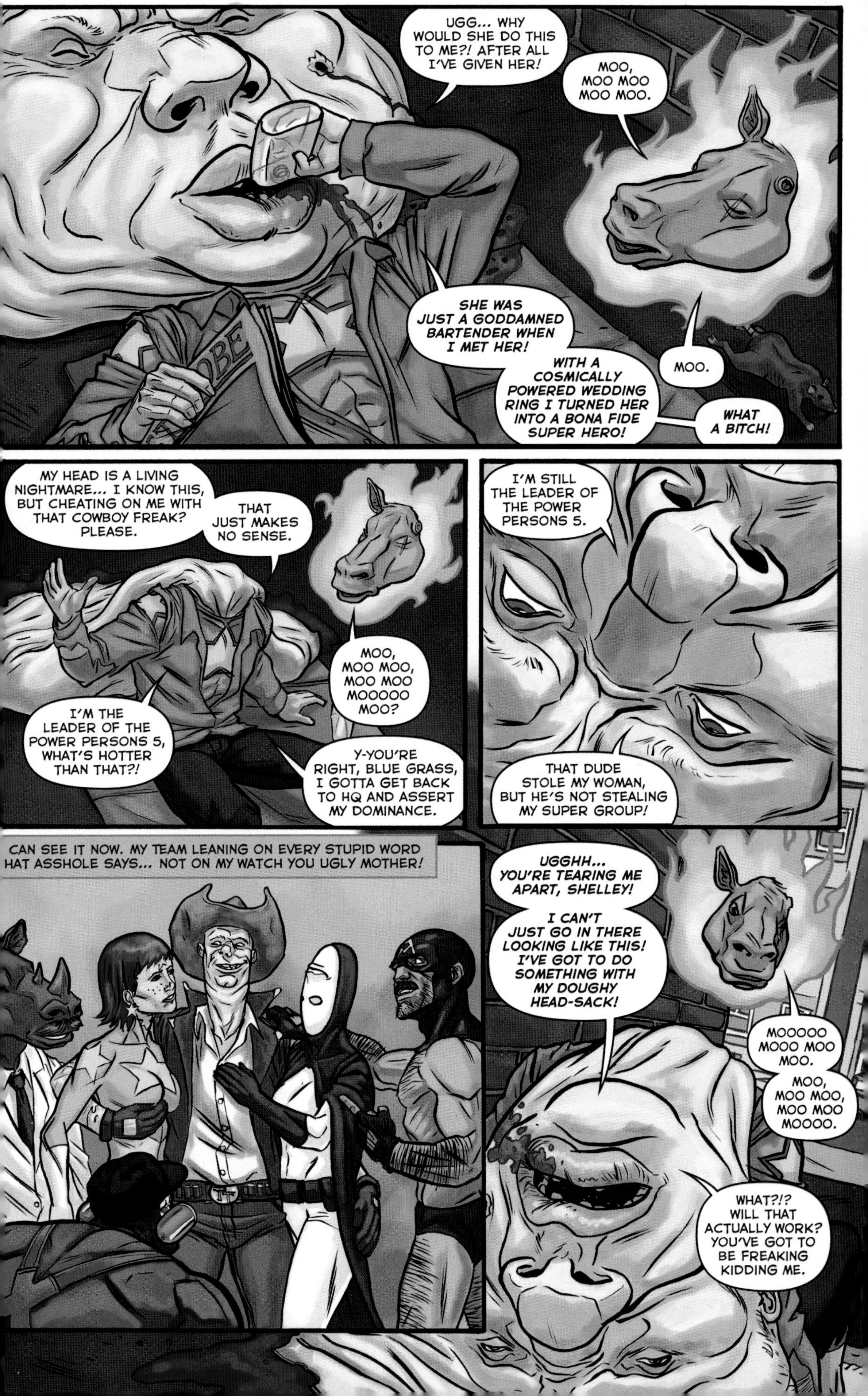
UGG... WHY WOULD SHE DO THIS TO ME?! AFTER ALL I'VE GIVEN HER!
MOO, MOO MOO MOO MOO.
SHE WAS JUST A GODDAMNED BARTENDER WHEN I MET HER!
WITH A COSMICALLY POWERED WEDDING RING I TURNED HER INTO A BONA FIDE SUPER HERO!
MOO.
WHAT A BITCH!
MY HEAD IS A LIVING NIGHTMARE... I KNOW THIS, BUT CHEATING ON ME WITH THAT COWBOY FREAK? PLEASE.
THAT JUST MAKES NO SENSE.
MOO, MOO MOO, MOO MOO MOOOOO MOO?
I'M THE LEADER OF THE POWER PERSONS 5, WHAT'S HOTTER THAN THAT?!
Y-YOU'RE RIGHT, BLUE GRASS, I GOTTA GET BACK TO HQ AND ASSERT MY DOMINANCE.
I'M STILL THE LEADER OF THE POWER PERSONS 5.
THAT DUDE STOLE MY WOMAN, BUT HE'S NOT STEALING MY SUPER GROUP!
CAN SEE IT NOW. MY TEAM LEANING ON EVERY STUPID WORD
HAT ASSHOLE SAYS... NOT ON MY WATCH YOU UGLY MOTHER!
UGGHH... YOU'RE TEARING ME APART, SHELLEY!
I CAN'T JUST GO IN THERE LOOKING LIKE THIS! I'VE GOT TO DO SOMETHING WITH MY DOUGHY HEAD-SACK!
MOOOOO MOOO MOO MOO.
MOO, MOO MOO, MOO MOO MOOOO.
WHAT?!? WILL THAT ACTUALLY WORK? YOU'VE GOT TO BE FREAKING KIDDING ME.

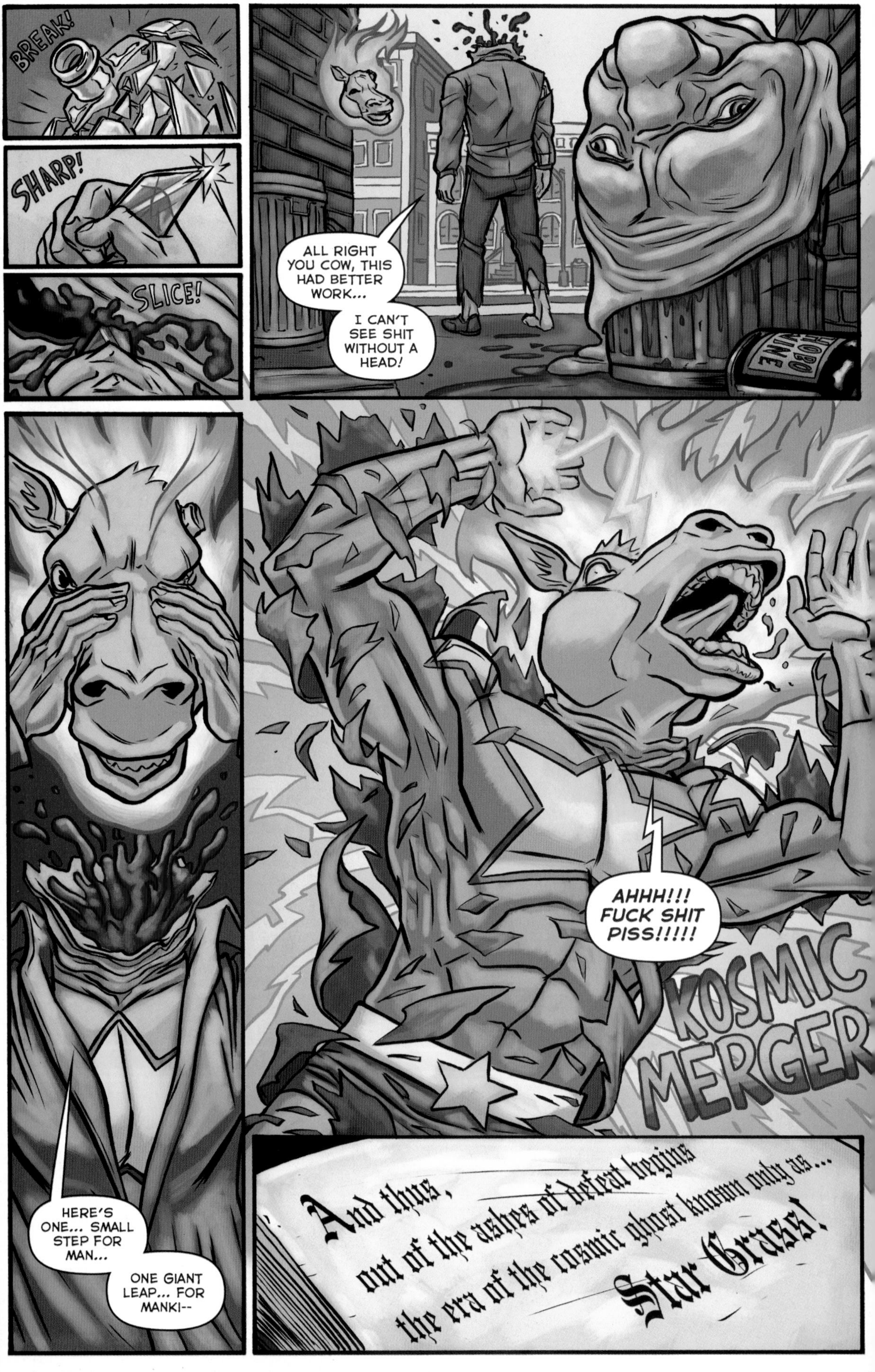
BREAK!
SHARP!
SLICE!
ALL RIGHT YOU COW, THIS HAD BETTER WORK...
I CAN'T SEE SHIT WITHOUT A HEAD!
HOBO WINE
HERE'S ONE... SMALL STEP FOR MAN...
ONE GIANT LEAP... FOR MANKI--
AHHH!!! FUCK SHIT PISS!!!!!
KOSMIC MERGER
And thus,
out of the ashes of defeat begins
the era of the cosmic ghost known only as...
Star Grass!

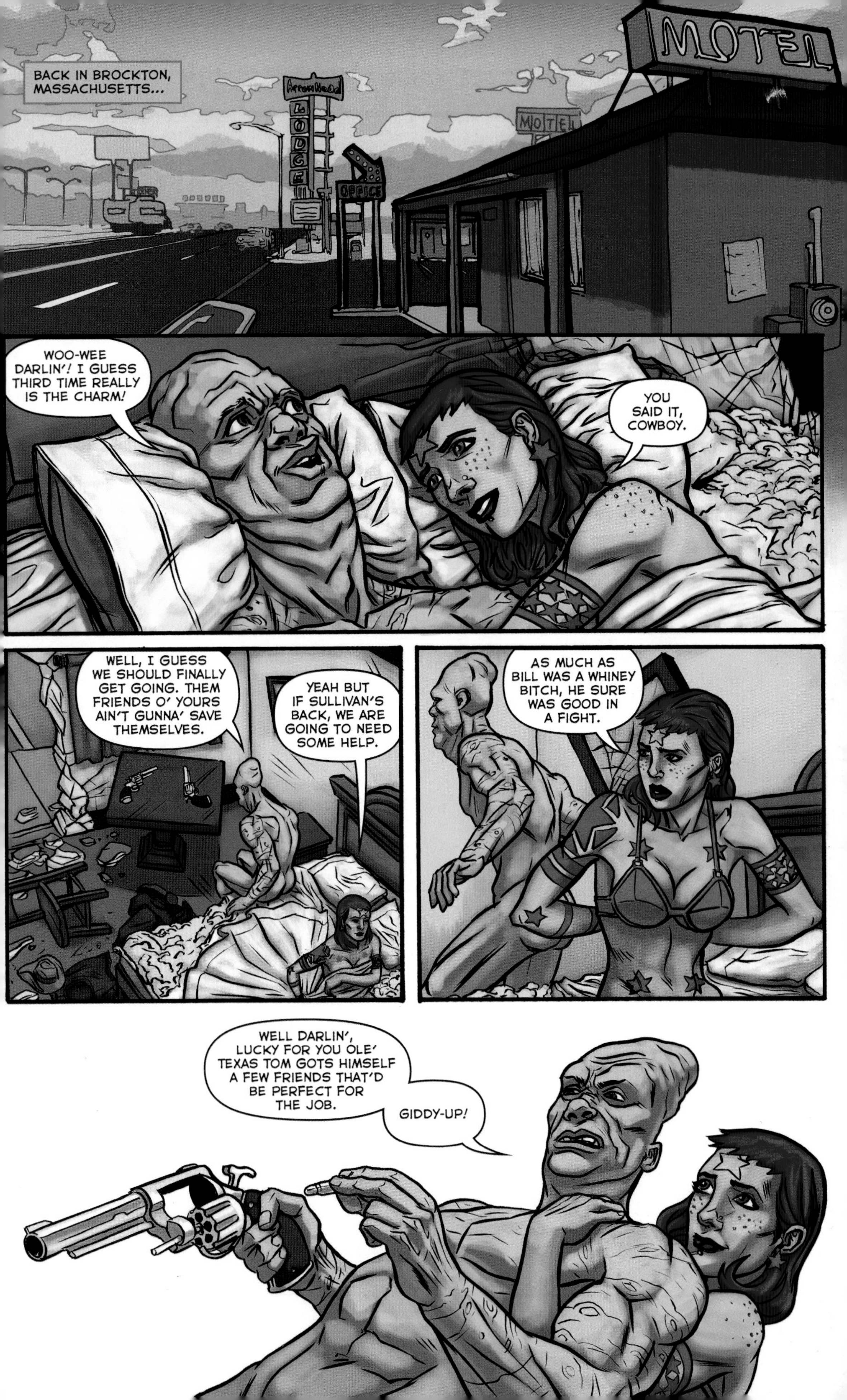
BACK IN BROCKTON, MASSACHUSETTS...
MOTEL
ArrowHead LODGE
MOTEL
OFFICE
WOO-WEE DARLIN'! I GUESS THIRD TIME REALLY IS THE CHARM!
YOU SAID IT, COWBOY.
WELL, I GUESS WE SHOULD FINALLY GET GOING. THEM FRIENDS O' YOURS AIN'T GUNNA' SAVE THEMSELVES.
YEAH BUT IF SULLIVAN'S BACK, WE ARE GOING TO NEED SOME HELP.
AS MUCH AS BILL WAS A WHINEY BITCH, HE SURE WAS GOOD IN A FIGHT.
WELL DARLIN', LUCKY FOR YOU OLE' TEXAS TOM GOTS HIMSELF A FEW FRIENDS THAT'D BE PERFECT FOR THE JOB.
GIDDY-UP!

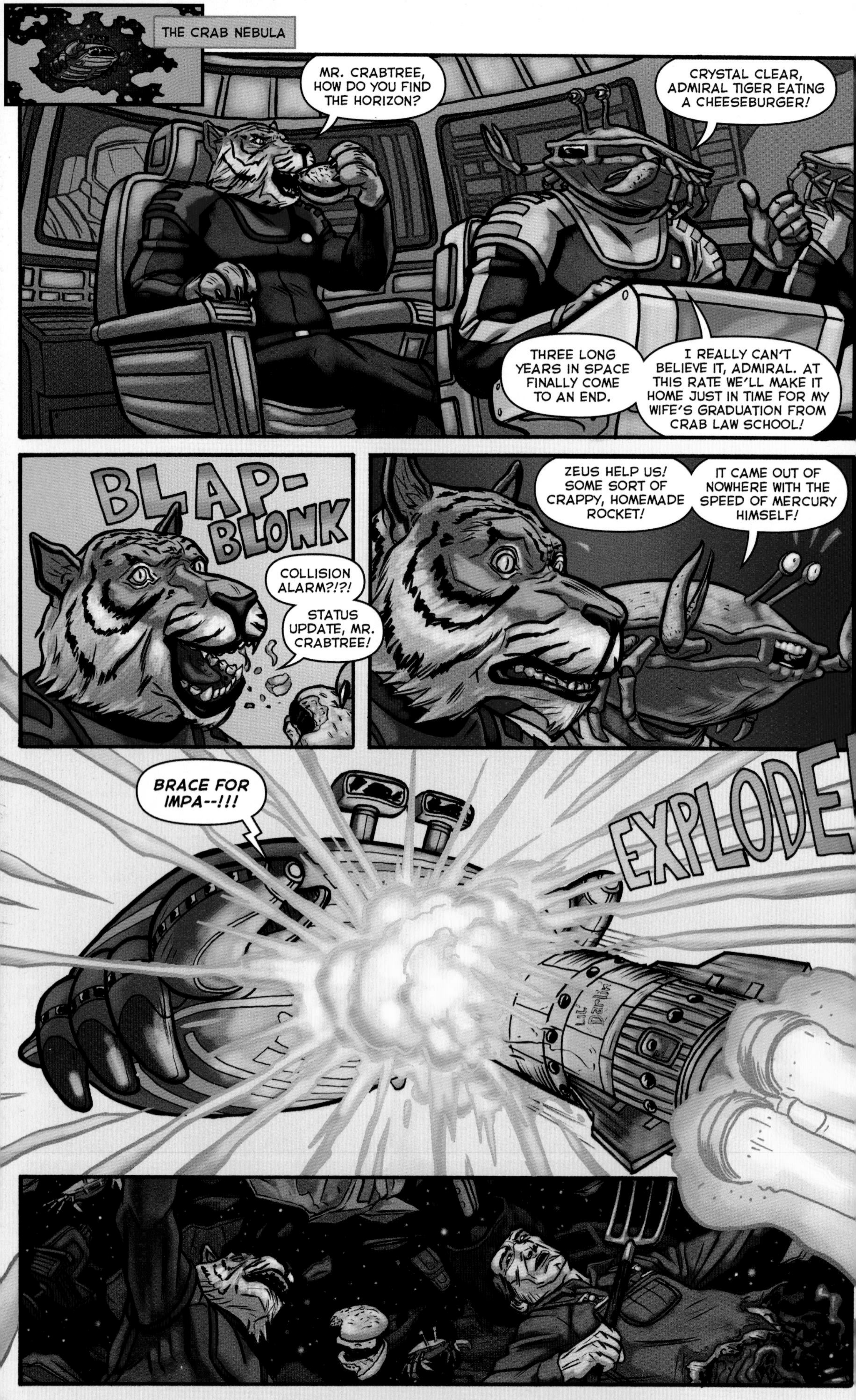
THE CRAB NEBULA
MR. CRABTREE, HOW DO YOU FIND THE HORIZON?
CRYSTAL CLEAR, ADMIRAL TIGER EATING A CHEESEBURGER!
THREE LONG YEARS IN SPACE FINALLY COME TO AN END.
I REALLY CAN'T BELIEVE IT, ADMIRAL. AT THIS RATE WE'LL MAKE IT HOME JUST IN TIME FOR MY WIFE'S GRADUATION FROM CRAB LAW SCHOOL!
BLAP-BLONK
COLLISION ALARM?!?!
STATUS UPDATE, MR. CRABTREE!
ZEUS HELP US! SOME SORT OF CRAPPY, HOMEMADE ROCKET!
IT CAME OUT OF NOWHERE WITH THE SPEED OF MERCURY HIMSELF!
BRACE FOR IMPA--!!!
EXPLODE

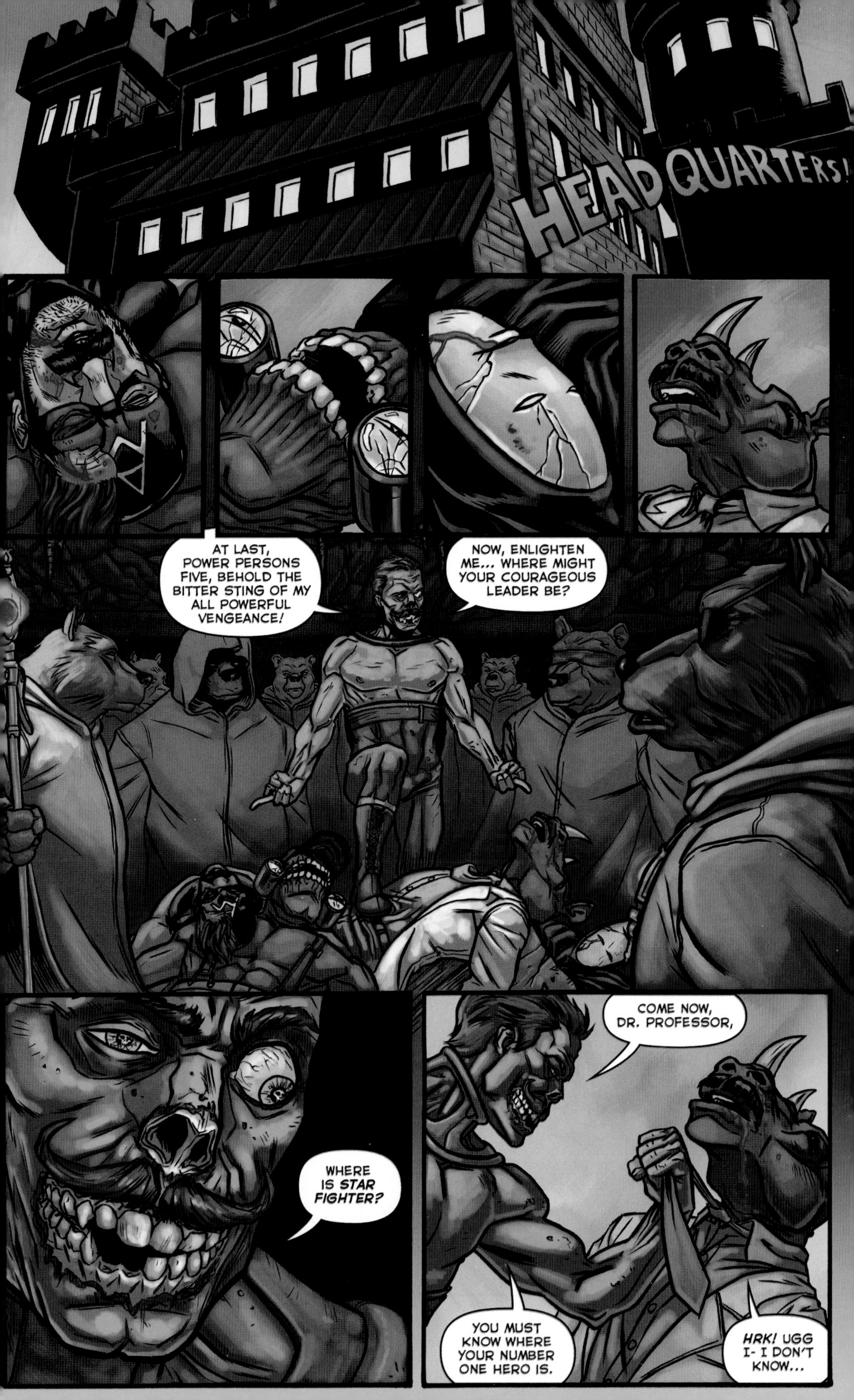
HEADQUARTERS!
AT LAST, POWER PERSONS FIVE, BEHOLD THE BITTER STING OF MY ALL POWERFUL VENGEANCE!
NOW, ENLIGHTEN ME... WHERE MIGHT YOUR COURAGEOUS LEADER BE?
WHERE IS STAR FIGHTER?
COME NOW, DR. PROFESSOR,
YOU MUST KNOW WHERE YOUR NUMBER ONE HERO IS.
HRK! UGG I- I DON'T KNOW...

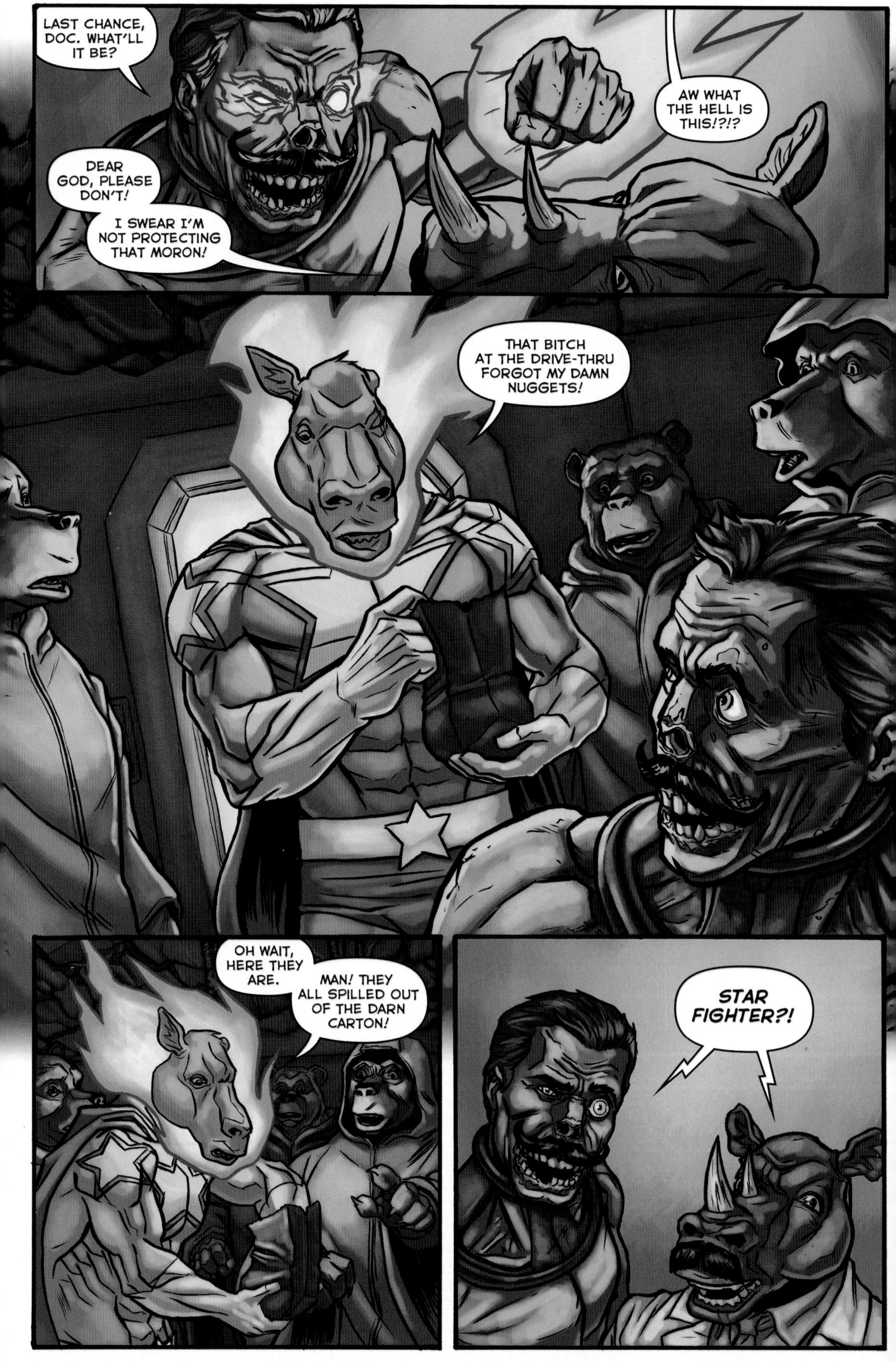
LAST CHANCE, DOC. WHAT'LL IT BE?
AW WHAT THE HELL IS THIS!?!?
DEAR GOD, PLEASE DON'T!
I SWEAR I'M NOT PROTECTING THAT MORON!
THAT BITCH AT THE DRIVE-THRU FORGOT MY DAMN NUGGETS!
OH WAIT, HERE THEY ARE.
MAN! THEY ALL SPILLED OUT OF THE DARN CARTON!
STAR FIGHTER?!

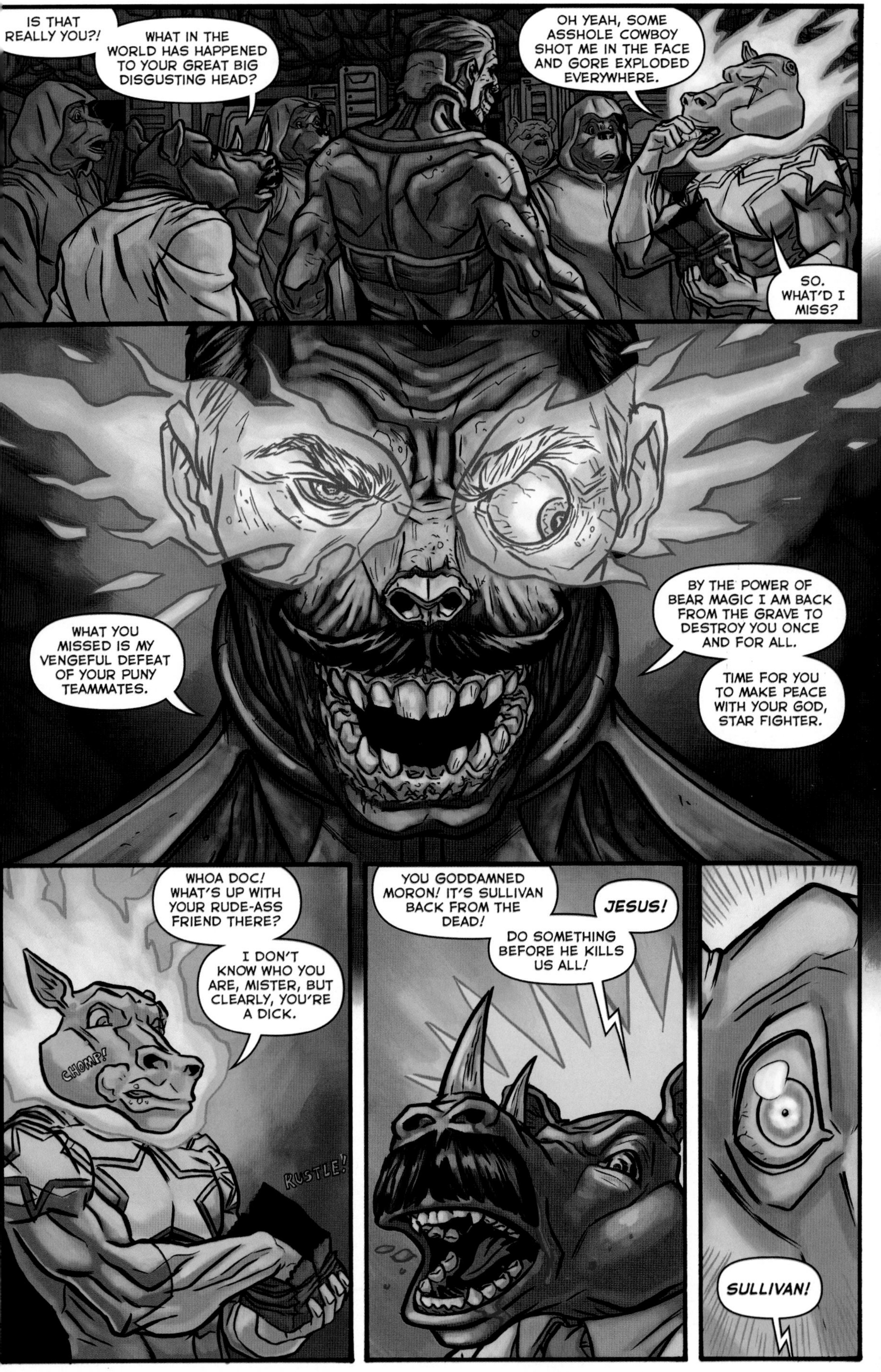
IS THAT REALLY YOU?!
WHAT IN THE WORLD HAS HAPPENED TO YOUR GREAT BIG DISGUSTING HEAD?
OH YEAH, SOME ASSHOLE COWBOY SHOT ME IN THE FACE AND GORE EXPLODED EVERYWHERE.
SO. WHAT'D I MISS?
WHAT YOU MISSED IS MY VENGEFUL DEFEAT OF YOUR PUNY TEAMMATES.
BY THE POWER OF BEAR MAGIC I AM BACK FROM THE GRAVE TO DESTROY YOU ONCE AND FOR ALL.
TIME FOR YOU TO MAKE PEACE WITH YOUR GOD, STAR FIGHTER.
WHOA DOC! WHAT'S UP WITH YOUR RUDE-ASS FRIEND THERE?
I DON'T KNOW WHO YOU ARE, MISTER, BUT CLEARLY, YOU'RE A DICK.
CHOMP!
RUSTLE!
YOU GODDAMNED MORON! IT'S SULLIVAN BACK FROM THE DEAD!
JESUS!
DO SOMETHING BEFORE HE KILLS US ALL!
SULLIVAN!

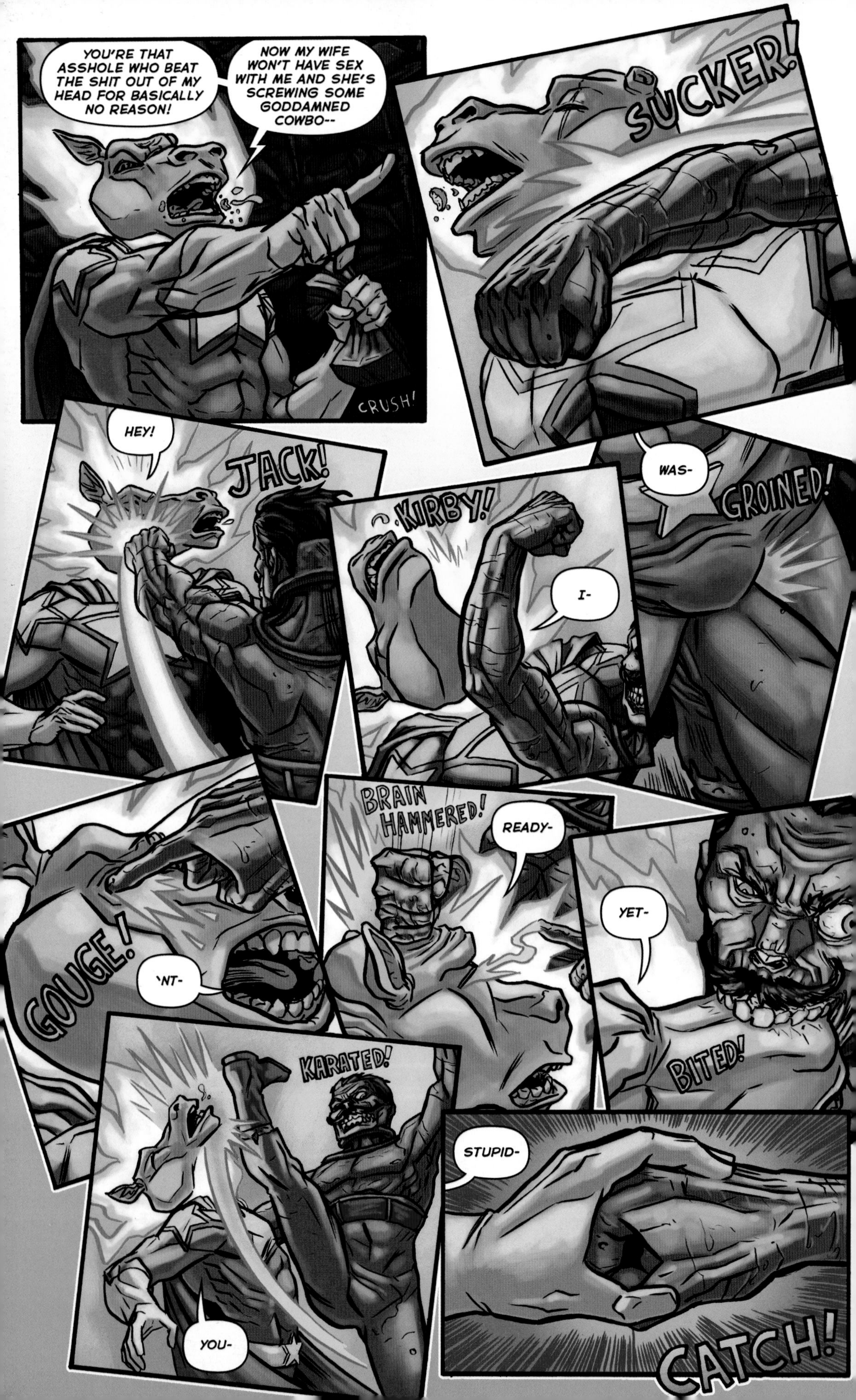

YOU'RE THAT ASSHOLE WHO BEAT THE SHIT OUT OF MY HEAD FOR BASICALLY NO REASON!
NOW MY WIFE WON'T HAVE SEX WITH ME AND SHE'S SCREWING SOME GODDAMNED COWBO--
CRUSH!
SUCKER!
HEY!
JACK!
KIRBY!
I-
WAS-
GROINED!
GOUGE!
'NT-
BRAIN HAMMERED!
READY-
YET-
BITED!
KARATED!
YOU-
STUPID-
CATCH!

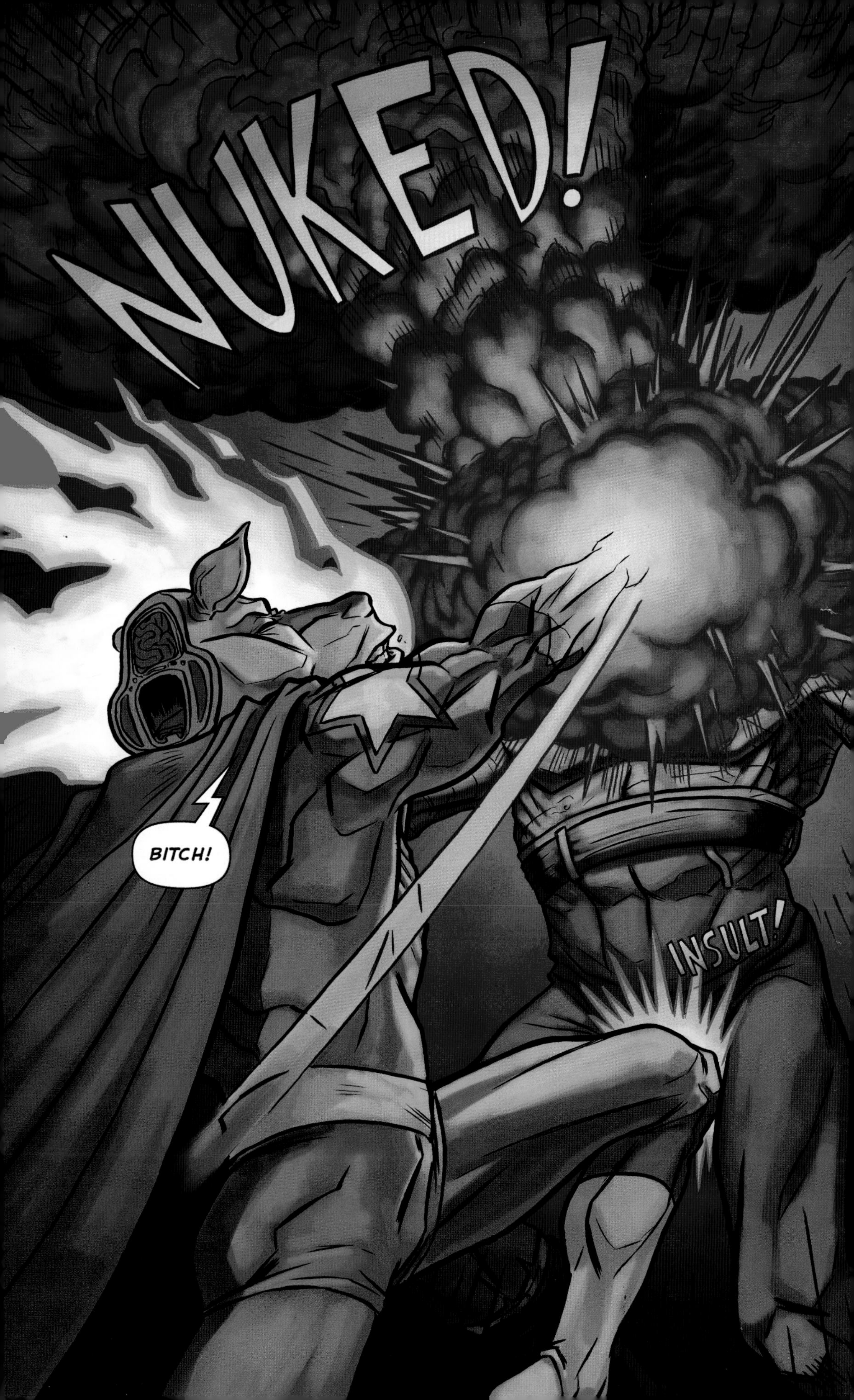
NUKED!
BITCH!
INSULT!

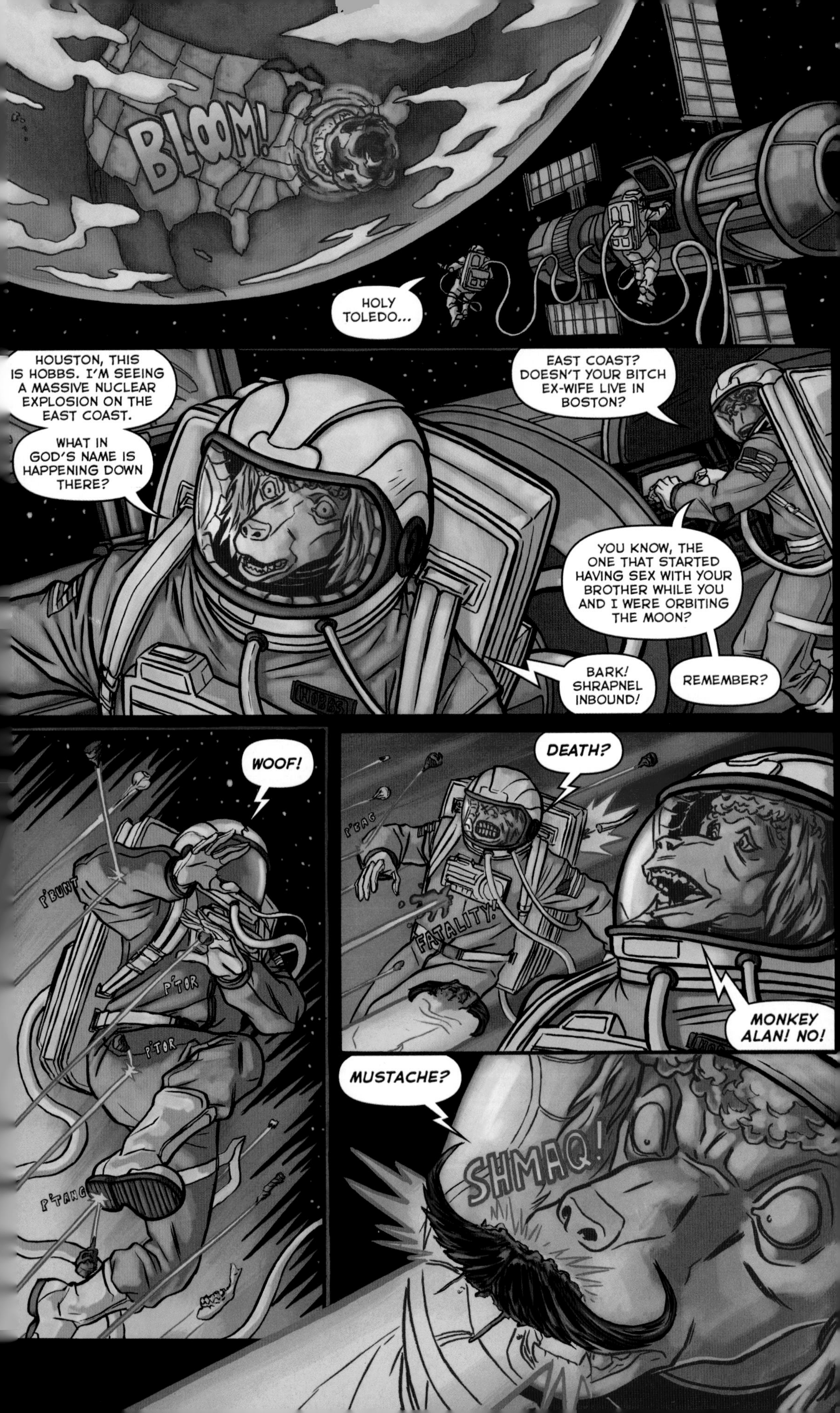
BLOOM!
HOLY TOLEDO...
HOUSTON, THIS IS HOBBS. I'M SEEING A MASSIVE NUCLEAR EXPLOSION ON THE EAST COAST.
WHAT IN GOD'S NAME IS HAPPENING DOWN THERE?
EAST COAST? DOESN'T YOUR BITCH EX-WIFE LIVE IN BOSTON?
YOU KNOW, THE ONE THAT STARTED HAVING SEX WITH YOUR BROTHER WHILE YOU AND I WERE ORBITING THE MOON?
REMEMBER?
BARK! SHRAPNEL INBOUND!
HOBBS
WOOF!
P'BUNT
P'TOR
P'TOR
P'TANG
DEATH?
P'BAG
FATALITY
MONKEY ALAN! NO!
MUSTACHE?
SHMAQ!

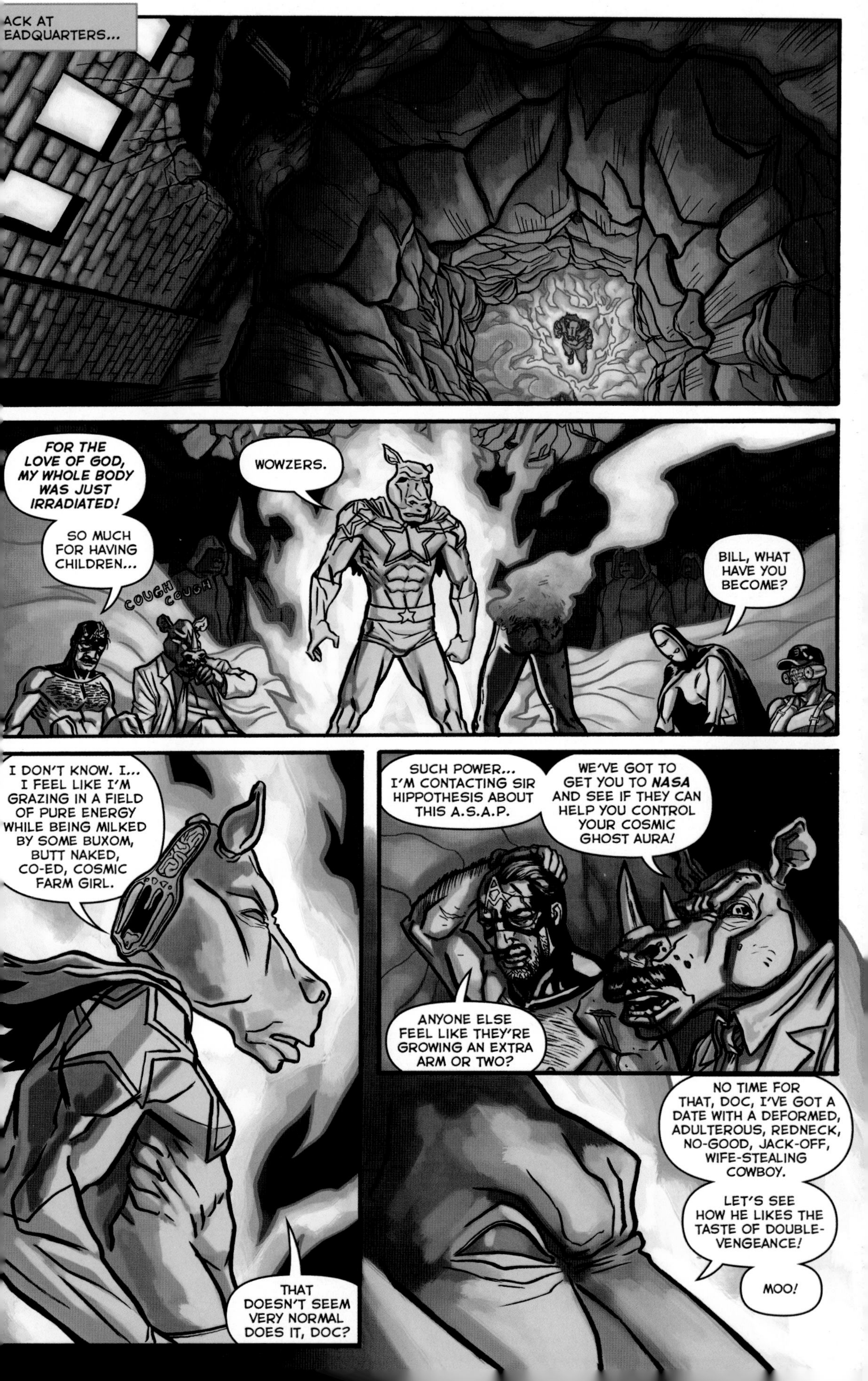
ACK AT EADQUARTERS...
FOR THE LOVE OF GOD, MY WHOLE BODY WAS JUST IRRADIATED!
SO MUCH FOR HAVING CHILDREN...
COUGH COUGH
WOWZERS.
BILL, WHAT HAVE YOU BECOME?
I DON'T KNOW. I... I FEEL LIKE I'M GRAZING IN A FIELD OF PURE ENERGY WHILE BEING MILKED BY SOME BUXOM, BUTT NAKED, CO-ED, COSMIC FARM GIRL.
THAT DOESN'T SEEM VERY NORMAL DOES IT, DOC?
SUCH POWER... I'M CONTACTING SIR HIPPOTHESIS ABOUT THIS A.S.A.P.
WE'VE GOT TO GET YOU TO NASA AND SEE IF THEY CAN HELP YOU CONTROL YOUR COSMIC GHOST AURA!
ANYONE ELSE FEEL LIKE THEY'RE GROWING AN EXTRA ARM OR TWO?
NO TIME FOR THAT, DOC, I'VE GOT A DATE WITH A DEFORMED, ADULTEROUS, REDNECK, NO-GOOD, JACK-OFF, WIFE-STEALING COWBOY.
LET'S SEE HOW HE LIKES THE TASTE OF DOUBLE-VENGEANCE!
MOO!

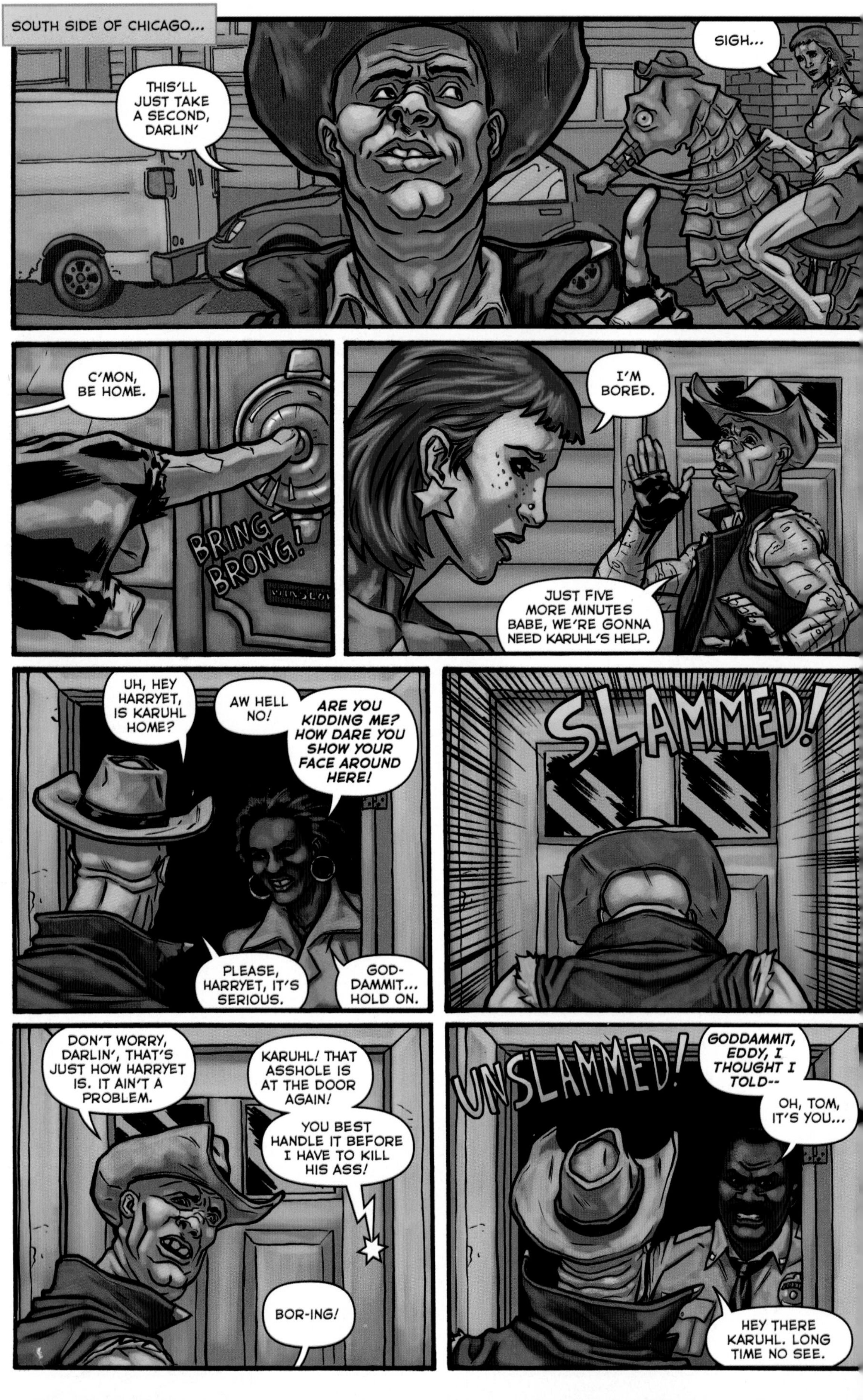
SOUTH SIDE OF CHICAGO...
THIS'LL JUST TAKE A SECOND, DARLIN'
SIGH...
C'MON, BE HOME.
BRING-BRONG!
I'M BORED.
JUST FIVE MORE MINUTES BABE, WE'RE GONNA NEED KARUHL'S HELP.
UH, HEY HARRYET, IS KARUHL HOME?
AW HELL NO!
ARE YOU KIDDING ME? HOW DARE YOU SHOW YOUR FACE AROUND HERE!
PLEASE, HARRYET, IT'S SERIOUS.
GOD-DAMMIT... HOLD ON.
SLAMMED!
DON'T WORRY, DARLIN', THAT'S JUST HOW HARRYET IS. IT AIN'T A PROBLEM.
KARUHL! THAT ASSHOLE IS AT THE DOOR AGAIN!
YOU BEST HANDLE IT BEFORE I HAVE TO KILL HIS ASS!
BOR-ING!
UNSLAMMED!
GODDAMMIT, EDDY, I THOUGHT I TOLD--
OH, TOM, IT'S YOU...
HEY THERE KARUHL. LONG TIME NO SEE.

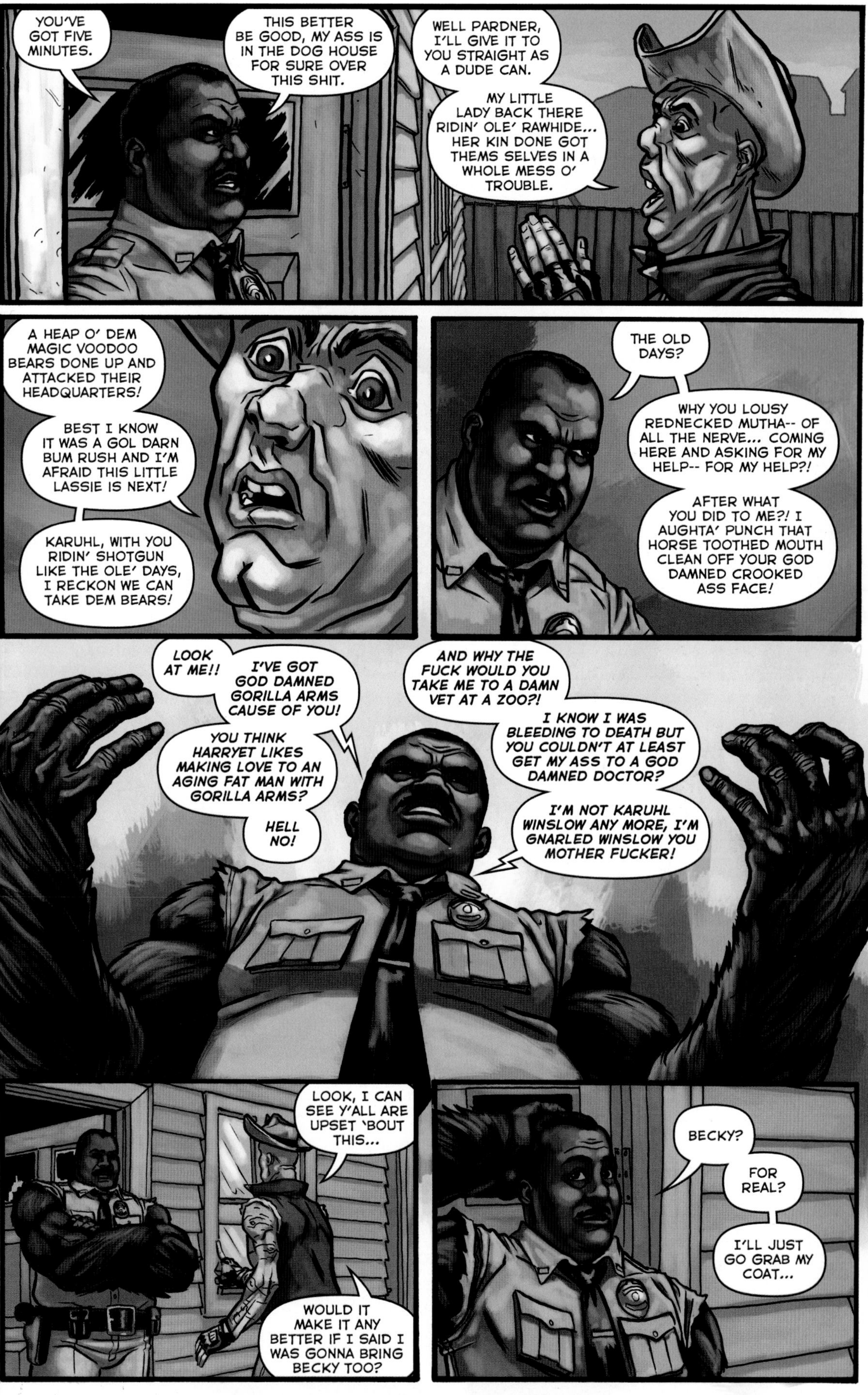
YOU'VE GOT FIVE MINUTES.
THIS BETTER BE GOOD, MY ASS IS IN THE DOG HOUSE FOR SURE OVER THIS SHIT.
WELL PARDNER, I'LL GIVE IT TO YOU STRAIGHT AS A DUDE CAN.
MY LITTLE LADY BACK THERE RIDIN' OLE' RAWHIDE... HER KIN DONE GOT THEMS SELVES IN A WHOLE MESS O' TROUBLE.
A HEAP O' DEM MAGIC VOODOO BEARS DONE UP AND ATTACKED THEIR HEADQUARTERS!
BEST I KNOW IT WAS A GOL DARN BUM RUSH AND I'M AFRAID THIS LITTLE LASSIE IS NEXT!
KARUHL, WITH YOU RIDIN' SHOTGUN LIKE THE OLE' DAYS, I RECKON WE CAN TAKE DEM BEARS!
THE OLD DAYS?
WHY YOU LOUSY REDNECKED MUTHA-- OF ALL THE NERVE... COMING HERE AND ASKING FOR MY HELP-- FOR MY HELP?!
AFTER WHAT YOU DID TO ME?! I AUGHTA' PUNCH THAT HORSE TOOTHED MOUTH CLEAN OFF YOUR GOD DAMNED CROOKED ASS FACE!
LOOK AT ME!!
I'VE GOT GOD DAMNED GORILLA ARMS CAUSE OF YOU!
YOU THINK HARRYET LIKES MAKING LOVE TO AN AGING FAT MAN WITH GORILLA ARMS?
HELL NO!
AND WHY THE FUCK WOULD YOU TAKE ME TO A DAMN VET AT A ZOO?!
I KNOW I WAS BLEEDING TO DEATH BUT YOU COULDN'T AT LEAST GET MY ASS TO A GOD DAMNED DOCTOR?
I'M NOT KARUHL WINSLOW ANY MORE, I'M GNARLED WINSLOW YOU MOTHER FUCKER!
LOOK, I CAN SEE Y'ALL ARE UPSET 'BOUT THIS...
WOULD IT MAKE IT ANY BETTER IF I SAID I WAS GONNA BRING BECKY TOO?
BECKY?
FOR REAL?
I'LL JUST GO GRAB MY COAT...

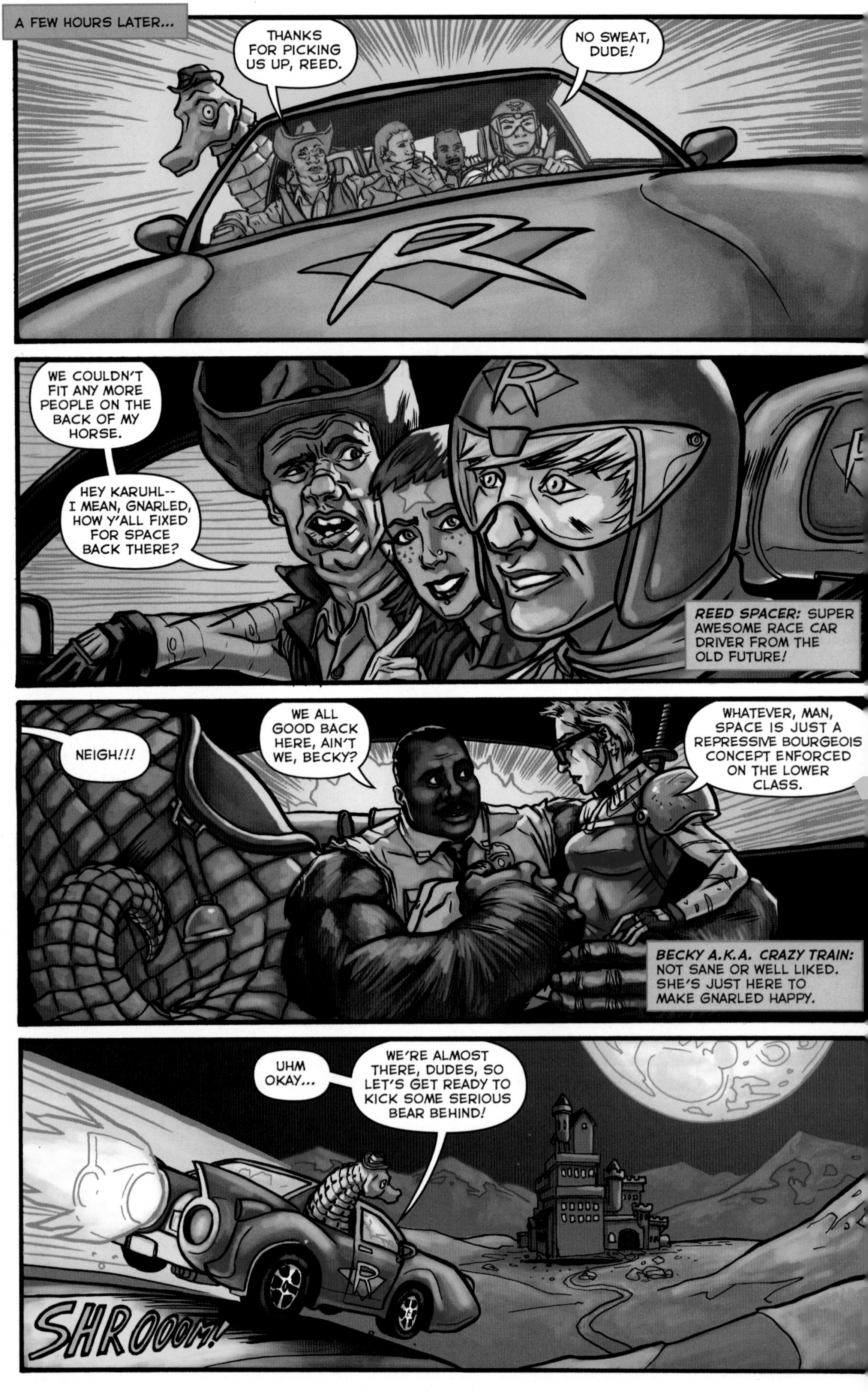
A FEW HOURS LATER...
THANKS FOR PICKING US UP, REED.
NO SWEAT, DUDE!
WE COULDN'T FIT ANY MORE PEOPLE ON THE BACK OF MY HORSE.
HEY KARUHL-- I MEAN, GNARLED, HOW Y'ALL FIXED FOR SPACE BACK THERE?
REED SPACER: SUPER AWESOME RACE CAR DRIVER FROM THE OLD FUTURE!
NEIGH!!!
WE ALL GOOD BACK HERE, AIN'T WE, BECKY?
WHATEVER, MAN, SPACE IS JUST A REPRESSIVE BOURGEOIS CONCEPT ENFORCED ON THE LOWER CLASS.
BECKY A.K.A. CRAZY TRAIN: NOT SANE OR WELL LIKED. SHE'S JUST HERE TO MAKE GNARLED HAPPY.
UHM OKAY...
WE'RE ALMOST THERE, DUDES, SO LET'S GET READY TO KICK SOME SERIOUS BEAR BEHIND!
SHROOOM!

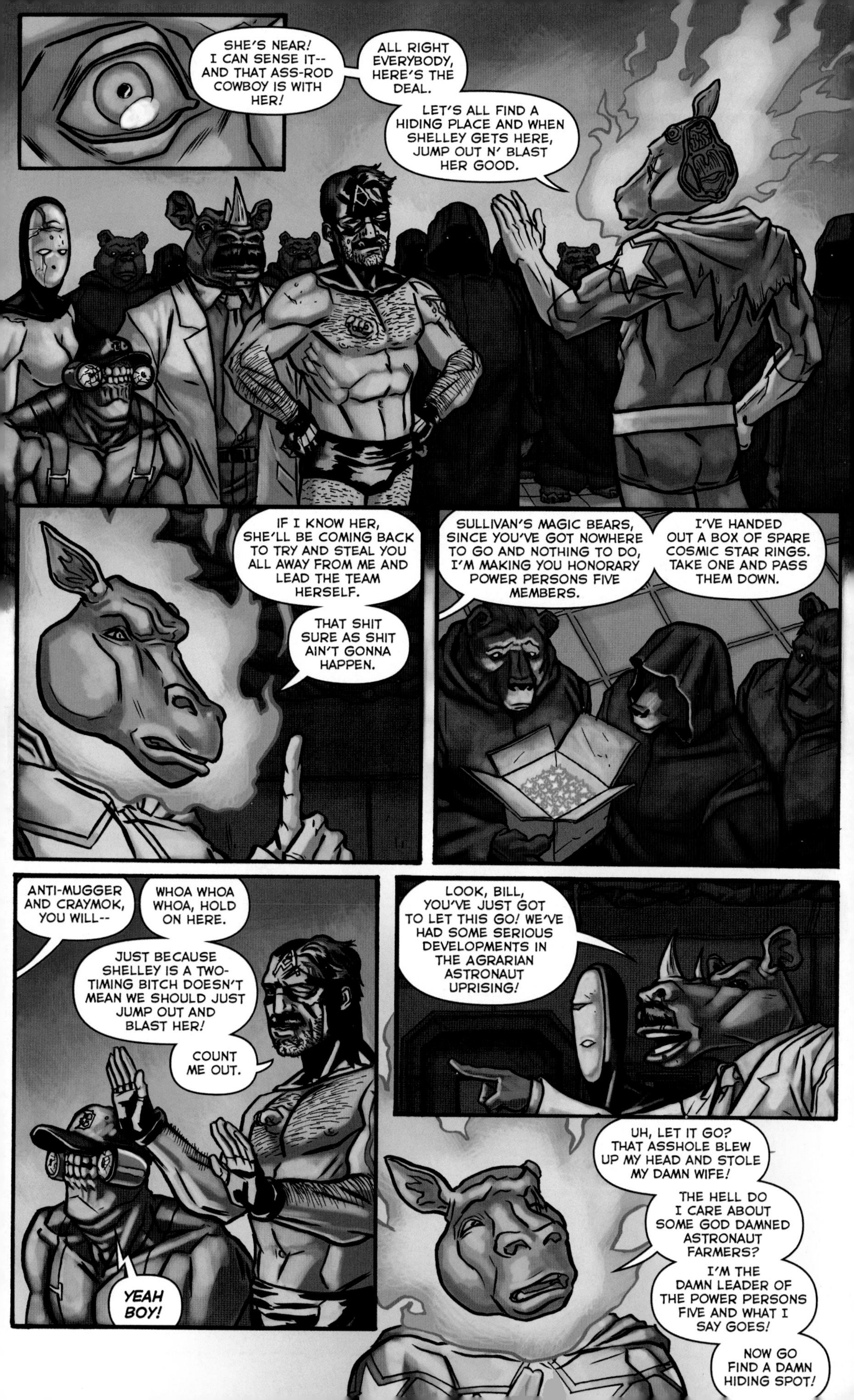
SHE'S NEAR! I CAN SENSE IT-- AND THAT ASS-ROD COWBOY IS WITH HER!
ALL RIGHT EVERYBODY, HERE'S THE DEAL.
LET'S ALL FIND A HIDING PLACE AND WHEN SHELLEY GETS HERE, JUMP OUT N' BLAST HER GOOD.
IF I KNOW HER, SHE'LL BE COMING BACK TO TRY AND STEAL YOU ALL AWAY FROM ME AND LEAD THE TEAM HERSELF.
THAT SHIT SURE AS SHIT AIN'T GONNA HAPPEN.
SULLIVAN'S MAGIC BEARS, SINCE YOU'VE GOT NOWHERE TO GO AND NOTHING TO DO, I'M MAKING YOU HONORARY POWER PERSONS FIVE MEMBERS.
I'VE HANDED OUT A BOX OF SPARE COSMIC STAR RINGS. TAKE ONE AND PASS THEM DOWN.
ANTI-MUGGER AND CRAYMOK, YOU WILL--
WHOA WHOA WHOA, HOLD ON HERE.
JUST BECAUSE SHELLEY IS A TWO-TIMING BITCH DOESN'T MEAN WE SHOULD JUST JUMP OUT AND BLAST HER!
COUNT ME OUT.
YEAH BOY!
LOOK, BILL, YOU'VE JUST GOT TO LET THIS GO! WE'VE HAD SOME SERIOUS DEVELOPMENTS IN THE AGRARIAN ASTRONAUT UPRISING!
UH, LET IT GO? THAT ASSHOLE BLEW UP MY HEAD AND STOLE MY DAMN WIFE!
THE HELL DO I CARE ABOUT SOME GOD DAMNED ASTRONAUT FARMERS?
I'M THE DAMN LEADER OF THE POWER PERSONS FIVE AND WHAT I SAY GOES!
NOW GO FIND A DAMN HIDING SPOT!

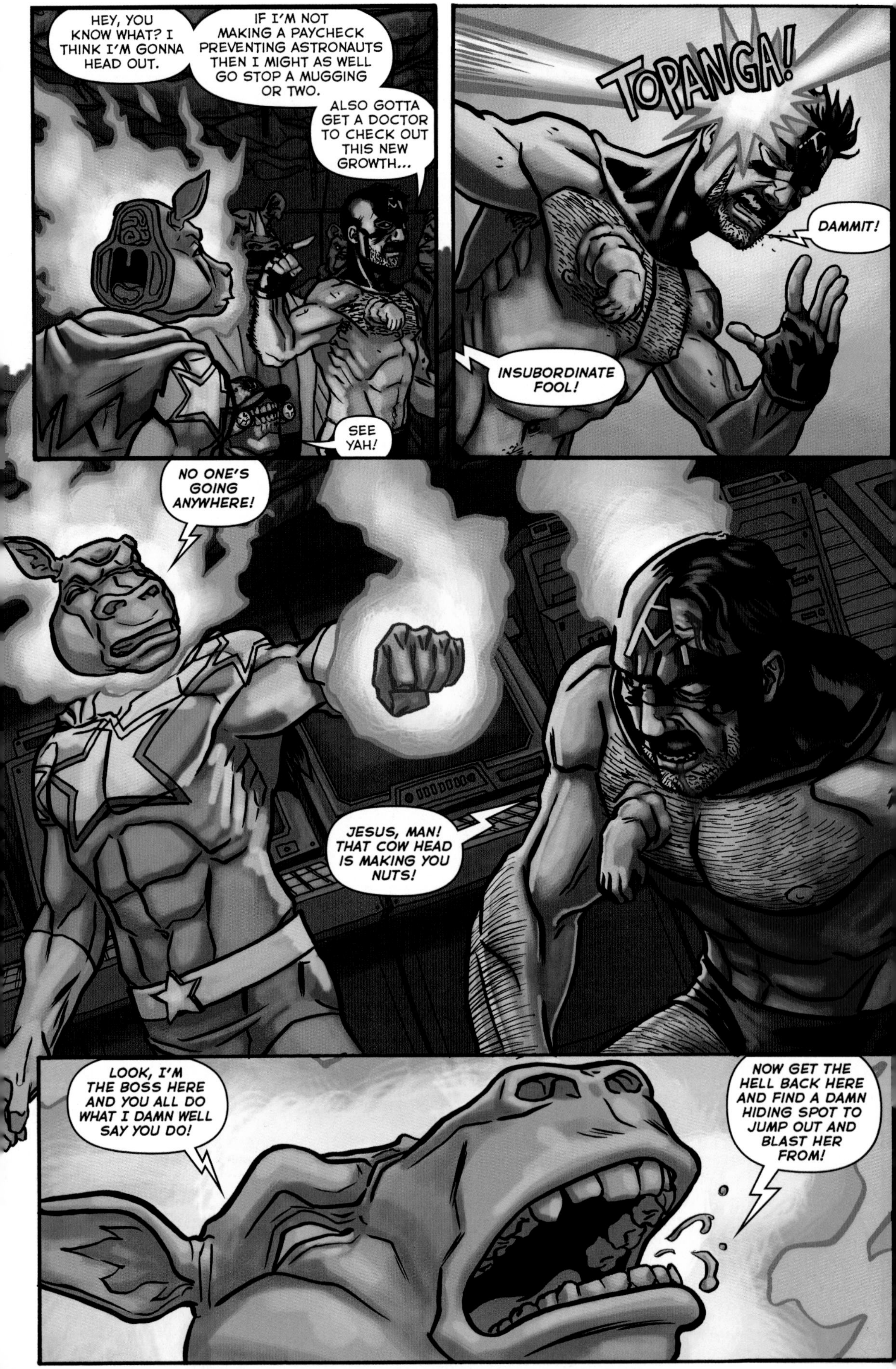
HEY, YOU KNOW WHAT? I THINK I'M GONNA HEAD OUT.
IF I'M NOT MAKING A PAYCHECK PREVENTING ASTRONAUTS THEN I MIGHT AS WELL GO STOP A MUGGING OR TWO.
ALSO GOTTA GET A DOCTOR TO CHECK OUT THIS NEW GROWTH...
SEE YAH!
TOPANGA!
DAMMIT!
INSUBORDINATE FOOL!
NO ONE'S GOING ANYWHERE!
JESUS, MAN! THAT COW HEAD IS MAKING YOU NUTS!
LOOK, I'M THE BOSS HERE AND YOU ALL DO WHAT I DAMN WELL SAY YOU DO!
NOW GET THE HELL BACK HERE AND FIND A DAMN HIDING SPOT TO JUMP OUT AND BLAST HER FROM!

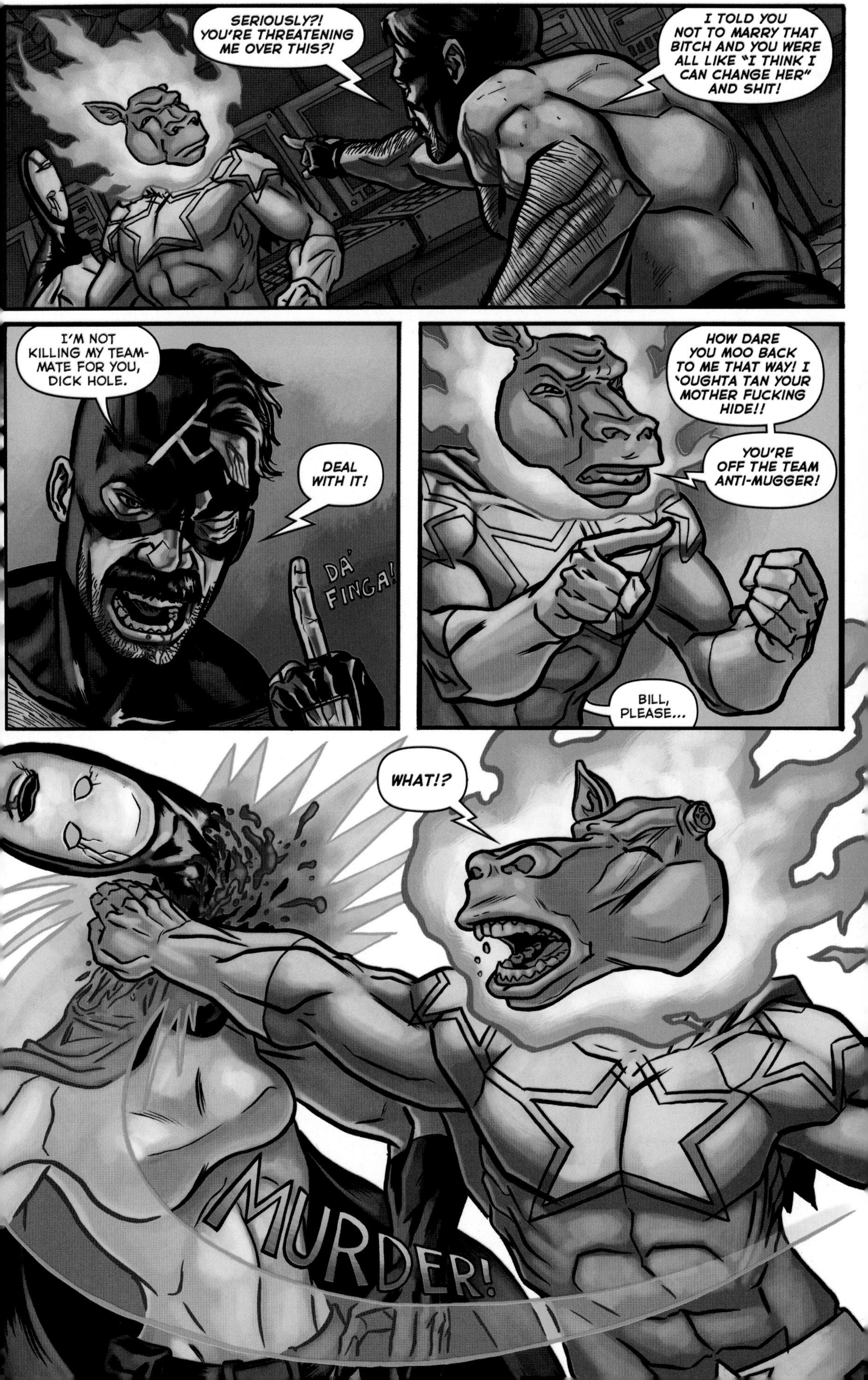
SERIOUSLY?! YOU'RE THREATENING ME OVER THIS?!
I TOLD YOU NOT TO MARRY THAT BITCH AND YOU WERE ALL LIKE "I THINK I CAN CHANGE HER" AND SHIT!
I'M NOT KILLING MY TEAM-MATE FOR YOU, DICK HOLE.
DEAL WITH IT!
DA' FINGA!
HOW DARE YOU MOO BACK TO ME THAT WAY! I 'OUGHTA TAN YOUR MOTHER FUCKING HIDE!!
YOU'RE OFF THE TEAM ANTI-MUGGER!
BILL, PLEASE...
WHAT!?
MURDER!

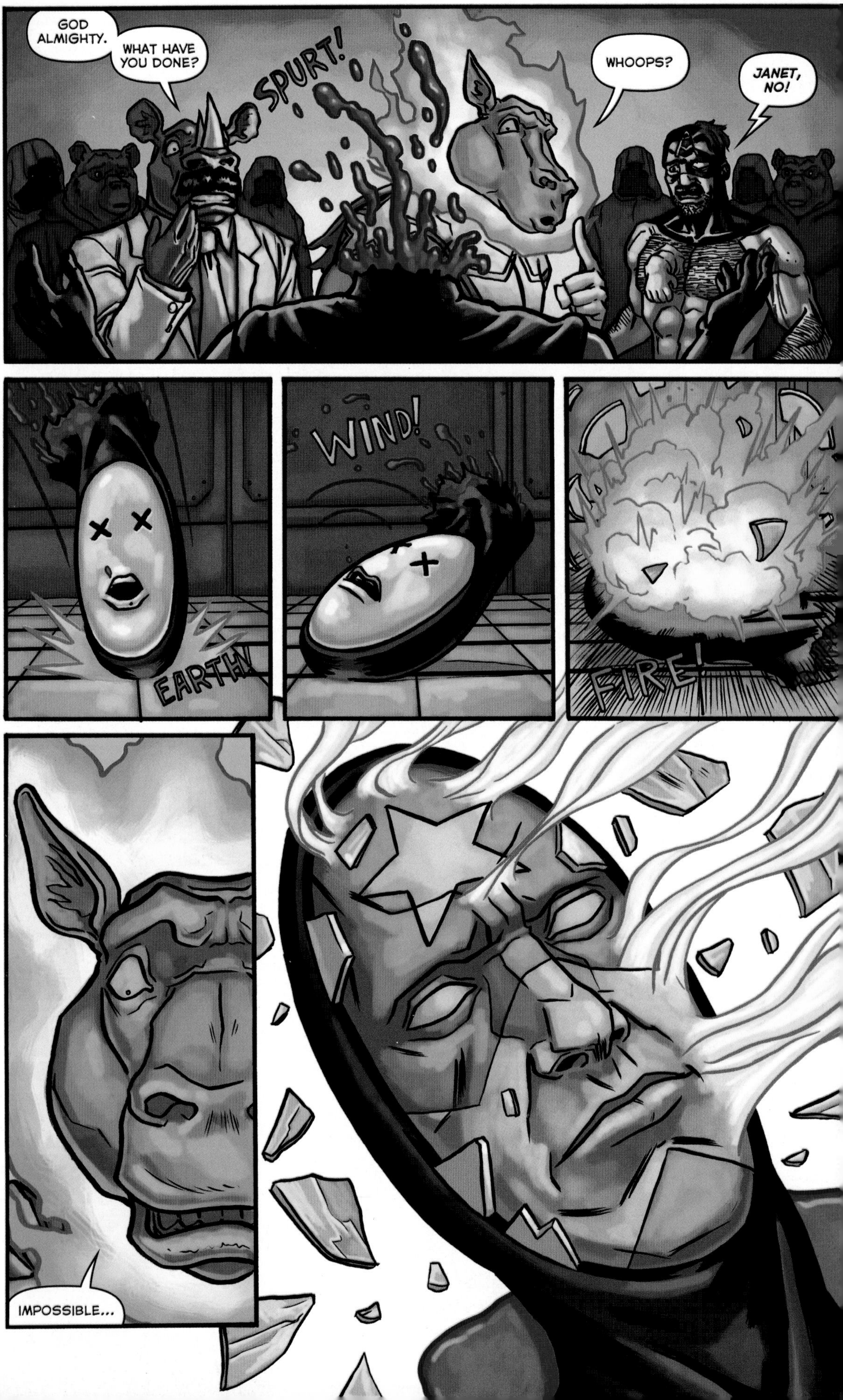
GOD ALMIGHTY.
WHAT HAVE YOU DONE?
SPURT!
WHOOPS?
JANET, NO!
EARTH!
WIND!
FIRE!
IMPOSSIBLE...

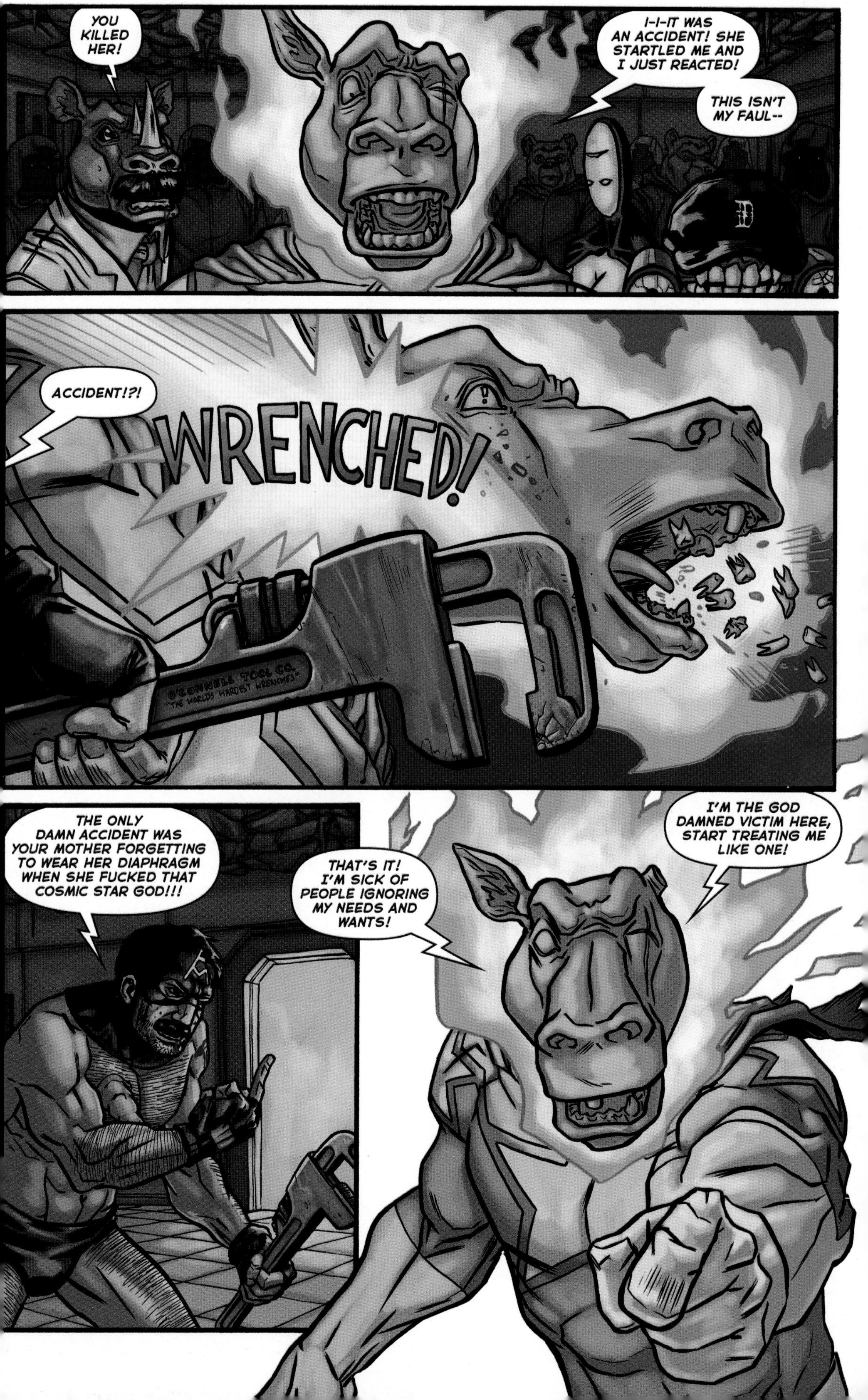
YOU KILLED HER!
I-I-IT WAS AN ACCIDENT! SHE STARTLED ME AND I JUST REACTED!
THIS ISN'T MY FAUL--
ACCIDENT!?!
WRENCHED!
O'CONNELL TOOL CO.
"THE WORLDS HARDEST WRENCHES"
THE ONLY DAMN ACCIDENT WAS YOUR MOTHER FORGETTING TO WEAR HER DIAPHRAGM WHEN SHE FUCKED THAT COSMIC STAR GOD!!!
THAT'S IT! I'M SICK OF PEOPLE IGNORING MY NEEDS AND WANTS!
I'M THE GOD DAMNED VICTIM HERE, START TREATING ME LIKE ONE!

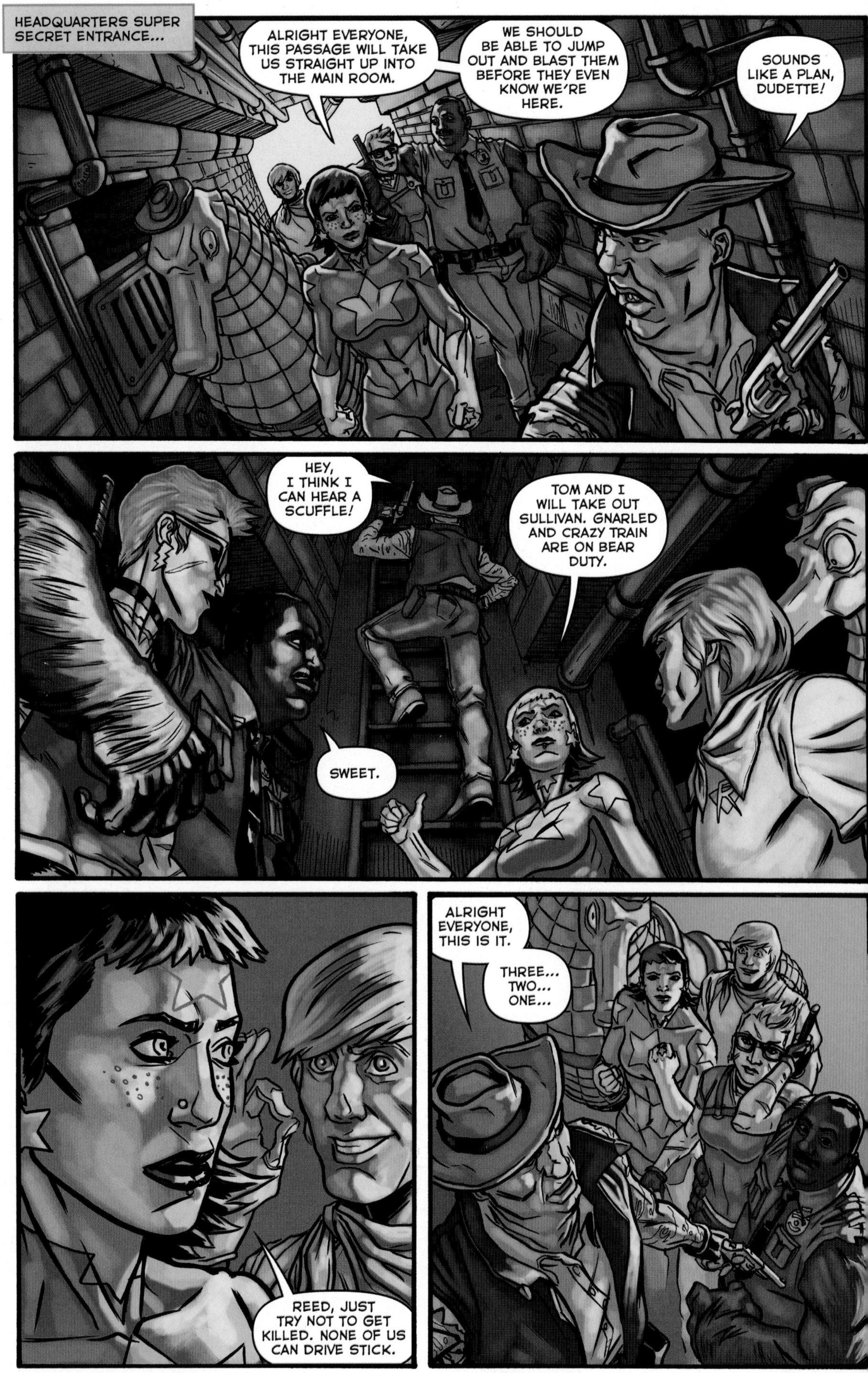
HEADQUARTERS SUPER SECRET ENTRANCE...
ALRIGHT EVERYONE, THIS PASSAGE WILL TAKE US STRAIGHT UP INTO THE MAIN ROOM.
WE SHOULD BE ABLE TO JUMP OUT AND BLAST THEM BEFORE THEY EVEN KNOW WE'RE HERE.
SOUNDS LIKE A PLAN, DUDETTE!
HEY, I THINK I CAN HEAR A SCUFFLE!
SWEET.
TOM AND I WILL TAKE OUT SULLIVAN. GNARLED AND CRAZY TRAIN ARE ON BEAR DUTY.
REED, JUST TRY NOT TO GET KILLED. NONE OF US CAN DRIVE STICK.
ALRIGHT EVERYONE, THIS IS IT.
THREE... TWO... ONE...

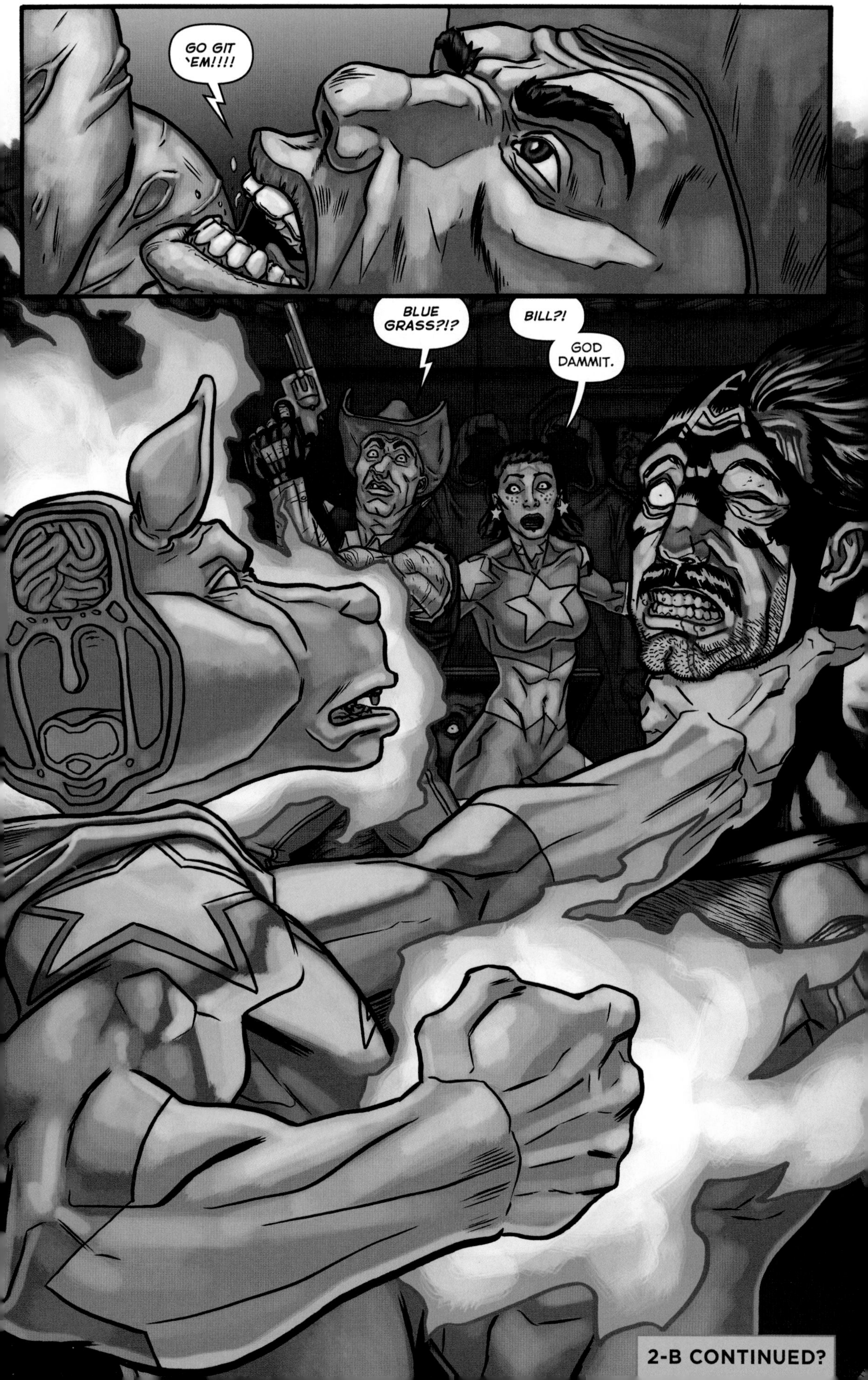
GO GIT `EM!!!!
BLUE GRASS?!?
BILL?!
GOD DAMMIT.
2-B CONTINUED?

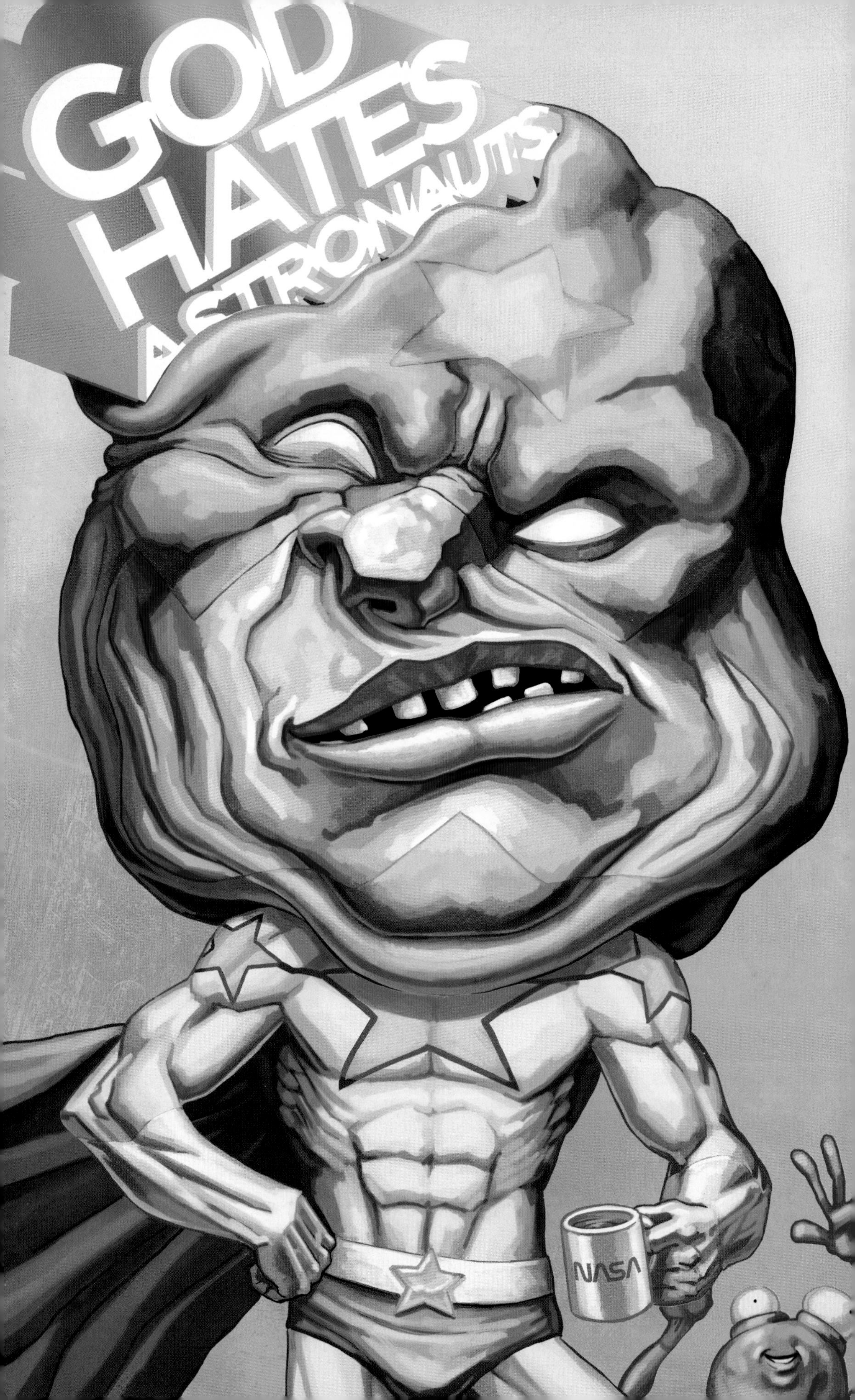
GOD
HATES
ASTRONAUTS
NASA

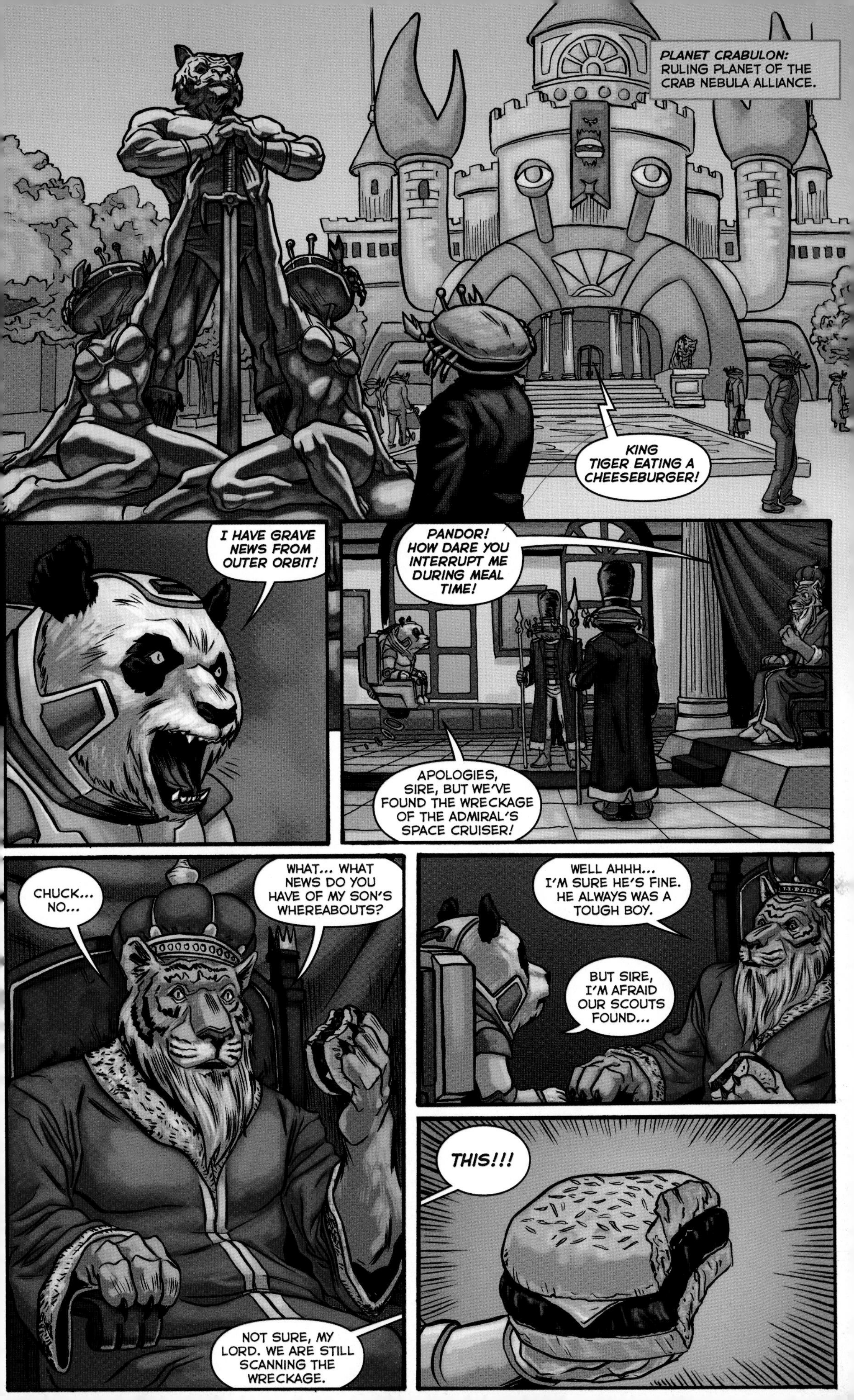
PLANET CRABULON: RULING PLANET OF THE CRAB NEBULA ALLIANCE.
KING TIGER EATING A CHEESEBURGER!
I HAVE GRAVE NEWS FROM OUTER ORBIT!
PANDOR! HOW DARE YOU INTERRUPT ME DURING MEAL TIME!
APOLOGIES, SIRE, BUT WE'VE FOUND THE WRECKAGE OF THE ADMIRAL'S SPACE CRUISER!
CHUCK... NO...
WHAT... WHAT NEWS DO YOU HAVE OF MY SON'S WHEREABOUTS?
NOT SURE, MY LORD. WE ARE STILL SCANNING THE WRECKAGE.
WELL AHHH... I'M SURE HE'S FINE. HE ALWAYS WAS A TOUGH BOY.
BUT SIRE, I'M AFRAID OUR SCOUTS FOUND...
THIS!!!

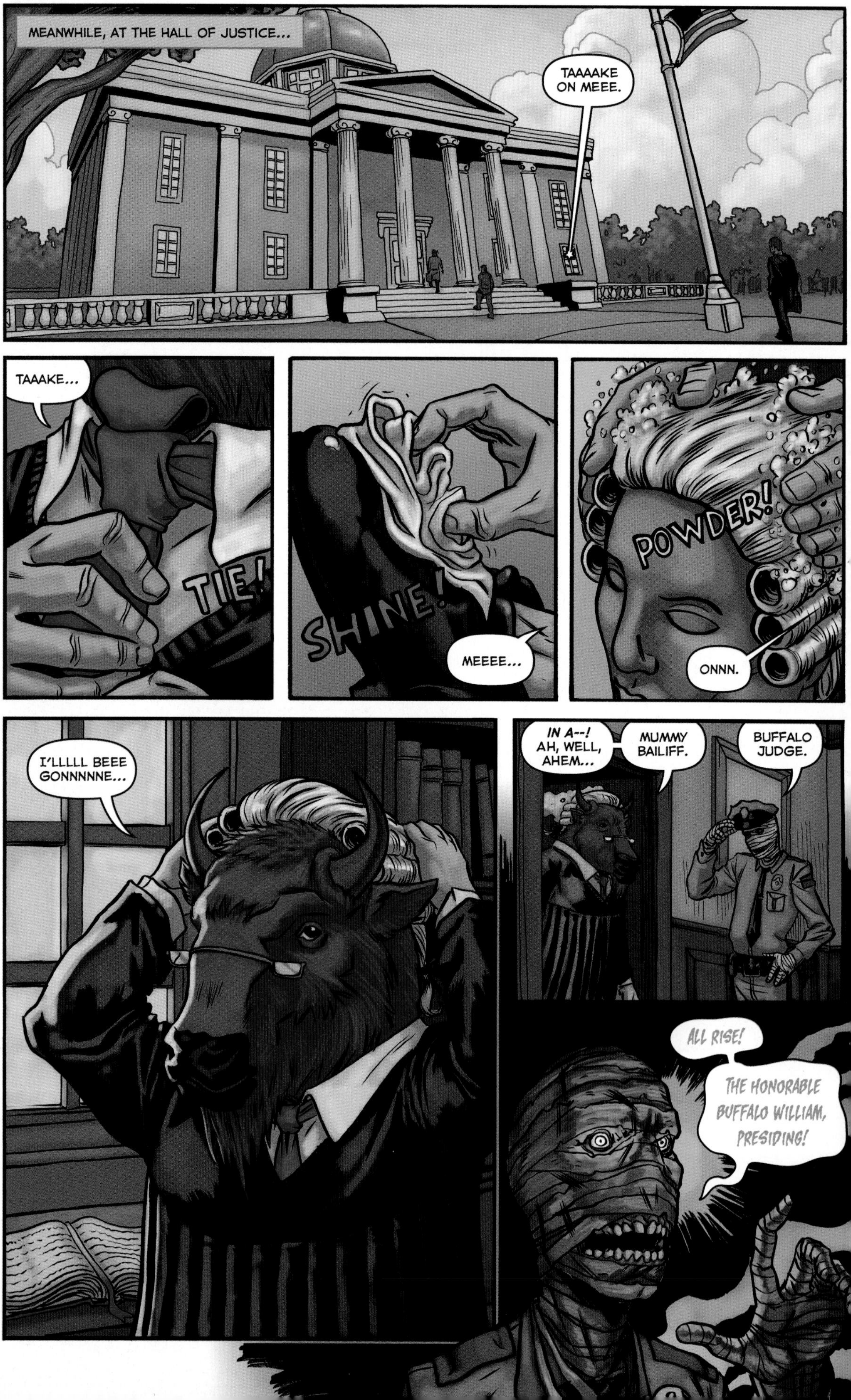
MEANWHILE, AT THE HALL OF JUSTICE...
TAAAAKE ON MEEE.
TAAAKE...
TIE!
SHINE!
MEEEE...
POWDER!
ONNN.
I'LLLLL BEEE GONNNNNE...
IN A--! AH, WELL, AHEM...
MUMMY BAILIFF.
BUFFALO JUDGE.
ALL RISE!
THE HONORABLE BUFFALO WILLIAM, PRESIDING!

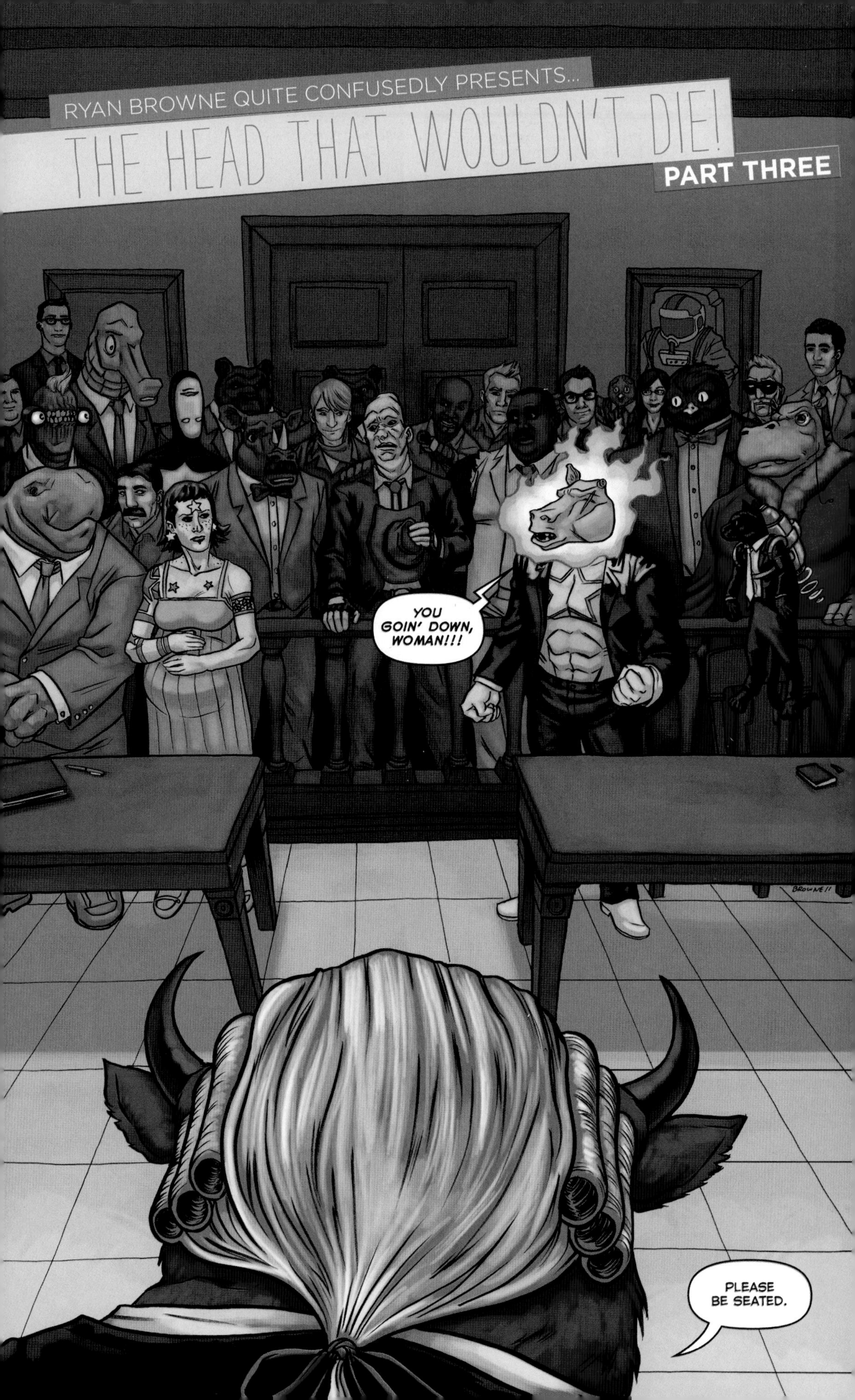
RYAN BROWNE QUITE CONFUSEDLY PRESENTS...
THE HEAD THAT WOULDN'T DIE!
PART THREE
YOU GOIN' DOWN, WOMAN!!!
BROWNE 11
PLEASE BE SEATED.

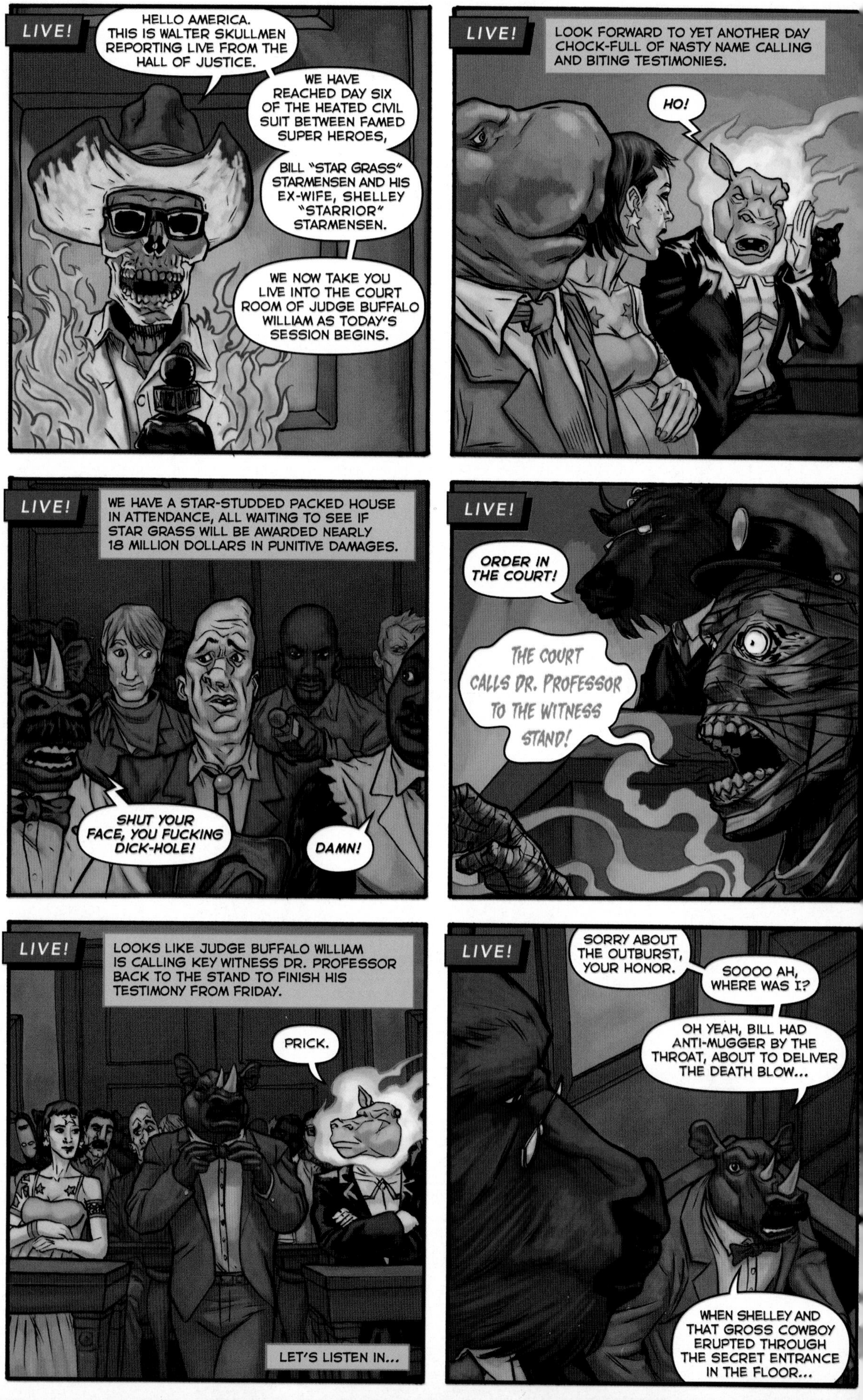
LIVE!
HELLO AMERICA. THIS IS WALTER SKULLMEN REPORTING LIVE FROM THE HALL OF JUSTICE.
WE HAVE REACHED DAY SIX OF THE HEATED CIVIL SUIT BETWEEN FAMED SUPER HEROES,
BILL "STAR GRASS" STARMENSEN AND HIS EX-WIFE, SHELLEY "STARRIOR" STARMENSEN.
WE NOW TAKE YOU LIVE INTO THE COURT ROOM OF JUDGE BUFFALO WILLIAM AS TODAY'S SESSION BEGINS.
LIVE!
LOOK FORWARD TO YET ANOTHER DAY CHOCK-FULL OF NASTY NAME CALLING AND BITING TESTIMONIES.
HO!
LIVE!
WE HAVE A STAR-STUDDED PACKED HOUSE IN ATTENDANCE, ALL WAITING TO SEE IF STAR GRASS WILL BE AWARDED NEARLY 18 MILLION DOLLARS IN PUNITIVE DAMAGES.
SHUT YOUR FACE, YOU FUCKING DICK-HOLE!
DAMN!
LIVE!
ORDER IN THE COURT!
THE COURT CALLS DR. PROFESSOR TO THE WITNESS STAND!
LIVE!
LOOKS LIKE JUDGE BUFFALO WILLIAM IS CALLING KEY WITNESS DR. PROFESSOR BACK TO THE STAND TO FINISH HIS TESTIMONY FROM FRIDAY.
PRICK.
LET'S LISTEN IN...
LIVE!
SORRY ABOUT THE OUTBURST, YOUR HONOR.
SOOOO AH, WHERE WAS I?
OH YEAH, BILL HAD ANTI-MUGGER BY THE THROAT, ABOUT TO DELIVER THE DEATH BLOW...
WHEN SHELLEY AND THAT GROSS COWBOY ERUPTED THROUGH THE SECRET ENTRANCE IN THE FLOOR...

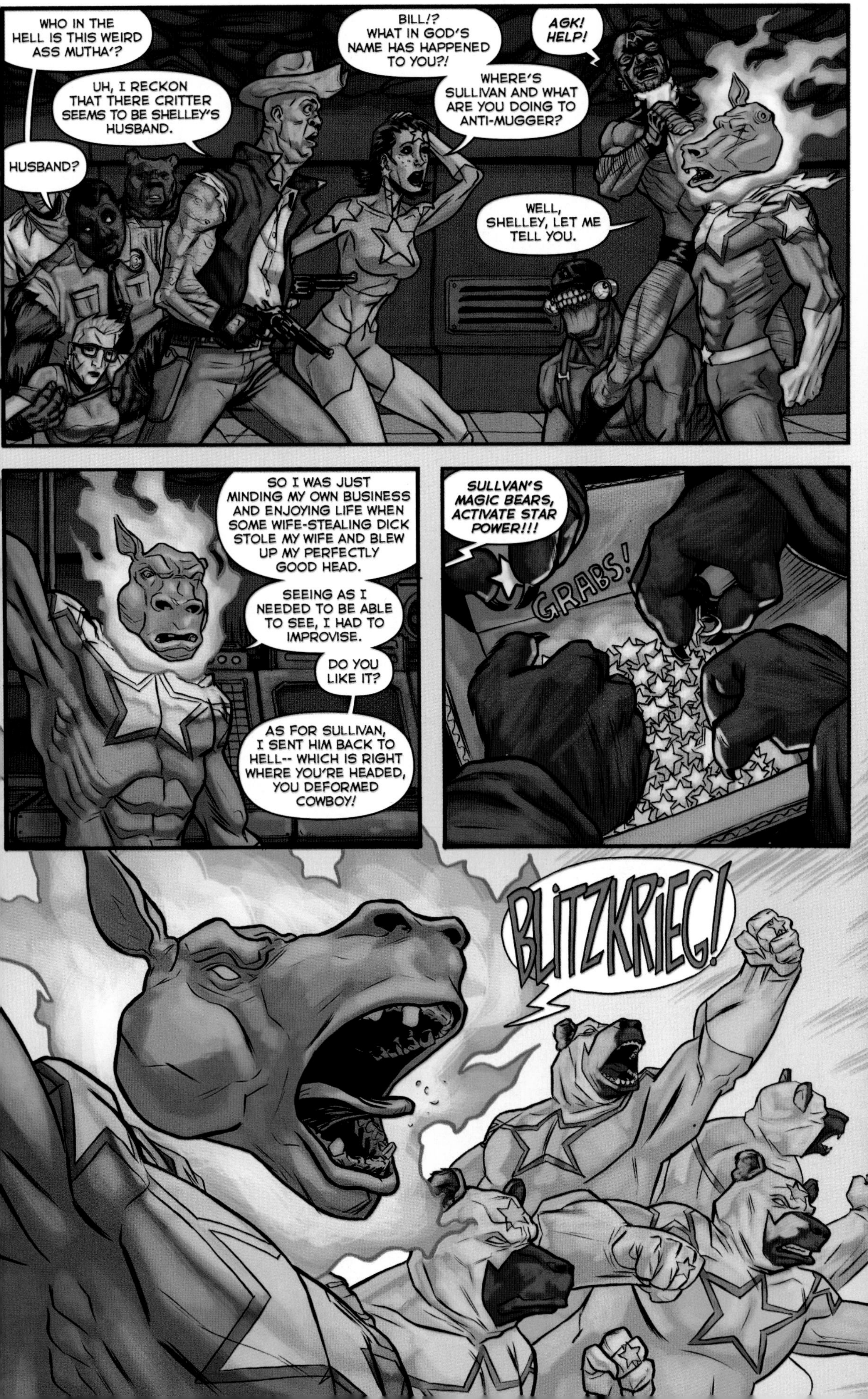
WHO IN THE HELL IS THIS WEIRD ASS MUTHA'?
UH, I RECKON THAT THERE CRITTER SEEMS TO BE SHELLEY'S HUSBAND.
HUSBAND?
BILL!? WHAT IN GOD'S NAME HAS HAPPENED TO YOU?!
WHERE'S SULLIVAN AND WHAT ARE YOU DOING TO ANTI-MUGGER?
AGK! HELP!
WELL, SHELLEY, LET ME TELL YOU.
SO I WAS JUST MINDING MY OWN BUSINESS AND ENJOYING LIFE WHEN SOME WIFE-STEALING DICK STOLE MY WIFE AND BLEW UP MY PERFECTLY GOOD HEAD.
SEEING AS I NEEDED TO BE ABLE TO SEE, I HAD TO IMPROVISE.
DO YOU LIKE IT?
AS FOR SULLIVAN, I SENT HIM BACK TO HELL-- WHICH IS RIGHT WHERE YOU'RE HEADED, YOU DEFORMED COWBOY!
SULLVAN'S MAGIC BEARS, ACTIVATE STAR POWER!!!
GRABS!
BLITZKRIEG!

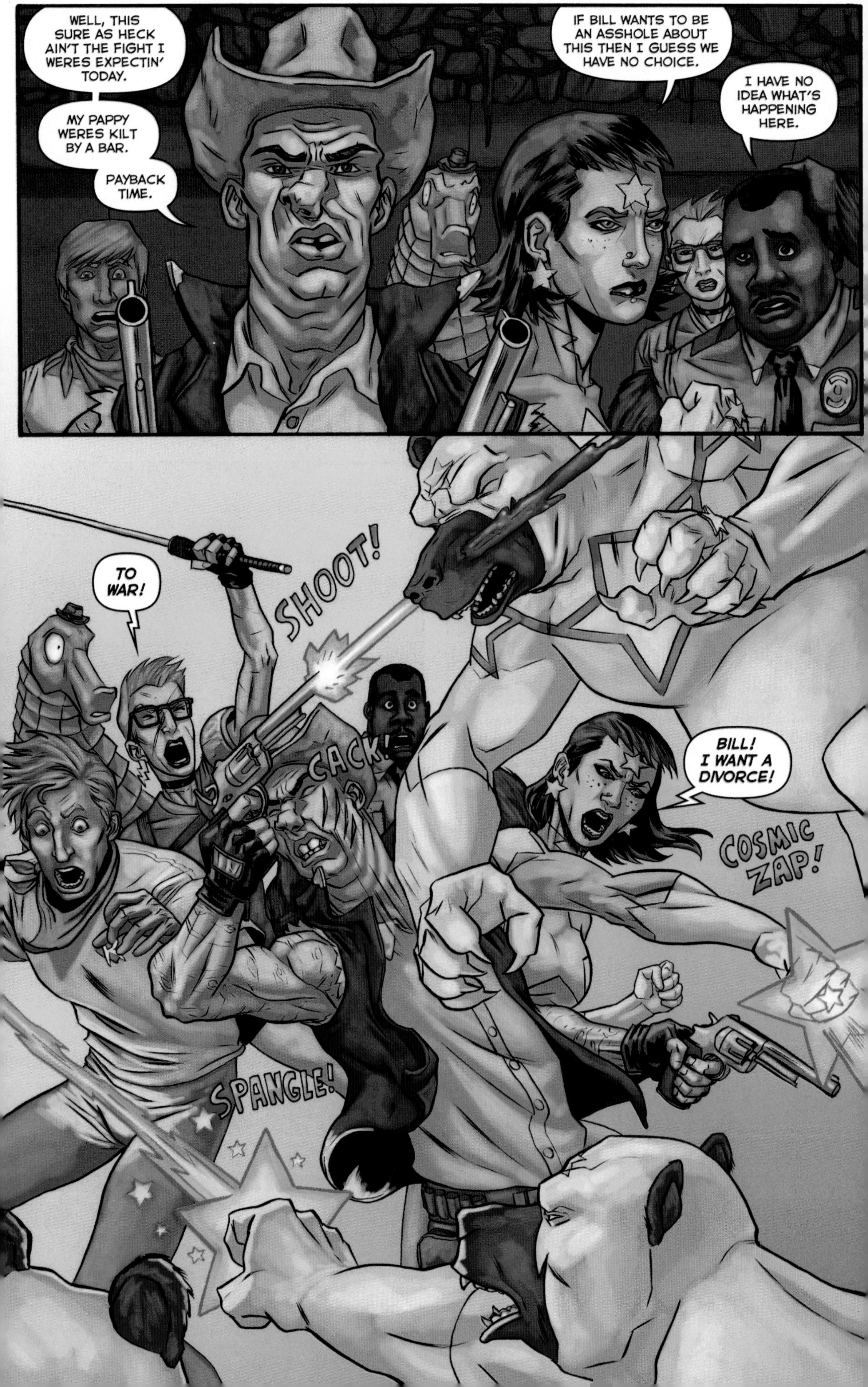
WELL, THIS SURE AS HECK AIN'T THE FIGHT I WERES EXPECTIN' TODAY.
MY PAPPY WERES KILT BY A BAR.
PAYBACK TIME.
IF BILL WANTS TO BE AN ASSHOLE ABOUT THIS THEN I GUESS WE HAVE NO CHOICE.
I HAVE NO IDEA WHAT'S HAPPENING HERE.
TO WAR!
SHOOT!
CACK!
BILL! I WANT A DIVORCE!
COSMIC ZAP!
SPANGLE!

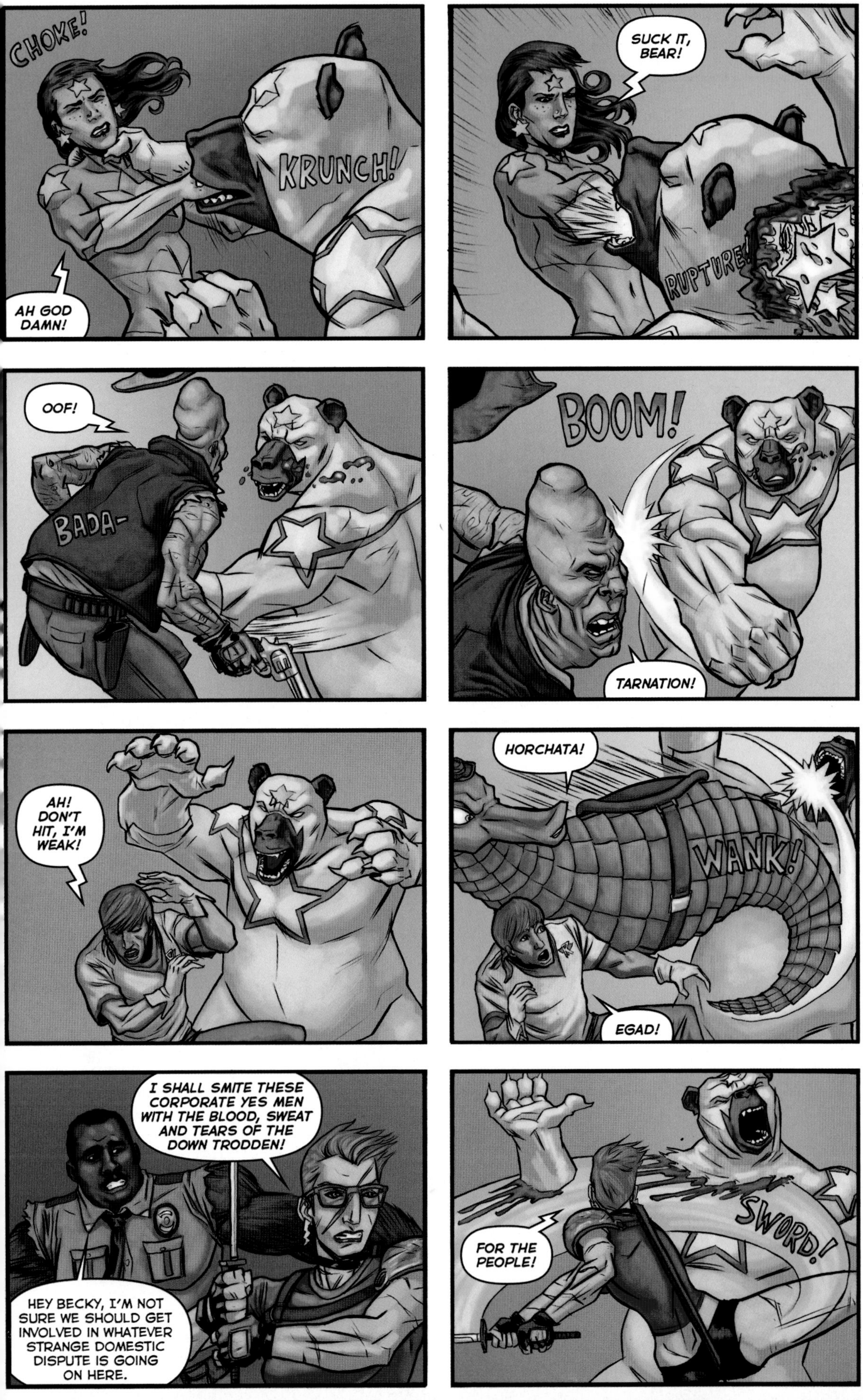
CHOKE!
KRUNCH!
AH GOD DAMN!
SUCK IT, BEAR!
RUPTURE!
OOF!
BADA-
BOOM!
TARNATION!
AH! DON'T HIT, I'M WEAK!
HORCHATA!
WANK!
EGAD!
I SHALL SMITE THESE CORPORATE YES MEN WITH THE BLOOD, SWEAT AND TEARS OF THE DOWN TRODDEN!
HEY BECKY, I'M NOT SURE WE SHOULD GET INVOLVED IN WHATEVER STRANGE DOMESTIC DISPUTE IS GOING ON HERE.
SWORD!
FOR THE PEOPLE!

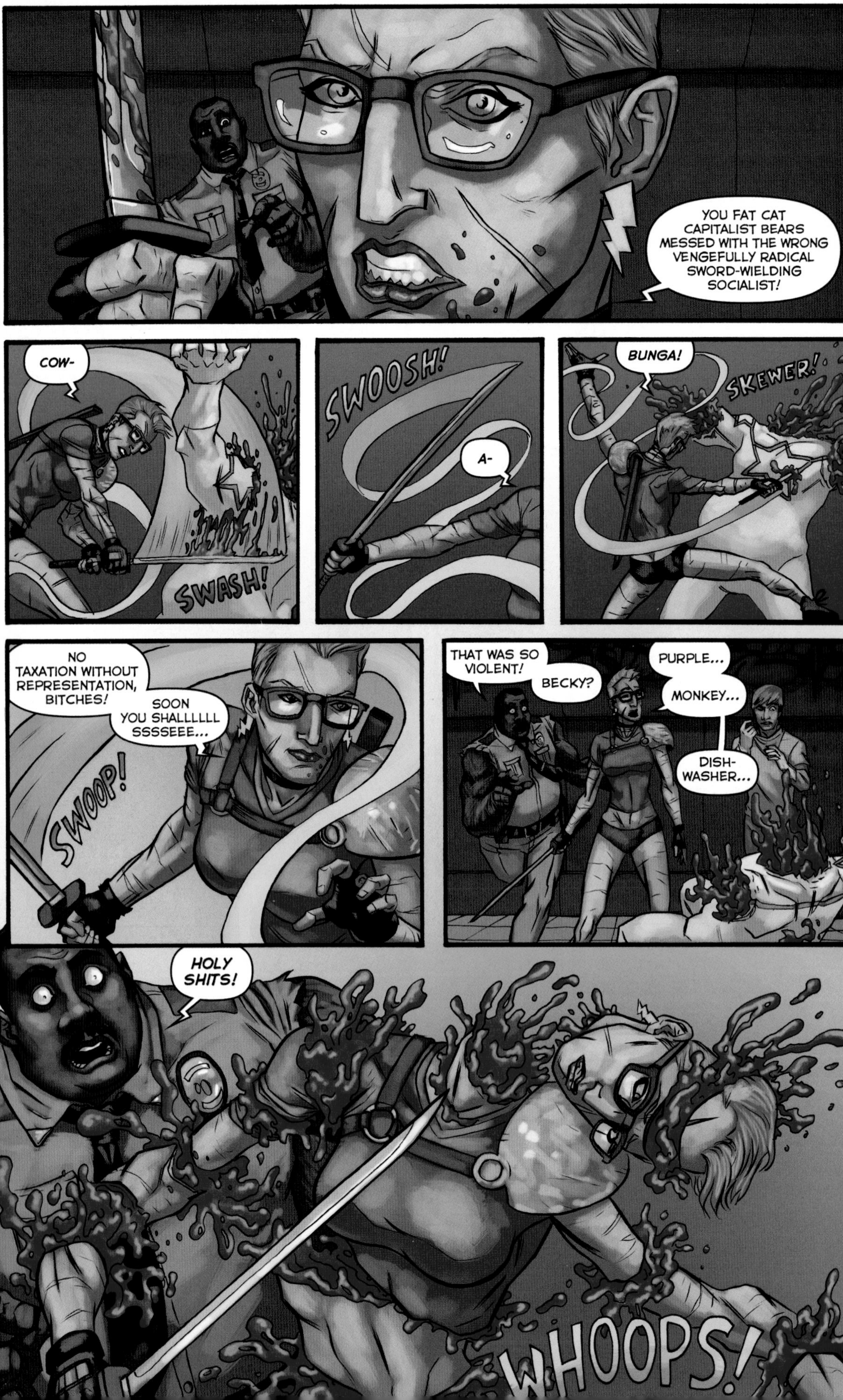
YOU FAT CAT CAPITALIST BEARS MESSED WITH THE WRONG VENGEFULLY RADICAL SWORD-WIELDING SOCIALIST!
COW-
SWASH!
SWOOSH!
A-
BUNGA!
SKEWER!
NO TAXATION WITHOUT REPRESENTATION, BITCHES!
SOON YOU SHALLLLLL SSSSEEE...
SWOOP!
THAT WAS SO VIOLENT!
BECKY?
PURPLE...
MONKEY...
DISH-WASHER...
HOLY SHITS!
WHOOPS!

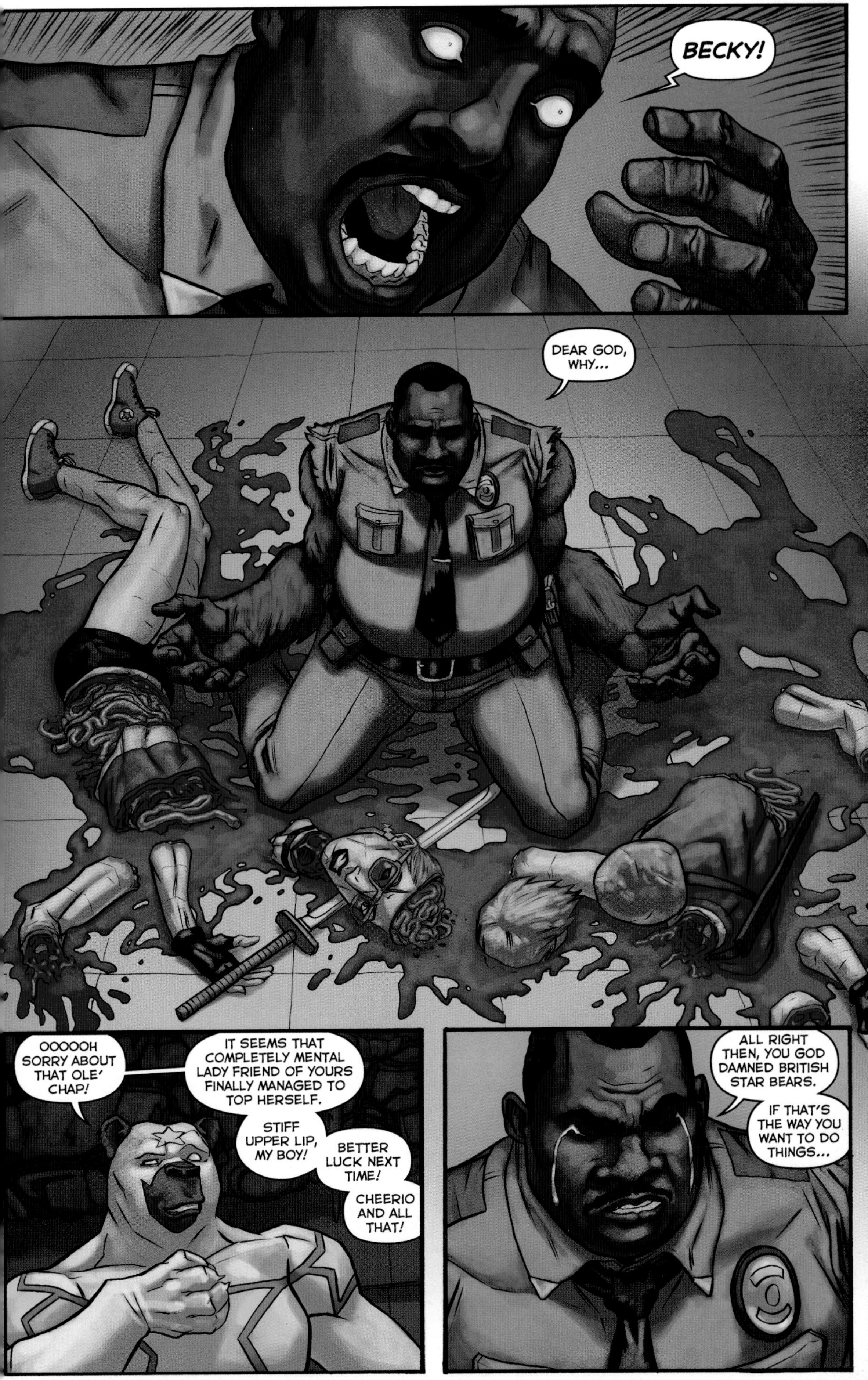
BECKY!
DEAR GOD, WHY...
OOOOOH SORRY ABOUT THAT OLE' CHAP!
IT SEEMS THAT COMPLETELY MENTAL LADY FRIEND OF YOURS FINALLY MANAGED TO TOP HERSELF.
STIFF UPPER LIP, MY BOY!
BETTER LUCK NEXT TIME!
CHEERIO AND ALL THAT!
ALL RIGHT THEN, YOU GOD DAMNED BRITISH STAR BEARS.
IF THAT'S THE WAY YOU WANT TO DO THINGS...

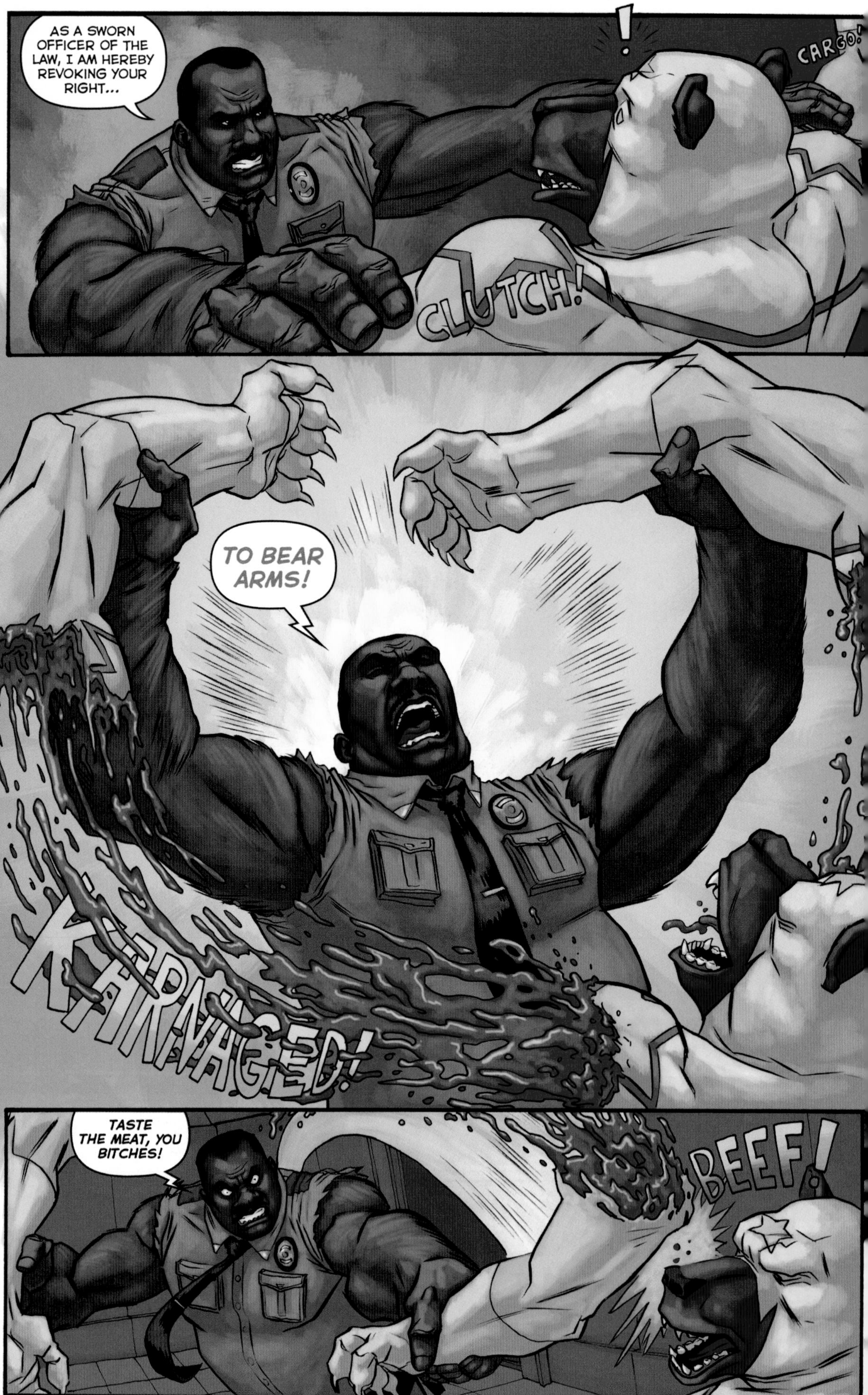
AS A SWORN OFFICER OF THE LAW, I AM HEREBY REVOKING YOUR RIGHT...
!
CARGO!
CLUTCH!
TO BEAR ARMS!
TASTE THE MEAT, YOU BITCHES!
BEEF!

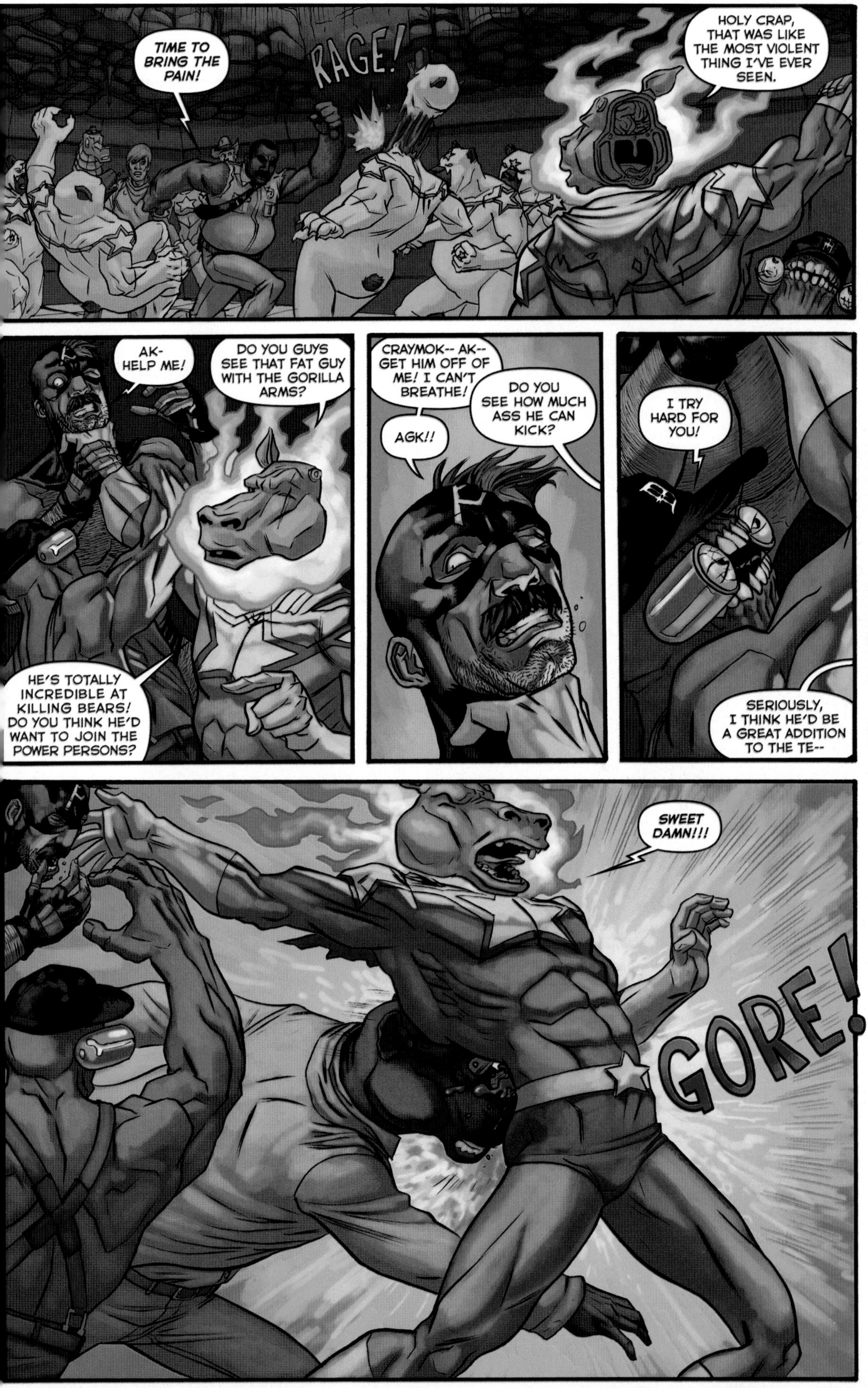
TIME TO BRING THE PAIN!
RAGE!
HOLY CRAP, THAT WAS LIKE THE MOST VIOLENT THING I'VE EVER SEEN.
AK- HELP ME!
DO YOU GUYS SEE THAT FAT GUY WITH THE GORILLA ARMS?
HE'S TOTALLY INCREDIBLE AT KILLING BEARS! DO YOU THINK HE'D WANT TO JOIN THE POWER PERSONS?
CRAYMOK-- AK-- GET HIM OFF OF ME! I CAN'T BREATHE!
AGK!!
DO YOU SEE HOW MUCH ASS HE CAN KICK?
I TRY HARD FOR YOU!
SERIOUSLY, I THINK HE'D BE A GREAT ADDITION TO THE TE--
SWEET DAMN!!!
GORE!

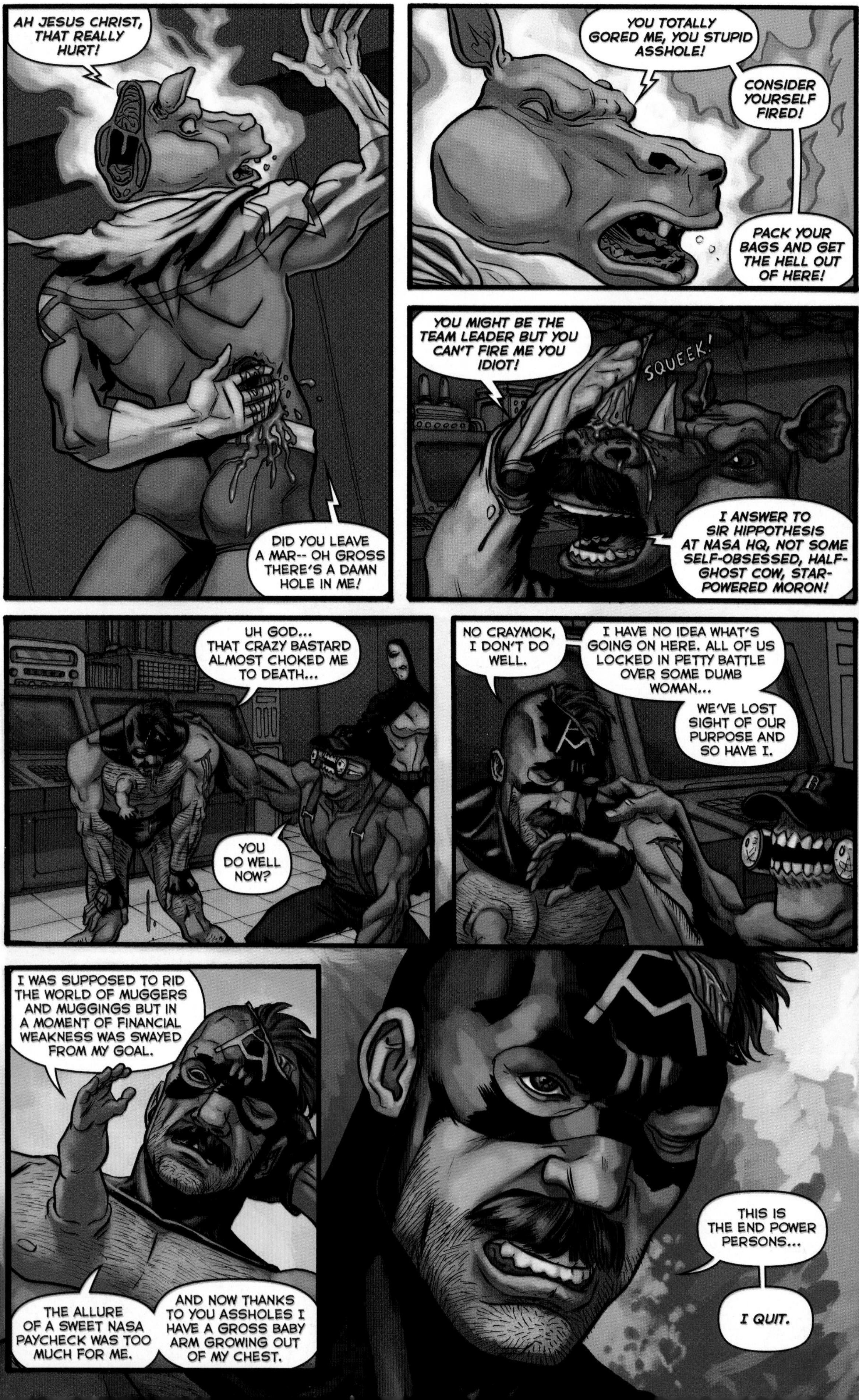
AH JESUS CHRIST, THAT REALLY HURT!
DID YOU LEAVE A MAR-- OH GROSS THERE'S A DAMN HOLE IN ME!
YOU TOTALLY GORED ME, YOU STUPID ASSHOLE!
CONSIDER YOURSELF FIRED!
PACK YOUR BAGS AND GET THE HELL OUT OF HERE!
YOU MIGHT BE THE TEAM LEADER BUT YOU CAN'T FIRE ME YOU IDIOT!
SQUEEK!
I ANSWER TO SIR HIPPOTHESIS AT NASA HQ, NOT SOME SELF-OBSESSED, HALF-GHOST COW, STAR-POWERED MORON!
UH GOD... THAT CRAZY BASTARD ALMOST CHOKED ME TO DEATH...
YOU DO WELL NOW?
NO CRAYMOK, I DON'T DO WELL.
I HAVE NO IDEA WHAT'S GOING ON HERE. ALL OF US LOCKED IN PETTY BATTLE OVER SOME DUMB WOMAN...
WE'VE LOST SIGHT OF OUR PURPOSE AND SO HAVE I.
I WAS SUPPOSED TO RID THE WORLD OF MUGGERS AND MUGGINGS BUT IN A MOMENT OF FINANCIAL WEAKNESS WAS SWAYED FROM MY GOAL.
THE ALLURE OF A SWEET NASA PAYCHECK WAS TOO MUCH FOR ME.
AND NOW THANKS TO YOU ASSHOLES I HAVE A GROSS BABY ARM GROWING OUT OF MY CHEST.
THIS IS THE END POWER PERSONS...
I QUIT.

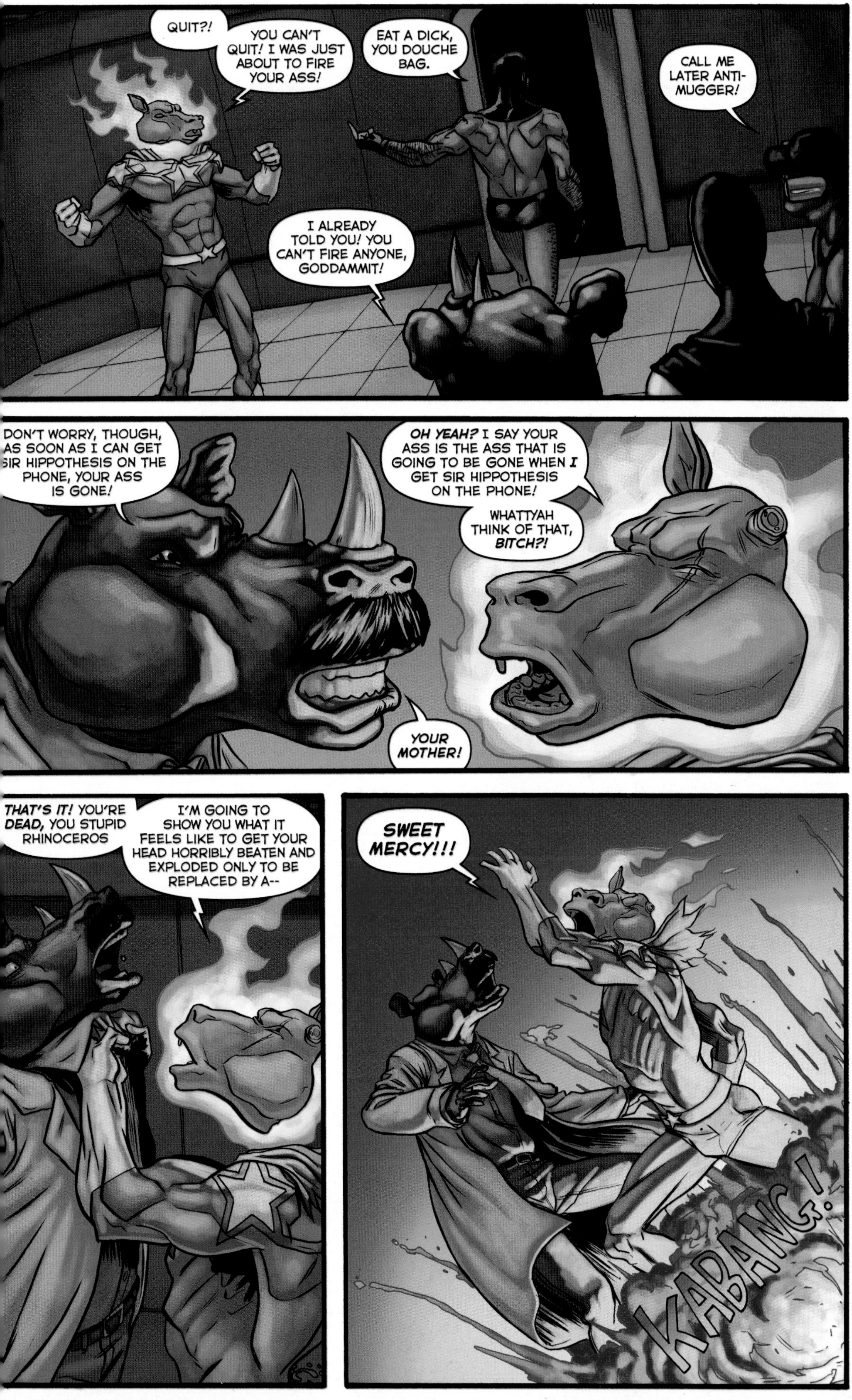
QUIT?!
YOU CAN'T QUIT! I WAS JUST ABOUT TO FIRE YOUR ASS!
EAT A DICK, YOU DOUCHE BAG.
CALL ME LATER ANTI-MUGGER!
I ALREADY TOLD YOU! YOU CAN'T FIRE ANYONE, GODDAMMIT!
DON'T WORRY, THOUGH, AS SOON AS I CAN GET SIR HIPPOTHESIS ON THE PHONE, YOUR ASS IS GONE!
OH YEAH? I SAY YOUR ASS IS THE ASS THAT IS GOING TO BE GONE WHEN I GET SIR HIPPOTHESIS ON THE PHONE!
WHATTYAH THINK OF THAT, BITCH?!
YOUR MOTHER!
THAT'S IT! YOU'RE DEAD, YOU STUPID RHINOCEROS
I'M GOING TO SHOW YOU WHAT IT FEELS LIKE TO GET YOUR HEAD HORRIBLY BEATEN AND EXPLODED ONLY TO BE REPLACED BY A--
SWEET MERCY!!!
KABANG!

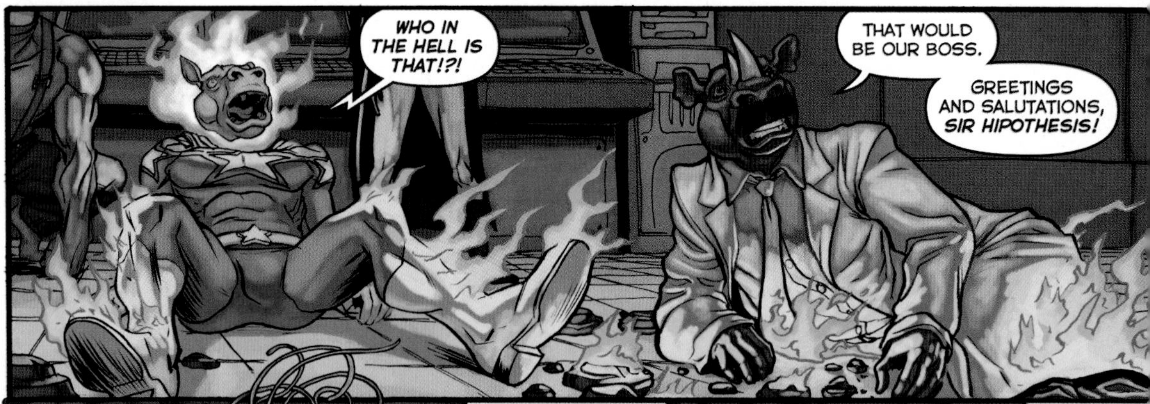
WHO IN THE HELL IS THAT!?!
THAT WOULD BE OUR BOSS.
GREETINGS AND SALUTATIONS, SIR HIPOTHESIS!

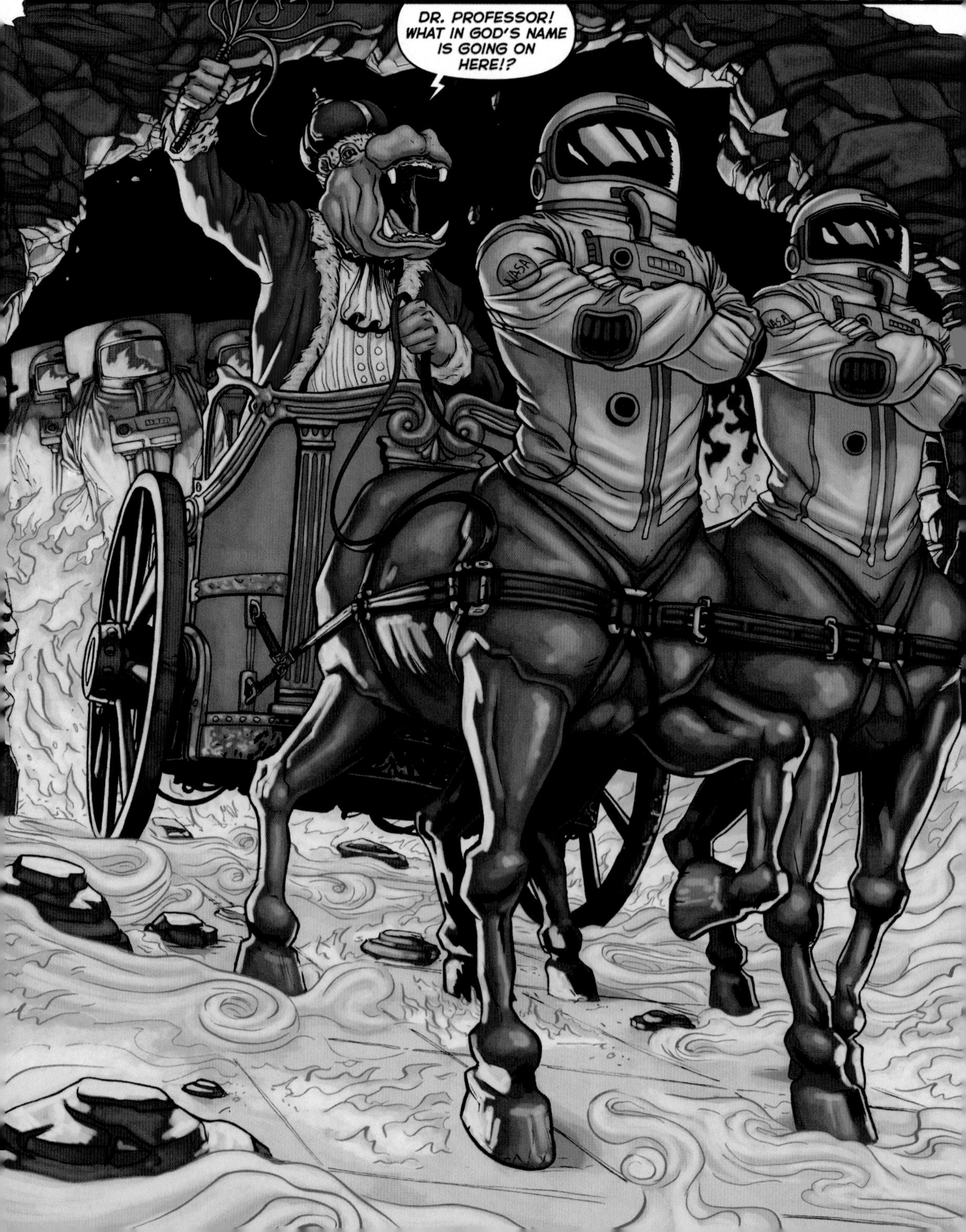
DR. PROFESSOR! WHAT IN GOD'S NAME IS GOING ON HERE!?

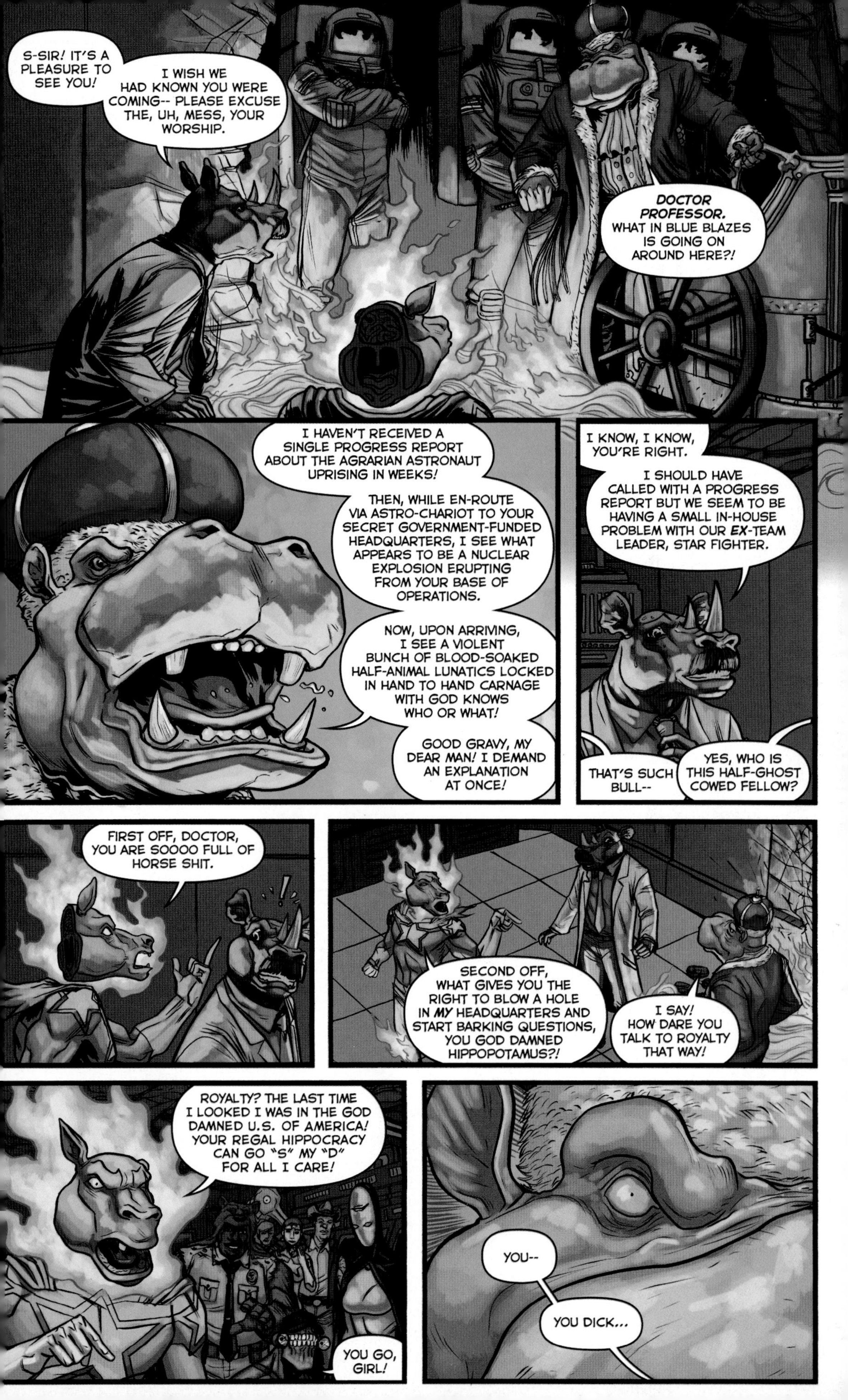
S-SIR! IT'S A PLEASURE TO SEE YOU!
I WISH WE HAD KNOWN YOU WERE COMING-- PLEASE EXCUSE THE, UH, MESS, YOUR WORSHIP.
DOCTOR PROFESSOR. WHAT IN BLUE BLAZES IS GOING ON AROUND HERE?!
I HAVEN'T RECEIVED A SINGLE PROGRESS REPORT ABOUT THE AGRARIAN ASTRONAUT UPRISING IN WEEKS!
THEN, WHILE EN-ROUTE VIA ASTRO-CHARIOT TO YOUR SECRET GOVERNMENT-FUNDED HEADQUARTERS, I SEE WHAT APPEARS TO BE A NUCLEAR EXPLOSION ERUPTING FROM YOUR BASE OF OPERATIONS.
NOW, UPON ARRIVING, I SEE A VIOLENT BUNCH OF BLOOD-SOAKED HALF-ANIMAL LUNATICS LOCKED IN HAND TO HAND CARNAGE WITH GOD KNOWS WHO OR WHAT!
GOOD GRAVY, MY DEAR MAN! I DEMAND AN EXPLANATION AT ONCE!
I KNOW, I KNOW, YOU'RE RIGHT.
I SHOULD HAVE CALLED WITH A PROGRESS REPORT BUT WE SEEM TO BE HAVING A SMALL IN-HOUSE PROBLEM WITH OUR EX-TEAM LEADER, STAR FIGHTER.
THAT'S SUCH BULL--
YES, WHO IS THIS HALF-GHOST COWED FELLOW?
FIRST OFF, DOCTOR, YOU ARE SOOOO FULL OF HORSE SHIT.
!
SECOND OFF, WHAT GIVES YOU THE RIGHT TO BLOW A HOLE IN MY HEADQUARTERS AND START BARKING QUESTIONS, YOU GOD DAMNED HIPPOPOTAMUS?!
I SAY! HOW DARE YOU TALK TO ROYALTY THAT WAY!
ROYALTY? THE LAST TIME I LOOKED I WAS IN THE GOD DAMNED U.S. OF AMERICA! YOUR REGAL HIPPOCRACY CAN GO "S" MY "D" FOR ALL I CARE!
YOU GO, GIRL!
YOU--
YOU DICK...

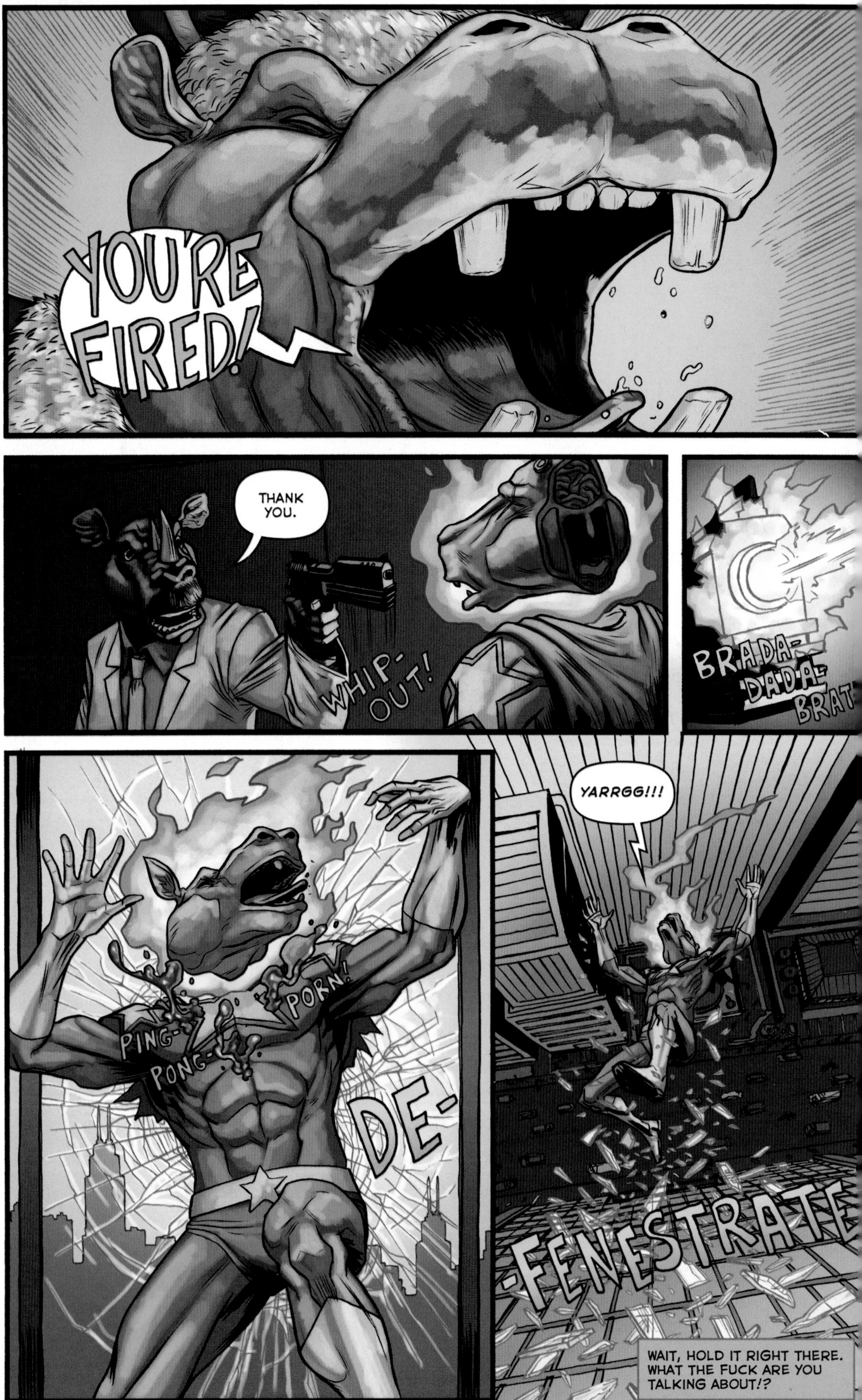
YOU'RE FIRED!
THANK YOU.
WHIP-OUT!
BRADA-DADA-BRAT
YARRGG!!!
PING-PONG-PORN!
DE-FENESTRATE
WAIT, HOLD IT RIGHT THERE. WHAT THE FUCK ARE YOU TALKING ABOUT!?

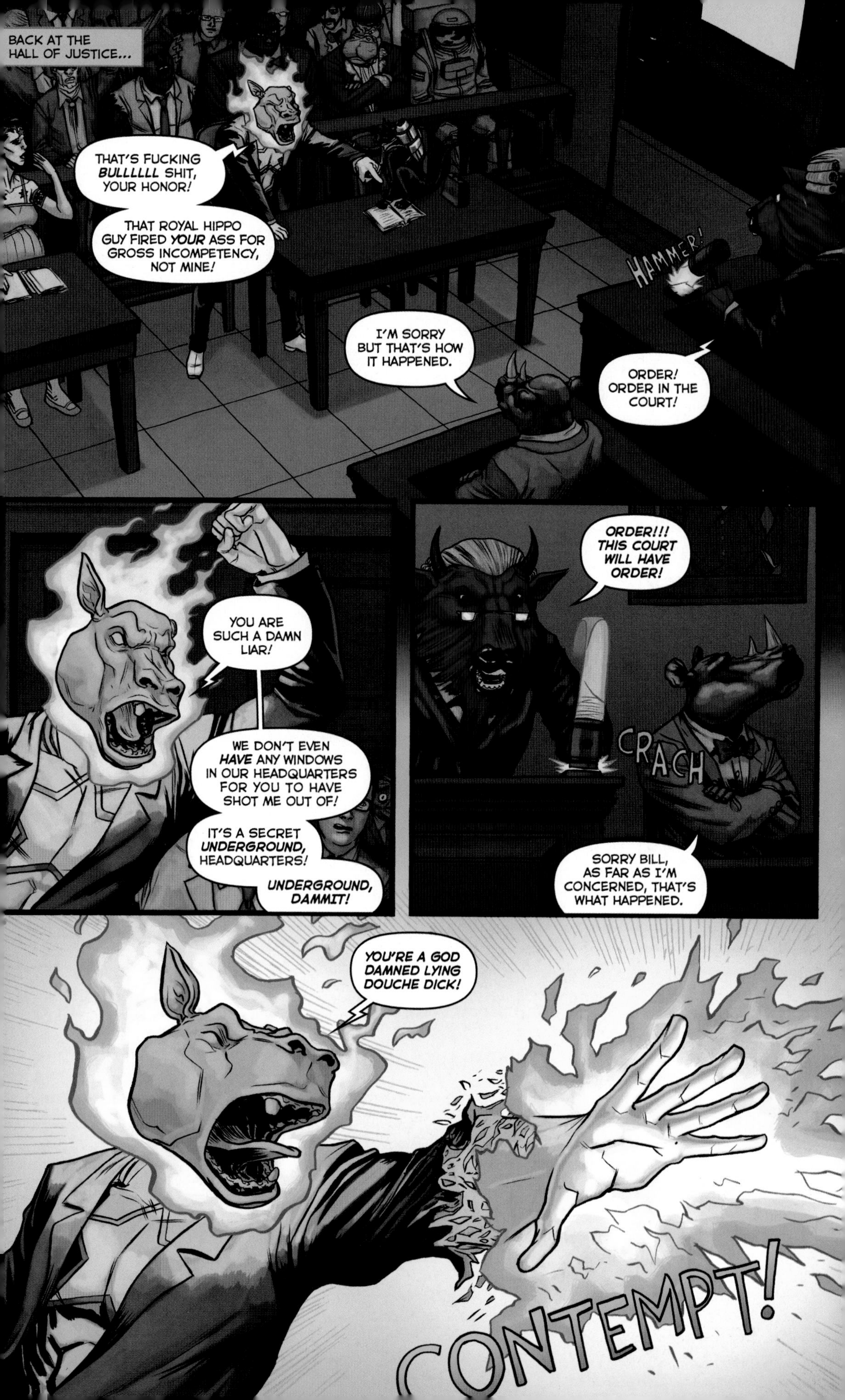
BACK AT THE HALL OF JUSTICE...
THAT'S FUCKING BULLLLLL SHIT, YOUR HONOR!
THAT ROYAL HIPPO GUY FIRED YOUR ASS FOR GROSS INCOMPETENCY, NOT MINE!
HAMMER!
I'M SORRY BUT THAT'S HOW IT HAPPENED.
ORDER! ORDER IN THE COURT!
YOU ARE SUCH A DAMN LIAR!
WE DON'T EVEN HAVE ANY WINDOWS IN OUR HEADQUARTERS FOR YOU TO HAVE SHOT ME OUT OF!
IT'S A SECRET UNDERGROUND, HEADQUARTERS!
UNDERGROUND, DAMMIT!
ORDER!!! THIS COURT WILL HAVE ORDER!
CRACH
SORRY BILL, AS FAR AS I'M CONCERNED, THAT'S WHAT HAPPENED.
YOU'RE A GOD DAMNED LYING DOUCHE DICK!
CONTEMPT!

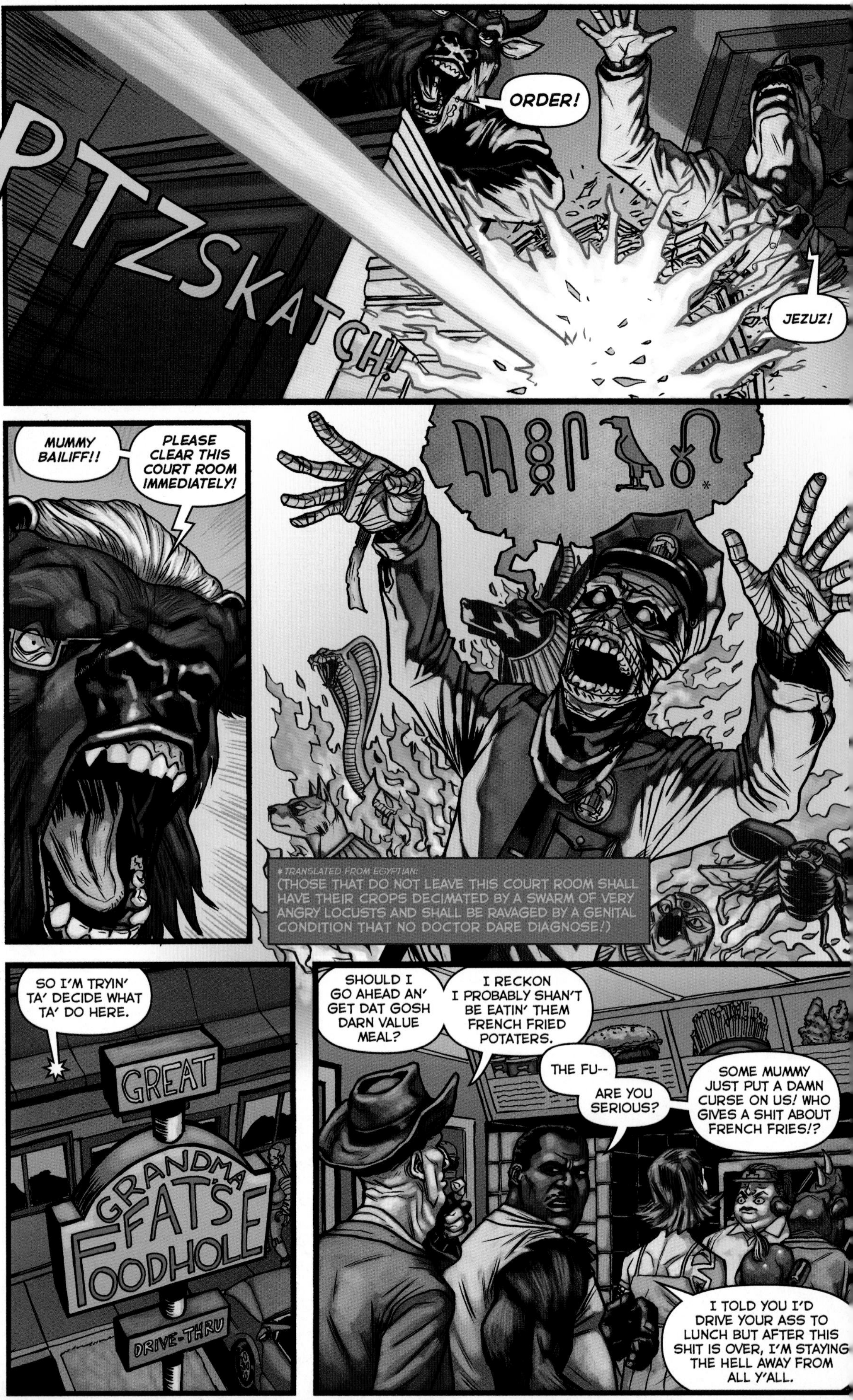

ORDER!
PTZSKATCH!
JEZUZ!
MUMMY BAILIFF!!
PLEASE CLEAR THIS COURT ROOM IMMEDIATELY!
*TRANSLATED FROM EGYPTIAN:
(THOSE THAT DO NOT LEAVE THIS COURT ROOM SHALL HAVE THEIR CROPS DECIMATED BY A SWARM OF VERY ANGRY LOCUSTS AND SHALL BE RAVAGED BY A GENITAL CONDITION THAT NO DOCTOR DARE DIAGNOSE!)
SO I'M TRYIN' TA' DECIDE WHAT TA' DO HERE.
GREAT
GRANDMA FAT'S E FOODHOLE
DRIVE-THRU
SHOULD I GO AHEAD AN' GET DAT GOSH DARN VALUE MEAL?
I RECKON I PROBABLY SHAN'T BE EATIN' THEM FRENCH FRIED POTATERS.
THE FU--
ARE YOU SERIOUS?
SOME MUMMY JUST PUT A DAMN CURSE ON US! WHO GIVES A SHIT ABOUT FRENCH FRIES!?
I TOLD YOU I'D DRIVE YOUR ASS TO LUNCH BUT AFTER THIS SHIT IS OVER, I'M STAYING THE HELL AWAY FROM ALL Y'ALL.

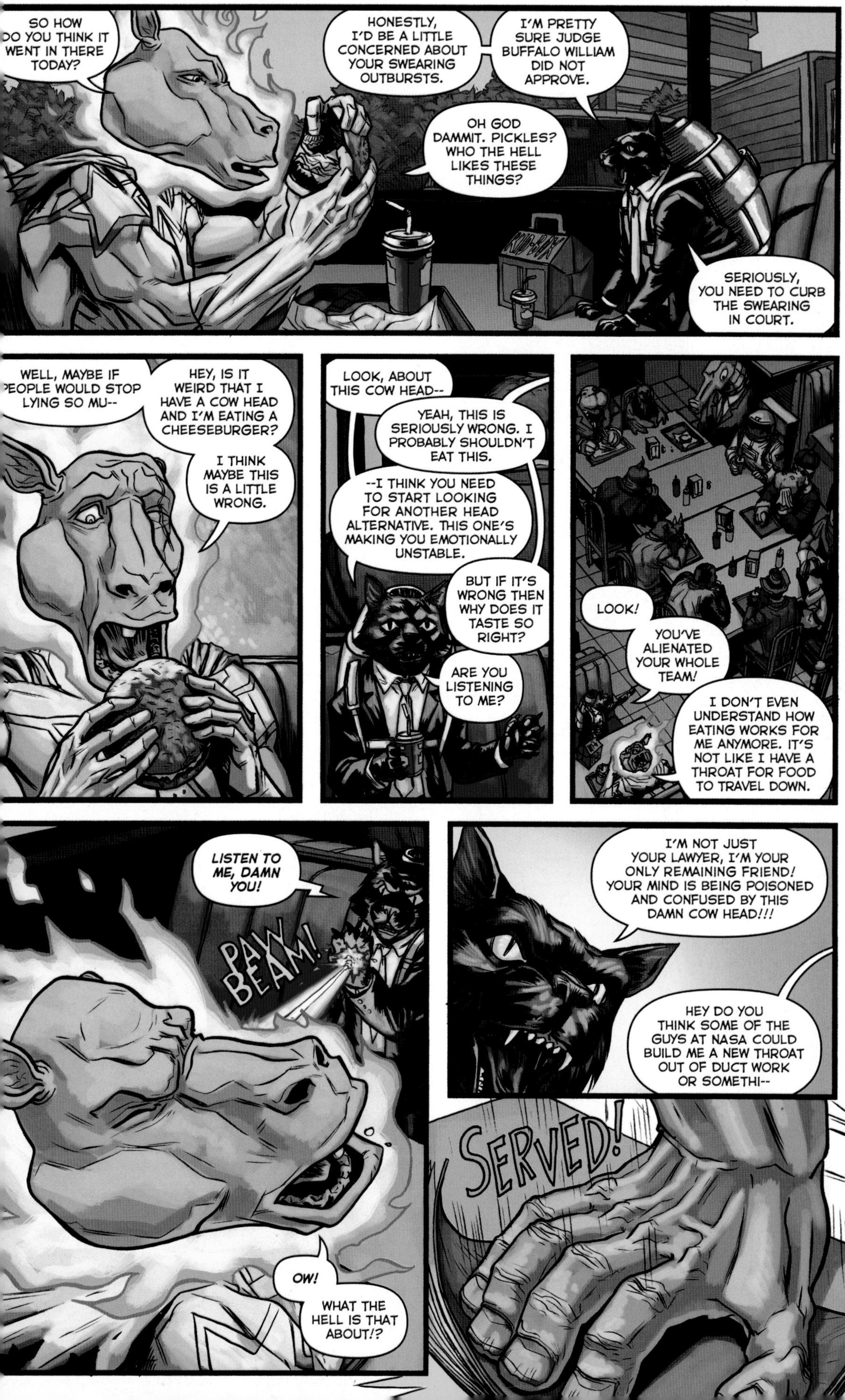

SO HOW DO YOU THINK IT WENT IN THERE TODAY?
HONESTLY, I'D BE A LITTLE CONCERNED ABOUT YOUR SWEARING OUTBURSTS.
I'M PRETTY SURE JUDGE BUFFALO WILLIAM DID NOT APPROVE.
OH GOD DAMMIT. PICKLES? WHO THE HELL LIKES THESE THINGS?
KID-BOX
SERIOUSLY, YOU NEED TO CURB THE SWEARING IN COURT.
WELL, MAYBE IF PEOPLE WOULD STOP LYING SO MU--
HEY, IS IT WEIRD THAT I HAVE A COW HEAD AND I'M EATING A CHEESEBURGER?
I THINK MAYBE THIS IS A LITTLE WRONG.
LOOK, ABOUT THIS COW HEAD--
YEAH, THIS IS SERIOUSLY WRONG. I PROBABLY SHOULDN'T EAT THIS.
--I THINK YOU NEED TO START LOOKING FOR ANOTHER HEAD ALTERNATIVE. THIS ONE'S MAKING YOU EMOTIONALLY UNSTABLE.
BUT IF IT'S WRONG THEN WHY DOES IT TASTE SO RIGHT?
ARE YOU LISTENING TO ME?
LOOK!
YOU'VE ALIENATED YOUR WHOLE TEAM!
I DON'T EVEN UNDERSTAND HOW EATING WORKS FOR ME ANYMORE. IT'S NOT LIKE I HAVE A THROAT FOR FOOD TO TRAVEL DOWN.
LISTEN TO ME, DAMN YOU!
PAW BEAM!
OW!
WHAT THE HELL IS THAT ABOUT!?
I'M NOT JUST YOUR LAWYER, I'M YOUR ONLY REMAINING FRIEND! YOUR MIND IS BEING POISONED AND CONFUSED BY THIS DAMN COW HEAD!!!
HEY DO YOU THINK SOME OF THE GUYS AT NASA COULD BUILD ME A NEW THROAT OUT OF DUCT WORK OR SOMETHI--
SERVED!

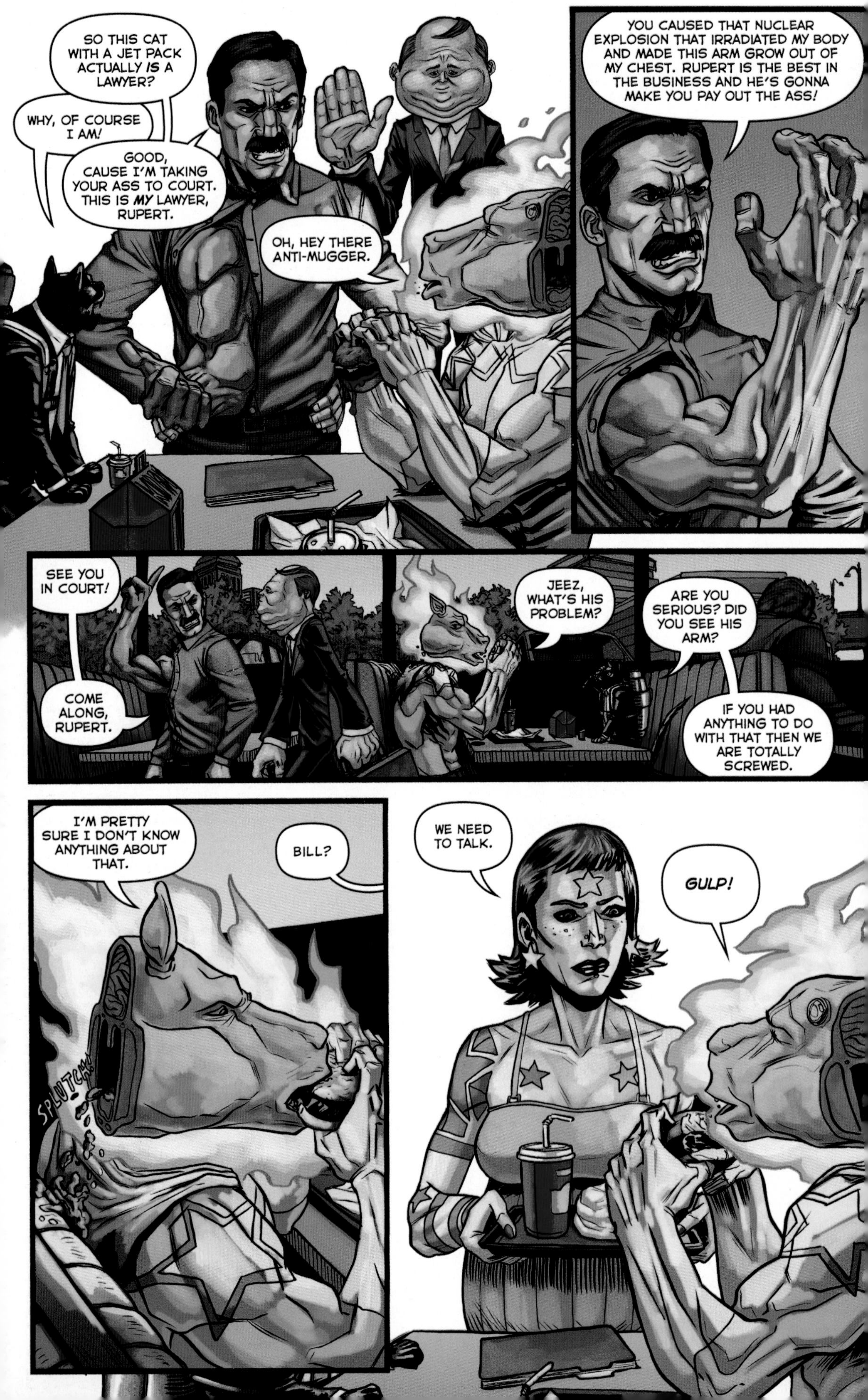
SO THIS CAT WITH A JET PACK ACTUALLY IS A LAWYER?
WHY, OF COURSE I AM!
GOOD, CAUSE I'M TAKING YOUR ASS TO COURT. THIS IS MY LAWYER, RUPERT.
OH, HEY THERE ANTI-MUGGER.
YOU CAUSED THAT NUCLEAR EXPLOSION THAT IRRADIATED MY BODY AND MADE THIS ARM GROW OUT OF MY CHEST. RUPERT IS THE BEST IN THE BUSINESS AND HE'S GONNA MAKE YOU PAY OUT THE ASS!
SEE YOU IN COURT!
COME ALONG, RUPERT.
JEEZ, WHAT'S HIS PROBLEM?
ARE YOU SERIOUS? DID YOU SEE HIS ARM?
IF YOU HAD ANYTHING TO DO WITH THAT THEN WE ARE TOTALLY SCREWED.
I'M PRETTY SURE I DON'T KNOW ANYTHING ABOUT THAT.
BILL?
SPLUTCH!
WE NEED TO TALK.
GULP!

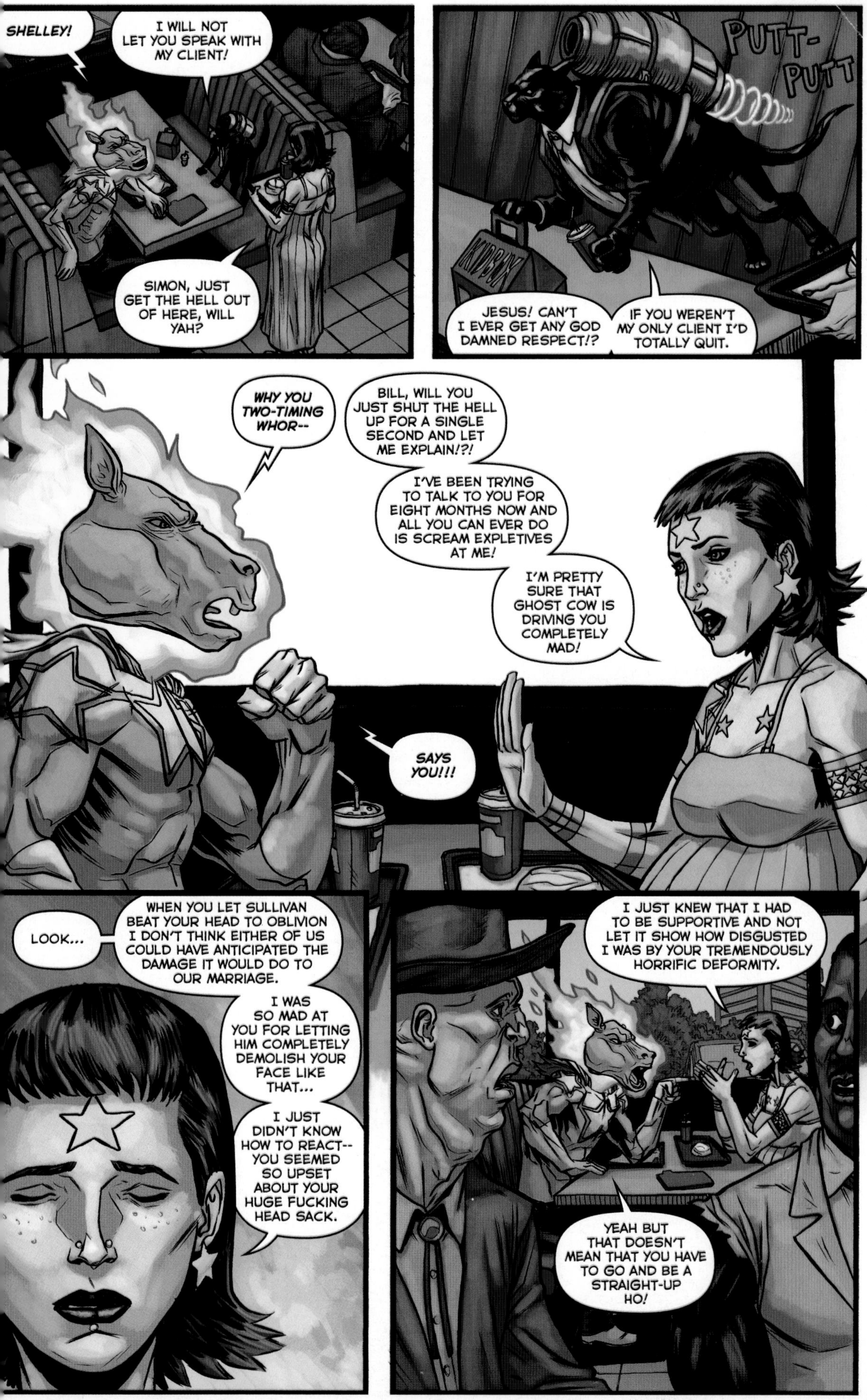
SHELLEY!
I WILL NOT LET YOU SPEAK WITH MY CLIENT!
SIMON, JUST GET THE HELL OUT OF HERE, WILL YAH?
PUTT-PUTT
JESUS! CAN'T I EVER GET ANY GOD DAMNED RESPECT!?
IF YOU WEREN'T MY ONLY CLIENT I'D TOTALLY QUIT.
WHY YOU TWO-TIMING WHOR--
BILL, WILL YOU JUST SHUT THE HELL UP FOR A SINGLE SECOND AND LET ME EXPLAIN!?!
I'VE BEEN TRYING TO TALK TO YOU FOR EIGHT MONTHS NOW AND ALL YOU CAN EVER DO IS SCREAM EXPLETIVES AT ME!
I'M PRETTY SURE THAT GHOST COW IS DRIVING YOU COMPLETELY MAD!
SAYS YOU!!!
LOOK...
WHEN YOU LET SULLIVAN BEAT YOUR HEAD TO OBLIVION I DON'T THINK EITHER OF US COULD HAVE ANTICIPATED THE DAMAGE IT WOULD DO TO OUR MARRIAGE.
I WAS SO MAD AT YOU FOR LETTING HIM COMPLETELY DEMOLISH YOUR FACE LIKE THAT...
I JUST DIDN'T KNOW HOW TO REACT-- YOU SEEMED SO UPSET ABOUT YOUR HUGE FUCKING HEAD SACK.
I JUST KNEW THAT I HAD TO BE SUPPORTIVE AND NOT LET IT SHOW HOW DISGUSTED I WAS BY YOUR TREMENDOUSLY HORRIFIC DEFORMITY.
YEAH BUT THAT DOESN'T MEAN THAT YOU HAVE TO GO AND BE A STRAIGHT-UP HO!

THAT NIGHT... NINE MONTHS AGO... I NEVER REALLY RECOVERED FROM THAT.

LOOK, BILL. I STILL LOVE YOU, AND I'M WILLING TO STICK WITH YOU THROUGH THIS.

I'M JUST NOT SURE HOW TO HANDLE YOUR GROSS DEFORMITY.

MAYBE WE SHOULD SEE A COUNSELOR OR THERAPIST OR SOMETHING.

YEAH, THAT SOUNDS GREAT.

WE'LL ASK DOC FIRST THING TOMORROW TO HOOK US UP WITH A COUNSELOR. I LOVE YOU. WE WILL FIGURE THIS OUT.

THANKS FOR TRYING, HONEY. I DO LOVE YOU SOOO MUCH.

UHM, SO SWEETIE... IS THERE REALLY *NOTHING* I CAN DO TO GET A LITTLE SEX TONIGHT?

I MEAN, IT'S BEEN LIKE A MONTH NOW SO I JUST...

UH, ALL RIGHT, I GUESS IF I JUST CLOSE MY EYES IT WON'T BE THAT BAD.

MOUNT

JUST BE CAREFUL WITH YOUR MISSHAPEN--

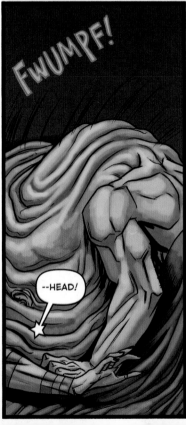

FWUMPF!

--HEAD!

OH SHIT! SORRY, HONEY!

ARE YOU OKAY UNDER THERE?

YUP, JUST GREAT. LET'S JUST DO THIS.

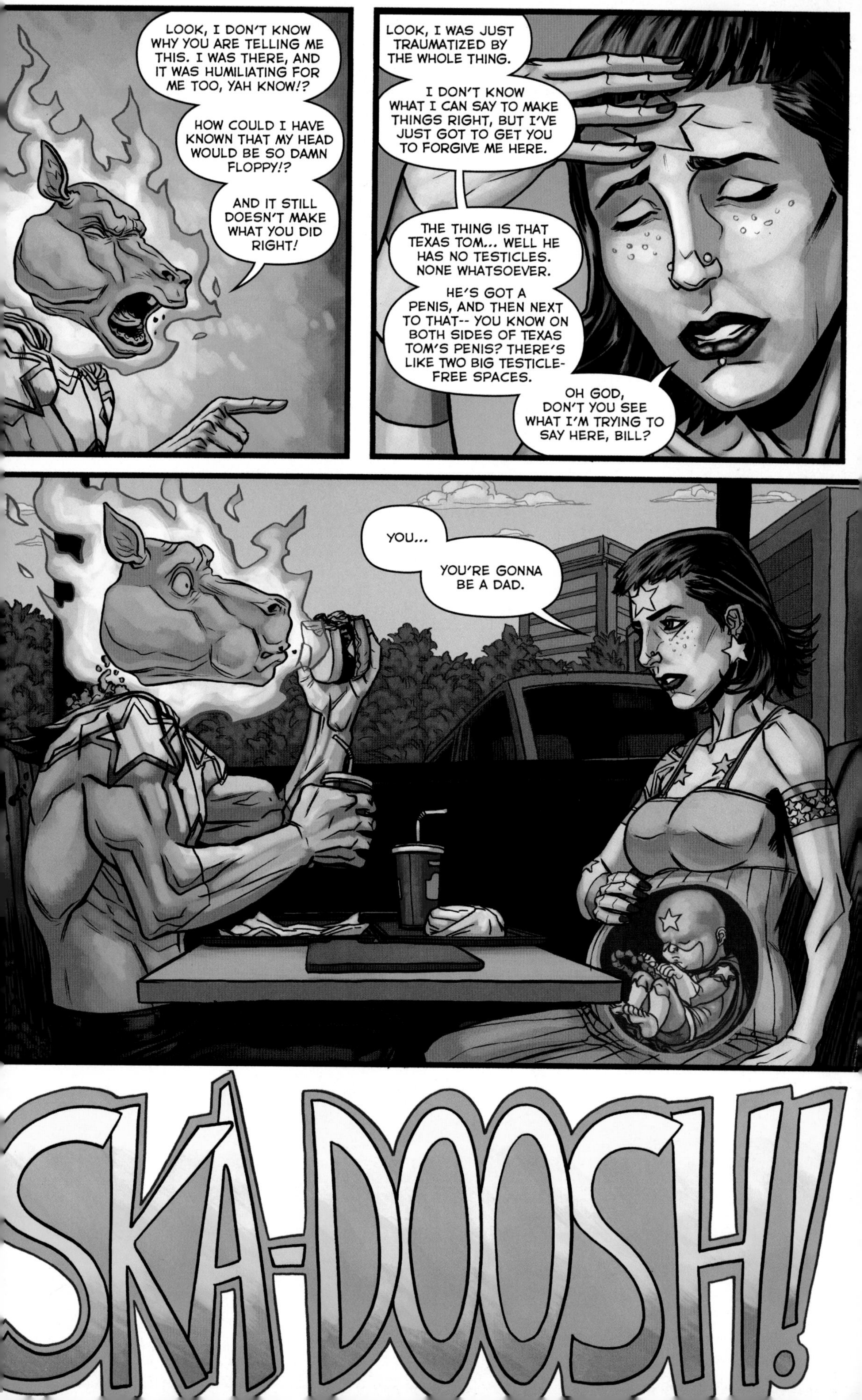
LOOK, I DON'T KNOW WHY YOU ARE TELLING ME THIS. I WAS THERE, AND IT WAS HUMILIATING FOR ME TOO, YAH KNOW!?
HOW COULD I HAVE KNOWN THAT MY HEAD WOULD BE SO DAMN FLOPPY!?
AND IT STILL DOESN'T MAKE WHAT YOU DID RIGHT!
LOOK, I WAS JUST TRAUMATIZED BY THE WHOLE THING.
I DON'T KNOW WHAT I CAN SAY TO MAKE THINGS RIGHT, BUT I'VE JUST GOT TO GET YOU TO FORGIVE ME HERE.
THE THING IS THAT TEXAS TOM... WELL HE HAS NO TESTICLES. NONE WHATSOEVER.
HE'S GOT A PENIS, AND THEN NEXT TO THAT-- YOU KNOW ON BOTH SIDES OF TEXAS TOM'S PENIS? THERE'S LIKE TWO BIG TESTICLE-FREE SPACES.
OH GOD, DON'T YOU SEE WHAT I'M TRYING TO SAY HERE, BILL?
YOU...
YOU'RE GONNA BE A DAD.
SKA-DOOSH!

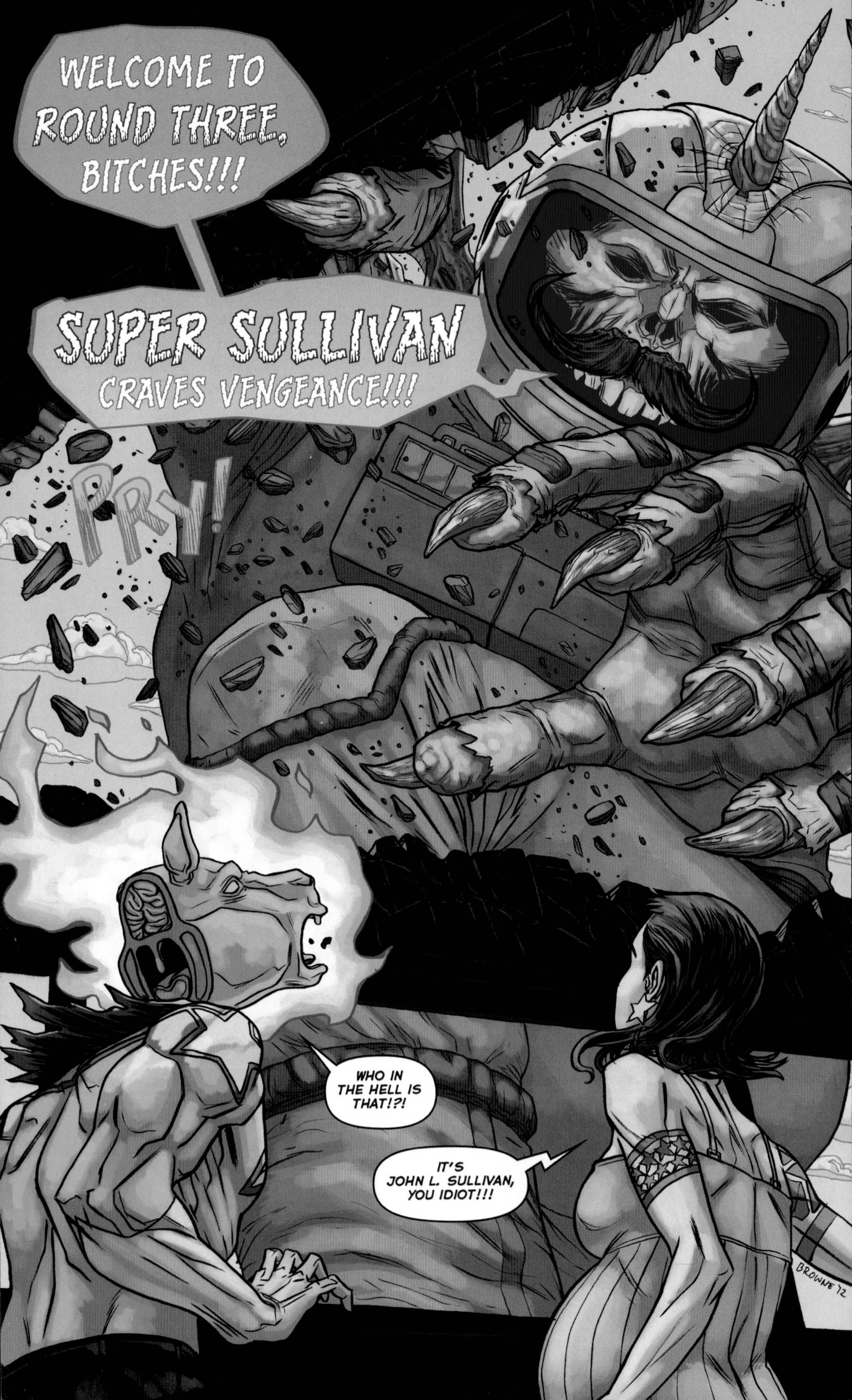
WELCOME TO ROUND THREE, BITCHES!!!
SUPER SULLIVAN CRAVES VENGEANCE!!!
PRY!
WHO IN THE HELL IS THAT!?!
IT'S JOHN L. SULLIVAN, YOU IDIOT!!!
BROWNE '12

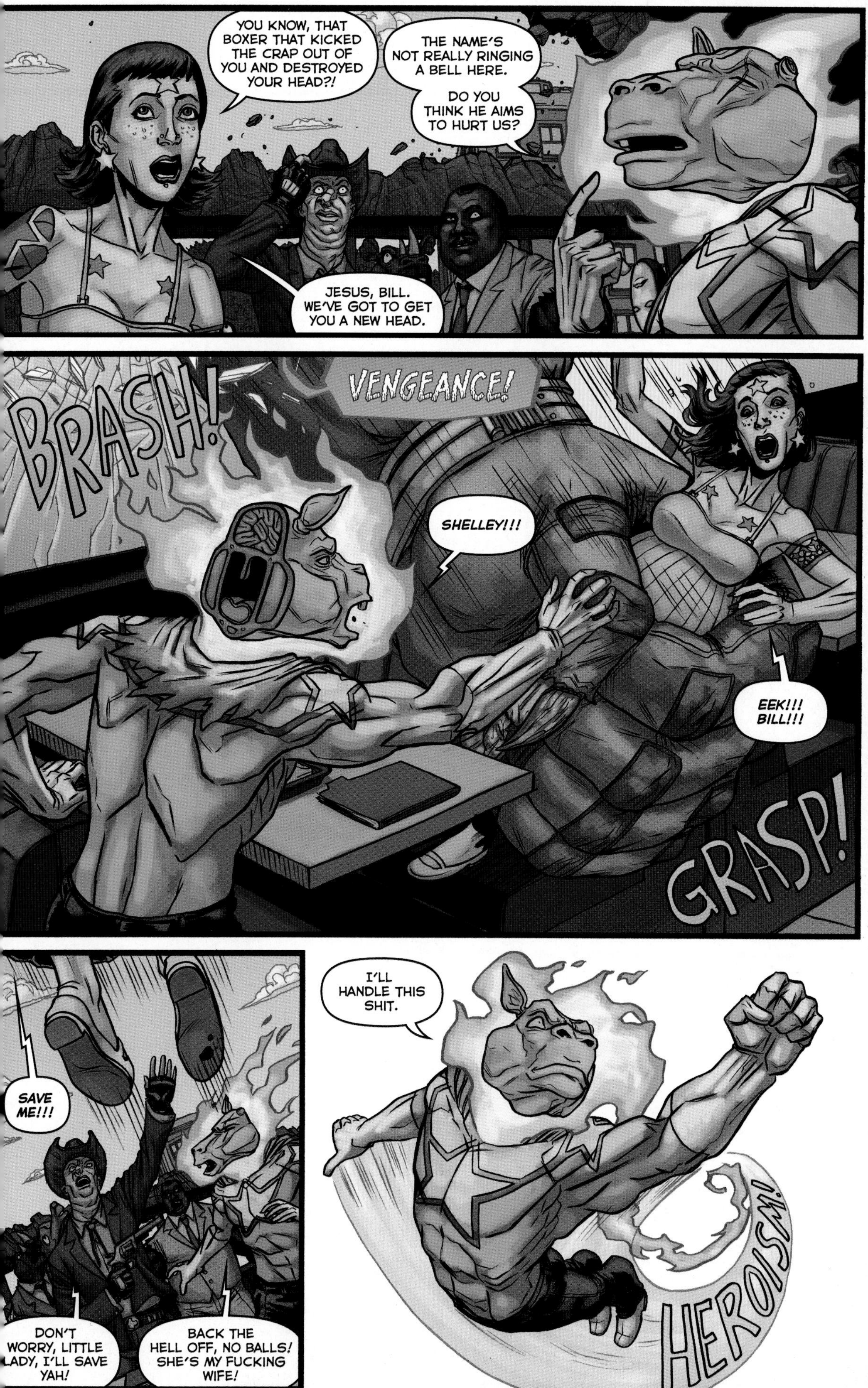
YOU KNOW, THAT BOXER THAT KICKED THE CRAP OUT OF YOU AND DESTROYED YOUR HEAD?!
THE NAME'S NOT REALLY RINGING A BELL HERE.
DO YOU THINK HE AIMS TO HURT US?
JESUS, BILL. WE'VE GOT TO GET YOU A NEW HEAD.
BRASH!
VENGEANCE!
SHELLEY!!!
EEK!!! BILL!!!
GRASP!
SAVE ME!!!
DON'T WORRY, LITTLE LADY, I'LL SAVE YAH!
BACK THE HELL OFF, NO BALLS! SHE'S MY FUCKING WIFE!
I'LL HANDLE THIS SHIT.
HEROISM!

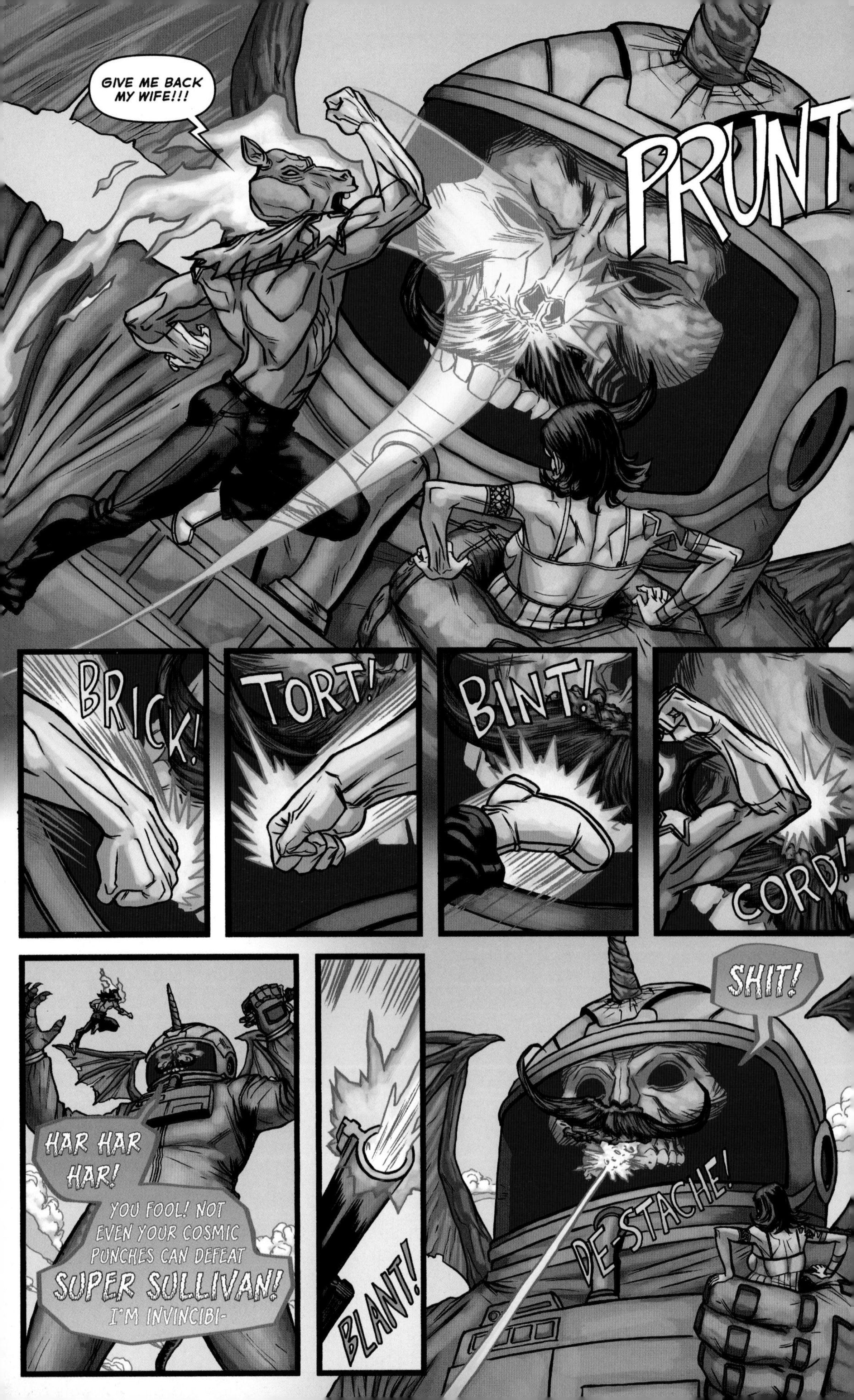
GIVE ME BACK MY WIFE!!!
PRUNT
BRICK!
TORT!
BINT!
CORD!
HAR HAR HAR!
YOU FOOL! NOT EVEN YOUR COSMIC PUNCHES CAN DEFEAT
SUPER SULLIVAN!
I'M INVINCIBI-
BLANT!
SHIT!
DE-STACHE!

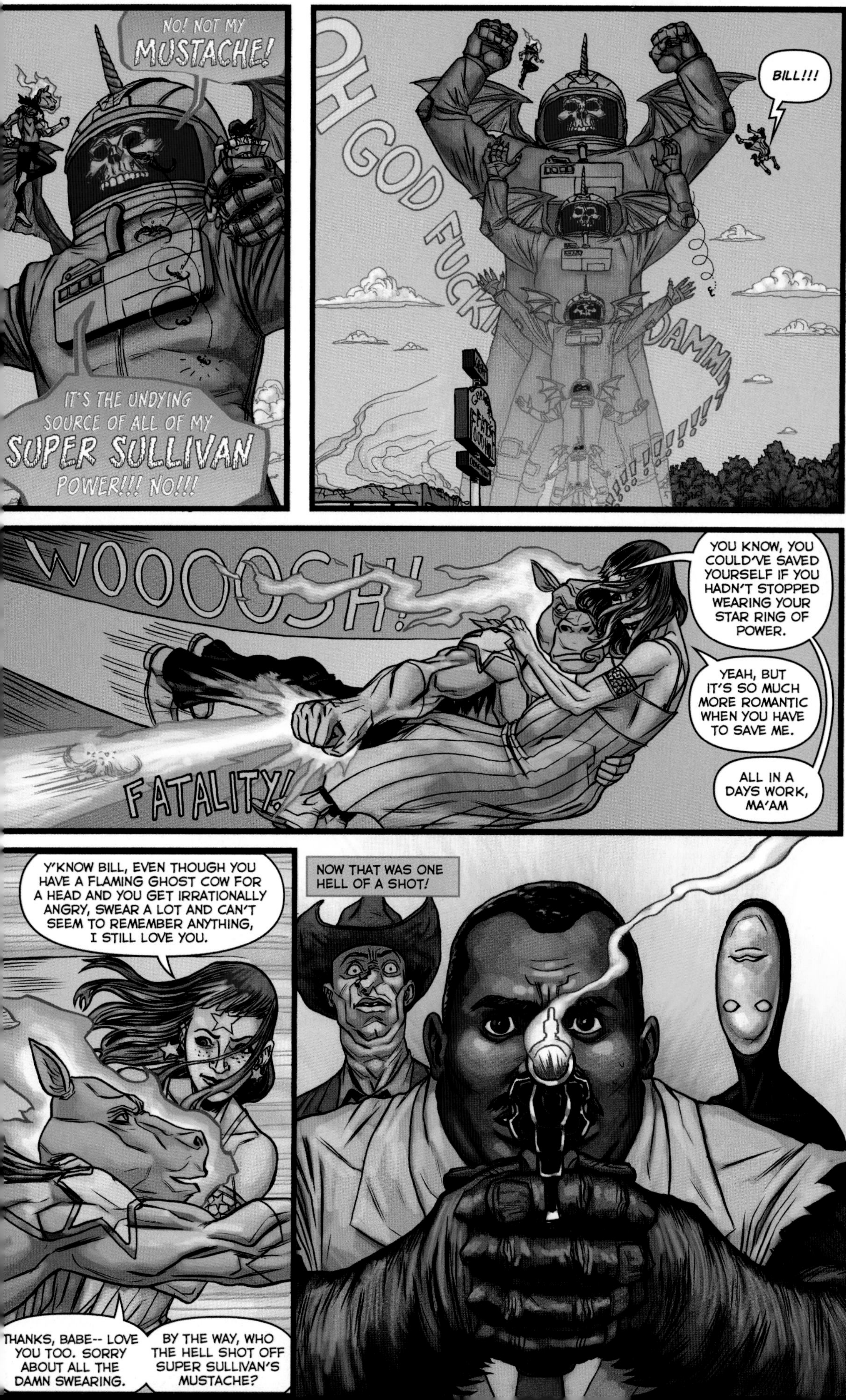
NO! NOT MY MUSTACHE!
IT'S THE UNDYING SOURCE OF ALL OF MY SUPER SULLIVAN POWER!!! NO!!!
OH GOD FUCKIN DAMN!!!!!!!!!
BILL!!!
WOOOOSH!
FATALITY!
YOU KNOW, YOU COULD'VE SAVED YOURSELF IF YOU HADN'T STOPPED WEARING YOUR STAR RING OF POWER.
YEAH, BUT IT'S SO MUCH MORE ROMANTIC WHEN YOU HAVE TO SAVE ME.
ALL IN A DAYS WORK, MA'AM
Y'KNOW BILL, EVEN THOUGH YOU HAVE A FLAMING GHOST COW FOR A HEAD AND YOU GET IRRATIONALLY ANGRY, SWEAR A LOT AND CAN'T SEEM TO REMEMBER ANYTHING, I STILL LOVE YOU.
THANKS, BABE-- LOVE YOU TOO. SORRY ABOUT ALL THE DAMN SWEARING.
BY THE WAY, WHO THE HELL SHOT OFF SUPER SULLIVAN'S MUSTACHE?
NOW THAT WAS ONE HELL OF A SHOT!

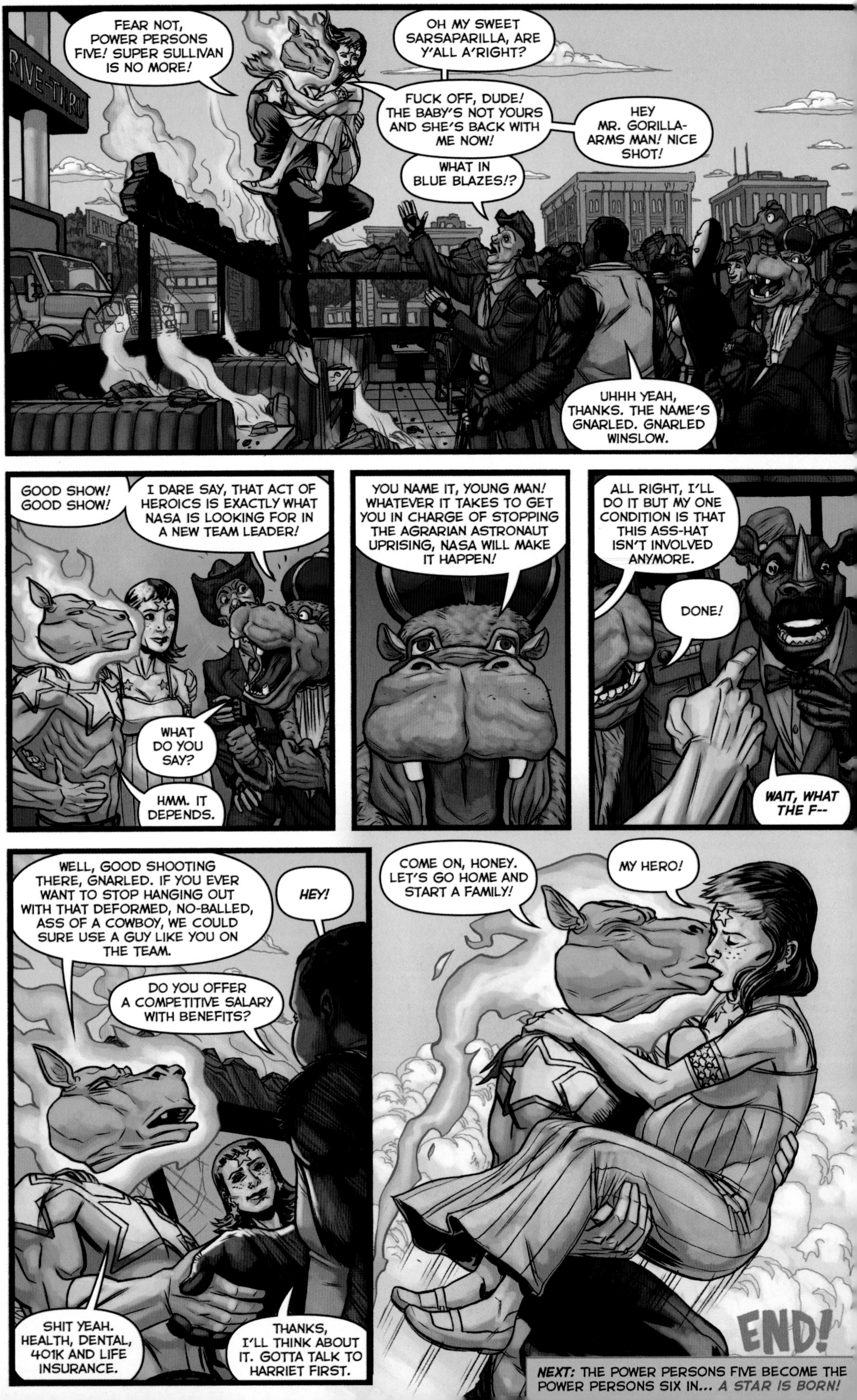

FEAR NOT, POWER PERSONS FIVE! SUPER SULLIVAN IS NO MORE!
OH MY SWEET SARSAPARILLA, ARE Y'ALL A'RIGHT?
FUCK OFF, DUDE! THE BABY'S NOT YOURS AND SHE'S BACK WITH ME NOW!
HEY MR. GORILLA-ARMS MAN! NICE SHOT!
WHAT IN BLUE BLAZES!?
UHHH YEAH, THANKS. THE NAME'S GNARLED. GNARLED WINSLOW.
GOOD SHOW! GOOD SHOW!
I DARE SAY, THAT ACT OF HEROICS IS EXACTLY WHAT NASA IS LOOKING FOR IN A NEW TEAM LEADER!
WHAT DO YOU SAY?
HMM. IT DEPENDS.
YOU NAME IT, YOUNG MAN! WHATEVER IT TAKES TO GET YOU IN CHARGE OF STOPPING THE AGRARIAN ASTRONAUT UPRISING, NASA WILL MAKE IT HAPPEN!
ALL RIGHT, I'LL DO IT BUT MY ONE CONDITION IS THAT THIS ASS-HAT ISN'T INVOLVED ANYMORE.
DONE!
WAIT, WHAT THE F--
WELL, GOOD SHOOTING THERE, GNARLED. IF YOU EVER WANT TO STOP HANGING OUT WITH THAT DEFORMED, NO-BALLED, ASS OF A COWBOY, WE COULD SURE USE A GUY LIKE YOU ON THE TEAM.
HEY!
DO YOU OFFER A COMPETITIVE SALARY WITH BENEFITS?
SHIT YEAH. HEALTH, DENTAL, 401K AND LIFE INSURANCE.
THANKS, I'LL THINK ABOUT IT. GOTTA TALK TO HARRIET FIRST.
COME ON, HONEY. LET'S GO HOME AND START A FAMILY!
MY HERO!
END!
NEXT: THE POWER PERSONS FIVE BECOME THE POWER PERSONS SIX IN... A STAR IS BORN!

THE ORIGINS OF GOD HATES ASTRONAUTS

The following section is a collection of two-page origin stories for many of the characters of God Hates Astronauts. All of these stories are written by me (Ryan Browne) and drawn by one of 18 different amazingly talented artists. I handled the coloring duties unless otherwise noted. Enjoy!!!

STAR FIGHTER
ART BY: TOM SCIOLI

STARRIOR
ART BY: JENNY FRISON

THE ANTI-MUGGER
ART BY: RYAN BROWNE

THE IMPOSSIBLE
DRAWN BY: TIM SEELEY

CRAYMOK
DRAWN BY: NICK PITARRA
COLORS BY: MEGAN WILSON

TEXAS TOM
DRAWN BY: CHRIS MITTEN

JOHN L. SULLIVAN
DRAWN BY: ANDY MACDONALD
COLORS BY: RICO RENZI

**JOHN L. SULLIVAN'S
CRIMINAL BEARS**
DRAWN BY: C.P. WILSON III

DR. PROFESSOR
ART BY: GABRIEL BAUTISTA

GNARLED WINSLOW
ART BY: GREG AND FAKE PETRE

CRAZY TRAIN
DRAWN BY: TRADD MOORE

SIR HIPPOTHESIS
DRAWN BY: CODY SCHIBI

REED SPACER
ART BY: ALEJANDRO BRUZZESE

MUMMY BAILIFF
DRAWN BY: KYLE STRAHM

**ADMIRAL TIGER EATING
A CHEESEBURGER**
DRAWN BY: RILEY ROSSMO

MR. CRABTREE
DRAWN BY: HILARY BARTA

OWLVIN
ART BY: ZANDER CANNON

HUGH MANATEE
ART BY: SEAN DOVE

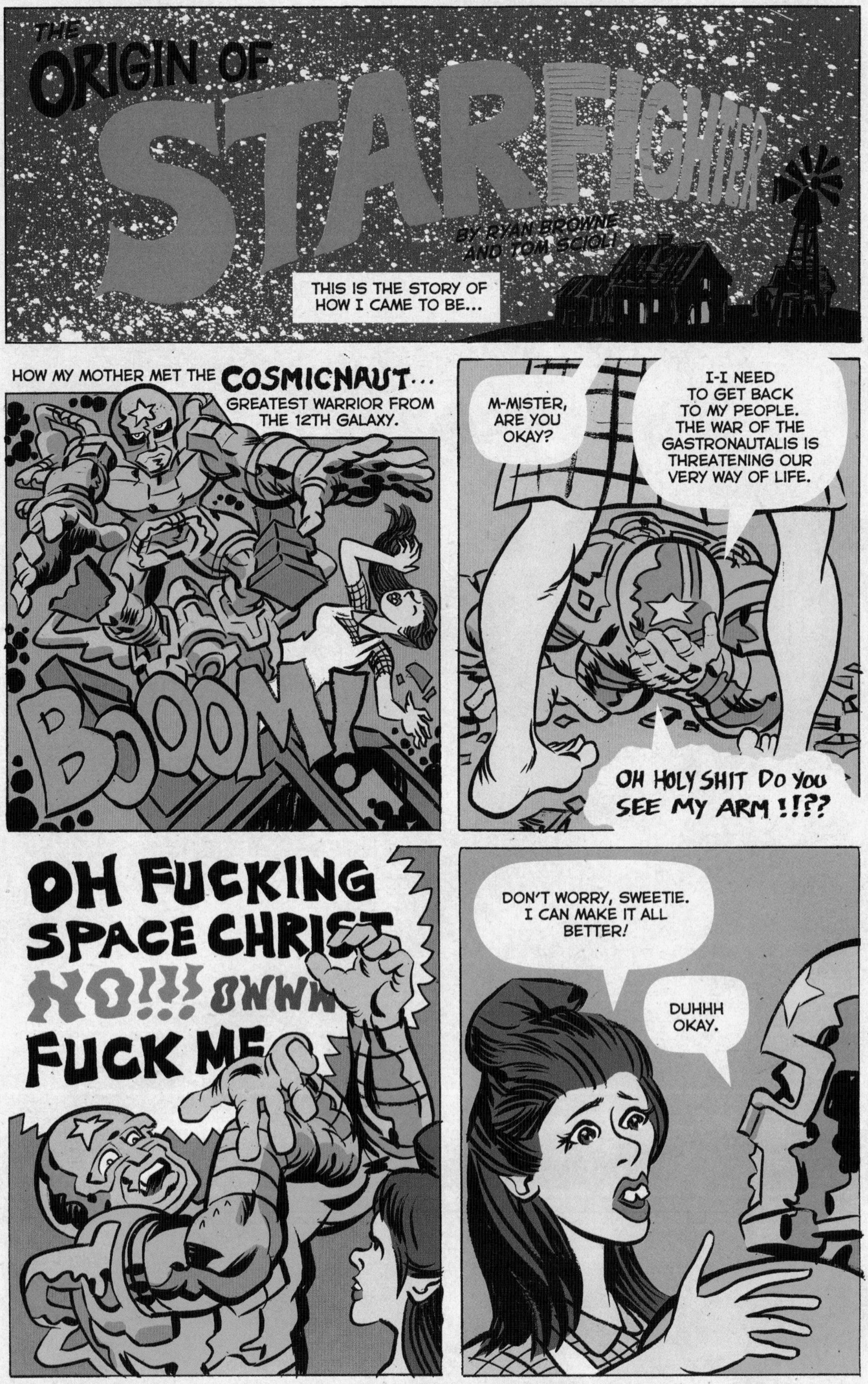
THE ORIGIN OF STARFIGHTER
BY RYAN BROWNE AND TOM SCIOLI
THIS IS THE STORY OF HOW I CAME TO BE...
HOW MY MOTHER MET THE COSMICNAUT...
GREATEST WARRIOR FROM THE 12TH GALAXY.
BOOOM!
M-MISTER, ARE YOU OKAY?
I-I NEED TO GET BACK TO MY PEOPLE. THE WAR OF THE GASTRONAUTALIS IS THREATENING OUR VERY WAY OF LIFE.
OH HOLY SHIT DO YOU SEE MY ARM!!??
OH FUCKING SPACE CHRIST NO!!! OWWW FUCK ME
DON'T WORRY, SWEETIE. I CAN MAKE IT ALL BETTER!
DUHHH OKAY.

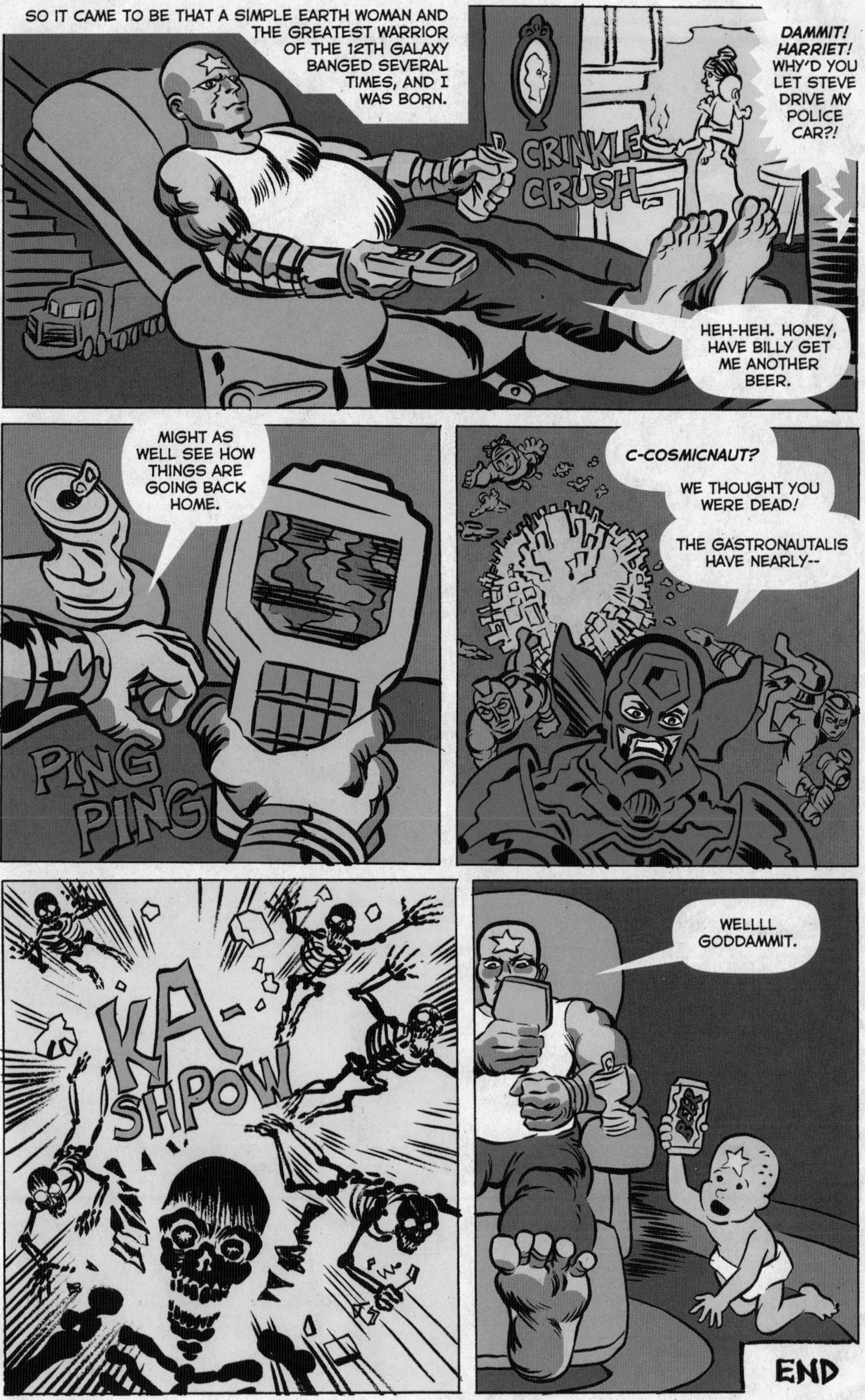
SO IT CAME TO BE THAT A SIMPLE EARTH WOMAN AND THE GREATEST WARRIOR OF THE 12TH GALAXY BANGED SEVERAL TIMES, AND I WAS BORN.
CRINKLE CRUSH
DAMMIT! HARRIET! WHY'D YOU LET STEVE DRIVE MY POLICE CAR?!
HEH-HEH. HONEY, HAVE BILLY GET ME ANOTHER BEER.
MIGHT AS WELL SEE HOW THINGS ARE GOING BACK HOME.
PING PING
C-COSMICNAUT?
WE THOUGHT YOU WERE DEAD!
THE GASTRONAUTALIS HAVE NEARLY--
KA-SHPOW
WELLLL GODDAMMIT.
BEER
END

TOM SCIOLI

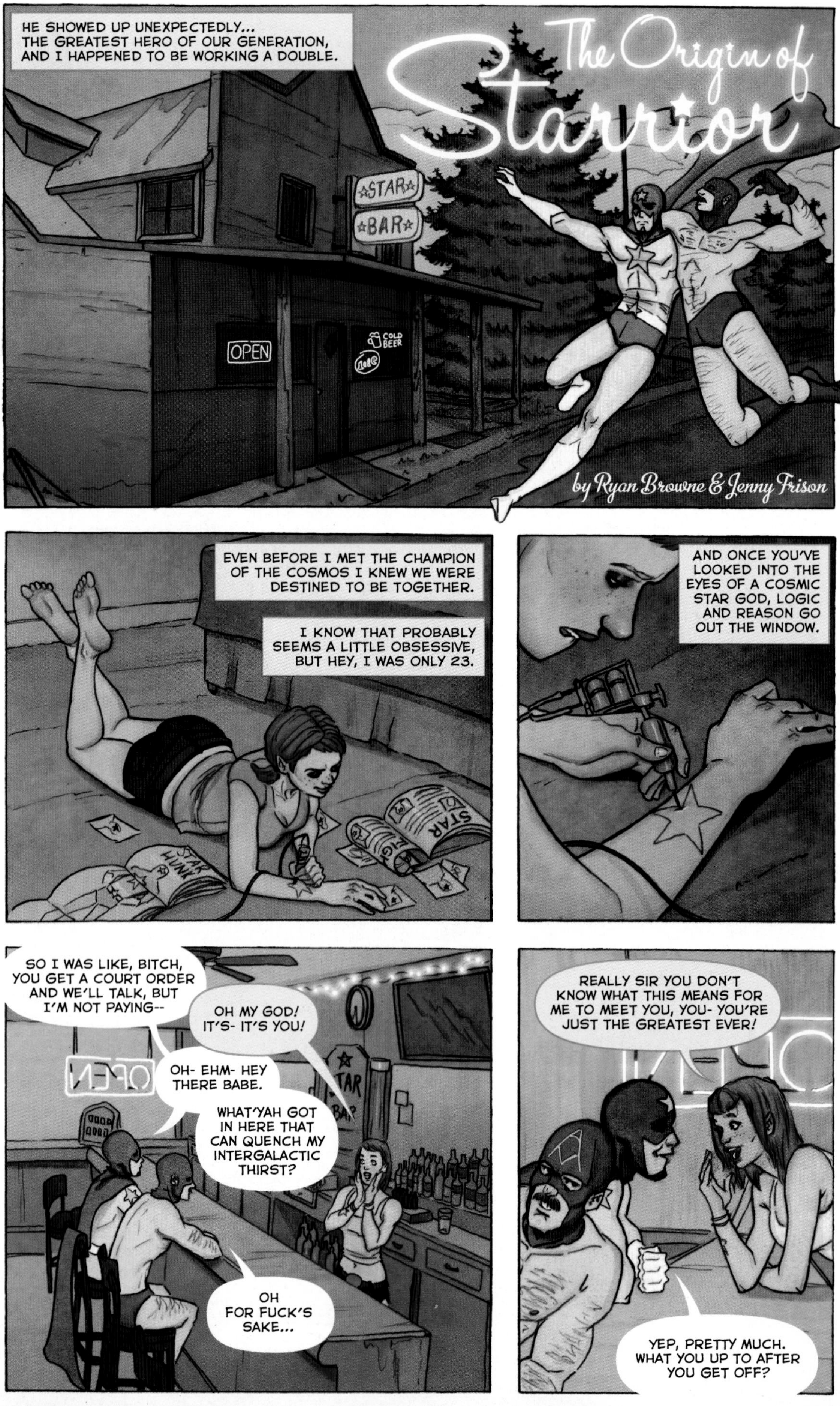

HE SHOWED UP UNEXPECTEDLY... THE GREATEST HERO OF OUR GENERATION, AND I HAPPENED TO BE WORKING A DOUBLE.
The Origin of Starrior
STAR
BAR
OPEN
COLD BEER
by Ryan Browne & Jenny Frison
EVEN BEFORE I MET THE CHAMPION OF THE COSMOS I KNEW WE WERE DESTINED TO BE TOGETHER.
I KNOW THAT PROBABLY SEEMS A LITTLE OBSESSIVE, BUT HEY, I WAS ONLY 23.
STAR HUNK
STAR
AND ONCE YOU'VE LOOKED INTO THE EYES OF A COSMIC STAR GOD, LOGIC AND REASON GO OUT THE WINDOW.
SO I WAS LIKE, BITCH, YOU GET A COURT ORDER AND WE'LL TALK, BUT I'M NOT PAYING--
OH MY GOD! IT'S- IT'S YOU!
OH- EHM- HEY THERE BABE.
WHAT'YAH GOT IN HERE THAT CAN QUENCH MY INTERGALACTIC THIRST?
OH FOR FUCK'S SAKE...
REALLY SIR YOU DON'T KNOW WHAT THIS MEANS FOR ME TO MEET YOU, YOU- YOU'RE JUST THE GREATEST EVER!
YEP, PRETTY MUCH. WHAT YOU UP TO AFTER YOU GET OFF?

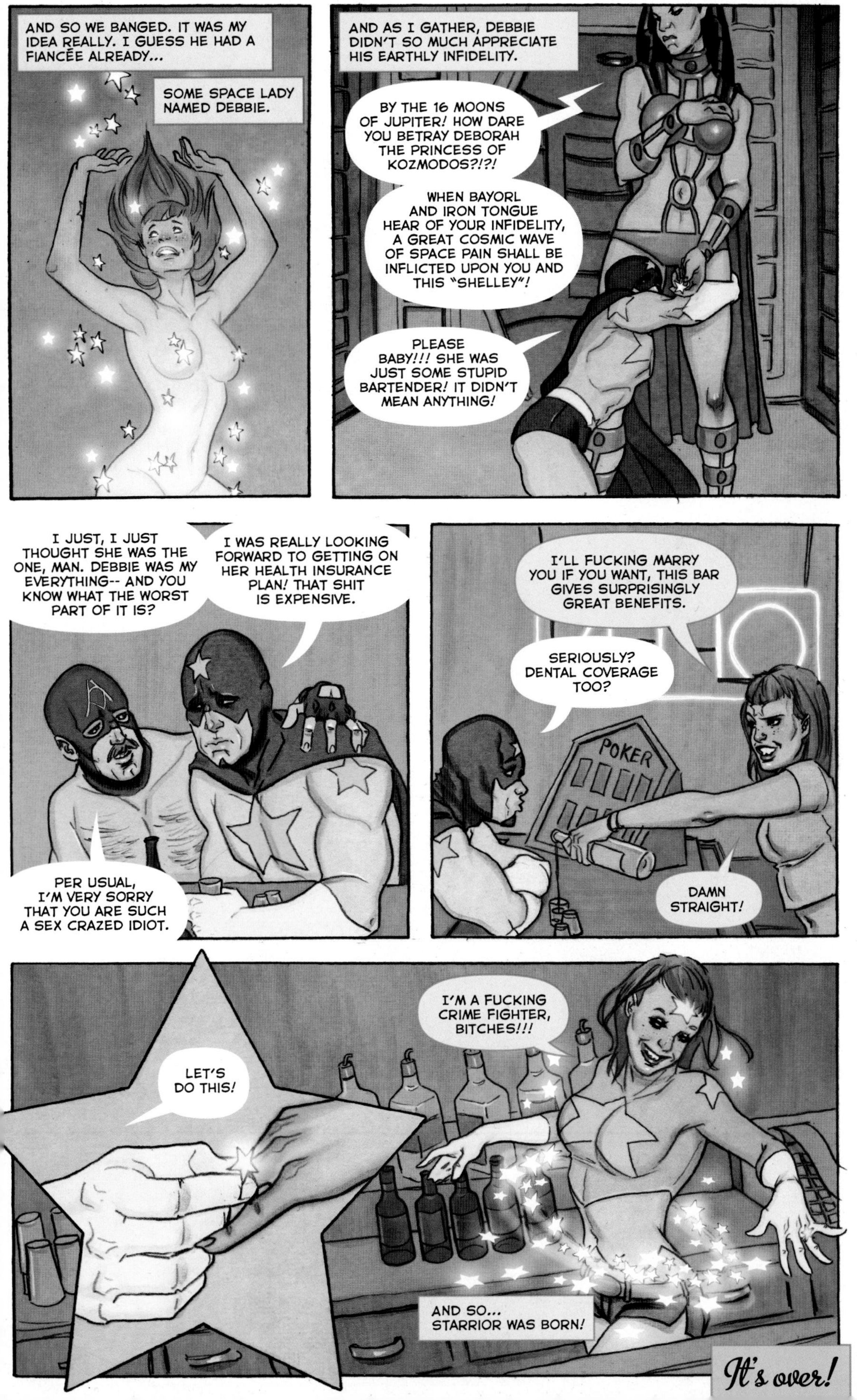
AND SO WE BANGED. IT WAS MY IDEA REALLY. I GUESS HE HAD A FIANCÉE ALREADY...
SOME SPACE LADY NAMED DEBBIE.
AND AS I GATHER, DEBBIE DIDN'T SO MUCH APPRECIATE HIS EARTHLY INFIDELITY.
BY THE 16 MOONS OF JUPITER! HOW DARE YOU BETRAY DEBORAH THE PRINCESS OF KOZMODOS?!?!
WHEN BAYORL AND IRON TONGUE HEAR OF YOUR INFIDELITY, A GREAT COSMIC WAVE OF SPACE PAIN SHALL BE INFLICTED UPON YOU AND THIS "SHELLEY"!
PLEASE BABY!!! SHE WAS JUST SOME STUPID BARTENDER! IT DIDN'T MEAN ANYTHING!
I JUST, I JUST THOUGHT SHE WAS THE ONE, MAN. DEBBIE WAS MY EVERYTHING-- AND YOU KNOW WHAT THE WORST PART OF IT IS?
I WAS REALLY LOOKING FORWARD TO GETTING ON HER HEALTH INSURANCE PLAN! THAT SHIT IS EXPENSIVE.
PER USUAL, I'M VERY SORRY THAT YOU ARE SUCH A SEX CRAZED IDIOT.
I'LL FUCKING MARRY YOU IF YOU WANT, THIS BAR GIVES SURPRISINGLY GREAT BENEFITS.
SERIOUSLY? DENTAL COVERAGE TOO?
POKER
DAMN STRAIGHT!
I'M A FUCKING CRIME FIGHTER, BITCHES!!!
LET'S DO THIS!
AND SO... STARRIOR WAS BORN!
It's over!

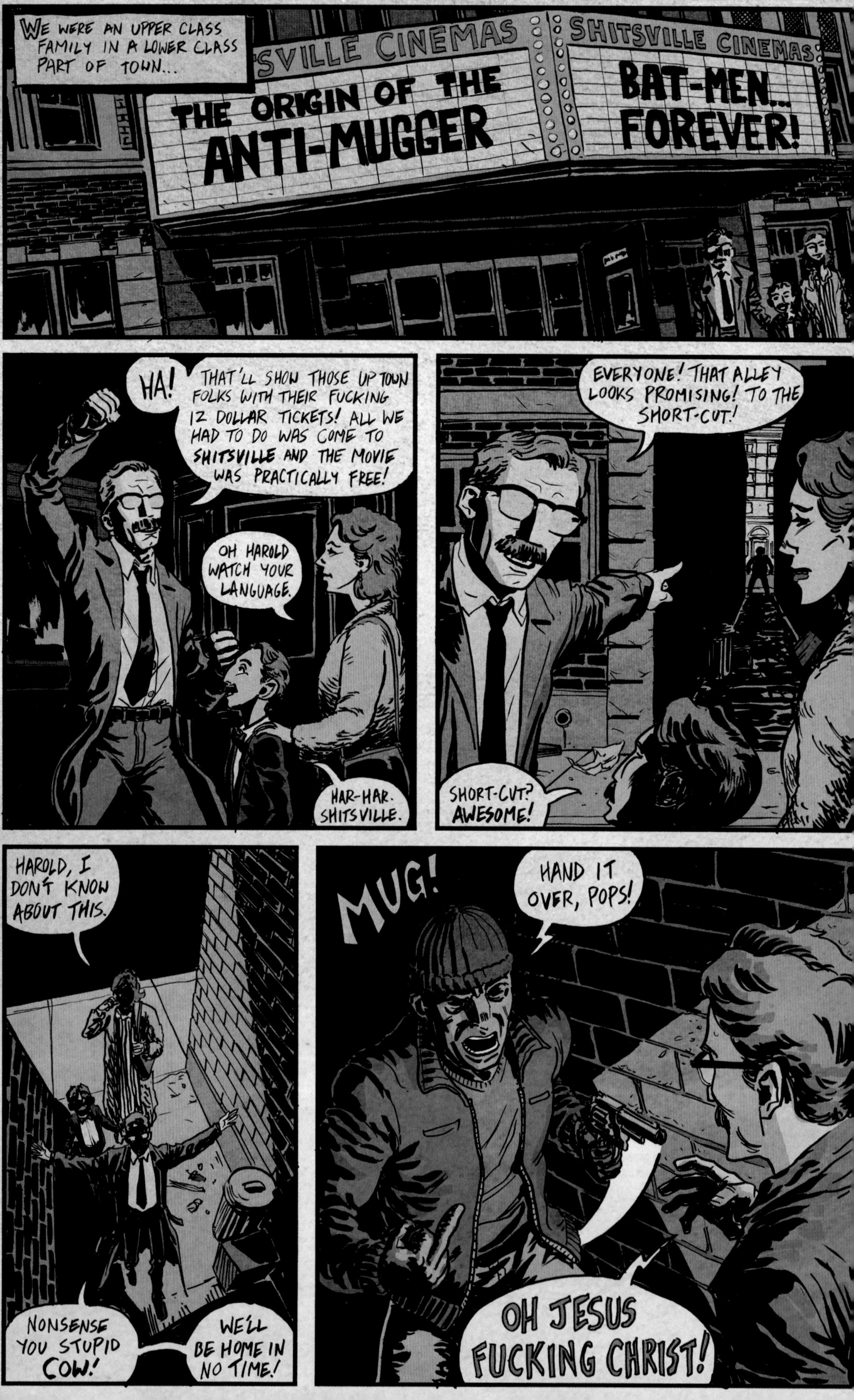
WE WERE AN UPPER CLASS FAMILY IN A LOWER CLASS PART OF TOWN...
SVILLE CINEMAS
THE ORIGIN OF THE ANTI-MUGGER
SHITSVILLE CINEMAS
BAT-MEN... FOREVER!
HA!
THAT'LL SHOW THOSE UPTOWN FOLKS WITH THEIR FUCKING 12 DOLLAR TICKETS! ALL WE HAD TO DO WAS COME TO SHITSVILLE AND THE MOVIE WAS PRACTICALLY FREE!
OH HAROLD WATCH YOUR LANGUAGE.
HAR-HAR. SHITSVILLE.
EVERYONE! THAT ALLEY LOOKS PROMISING! TO THE SHORT-CUT!
SHORT-CUT? AWESOME!
HAROLD, I DON'T KNOW ABOUT THIS.
NONSENSE YOU STUPID COW!
WE'LL BE HOME IN NO TIME!
MUG!
HAND IT OVER, POPS!
OH JESUS FUCKING CHRIST!

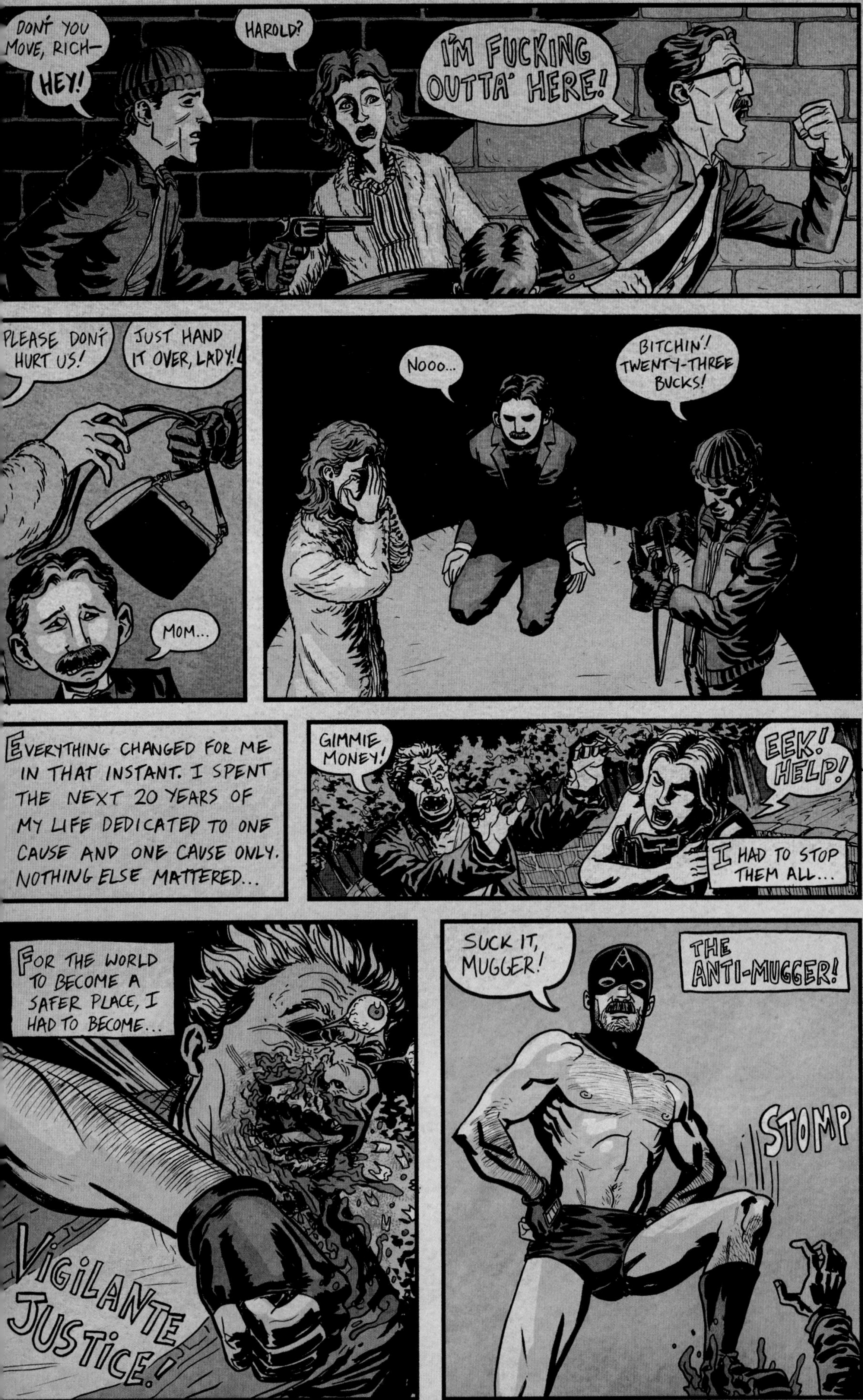
DON'T YOU MOVE, RICH— HEY!
HAROLD?
I'M FUCKING OUTTA' HERE!
PLEASE DON'T HURT US!
JUST HAND IT OVER, LADY!
MOM...
NOOO...
BITCHIN'! TWENTY-THREE BUCKS!
EVERYTHING CHANGED FOR ME IN THAT INSTANT. I SPENT THE NEXT 20 YEARS OF MY LIFE DEDICATED TO ONE CAUSE AND ONE CAUSE ONLY. NOTHING ELSE MATTERED...
GIMMIE MONEY!
EEK! HELP!
I HAD TO STOP THEM ALL...
FOR THE WORLD TO BECOME A SAFER PLACE, I HAD TO BECOME...
VIGILANTE JUSTICE!
SUCK IT, MUGGER!
THE ANTI-MUGGER!
STOMP

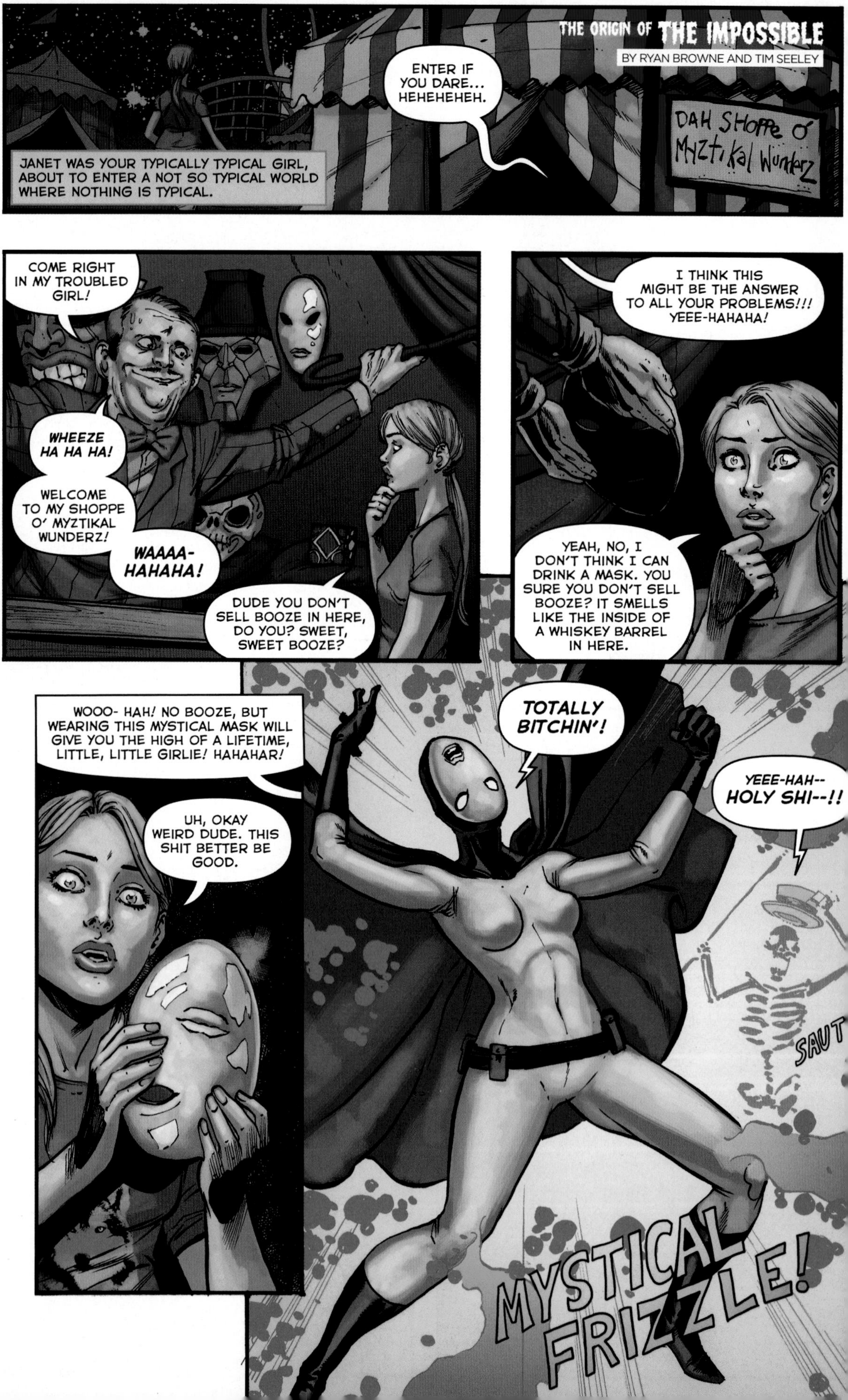
THE ORIGIN OF THE IMPOSSIBLE
BY RYAN BROWNE AND TIM SEELEY
ENTER IF YOU DARE... HEHEHEHEH.
DAH SHOPPE O' MYZTIKAL WUNDERZ
JANET WAS YOUR TYPICALLY TYPICAL GIRL, ABOUT TO ENTER A NOT SO TYPICAL WORLD WHERE NOTHING IS TYPICAL.
COME RIGHT IN MY TROUBLED GIRL!
WHEEZE HA HA HA!
WELCOME TO MY SHOPPE O' MYZTIKAL WUNDERZ!
WAAAA-HAHAHA!
DUDE YOU DON'T SELL BOOZE IN HERE, DO YOU? SWEET, SWEET BOOZE?
I THINK THIS MIGHT BE THE ANSWER TO ALL YOUR PROBLEMS!!! YEEE-HAHAHA!
YEAH, NO, I DON'T THINK I CAN DRINK A MASK. YOU SURE YOU DON'T SELL BOOZE? IT SMELLS LIKE THE INSIDE OF A WHISKEY BARREL IN HERE.
WOOO- HAH! NO BOOZE, BUT WEARING THIS MYSTICAL MASK WILL GIVE YOU THE HIGH OF A LIFETIME, LITTLE, LITTLE GIRLIE! HAHAHAR!
UH, OKAY WEIRD DUDE. THIS SHIT BETTER BE GOOD.
TOTALLY BITCHIN'!
YEEE-HAH-- HOLY SHI--!!
SAUT
MYSTICAL FRIZZLE!

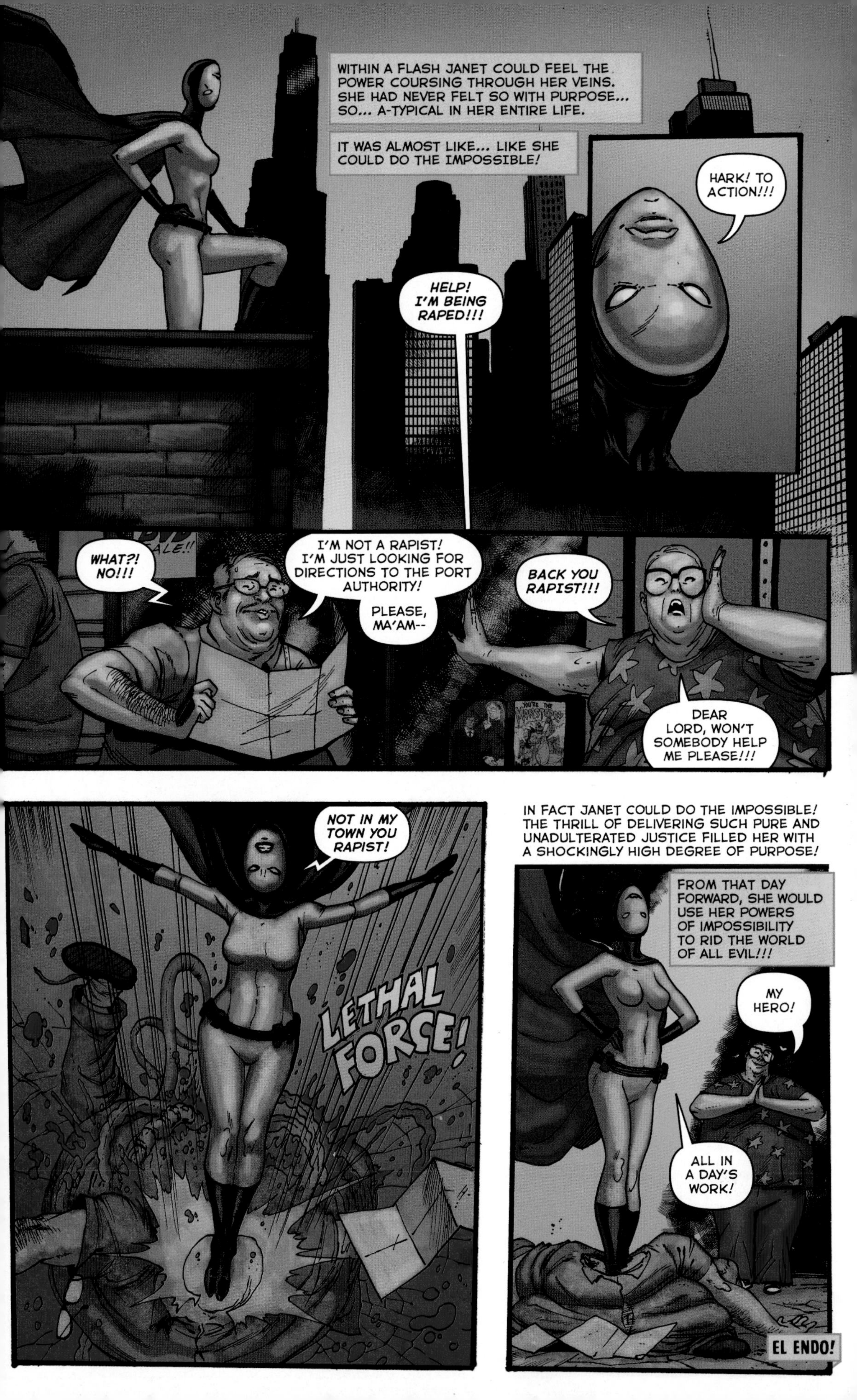

WITHIN A FLASH JANET COULD FEEL THE POWER COURSING THROUGH HER VEINS. SHE HAD NEVER FELT SO WITH PURPOSE... SO... A-TYPICAL IN HER ENTIRE LIFE.
IT WAS ALMOST LIKE... LIKE SHE COULD DO THE IMPOSSIBLE!
HARK! TO ACTION!!!
HELP! I'M BEING RAPED!!!
WHAT?! NO!!!
I'M NOT A RAPIST! I'M JUST LOOKING FOR DIRECTIONS TO THE PORT AUTHORITY!
PLEASE, MA'AM--
BACK YOU RAPIST!!!
DEAR LORD, WON'T SOMEBODY HELP ME PLEASE!!!
NOT IN MY TOWN YOU RAPIST!
LETHAL FORCE!
IN FACT JANET COULD DO THE IMPOSSIBLE! THE THRILL OF DELIVERING SUCH PURE AND UNADULTERATED JUSTICE FILLED HER WITH A SHOCKINGLY HIGH DEGREE OF PURPOSE!
FROM THAT DAY FORWARD, SHE WOULD USE HER POWERS OF IMPOSSIBILITY TO RID THE WORLD OF ALL EVIL!!!
MY HERO!
ALL IN A DAY'S WORK!
EL ENDO!

THE ORIGIN OF CRAYMOK

BY RYAN BROWNE, NICK PITARRA + MEGAN WILSON

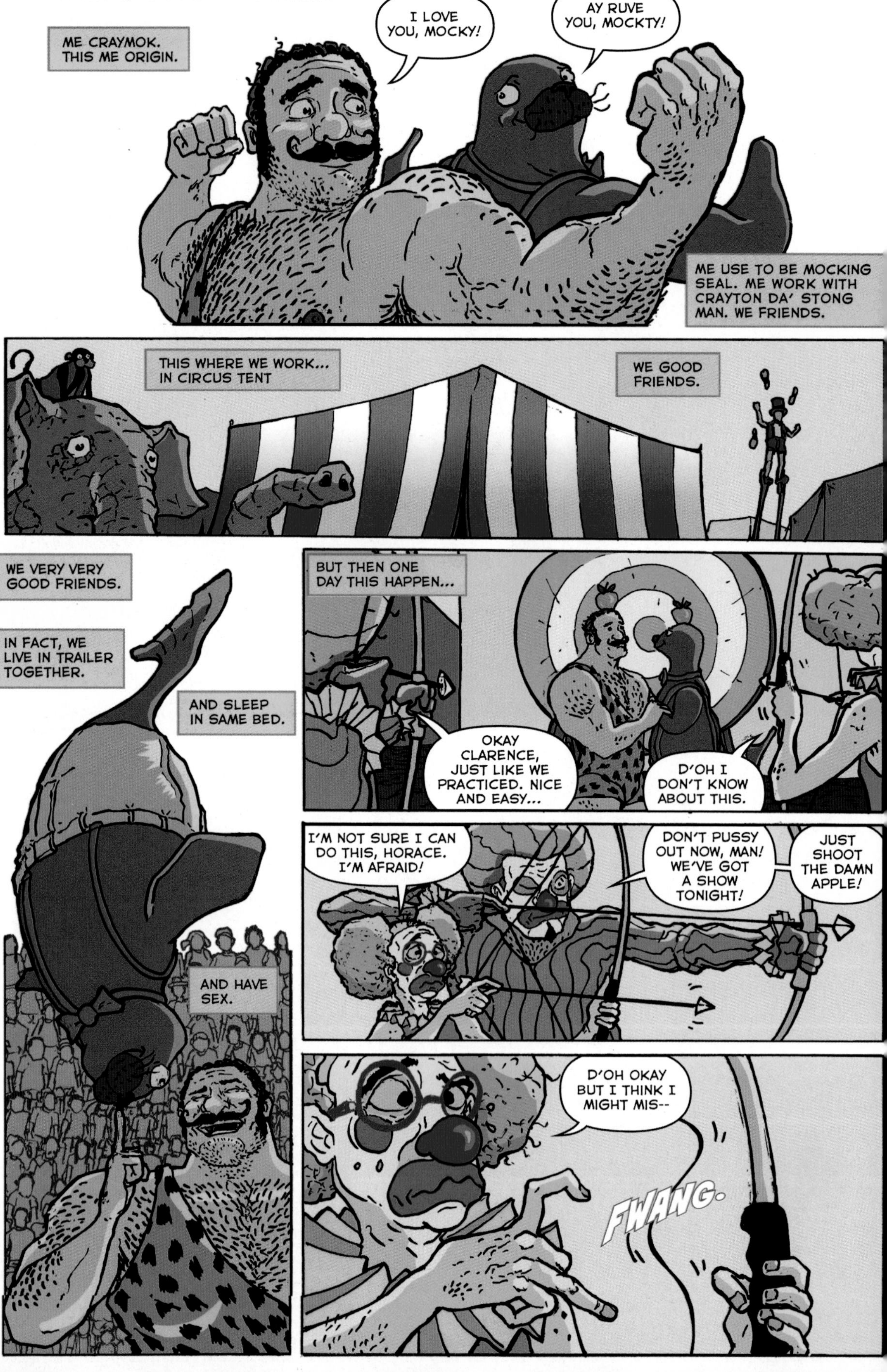

ME CRAYMOK. THIS ME ORIGIN.
I LOVE YOU, MOCKY!
AY RUVE YOU, MOCKTY!
ME USE TO BE MOCKING SEAL. ME WORK WITH CRAYTON DA' STONG MAN. WE FRIENDS.
THIS WHERE WE WORK... IN CIRCUS TENT
WE GOOD FRIENDS.
WE VERY VERY GOOD FRIENDS.
IN FACT, WE LIVE IN TRAILER TOGETHER.
AND SLEEP IN SAME BED.
AND HAVE SEX.
BUT THEN ONE DAY THIS HAPPEN...
OKAY CLARENCE, JUST LIKE WE PRACTICED. NICE AND EASY...
D'OH I DON'T KNOW ABOUT THIS.
I'M NOT SURE I CAN DO THIS, HORACE. I'M AFRAID!
DON'T PUSSY OUT NOW, MAN! WE'VE GOT A SHOW TONIGHT!
JUST SHOOT THE DAMN APPLE!
D'OH OKAY BUT I THINK I MIGHT MIS--
FWANG.

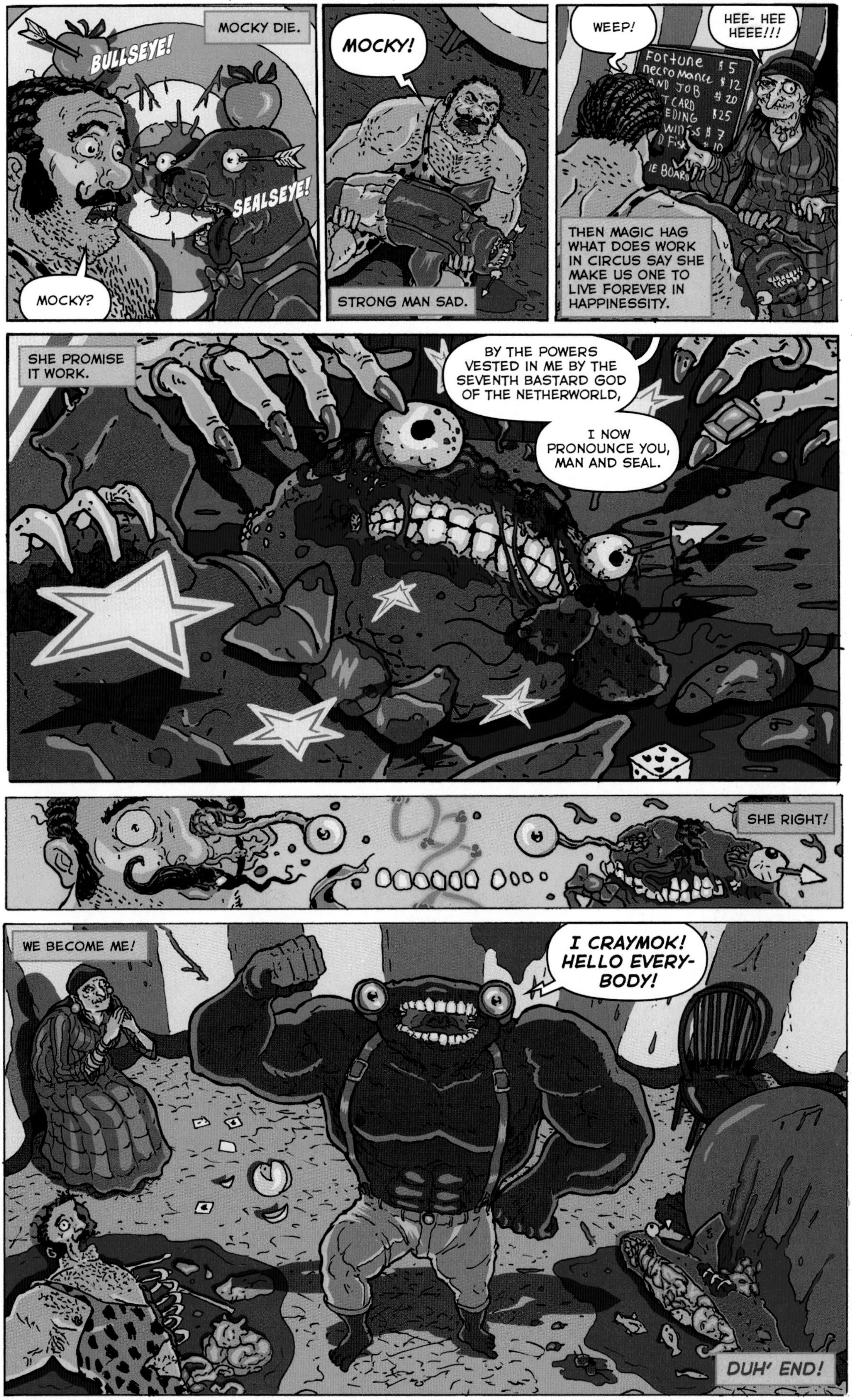
MOCKY DIE.
BULLSEYE!
SEALSEYE!
MOCKY?
MOCKY!
STRONG MAN SAD.
WEEP!
HEE- HEE HEEE!!!
Fortune $5
necroMance $12
THEN MAGIC HAG WHAT DOES WORK IN CIRCUS SAY SHE MAKE US ONE TO LIVE FOREVER IN HAPPINESSITY.
SHE PROMISE IT WORK.
BY THE POWERS VESTED IN ME BY THE SEVENTH BASTARD GOD OF THE NETHERWORLD,
I NOW PRONOUNCE YOU, MAN AND SEAL.
SHE RIGHT!
WE BECOME ME!
I CRAYMOK! HELLO EVERY-BODY!
DUH' END!

The Origin of TEXAS TOM by Ryan Browne and Chris Mitten

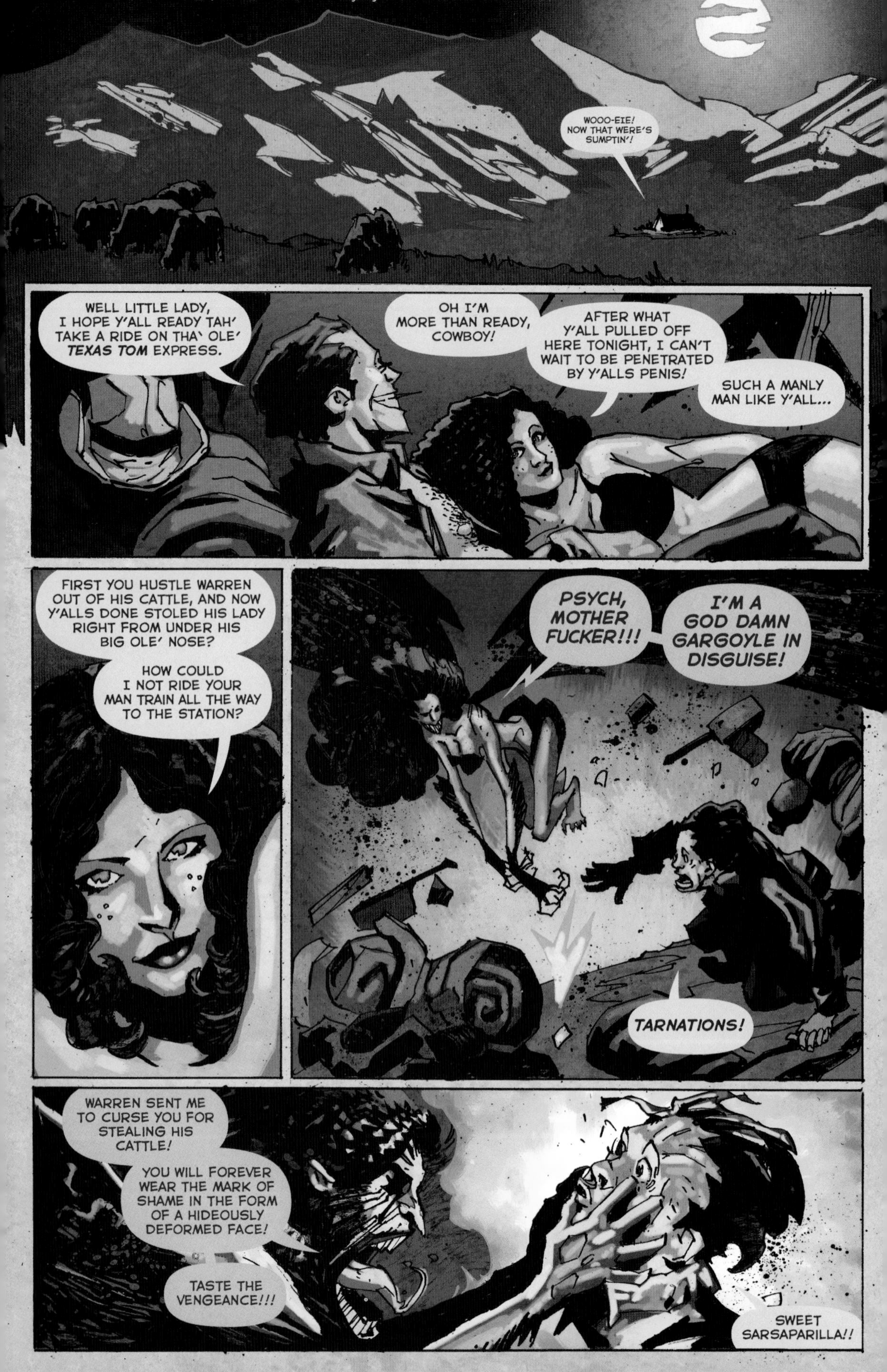
WOOO-EIE! NOW THAT WERE'S SUMPTIN'!
WELL LITTLE LADY, I HOPE Y'ALL READY TAH' TAKE A RIDE ON THA' OLE' TEXAS TOM EXPRESS.
OH I'M MORE THAN READY, COWBOY!
AFTER WHAT Y'ALL PULLED OFF HERE TONIGHT, I CAN'T WAIT TO BE PENETRATED BY Y'ALLS PENIS!
SUCH A MANLY MAN LIKE Y'ALL...
FIRST YOU HUSTLE WARREN OUT OF HIS CATTLE, AND NOW Y'ALLS DONE STOLED HIS LADY RIGHT FROM UNDER HIS BIG OLE' NOSE?
HOW COULD I NOT RIDE YOUR MAN TRAIN ALL THE WAY TO THE STATION?
PSYCH, MOTHER FUCKER!!!
I'M A GOD DAMN GARGOYLE IN DISGUISE!
TARNATIONS!
WARREN SENT ME TO CURSE YOU FOR STEALING HIS CATTLE!
YOU WILL FOREVER WEAR THE MARK OF SHAME IN THE FORM OF A HIDEOUSLY DEFORMED FACE!
TASTE THE VENGEANCE!!!
SWEET SARSAPARILLA!!

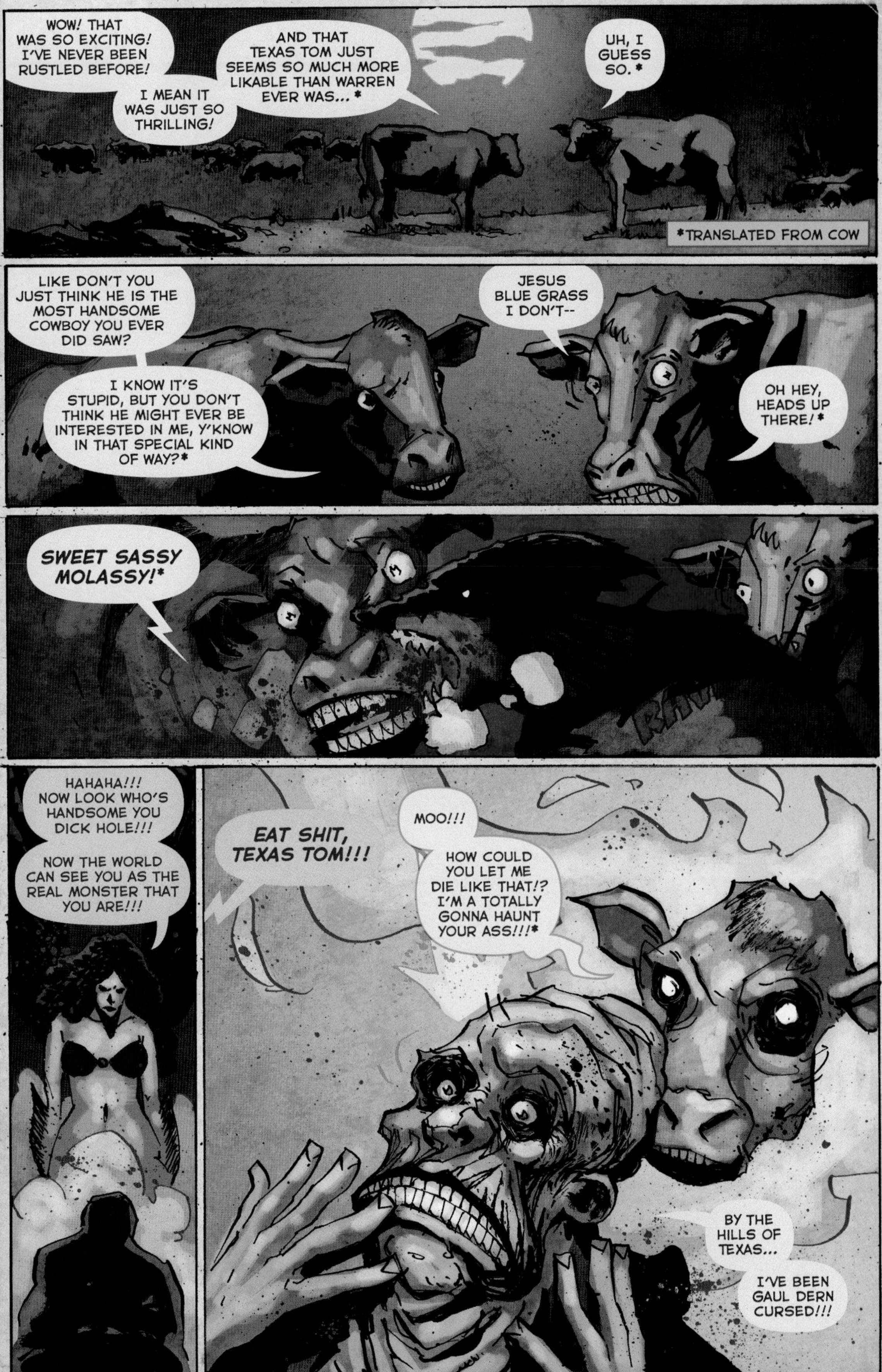
WOW! THAT WAS SO EXCITING! I'VE NEVER BEEN RUSTLED BEFORE!
I MEAN IT WAS JUST SO THRILLING!
AND THAT TEXAS TOM JUST SEEMS SO MUCH MORE LIKABLE THAN WARREN EVER WAS... *
UH, I GUESS SO. *
*TRANSLATED FROM COW
LIKE DON'T YOU JUST THINK HE IS THE MOST HANDSOME COWBOY YOU EVER DID SAW?
I KNOW IT'S STUPID, BUT YOU DON'T THINK HE MIGHT EVER BE INTERESTED IN ME, Y'KNOW IN THAT SPECIAL KIND OF WAY?*
JESUS BLUE GRASS I DON'T--
OH HEY, HEADS UP THERE!*
SWEET SASSY MOLASSY!*
HAHAHA!!! NOW LOOK WHO'S HANDSOME YOU DICK HOLE!!!
NOW THE WORLD CAN SEE YOU AS THE REAL MONSTER THAT YOU ARE!!!
EAT SHIT, TEXAS TOM!!!
MOO!!!
HOW COULD YOU LET ME DIE LIKE THAT!? I'M A TOTALLY GONNA HAUNT YOUR ASS!!!*
BY THE HILLS OF TEXAS...
I'VE BEEN GAUL DERN CURSED!!!
DAH' END!

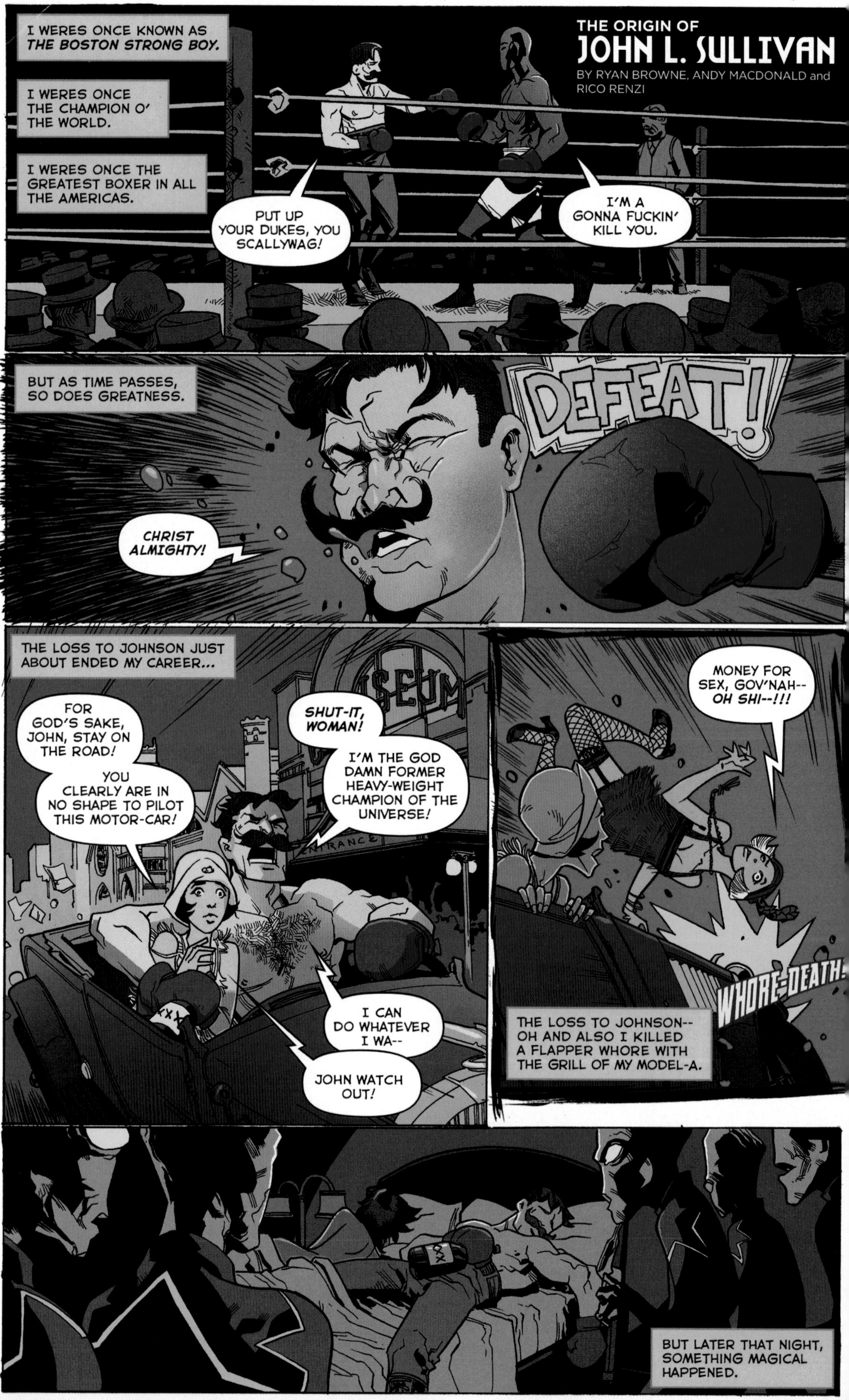
THE ORIGIN OF
JOHN L. SULLIVAN
BY RYAN BROWNE, ANDY MACDONALD and RICO RENZI
I WERES ONCE KNOWN AS *THE BOSTON STRONG BOY.*
I WERES ONCE THE CHAMPION O' THE WORLD.
I WERES ONCE THE GREATEST BOXER IN ALL THE AMERICAS.
PUT UP YOUR DUKES, YOU SCALLYWAG!
I'M A GONNA FUCKIN' KILL YOU.
BUT AS TIME PASSES, SO DOES GREATNESS.
DEFEAT!
CHRIST ALMIGHTY!
THE LOSS TO JOHNSON JUST ABOUT ENDED MY CAREER...
FOR GOD'S SAKE, JOHN, STAY ON THE ROAD!
YOU CLEARLY ARE IN NO SHAPE TO PILOT THIS MOTOR-CAR!
SHUT-IT, WOMAN!
I'M THE GOD DAMN FORMER HEAVY-WEIGHT CHAMPION OF THE UNIVERSE!
I CAN DO WHATEVER I WA--
JOHN WATCH OUT!
MONEY FOR SEX, GOV'NAH-- *OH SHI--!!!*
WHORE-DEATH!
THE LOSS TO JOHNSON-- OH AND ALSO I KILLED A FLAPPER WHORE WITH THE GRILL OF MY MODEL-A.
BUT LATER THAT NIGHT, SOMETHING MAGICAL HAPPENED.

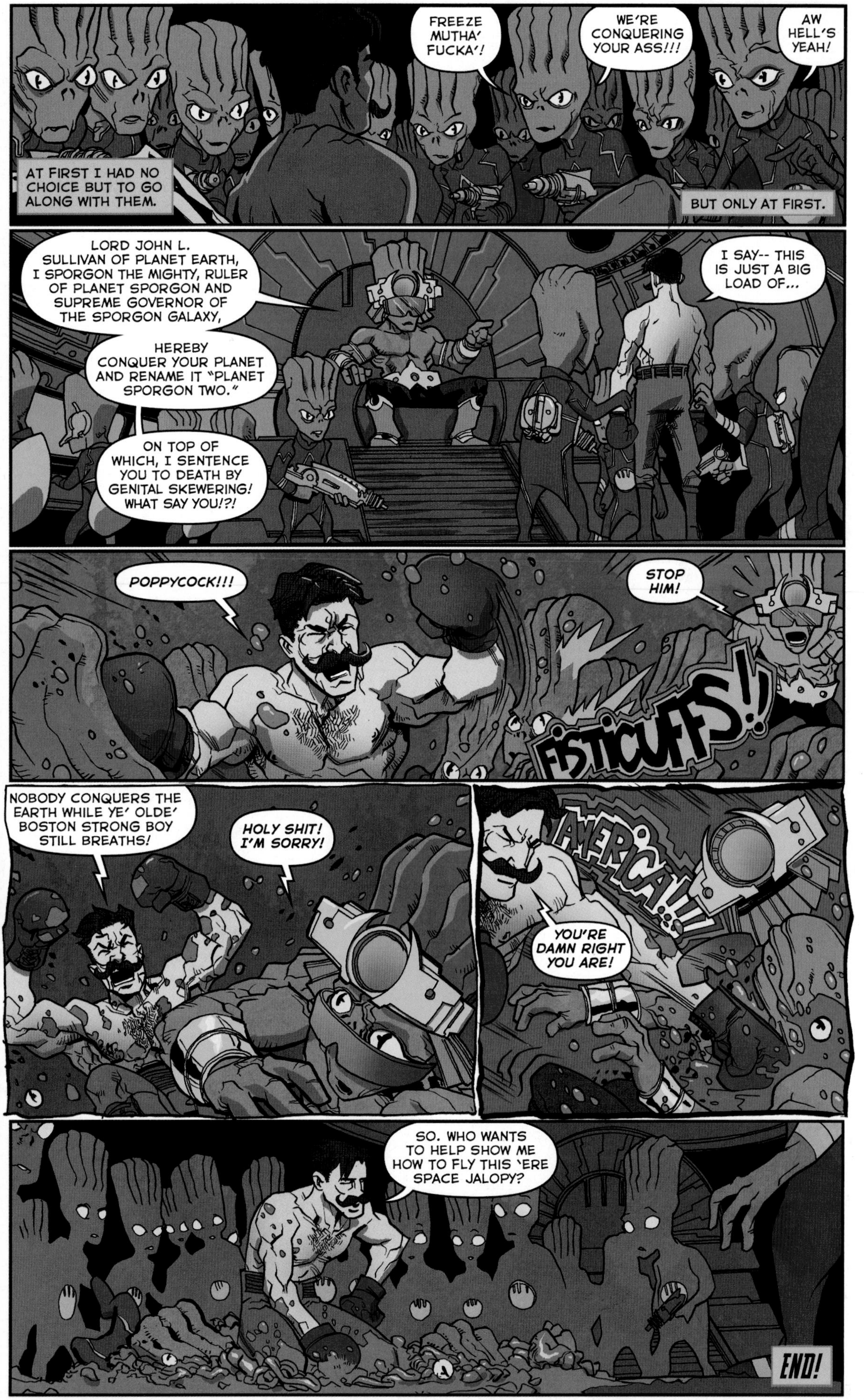
AT FIRST I HAD NO CHOICE BUT TO GO ALONG WITH THEM.
FREEZE MUTHA' FUCKA'!
WE'RE CONQUERING YOUR ASS!!!
AW HELL'S YEAH!
BUT ONLY AT FIRST.
LORD JOHN L. SULLIVAN OF PLANET EARTH, I SPORGON THE MIGHTY, RULER OF PLANET SPORGON AND SUPREME GOVERNOR OF THE SPORGON GALAXY,
HEREBY CONQUER YOUR PLANET AND RENAME IT "PLANET SPORGON TWO."
ON TOP OF WHICH, I SENTENCE YOU TO DEATH BY GENITAL SKEWERING! WHAT SAY YOU!?!
I SAY-- THIS IS JUST A BIG LOAD OF...
POPPYCOCK!!!
STOP HIM!
FISTICUFFS!!
NOBODY CONQUERS THE EARTH WHILE YE' OLDE' BOSTON STRONG BOY STILL BREATHS!
HOLY SHIT! I'M SORRY!
AMERICA!!!
YOU'RE DAMN RIGHT YOU ARE!
SO. WHO WANTS TO HELP SHOW ME HOW TO FLY THIS 'ERE SPACE JALOPY?
END!

THE ORIGIN OF...

JOHN L. SULLIVAN'S CRIMINAL BEARS!

BY RYAN BROWNE & C.P. WILSON III

HONEY...

SALMON...

HOLY SCHMOLY, DER' HE BE!

CRIPES!

TINK TINK

GRRR?

MY DAMN BULLETS AIN'T A SHOOTIN'!

IS THIS THAT LIBERAL VOODOO AGAIN?

WHAT IN THE GOD DAMNED HELL IS GOIN' ON H—

SHOOTIN'S A HOOT!!!

YARRG!!!

I'M A COMIN', PA!!!

ABDUCT!

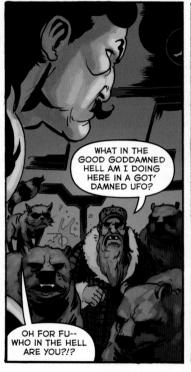

DEAR BEAR FRIENDS, I, JOHN L. SULLIVAN, SHALL BE YOUR NEW, UNQUESTIONED MASTER!

YOU SHALL LEARN THE WAYS OF COMBAT BOXING AT THE HAND OF THE GREATEST PUGILIST THIS WORLD HAS EVER SEEN!

TOGETHER WE SHALL ROB MANY A BANK AND FINALLY SHOW THE WORLD THAT JOH—

WHAT IN THE GOOD GODDAMNED HELL AM I DOING HERE IN A GOT' DAMNED UFO?

OH FOR FU-- WHO IN THE HELL ARE YOU?!?

ME? I'M A GOD DAMNED RED BLOODED AMERICAN PERFORMING HIS GOD GIVEN RIGHT OF HUNTING THE HELL OUT OF THEM THERE GRIZZLY BEARS.

YOU THINK YOU ALIENS CAN JUST INVADE THE UNITED STATES OF A. AND JUST GET AWAY WITH IT?

NOT ON MY WATCH YOU YELLER--

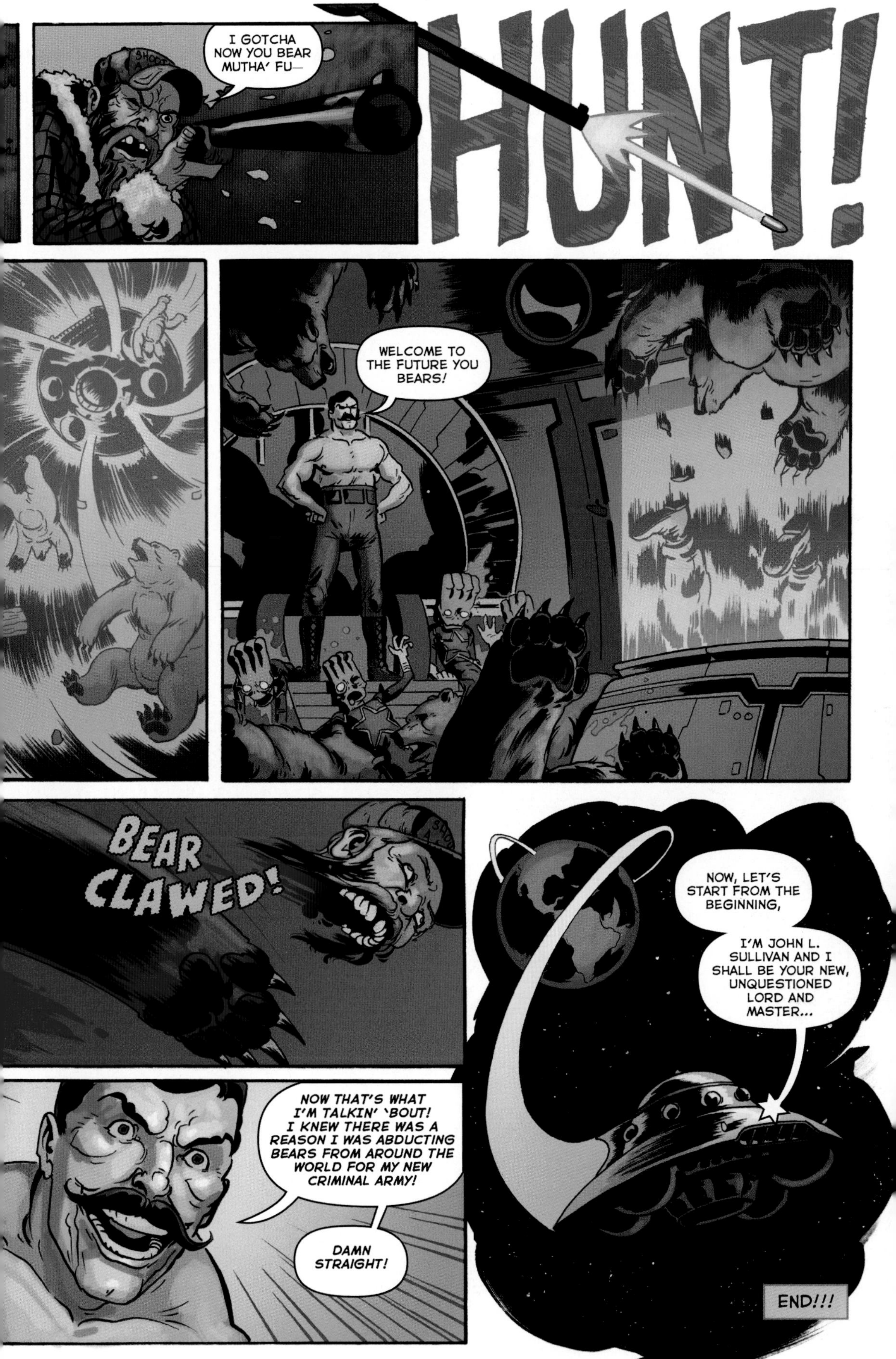
I GOTCHA NOW YOU BEAR MUTHA' FU—
HUNT!
WELCOME TO THE FUTURE YOU BEARS!
BEAR CLAWED!
NOW, LET'S START FROM THE BEGINNING,
I'M JOHN L. SULLIVAN AND I SHALL BE YOUR NEW, UNQUESTIONED LORD AND MASTER...
NOW THAT'S WHAT I'M TALKIN' 'BOUT! I KNEW THERE WAS A REASON I WAS ABDUCTING BEARS FROM AROUND THE WORLD FOR MY NEW CRIMINAL ARMY!
DAMN STRAIGHT!
END!!!

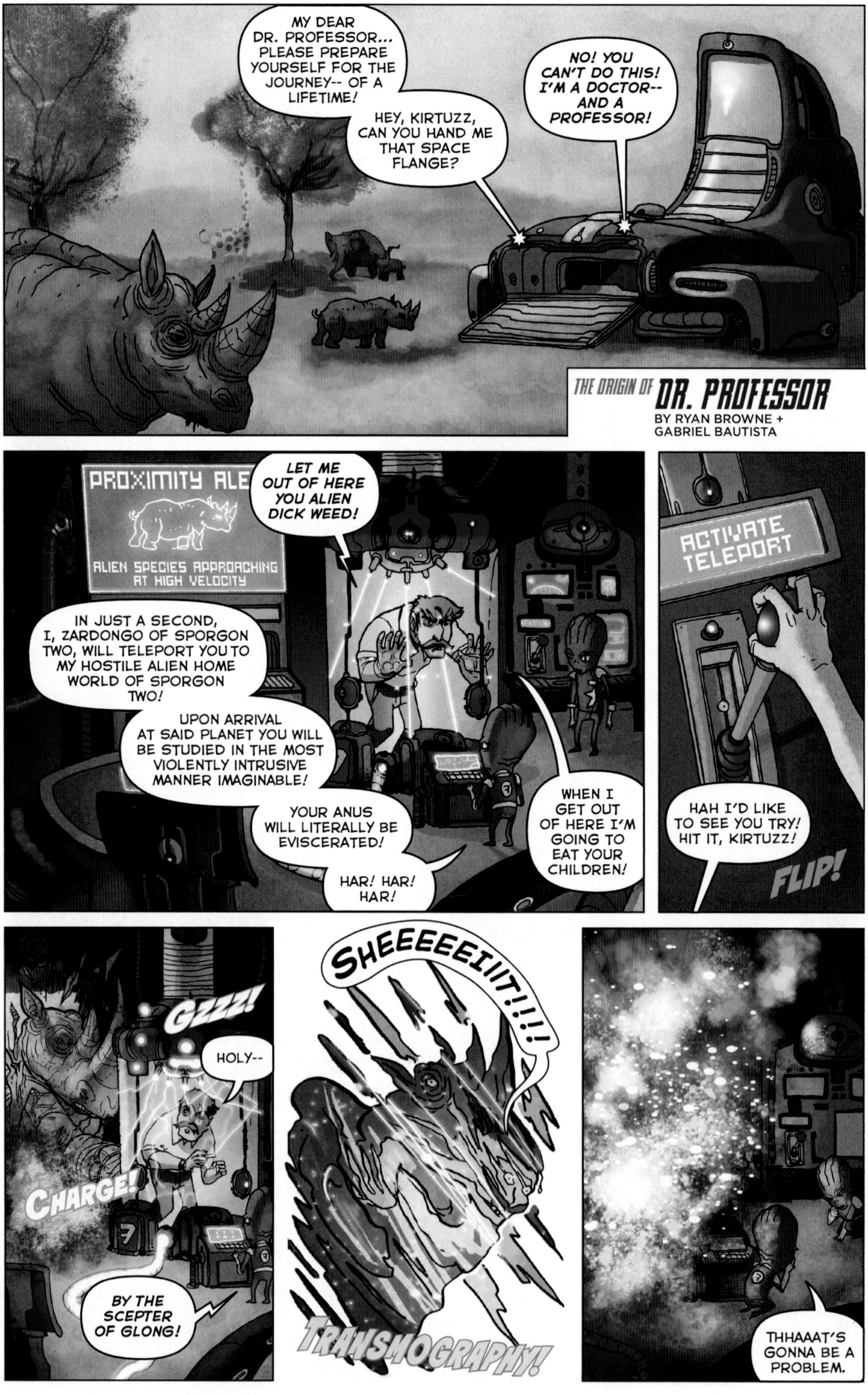
MY DEAR DR. PROFESSOR... PLEASE PREPARE YOURSELF FOR THE JOURNEY-- OF A LIFETIME!
HEY, KIRTUZZ, CAN YOU HAND ME THAT SPACE FLANGE?
NO! YOU CAN'T DO THIS! I'M A DOCTOR-- AND A PROFESSOR!
THE ORIGIN OF DR. PROFESSOR
BY RYAN BROWNE + GABRIEL BAUTISTA
PROXIMITY ALE
ALIEN SPECIES APPROACHING AT HIGH VELOCITY
LET ME OUT OF HERE YOU ALIEN DICK WEED!
IN JUST A SECOND, I, ZARDONGO OF SPORGON TWO, WILL TELEPORT YOU TO MY HOSTILE ALIEN HOME WORLD OF SPORGON TWO!
UPON ARRIVAL AT SAID PLANET YOU WILL BE STUDIED IN THE MOST VIOLENTLY INTRUSIVE MANNER IMAGINABLE!
YOUR ANUS WILL LITERALLY BE EVISCERATED!
HAR! HAR! HAR!
WHEN I GET OUT OF HERE I'M GOING TO EAT YOUR CHILDREN!
ACTIVATE TELEPORT
HAH I'D LIKE TO SEE YOU TRY! HIT IT, KIRTUZZ!
FLIP!
GZZZ!
HOLY--
CHARGE!
BY THE SCEPTER OF GLONG!
SHEEEEEIIIT!!!!
TRANSMOGRAPHY!
THHAAAT'S GONNA BE A PROBLEM.

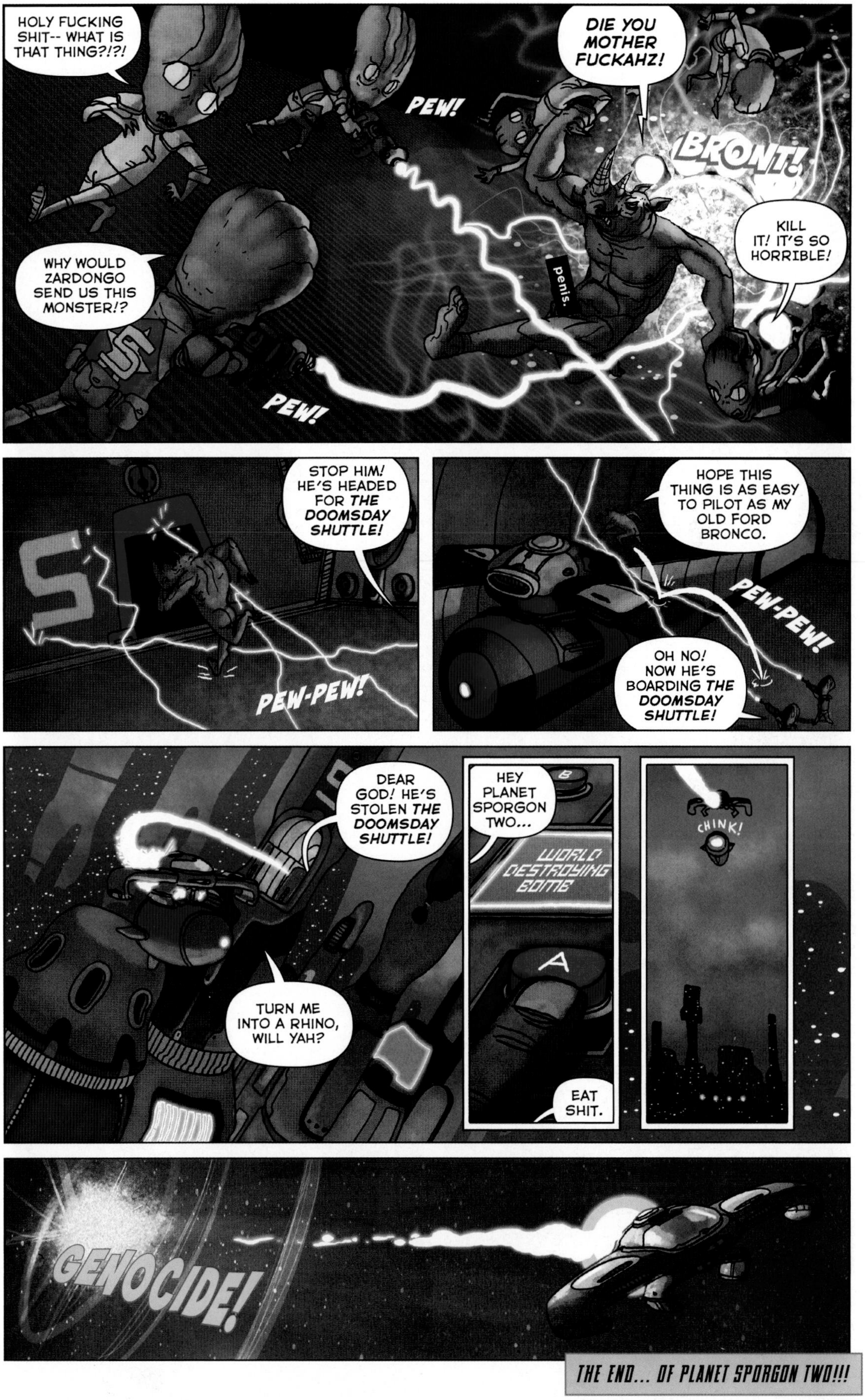
HOLY FUCKING SHIT-- WHAT IS THAT THING?!?!
PEW!
DIE YOU MOTHER FUCKAHZ!
BRONT!
WHY WOULD ZARDONGO SEND US THIS MONSTER!?
penis.
KILL IT! IT'S SO HORRIBLE!
PEW!
STOP HIM! HE'S HEADED FOR THE DOOMSDAY SHUTTLE!
PEW-PEW!
HOPE THIS THING IS AS EASY TO PILOT AS MY OLD FORD BRONCO.
PEW-PEW!
OH NO! NOW HE'S BOARDING THE DOOMSDAY SHUTTLE!
DEAR GOD! HE'S STOLEN THE DOOMSDAY SHUTTLE!
TURN ME INTO A RHINO, WILL YAH?
HEY PLANET SPORGON TWO...
B
WORLD DESTROYING BOMB
A
EAT SHIT.
CHINK!
GENOCIDE!
THE END... OF PLANET SPORGON TWO!!!

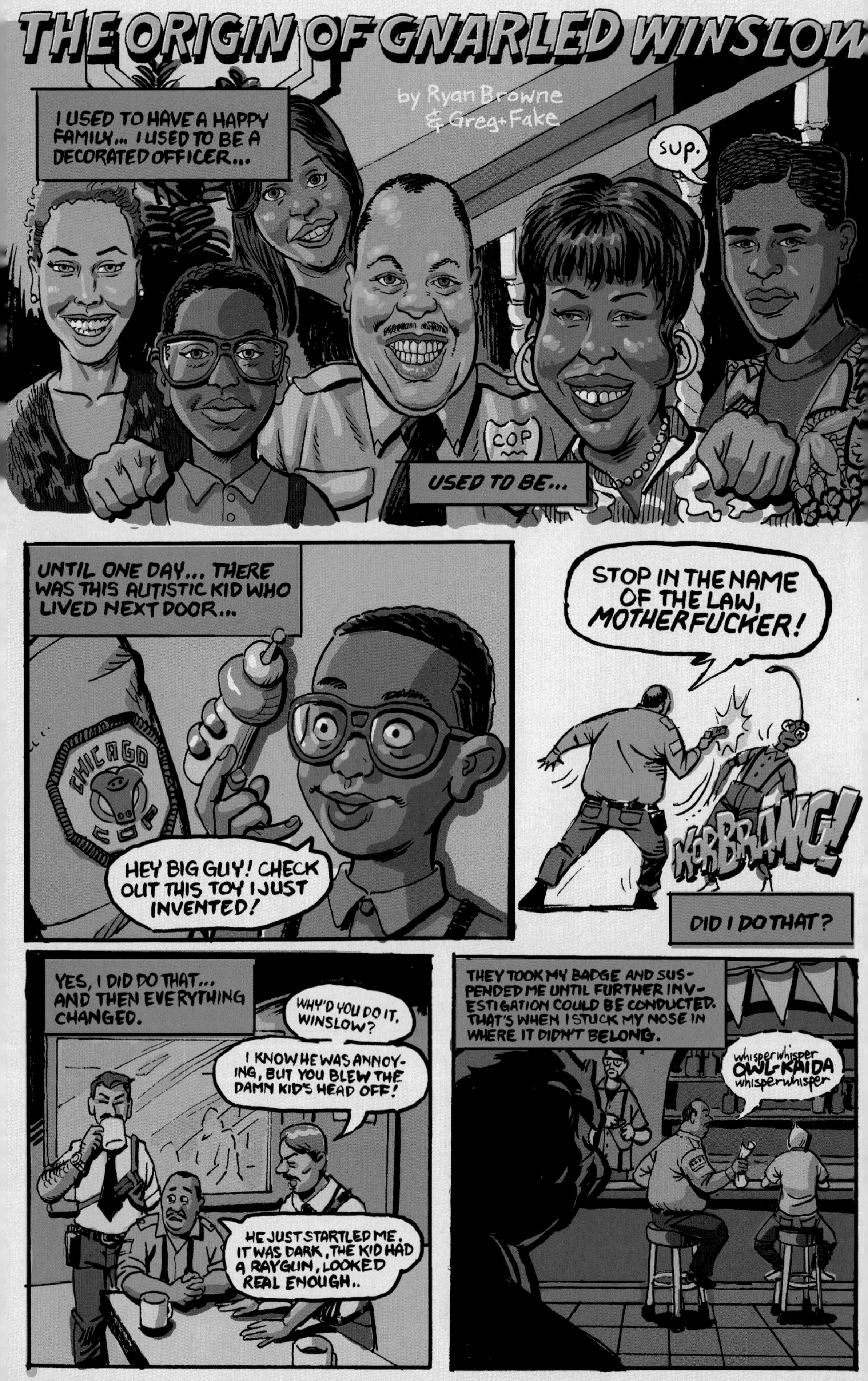
THE ORIGIN OF GNARLED WINSLOW
by Ryan Browne & Greg+Fake
I USED TO HAVE A HAPPY FAMILY... I USED TO BE A DECORATED OFFICER...
SUP.
COP
USED TO BE...
UNTIL ONE DAY... THERE WAS THIS AUTISTIC KID WHO LIVED NEXT DOOR...
CHICAGO COP
HEY BIG GUY! CHECK OUT THIS TOY I JUST INVENTED!
STOP IN THE NAME OF THE LAW, MOTHERFUCKER!
KA-BRANG!
DID I DO THAT?
YES, I DID DO THAT... AND THEN EVERYTHING CHANGED.
WHY'D YOU DO IT, WINSLOW?
I KNOW HE WAS ANNOYING, BUT YOU BLEW THE DAMN KID'S HEAD OFF!
HE JUST STARTLED ME. IT WAS DARK, THE KID HAD A RAYGUN, LOOKED REAL ENOUGH..
THEY TOOK MY BADGE AND SUSPENDED ME UNTIL FURTHER INVESTIGATION COULD BE CONDUCTED. THAT'S WHEN I STUCK MY NOSE IN WHERE IT DIDN'T BELONG.
whisperwhisper OWL-KAIDA whisperwhisper

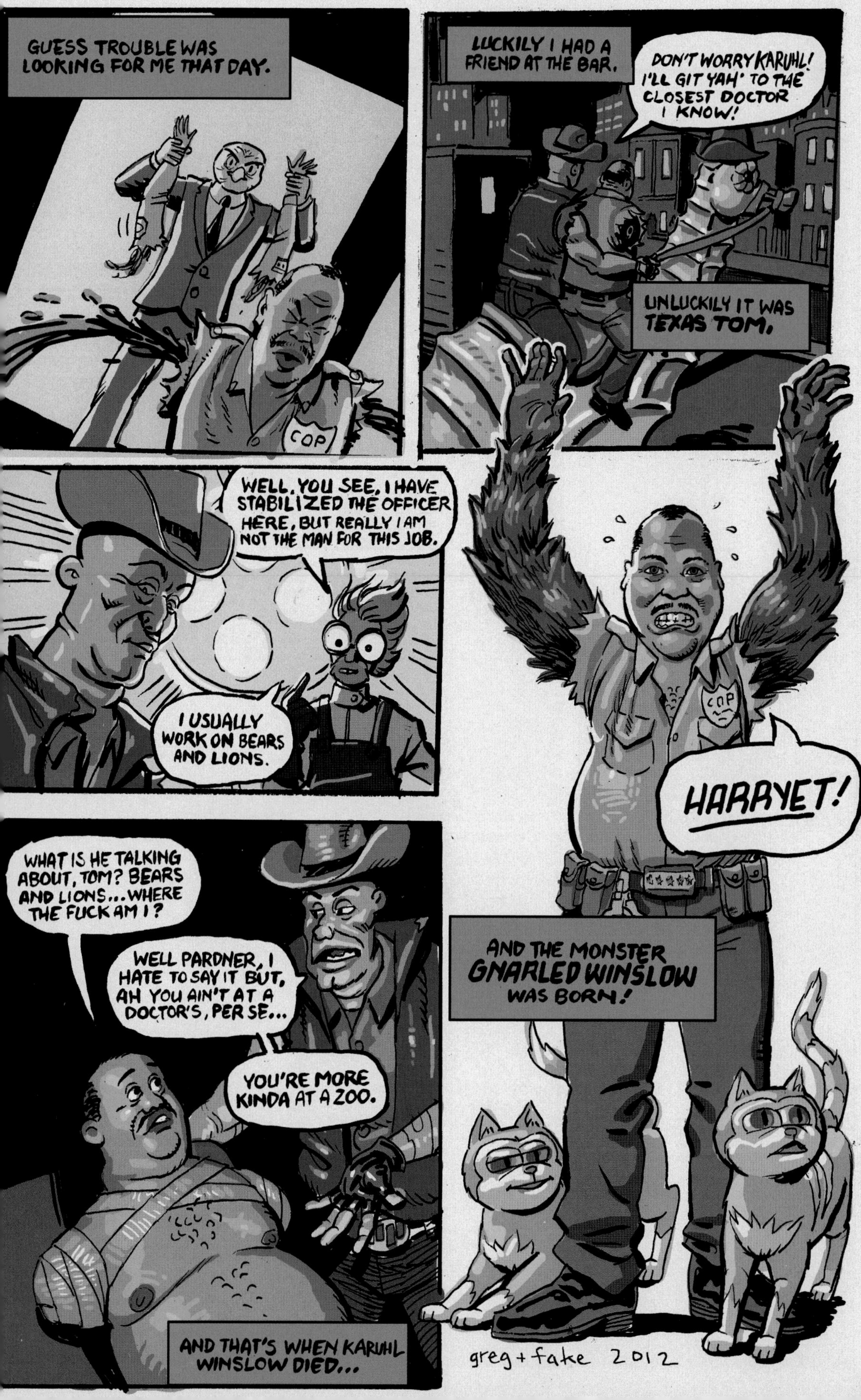
GUESS TROUBLE WAS LOOKING FOR ME THAT DAY.
COP
LUCKILY I HAD A FRIEND AT THE BAR.
DON'T WORRY KARUHL! I'LL GIT YAH' TO THE CLOSEST DOCTOR I KNOW!
UNLUCKILY IT WAS TEXAS TOM.
WELL, YOU SEE, I HAVE STABILIZED THE OFFICER HERE, BUT REALLY I AM NOT THE MAN FOR THIS JOB.
I USUALLY WORK ON BEARS AND LIONS.
WHAT IS HE TALKING ABOUT, TOM? BEARS AND LIONS... WHERE THE FUCK AM I?
WELL PARDNER, I HATE TO SAY IT BUT, AH YOU AIN'T AT A DOCTOR'S, PER SE...
YOU'RE MORE KINDA AT A ZOO.
AND THAT'S WHEN KARUHL WINSLOW DIED...
COP
HARRYET!
AND THE MONSTER GNARLED WINSLOW WAS BORN!
greg + fake 2012

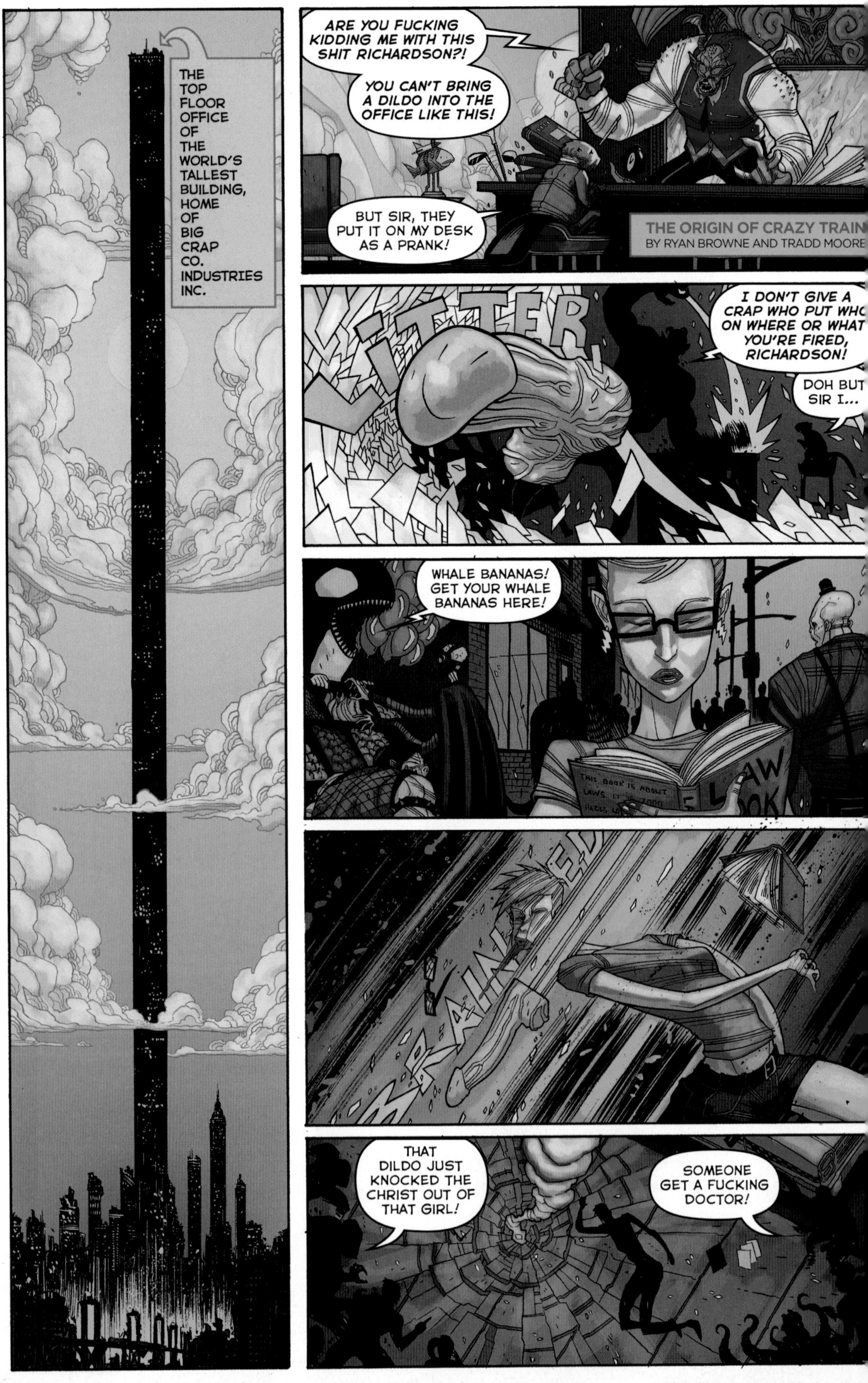
THE TOP FLOOR OFFICE OF THE WORLD'S TALLEST BUILDING, HOME OF BIG CRAP CO. INDUSTRIES INC.
ARE YOU FUCKING KIDDING ME WITH THIS SHIT RICHARDSON?!
YOU CAN'T BRING A DILDO INTO THE OFFICE LIKE THIS!
BUT SIR, THEY PUT IT ON MY DESK AS A PRANK!
THE ORIGIN OF CRAZY TRAIN
BY RYAN BROWNE AND TRADD MOORE
I DON'T GIVE A CRAP WHO PUT WHO ON WHERE OR WHAT YOU'RE FIRED, RICHARDSON!
DOH BUT SIR I...
WHALE BANANAS! GET YOUR WHALE BANANAS HERE!
THAT DILDO JUST KNOCKED THE CHRIST OUT OF THAT GIRL!
SOMEONE GET A FUCKING DOCTOR!

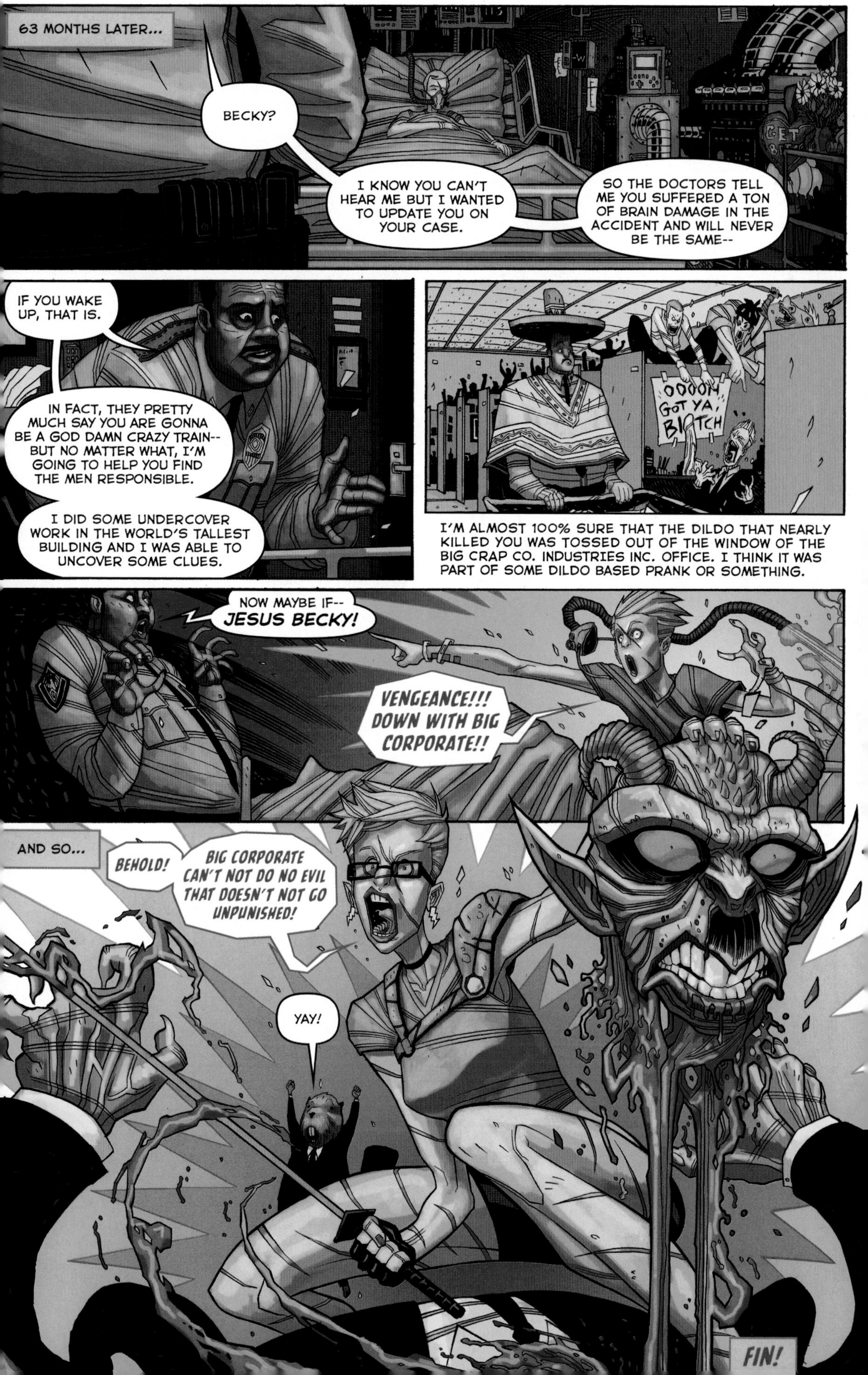
63 MONTHS LATER...
BECKY?
I KNOW YOU CAN'T HEAR ME BUT I WANTED TO UPDATE YOU ON YOUR CASE.
SO THE DOCTORS TELL ME YOU SUFFERED A TON OF BRAIN DAMAGE IN THE ACCIDENT AND WILL NEVER BE THE SAME--
IF YOU WAKE UP, THAT IS.
IN FACT, THEY PRETTY MUCH SAY YOU ARE GONNA BE A GOD DAMN CRAZY TRAIN--
BUT NO MATTER WHAT, I'M GOING TO HELP YOU FIND THE MEN RESPONSIBLE.
I DID SOME UNDERCOVER WORK IN THE WORLD'S TALLEST BUILDING AND I WAS ABLE TO UNCOVER SOME CLUES.
OOOOH GOT YA, BITCH
I'M ALMOST 100% SURE THAT THE DILDO THAT NEARLY KILLED YOU WAS TOSSED OUT OF THE WINDOW OF THE BIG CRAP CO. INDUSTRIES INC. OFFICE. I THINK IT WAS PART OF SOME DILDO BASED PRANK OR SOMETHING.
NOW MAYBE IF--
JESUS BECKY!
VENGEANCE!!! DOWN WITH BIG CORPORATE!!
AND SO...
BEHOLD!
BIG CORPORATE CAN'T NOT DO NO EVIL THAT DOESN'T NOT GO UNPUNISHED!
YAY!
FIN!

THE SECRET UNDERGROUND LABORATORY OF LOUIS PASTEUR.

JUNE 26TH, 1955-- THE NIGHT THAT WOULD SET ME ON MY QUEST FOR GREATNESS.

MR. PASTEUR! MR. PASTEUR!

I STOLED THAT NEWBORN BABY YAH WANTED!

AW HELLS YEAH! BRING IT HERE, MONSIEUR BRILDOR.

CALL ME CRAZY, WILL THEY? ZIS SHIT IZ GONNA BE THE BOMB!!!

THE ORIGIN OF SIR HIPPOTHESIS
BY: RYAN BROWNE + CODY SCHIBI

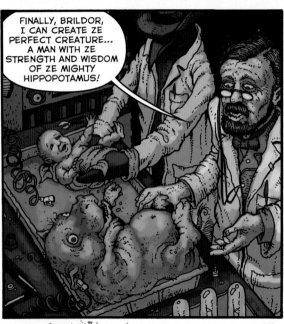

FINALLY, BRILDOR, I CAN CREATE ZE PERFECT CREATURE... A MAN WITH ZE STRENGTH AND WISDOM OF ZE MIGHTY HIPPOPOTAMUS!

SNACK!

WHO GIVES A SHIT ABOUT MILK WHEN YOU CAN CREATE AN ENTIRELY NEW SPECIES!?

FLIP

ON
OFF

I'LL FLIP THE SWITCH FOR YAH, BOSS!

BRILDOR! NO--

FRIZZLE FRY

SACRE BLEU!!!

MAMA?

AHHHHH JEEZE.

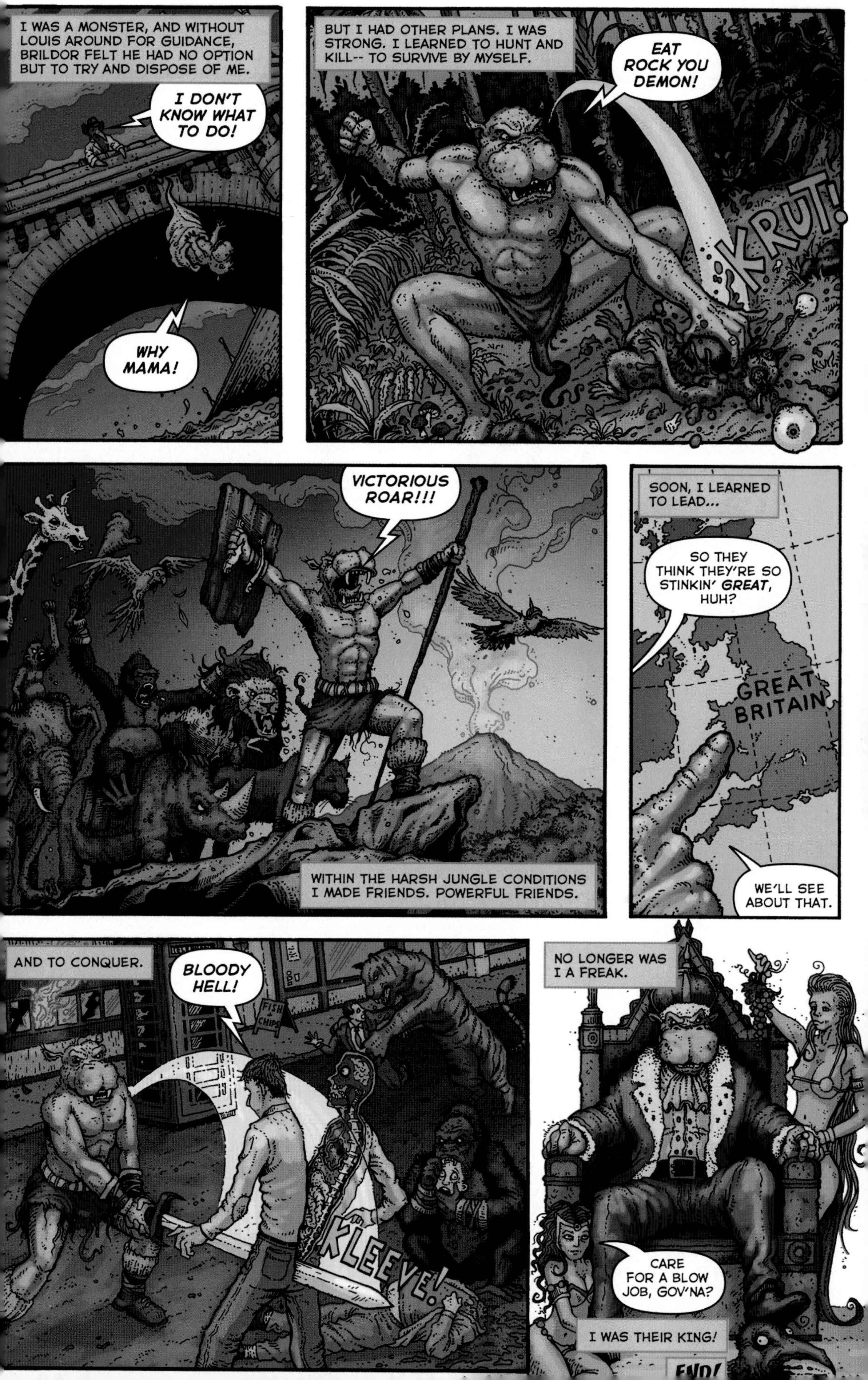

I WAS A MONSTER, AND WITHOUT LOUIS AROUND FOR GUIDANCE, BRILDOR FELT HE HAD NO OPTION BUT TO TRY AND DISPOSE OF ME.
I DON'T KNOW WHAT TO DO!
WHY MAMA!
BUT I HAD OTHER PLANS. I WAS STRONG. I LEARNED TO HUNT AND KILL-- TO SURVIVE BY MYSELF.
EAT ROCK YOU DEMON!
KRUT!
VICTORIOUS ROAR!!!
WITHIN THE HARSH JUNGLE CONDITIONS I MADE FRIENDS. POWERFUL FRIENDS.
SOON, I LEARNED TO LEAD...
SO THEY THINK THEY'RE SO STINKIN' GREAT, HUH?
GREAT BRITAIN
WE'LL SEE ABOUT THAT.
AND TO CONQUER.
BLOODY HELL!
FISH CHIPS
KLEEVE!
NO LONGER WAS I A FREAK.
CARE FOR A BLOW JOB, GOV'NA?
I WAS THEIR KING!
END!

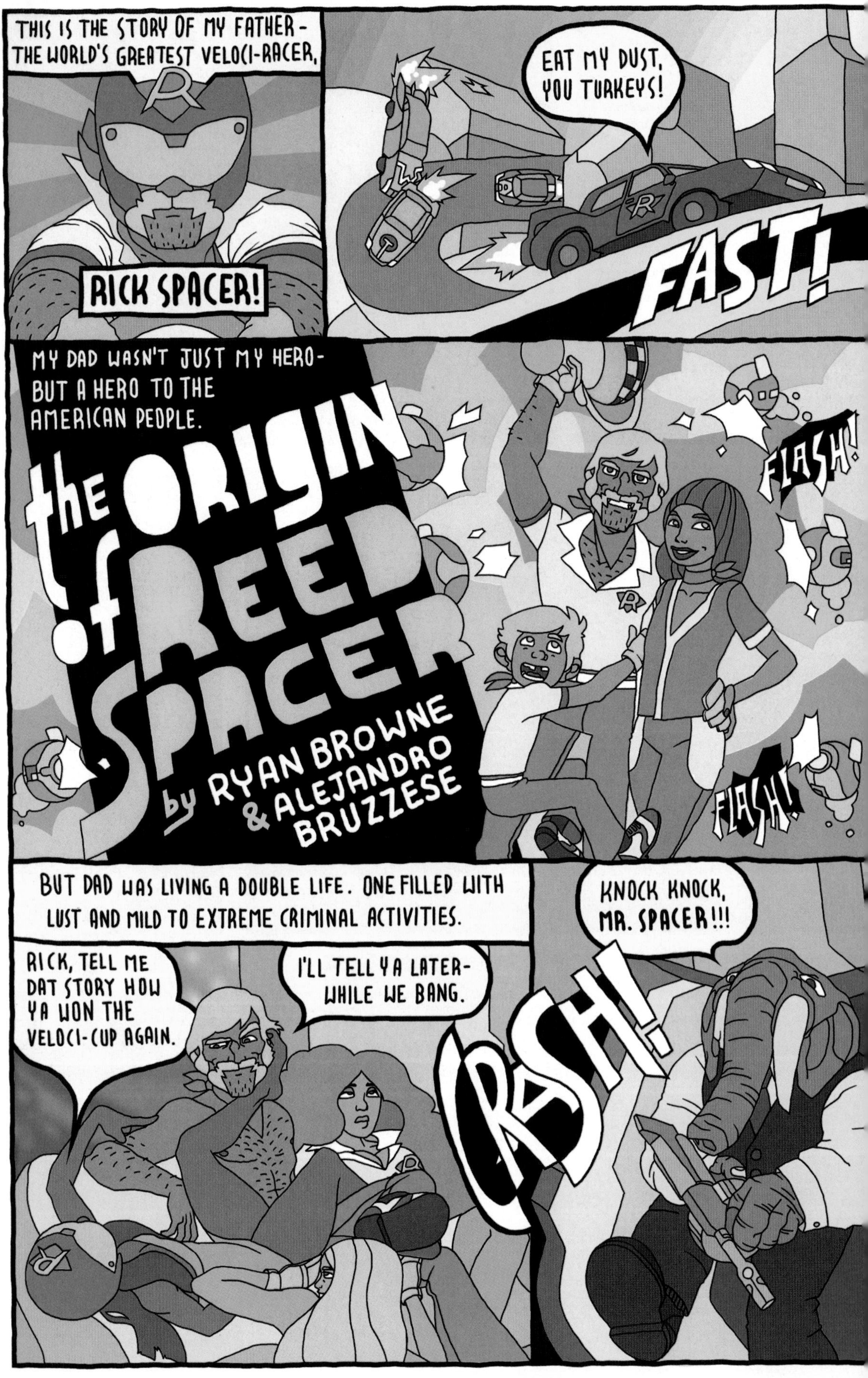
THIS IS THE STORY OF MY FATHER - THE WORLD'S GREATEST VELOCI-RACER,
RICK SPACER!
EAT MY DUST, YOU TURKEYS!
FAST!
MY DAD WASN'T JUST MY HERO- BUT A HERO TO THE AMERICAN PEOPLE.
the ORIGIN of REED SPACER
by RYAN BROWNE & ALEJANDRO BRUZZESE
FLASH!
FLASH!
BUT DAD WAS LIVING A DOUBLE LIFE. ONE FILLED WITH LUST AND MILD TO EXTREME CRIMINAL ACTIVITIES.
RICK, TELL ME DAT STORY HOW YA WON THE VELOCI-CUP AGAIN.
I'LL TELL YA LATER- WHILE WE BANG.
KNOCK KNOCK, MR. SPACER!!!
CRASH!

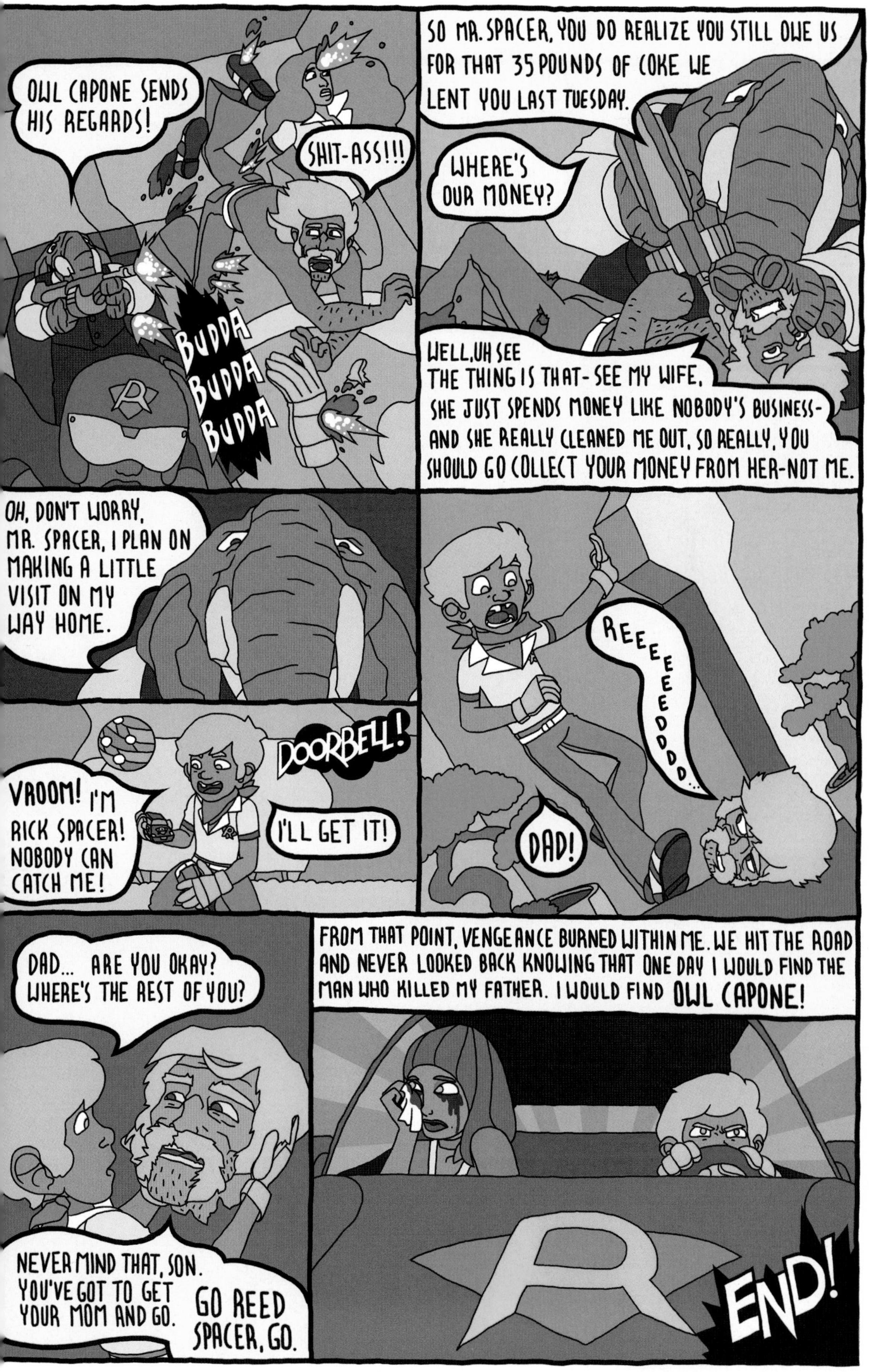
OWL CAPONE SENDS HIS REGARDS!
SHIT-ASS!!!
BUDDA BUDDA BUDDA
SO MR. SPACER, YOU DO REALIZE YOU STILL OWE US FOR THAT 35 POUNDS OF COKE WE LENT YOU LAST TUESDAY.
WHERE'S OUR MONEY?
WELL, UH SEE THE THING IS THAT- SEE MY WIFE, SHE JUST SPENDS MONEY LIKE NOBODY'S BUSINESS- AND SHE REALLY CLEANED ME OUT, SO REALLY, YOU SHOULD GO COLLECT YOUR MONEY FROM HER-NOT ME.
OH, DON'T WORRY, MR. SPACER, I PLAN ON MAKING A LITTLE VISIT ON MY WAY HOME.
VROOM! I'M RICK SPACER! NOBODY CAN CATCH ME!
DOORBELL!
I'LL GET IT!
REEEEEEEDDDD...
DAD!
DAD... ARE YOU OKAY? WHERE'S THE REST OF YOU?
NEVER MIND THAT, SON. YOU'VE GOT TO GET YOUR MOM AND GO.
GO REED SPACER, GO.
FROM THAT POINT, VENGEANCE BURNED WITHIN ME. WE HIT THE ROAD AND NEVER LOOKED BACK KNOWING THAT ONE DAY I WOULD FIND THE MAN WHO KILLED MY FATHER. I WOULD FIND OWL CAPONE!
END!

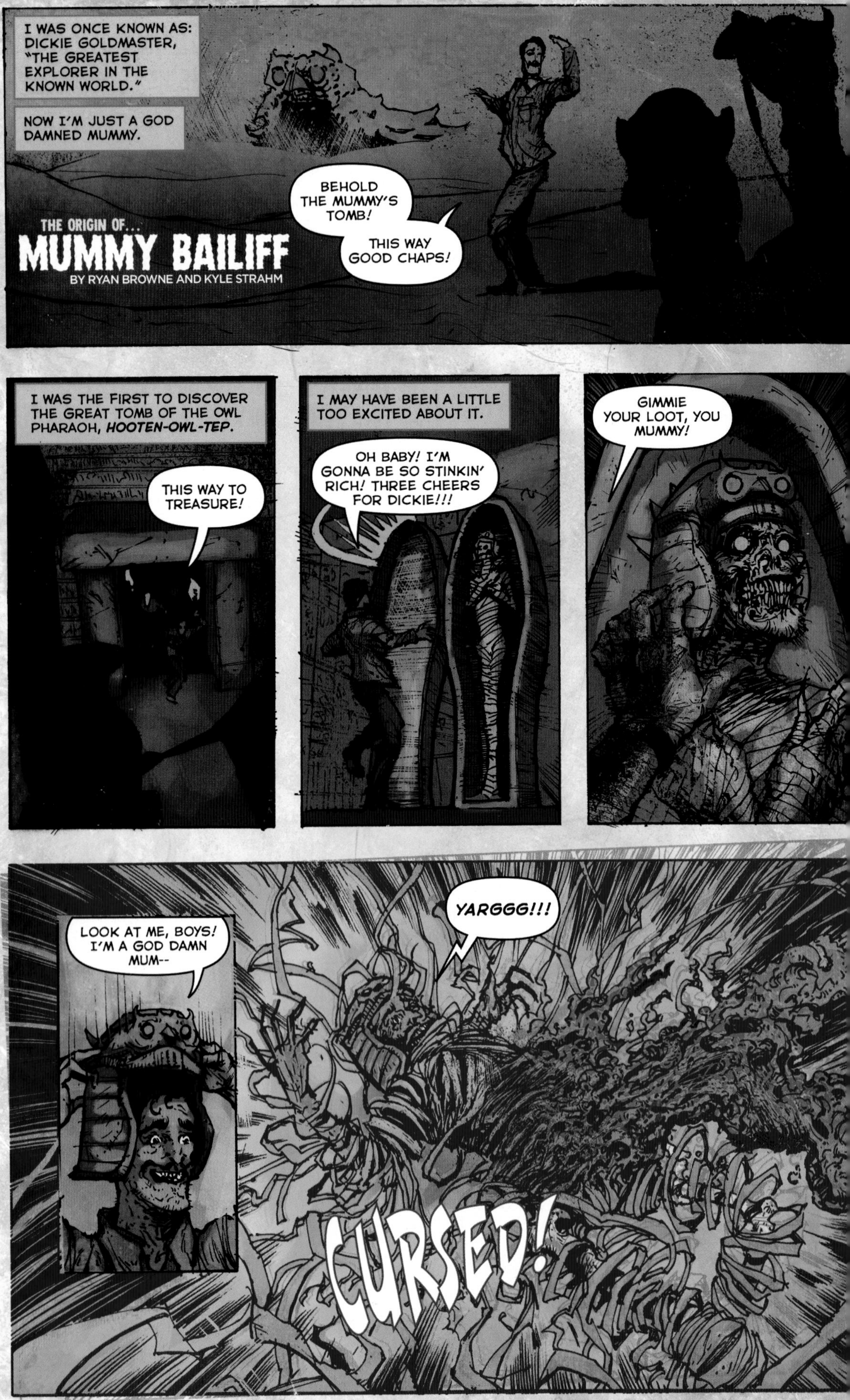
I WAS ONCE KNOWN AS: DICKIE GOLDMASTER, "THE GREATEST EXPLORER IN THE KNOWN WORLD."
NOW I'M JUST A GOD DAMNED MUMMY.
THE ORIGIN OF...
MUMMY BAILIFF
BY RYAN BROWNE AND KYLE STRAHM
BEHOLD THE MUMMY'S TOMB!
THIS WAY GOOD CHAPS!
I WAS THE FIRST TO DISCOVER THE GREAT TOMB OF THE OWL PHARAOH, *HOOTEN-OWL-TEP*.
THIS WAY TO TREASURE!
I MAY HAVE BEEN A LITTLE TOO EXCITED ABOUT IT.
OH BABY! I'M GONNA BE SO STINKIN' RICH! THREE CHEERS FOR DICKIE!!!
GIMMIE YOUR LOOT, YOU MUMMY!
LOOK AT ME, BOYS! I'M A GOD DAMN MUM--
YARGGG!!!
CURSED!

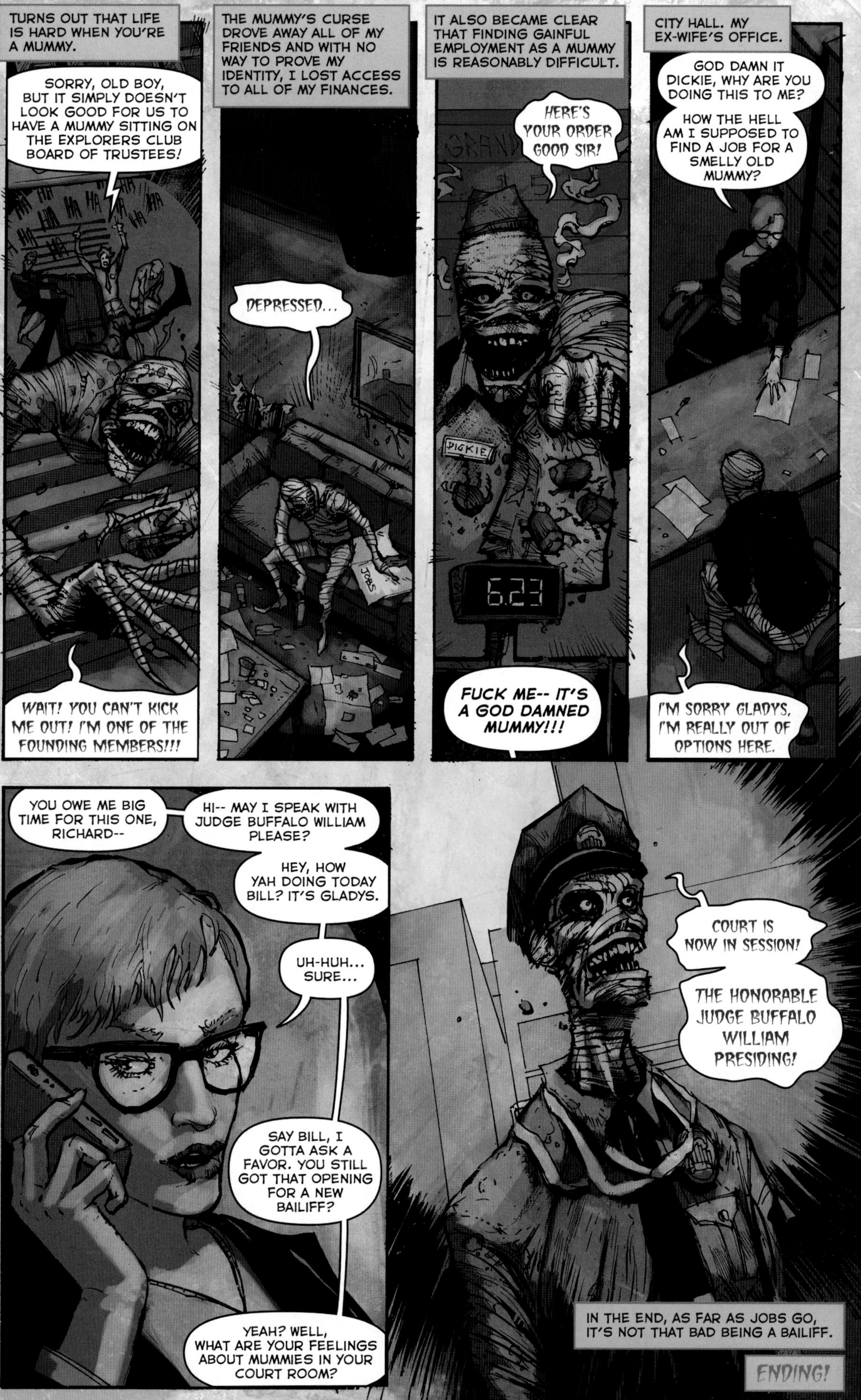
TURNS OUT THAT LIFE IS HARD WHEN YOU'RE A MUMMY.
SORRY, OLD BOY, BUT IT SIMPLY DOESN'T LOOK GOOD FOR US TO HAVE A MUMMY SITTING ON THE EXPLORERS CLUB BOARD OF TRUSTEES!
WAIT! YOU CAN'T KICK ME OUT! I'M ONE OF THE FOUNDING MEMBERS!!!
THE MUMMY'S CURSE DROVE AWAY ALL OF MY FRIENDS AND WITH NO WAY TO PROVE MY IDENTITY, I LOST ACCESS TO ALL OF MY FINANCES.
DEPRESSED...
JOBS
IT ALSO BECAME CLEAR THAT FINDING GAINFUL EMPLOYMENT AS A MUMMY IS REASONABLY DIFFICULT.
HERE'S YOUR ORDER GOOD SIR!
DICKIE
6.23
FUCK ME-- IT'S A GOD DAMNED MUMMY!!!
CITY HALL. MY EX-WIFE'S OFFICE.
GOD DAMN IT DICKIE, WHY ARE YOU DOING THIS TO ME?
HOW THE HELL AM I SUPPOSED TO FIND A JOB FOR A SMELLY OLD MUMMY?
I'M SORRY GLADYS, I'M REALLY OUT OF OPTIONS HERE.
YOU OWE ME BIG TIME FOR THIS ONE, RICHARD--
HI-- MAY I SPEAK WITH JUDGE BUFFALO WILLIAM PLEASE?
HEY, HOW YAH DOING TODAY BILL? IT'S GLADYS.
UH-HUH... SURE...
SAY BILL, I GOTTA ASK A FAVOR. YOU STILL GOT THAT OPENING FOR A NEW BAILIFF?
YEAH? WELL, WHAT ARE YOUR FEELINGS ABOUT MUMMIES IN YOUR COURT ROOM?
COURT IS NOW IN SESSION!
THE HONORABLE JUDGE BUFFALO WILLIAM PRESIDING!
IN THE END, AS FAR AS JOBS GO, IT'S NOT THAT BAD BEING A BAILIFF.
ENDING!

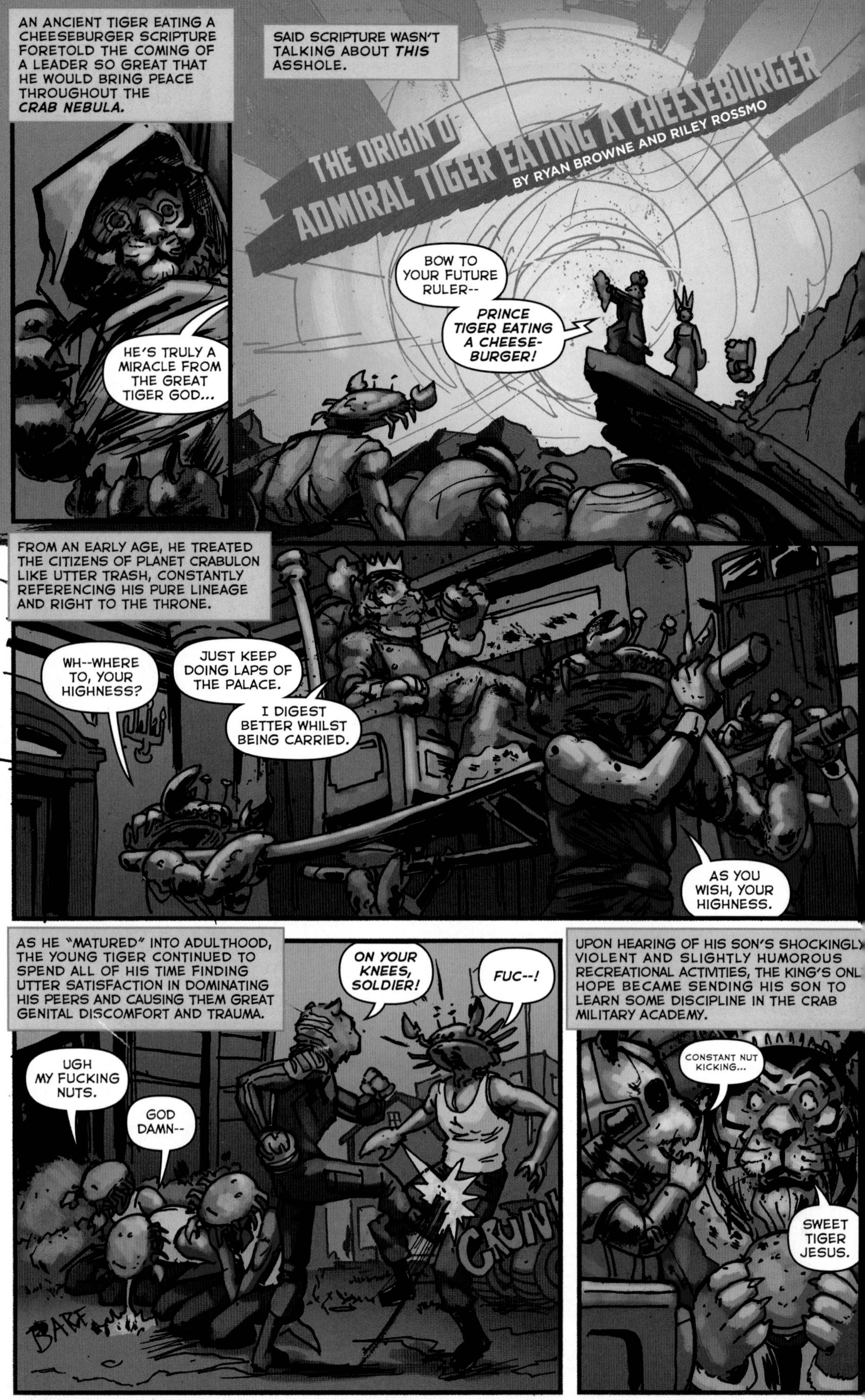

AN ANCIENT TIGER EATING A CHEESEBURGER SCRIPTURE FORETOLD THE COMING OF A LEADER SO GREAT THAT HE WOULD BRING PEACE THROUGHOUT THE *CRAB NEBULA.*
SAID SCRIPTURE WASN'T TALKING ABOUT *THIS* ASSHOLE.
THE ORIGIN O' ADMIRAL TIGER EATING A CHEESEBURGER
BY RYAN BROWNE AND RILEY ROSSMO
HE'S TRULY A MIRACLE FROM THE GREAT TIGER GOD...
BOW TO YOUR FUTURE RULER--
PRINCE TIGER EATING A CHEESE-BURGER!
FROM AN EARLY AGE, HE TREATED THE CITIZENS OF PLANET CRABULON LIKE UTTER TRASH, CONSTANTLY REFERENCING HIS PURE LINEAGE AND RIGHT TO THE THRONE.
WH--WHERE TO, YOUR HIGHNESS?
JUST KEEP DOING LAPS OF THE PALACE.
I DIGEST BETTER WHILST BEING CARRIED.
AS YOU WISH, YOUR HIGHNESS.
AS HE "MATURED" INTO ADULTHOOD, THE YOUNG TIGER CONTINUED TO SPEND ALL OF HIS TIME FINDING UTTER SATISFACTION IN DOMINATING HIS PEERS AND CAUSING THEM GREAT GENITAL DISCOMFORT AND TRAUMA.
ON YOUR KNEES, SOLDIER!
FUC--!
UGH MY FUCKING NUTS.
GOD DAMN--
CRUN
BARF
UPON HEARING OF HIS SON'S SHOCKINGLY VIOLENT AND SLIGHTLY HUMOROUS RECREATIONAL ACTIVITIES, THE KING'S ONL HOPE BECAME SENDING HIS SON TO LEARN SOME DISCIPLINE IN THE CRAB MILITARY ACADEMY.
CONSTANT NUT KICKING...
SWEET TIGER JESUS.

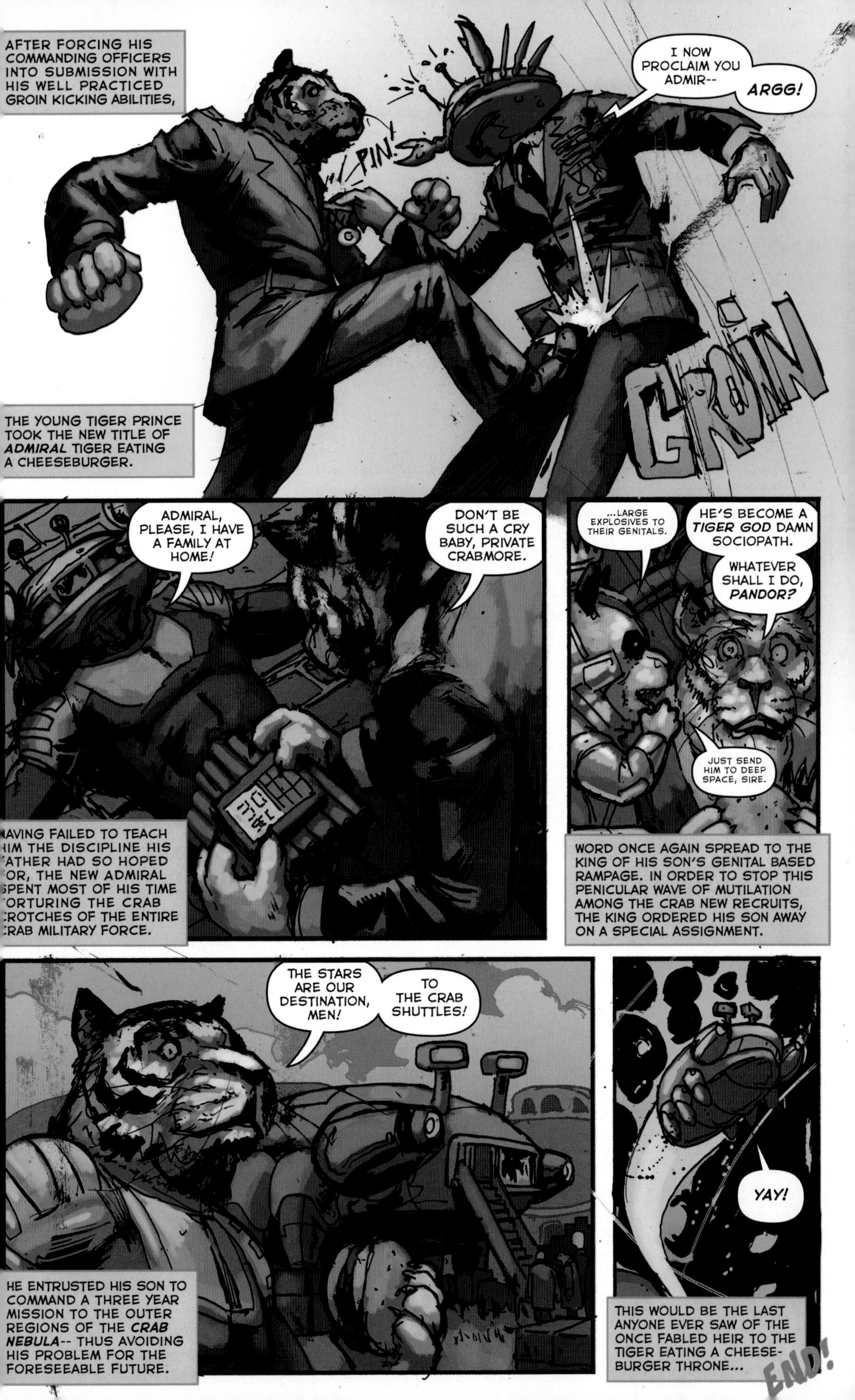
AFTER FORCING HIS COMMANDING OFFICERS INTO SUBMISSION WITH HIS WELL PRACTICED GROIN KICKING ABILITIES,
I NOW PROCLAIM YOU ADMIR--
ARGG!
PIN!
GROIN
THE YOUNG TIGER PRINCE TOOK THE NEW TITLE OF ADMIRAL TIGER EATING A CHEESEBURGER.
ADMIRAL, PLEASE, I HAVE A FAMILY AT HOME!
DON'T BE SUCH A CRY BABY, PRIVATE CRABMORE.
HAVING FAILED TO TEACH HIM THE DISCIPLINE HIS FATHER HAD SO HOPED FOR, THE NEW ADMIRAL SPENT MOST OF HIS TIME TORTURING THE CRAB CROTCHES OF THE ENTIRE CRAB MILITARY FORCE.
...LARGE EXPLOSIVES TO THEIR GENITALS.
HE'S BECOME A TIGER GOD DAMN SOCIOPATH.
WHATEVER SHALL I DO, PANDOR?
JUST SEND HIM TO DEEP SPACE, SIRE.
WORD ONCE AGAIN SPREAD TO THE KING OF HIS SON'S GENITAL BASED RAMPAGE. IN ORDER TO STOP THIS PENICULAR WAVE OF MUTILATION AMONG THE CRAB NEW RECRUITS, THE KING ORDERED HIS SON AWAY ON A SPECIAL ASSIGNMENT.
THE STARS ARE OUR DESTINATION, MEN!
TO THE CRAB SHUTTLES!
HE ENTRUSTED HIS SON TO COMMAND A THREE YEAR MISSION TO THE OUTER REGIONS OF THE CRAB NEBULA-- THUS AVOIDING HIS PROBLEM FOR THE FORESEEABLE FUTURE.
YAY!
THIS WOULD BE THE LAST ANYONE EVER SAW OF THE ONCE FABLED HEIR TO THE TIGER EATING A CHEESE-BURGER THRONE...
END!

A BIZARRE ALIEN WORLD, MILLIONS OF SPACE-MILES FROM *THE CRAB NEBULA*.

THE INTREPID CRAB SPACE EXPLORER, *MR. CRABTREE*, LEADS A HEROIC AWAY TEAM DEEP INTO HOSTILE TERRITORY!

STAY SHARP MEN,

YOU NEVER KNOW WHAT YOU WILL FIND ON...

PLANET WHORE-ZONG TWELVE!!!

THE ORIGIN OF **MR. CRABTREE!**

BY RYAN BROWNE & HILARY BARTA

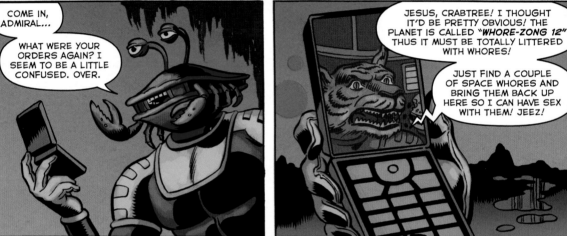

COME IN, ADMIRAL...

WHAT WERE YOUR ORDERS AGAIN? I SEEM TO BE A LITTLE CONFUSED. OVER.

JESUS, CRABTREE! I THOUGHT IT'D BE PRETTY OBVIOUS! THE PLANET IS CALLED *"WHORE-ZONG 12"* THUS IT MUST BE TOTALLY LITTERED WITH WHORES!

JUST FIND A COUPLE OF SPACE WHORES AND BRING THEM BACK UP HERE SO I CAN HAVE SEX WITH THEM! JEEZ!

I'M SORRY SIR, WE'VE BEEN SCANNING THE SURFACE OF THE PLANET AND SO FAR WE HAVEN'T SEEN ANY--

MONEY FOR SEX?!?!

--SPACE WHORES!

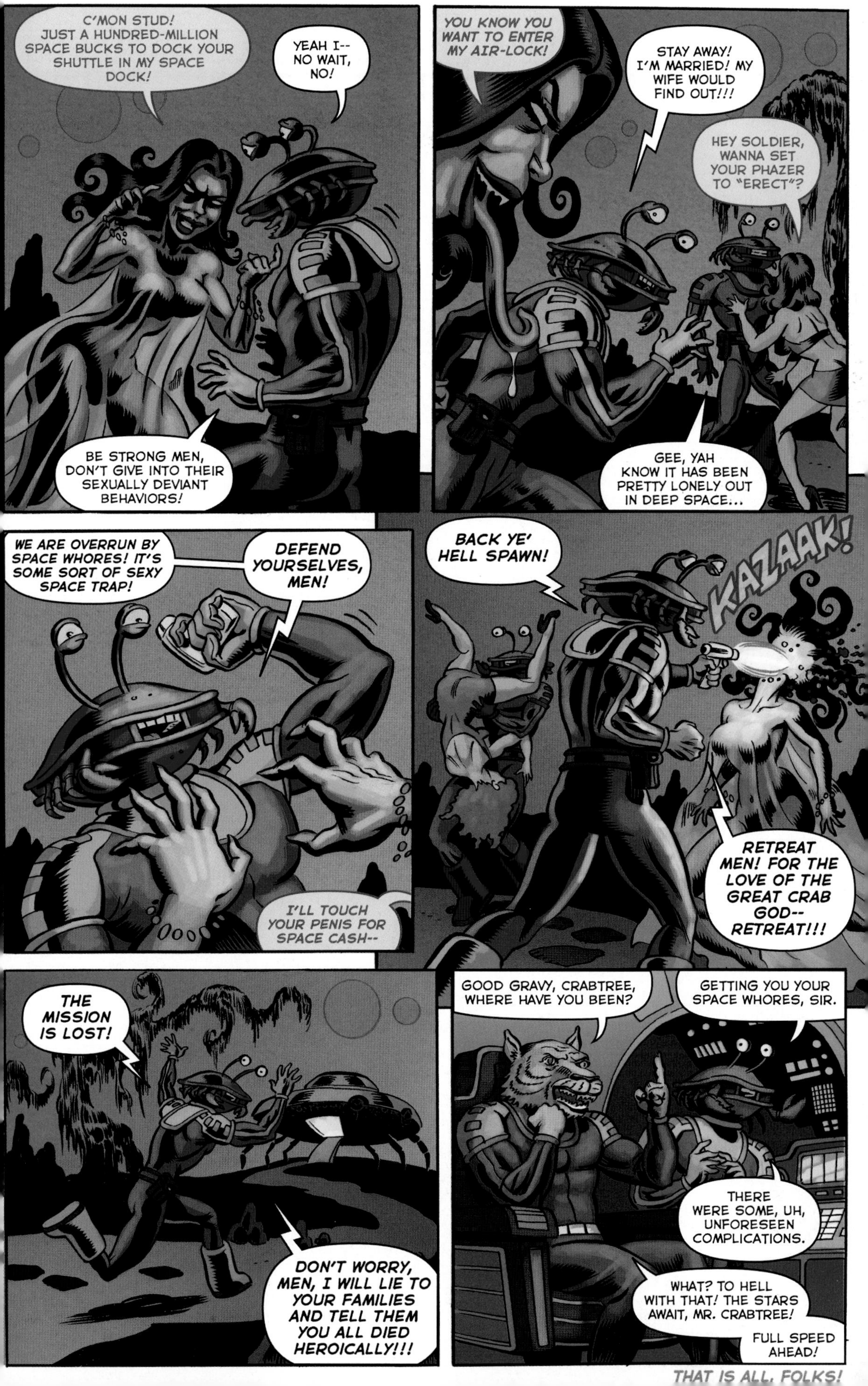
C'MON STUD! JUST A HUNDRED-MILLION SPACE BUCKS TO DOCK YOUR SHUTTLE IN MY SPACE DOCK!
YEAH I-- NO WAIT, NO!
BE STRONG MEN, DON'T GIVE INTO THEIR SEXUALLY DEVIANT BEHAVIORS!
YOU KNOW YOU WANT TO ENTER MY AIR-LOCK!
STAY AWAY! I'M MARRIED! MY WIFE WOULD FIND OUT!!!
HEY SOLDIER, WANNA SET YOUR PHAZER TO "ERECT"?
GEE, YAH KNOW IT HAS BEEN PRETTY LONELY OUT IN DEEP SPACE...
WE ARE OVERRUN BY SPACE WHORES! IT'S SOME SORT OF SEXY SPACE TRAP!
DEFEND YOURSELVES, MEN!
I'LL TOUCH YOUR PENIS FOR SPACE CASH--
BACK YE' HELL SPAWN!
KAZAAK!
RETREAT MEN! FOR THE LOVE OF THE GREAT CRAB GOD-- RETREAT!!!
THE MISSION IS LOST!
DON'T WORRY, MEN, I WILL LIE TO YOUR FAMILIES AND TELL THEM YOU ALL DIED HEROICALLY!!!
GOOD GRAVY, CRABTREE, WHERE HAVE YOU BEEN?
GETTING YOU YOUR SPACE WHORES, SIR.
THERE WERE SOME, UH, UNFORESEEN COMPLICATIONS.
WHAT? TO HELL WITH THAT! THE STARS AWAIT, MR. CRABTREE!
FULL SPEED AHEAD!
THAT IS ALL, FOLKS!

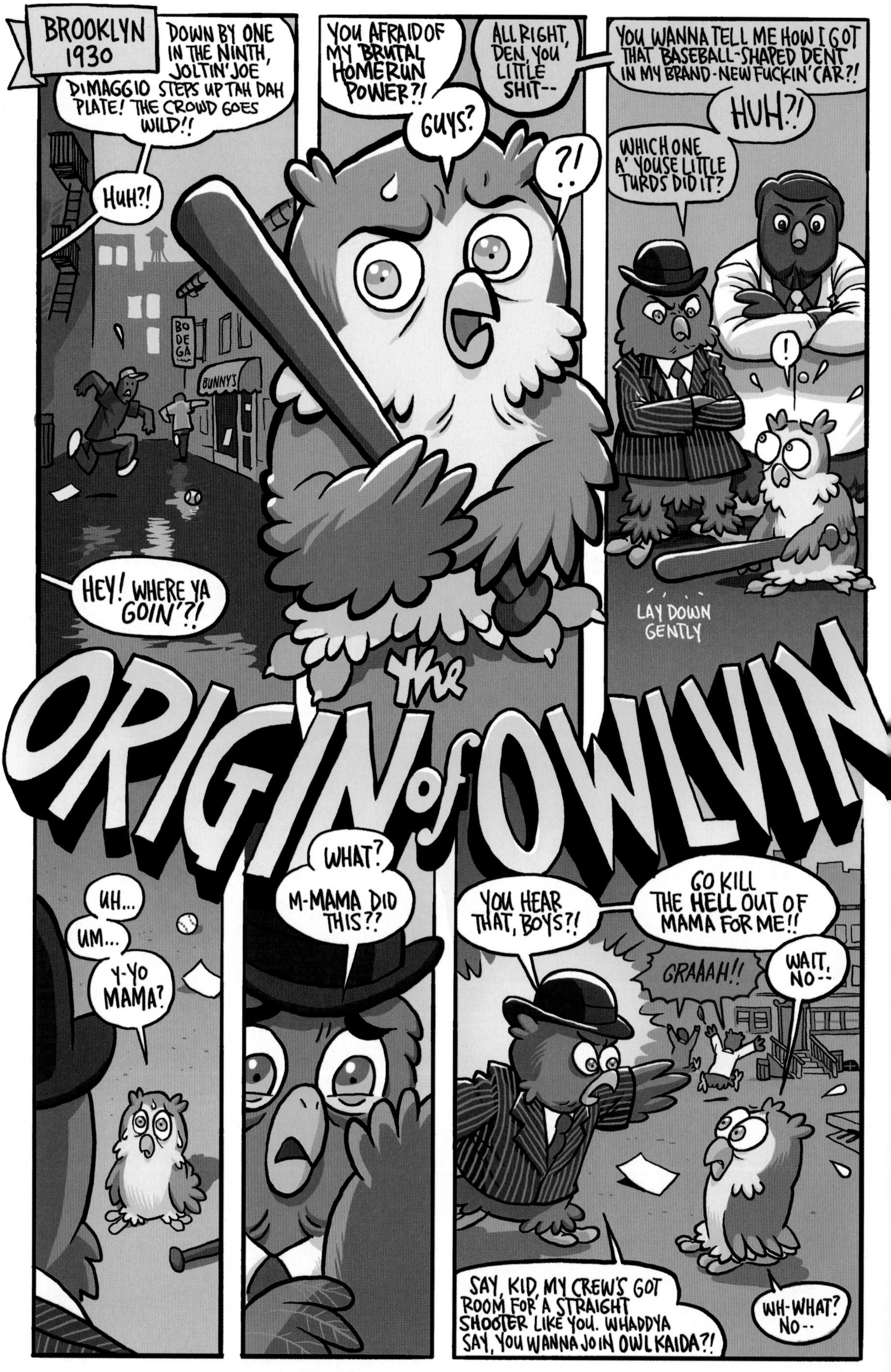
BROOKLYN 1930
DOWN BY ONE IN THE NINTH, JOLTIN' JOE DIMAGGIO STEPS UP TAH DAH PLATE! THE CROWD GOES WILD!!
HUH?!
BO DE GA
BUNNY'S
HEY! WHERE YA GOIN'?!
YOU AFRAID OF MY BRUTAL HOMERUN POWER?!
GUYS?
?!
ALL RIGHT, DEN, YOU LITTLE SHIT--
YOU WANNA TELL ME HOW I GOT THAT BASEBALL-SHAPED DENT IN MY BRAND-NEW FUCKIN' CAR?!
HUH?!
WHICH ONE A' YOUSE LITTLE TURDS DID IT?
!
LAY DOWN GENTLY
THE ORIGIN OF OWLVIN
UH...
UM...
Y-YO MAMA?
WHAT?
M-MAMA DID THIS??
YOU HEAR THAT, BOYS?!
GO KILL THE HELL OUT OF MAMA FOR ME!!
GRAAAH!!
WAIT, NO--
SAY, KID, MY CREW'S GOT ROOM FOR A STRAIGHT SHOOTER LIKE YOU. WHADDYA SAY, YOU WANNA JOIN OWL KAIDA?!
WH-WHAT? NO--

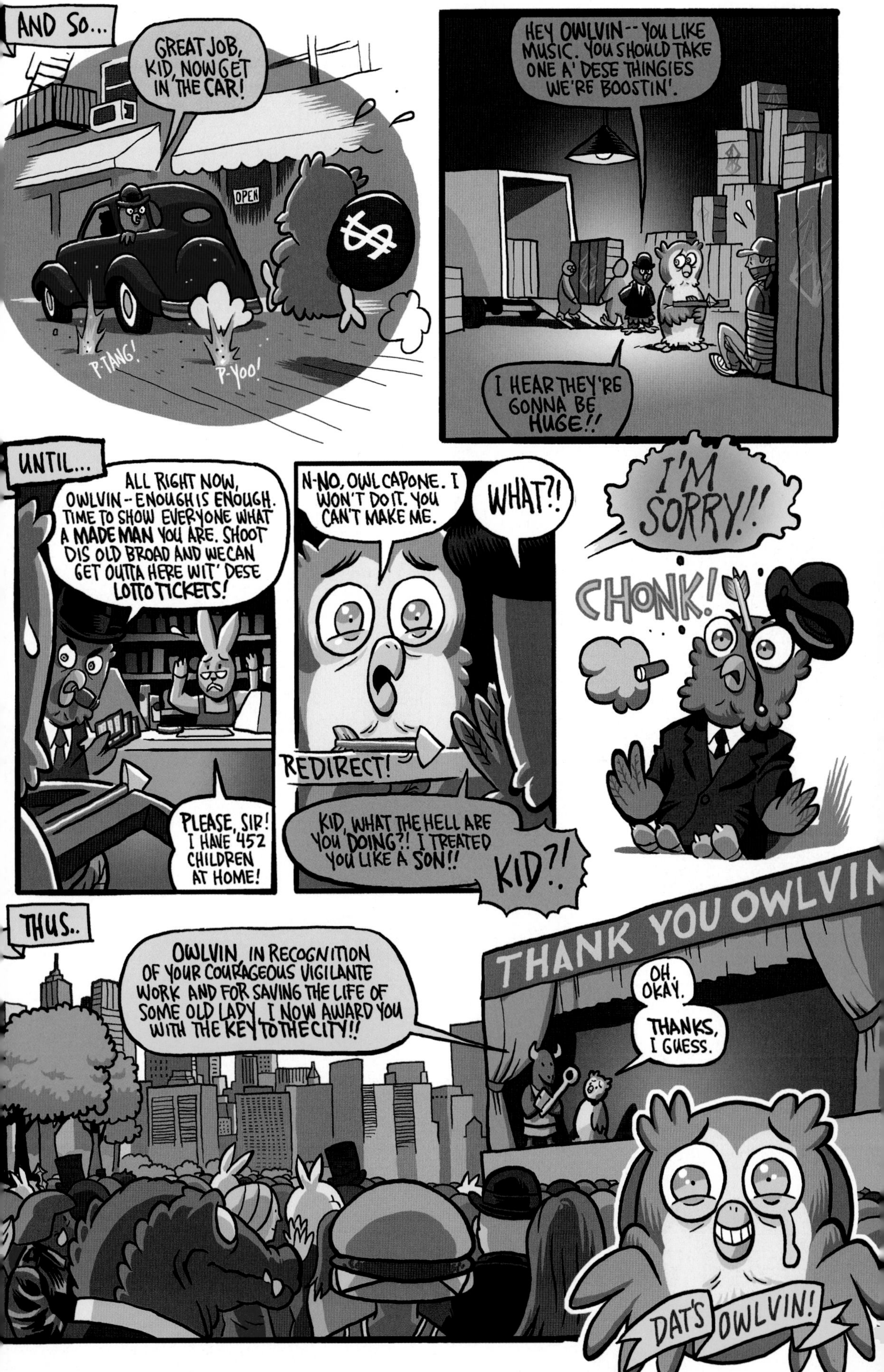
AND SO...
GREAT JOB, KID, NOW GET IN THE CAR!
OPEN
P-TANG!
P-YOO!
HEY OWLVIN-- YOU LIKE MUSIC. YOU SHOULD TAKE ONE A' DESE THINGIES WE'RE BOOSTIN'.
I HEAR THEY'RE GONNA BE HUGE!!
UNTIL...
ALL RIGHT NOW, OWLVIN-- ENOUGH IS ENOUGH. TIME TO SHOW EVERYONE WHAT A MADE MAN YOU ARE. SHOOT DIS OLD BROAD AND WE CAN GET OUTTA HERE WIT' DESE LOTTO TICKETS!
PLEASE, SIR! I HAVE 452 CHILDREN AT HOME!
N-NO, OWL CAPONE. I WON'T DO IT. YOU CAN'T MAKE ME.
WHAT?!
REDIRECT!
KID, WHAT THE HELL ARE YOU DOING?! I TREATED YOU LIKE A SON!!
KID?!
I'M SORRY!!
CHONK!
THUS..
OWLVIN, IN RECOGNITION OF YOUR COURAGEOUS VIGILANTE WORK AND FOR SAVING THE LIFE OF SOME OLD LADY, I NOW AWARD YOU WITH THE KEY TO THE CITY!!
THANK YOU OWLVIN
OH. OKAY.
THANKS, I GUESS.
DAT'S OWLVIN!

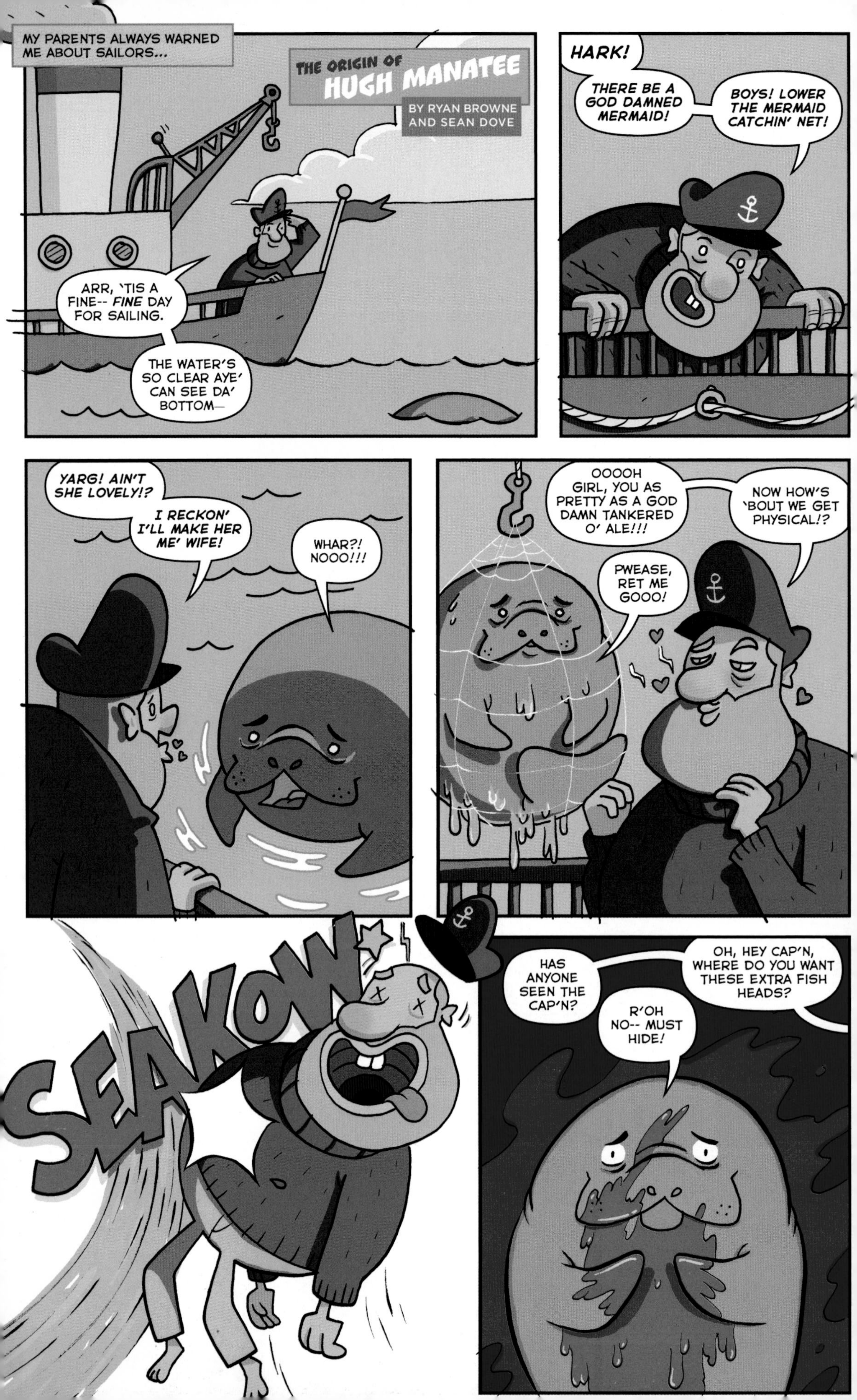
MY PARENTS ALWAYS WARNED ME ABOUT SAILORS...
THE ORIGIN OF HUGH MANATEE
BY RYAN BROWNE AND SEAN DOVE
ARR, 'TIS A FINE-- FINE DAY FOR SAILING.
THE WATER'S SO CLEAR AYE' CAN SEE DA' BOTTOM—
HARK!
THERE BE A GOD DAMNED MERMAID!
BOYS! LOWER THE MERMAID CATCHIN' NET!
YARG! AIN'T SHE LOVELY!?
I RECKON' I'LL MAKE HER ME' WIFE!
WHAR?! NOOO!!!
OOOOH GIRL, YOU AS PRETTY AS A GOD DAMN TANKERED O' ALE!!!
NOW HOW'S 'BOUT WE GET PHYSICAL!?
PWEASE, RET ME GOOO!
SEAKOW
HAS ANYONE SEEN THE CAP'N?
OH, HEY CAP'N, WHERE DO YOU WANT THESE EXTRA FISH HEADS?
R'OH NO-- MUST HIDE!

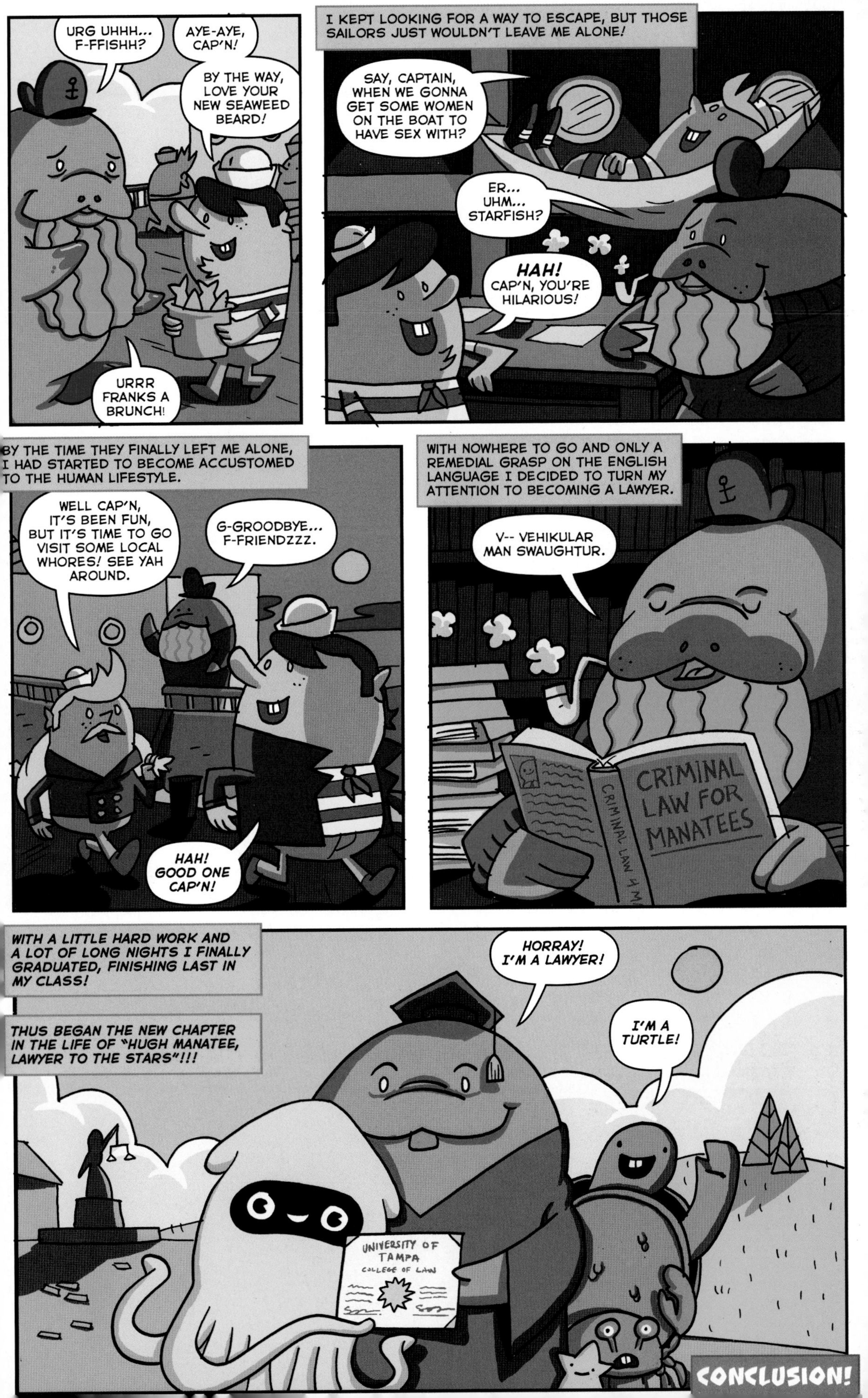
URG UHHH... F-FFISHH?
AYE-AYE, CAP'N!
BY THE WAY, LOVE YOUR NEW SEAWEED BEARD!
URRR FRANKS A BRUNCH!
I KEPT LOOKING FOR A WAY TO ESCAPE, BUT THOSE SAILORS JUST WOULDN'T LEAVE ME ALONE!
SAY, CAPTAIN, WHEN WE GONNA GET SOME WOMEN ON THE BOAT TO HAVE SEX WITH?
ER... UHM... STARFISH?
HAH! CAP'N, YOU'RE HILARIOUS!
BY THE TIME THEY FINALLY LEFT ME ALONE, I HAD STARTED TO BECOME ACCUSTOMED TO THE HUMAN LIFESTYLE.
WELL CAP'N, IT'S BEEN FUN, BUT IT'S TIME TO GO VISIT SOME LOCAL WHORES! SEE YAH AROUND.
G-GROODBYE... F-FRIENDZZZ.
HAH! GOOD ONE CAP'N!
WITH NOWHERE TO GO AND ONLY A REMEDIAL GRASP ON THE ENGLISH LANGUAGE I DECIDED TO TURN MY ATTENTION TO BECOMING A LAWYER.
V-- VEHIKULAR MAN SWAUGHTUR.
CRIMINAL LAW FOR MANATEES
CRIMINAL LAW 4 M
WITH A LITTLE HARD WORK AND A LOT OF LONG NIGHTS I FINALLY GRADUATED, FINISHING LAST IN MY CLASS!
THUS BEGAN THE NEW CHAPTER IN THE LIFE OF "HUGH MANATEE, LAWYER TO THE STARS"!!!
HORRAY! I'M A LAWYER!
I'M A TURTLE!
UNIVERSITY OF TAMPA COLLEGE OF LAW
CONCLUSION!

THE PIN-UPS OF GOD HATES ASTRONAUTS

The following section is a collection of kick-ass pin-ups from a bunch of sweet dudes, one dudette and one dude who kind of looks like a dudette. Also be witness to the Canadian powerhouse who is Tom Fowler—who has actually contributed two pin-ups to this collection as did the bearded wonder known only as Steve Seeley. Enjoy the visual feast!

"Bheargavad Gita" is the creation of Tom Fowler and is printed with the artist's permission.

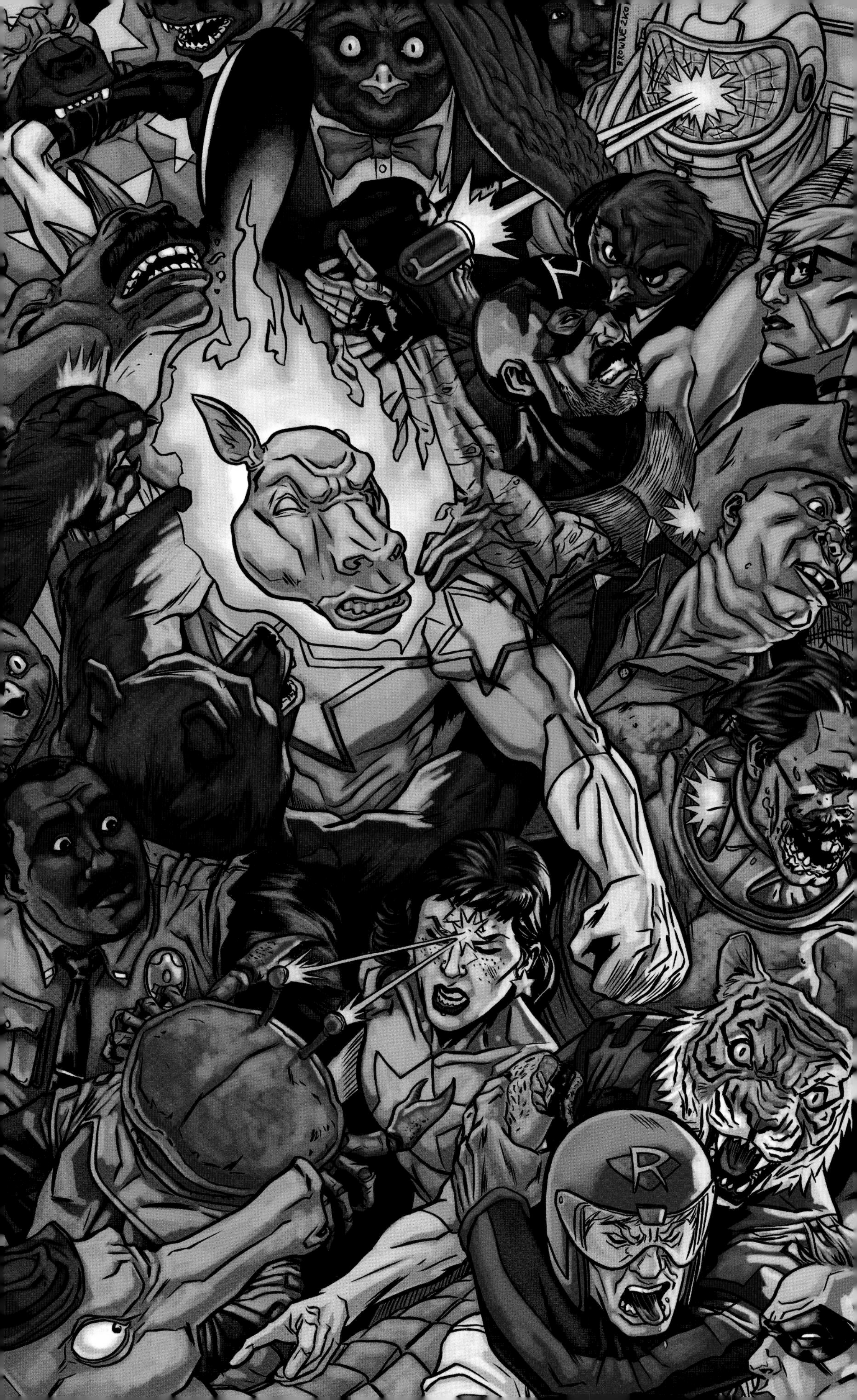
BROWNE 2K10
R

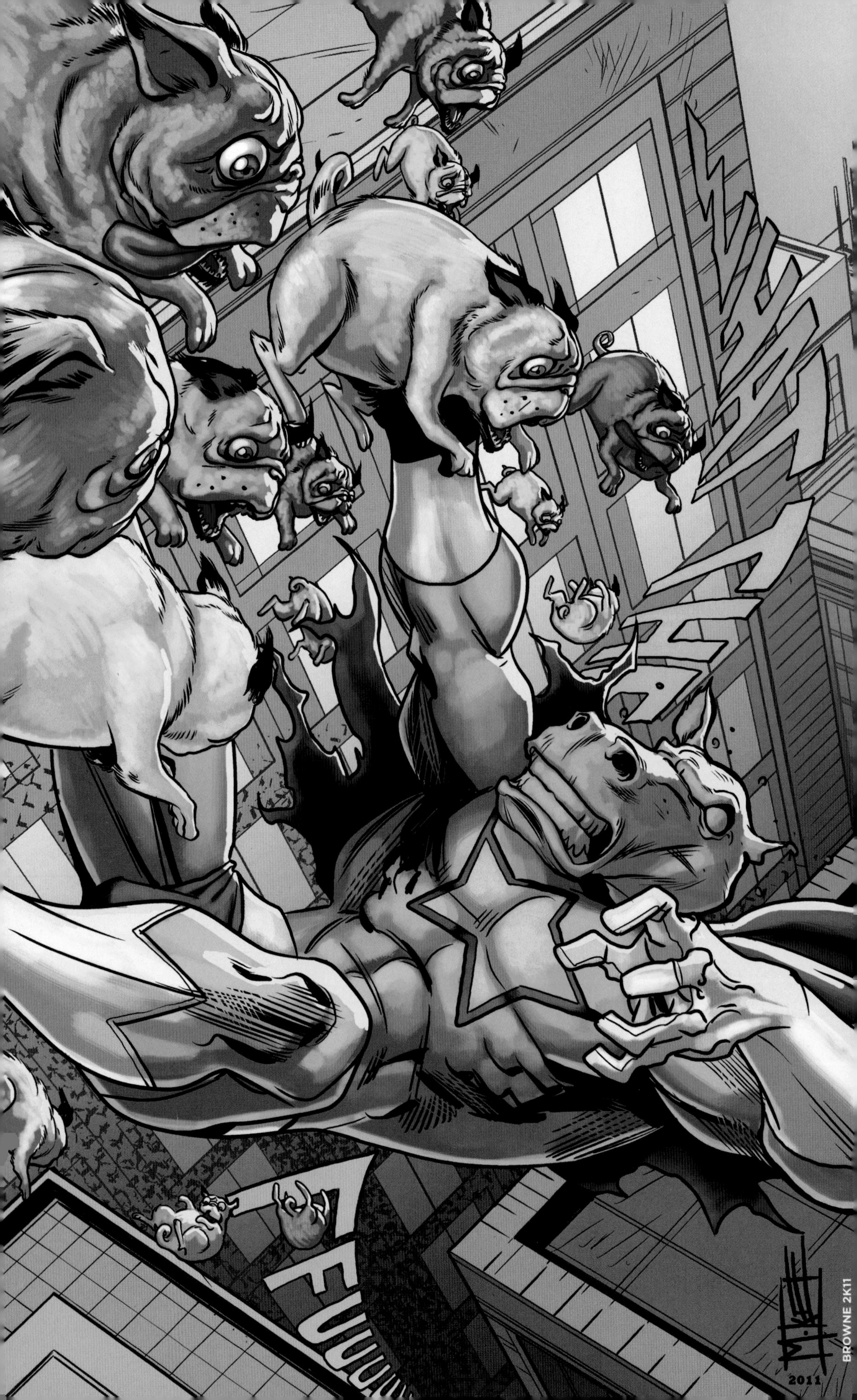
FUUU
BROWNE 2K11
2011

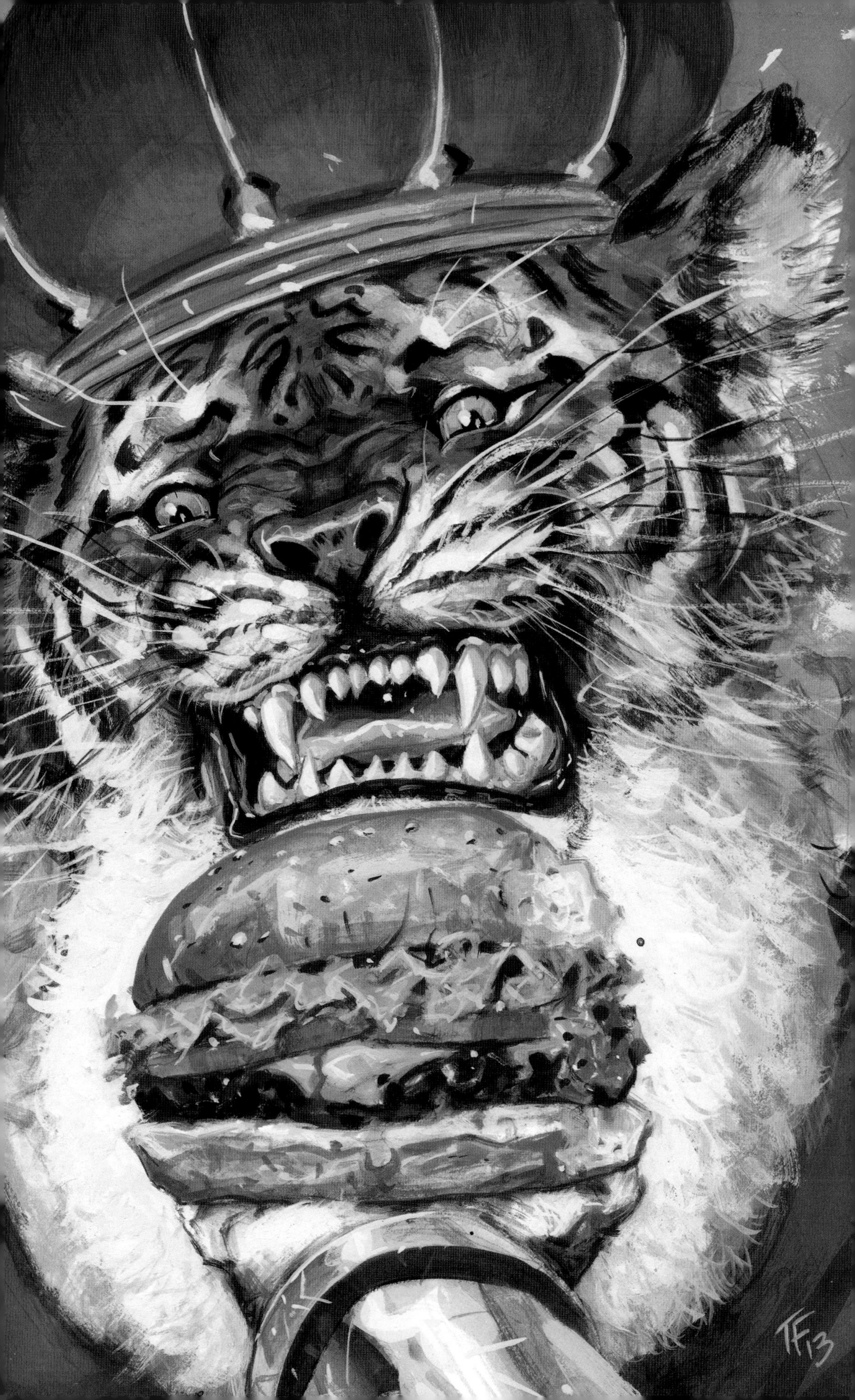
TF 13

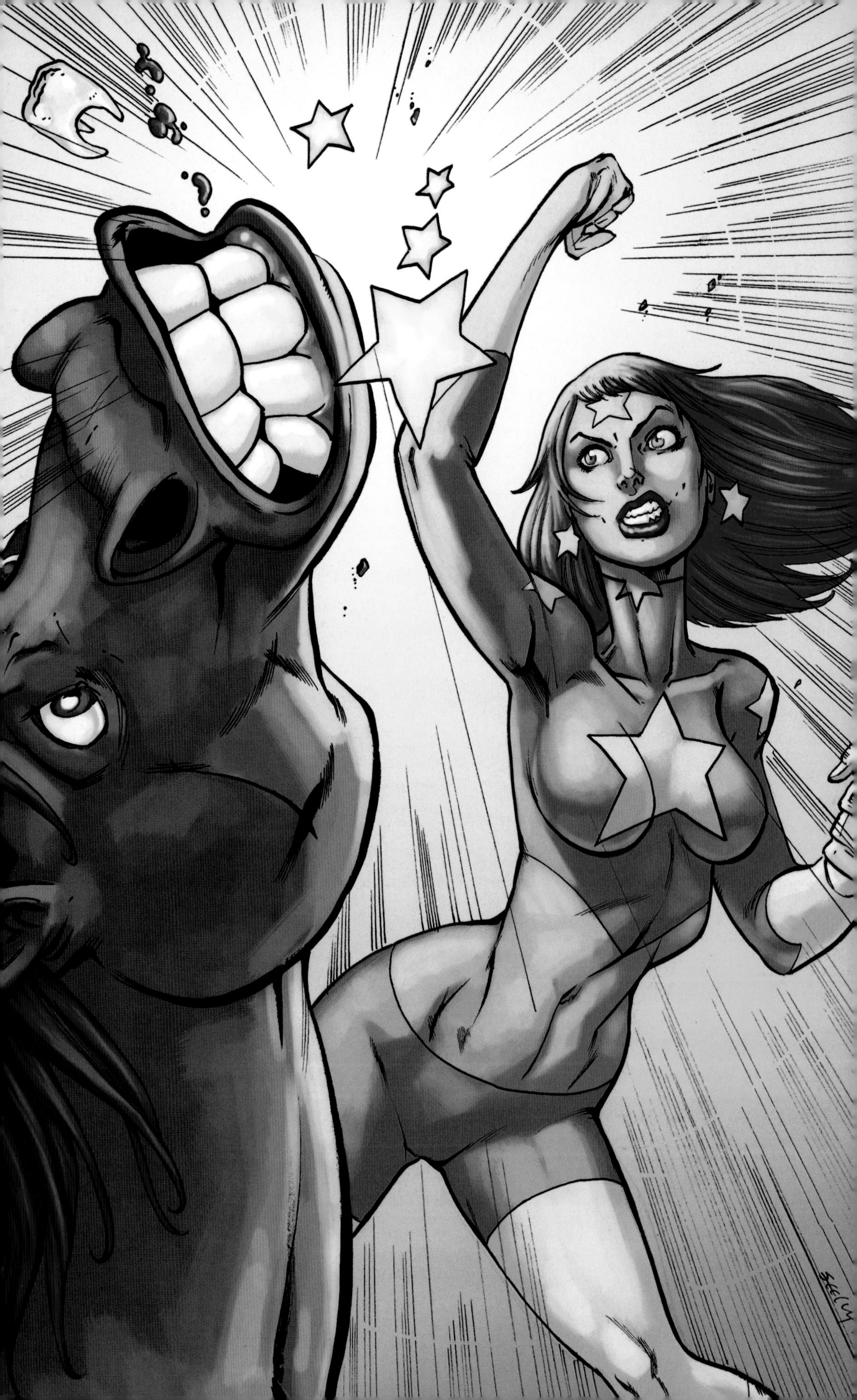

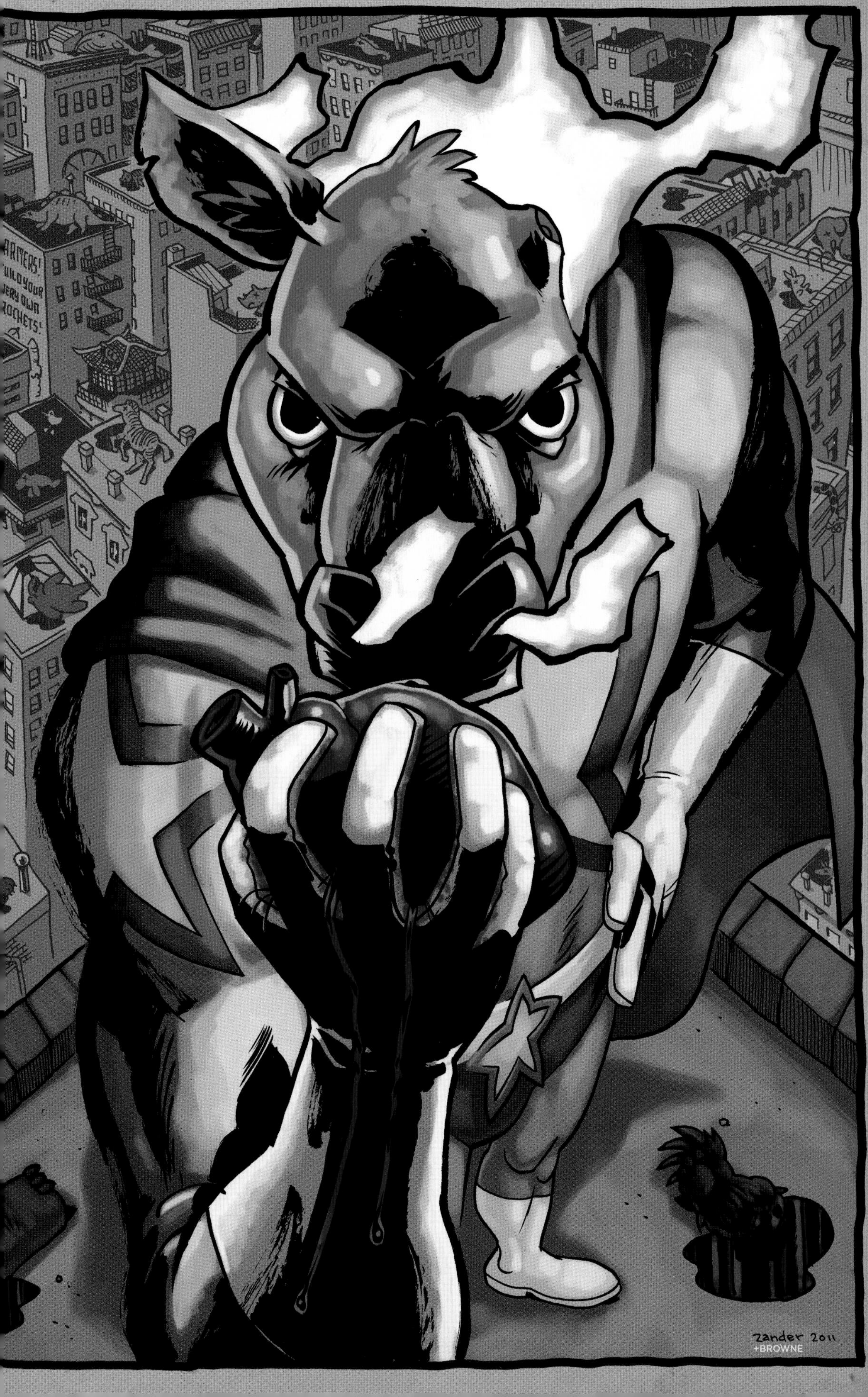

ARMERS!
UILD YOUR
ERY OWN
ROCHETS!
Zander 2011
+BROWNE

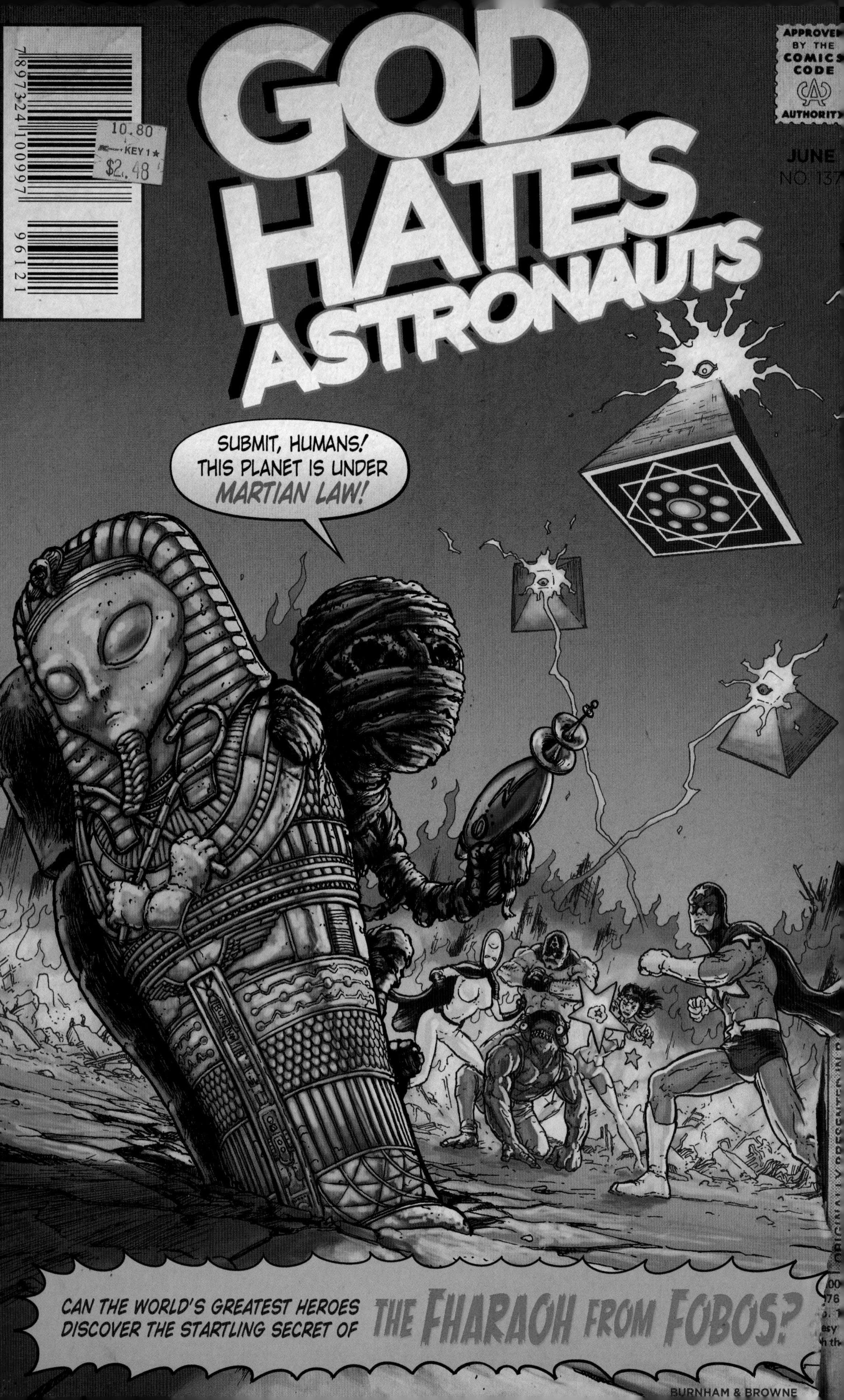
GOD HATES ASTRONAUTS
APPROVED BY THE COMICS CODE AUTHORITY
JUNE
NO. 137
SUBMIT, HUMANS! THIS PLANET IS UNDER MARTIAN LAW!
CAN THE WORLD'S GREATEST HEROES DISCOVER THE STARTLING SECRET OF
THE FHARAOH FROM FOBOS?
BURNHAM & BROWNE

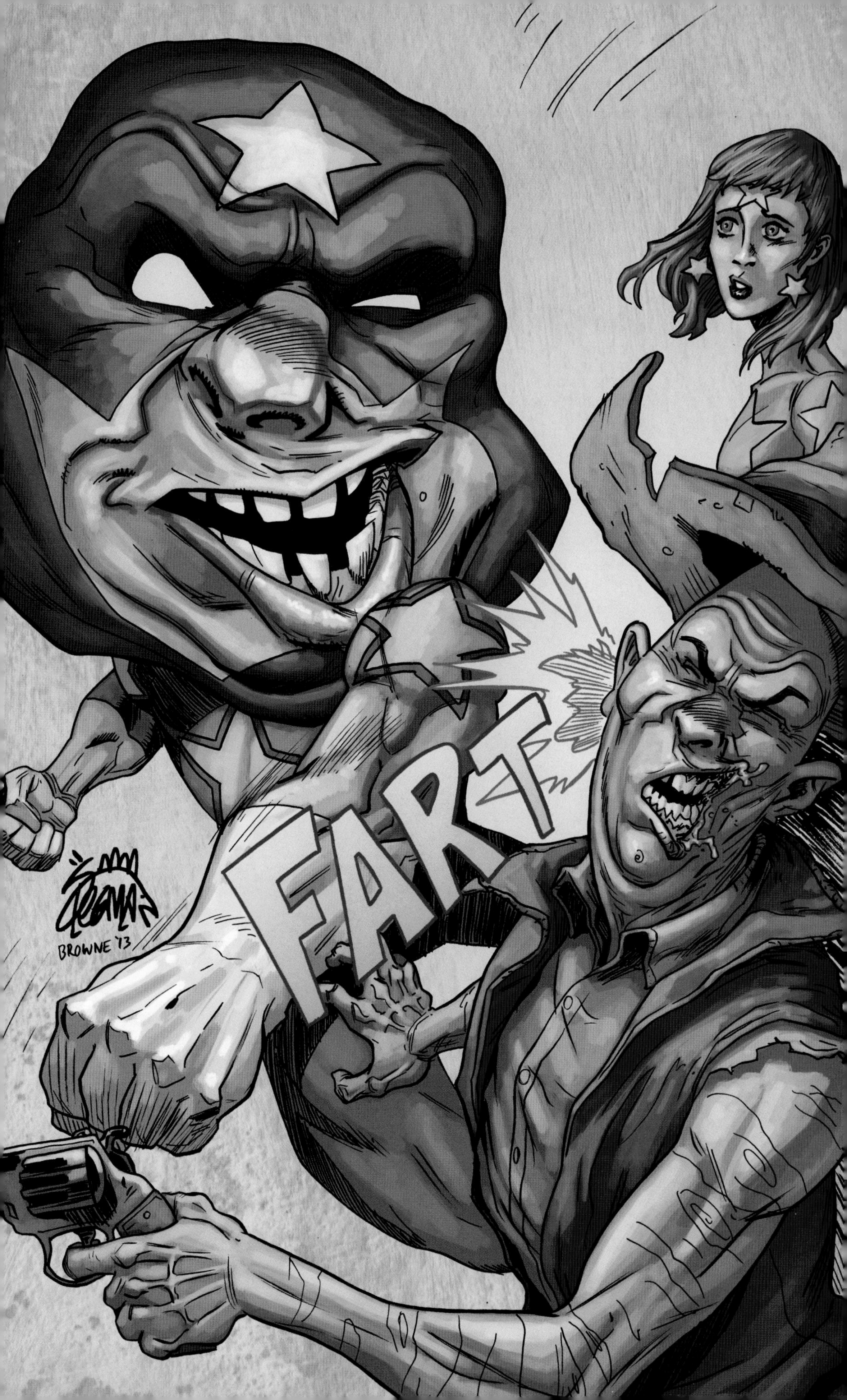
FART
BROWNE '13

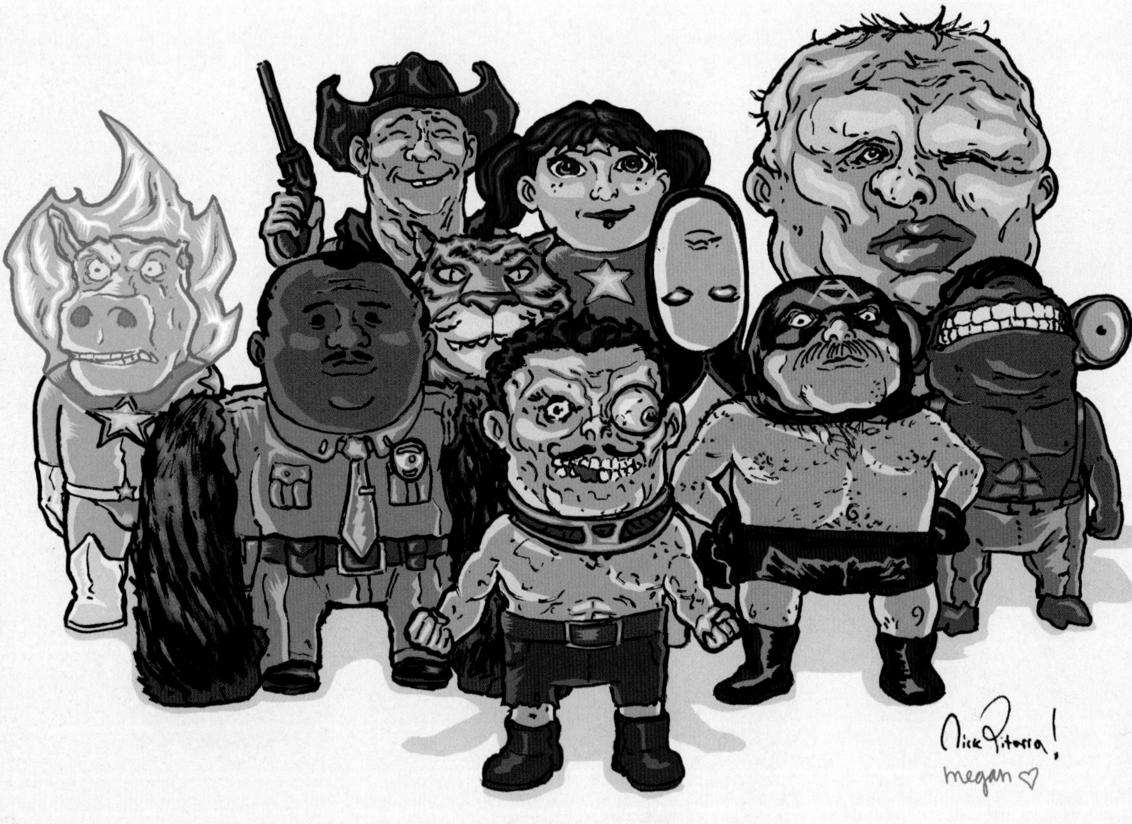
Nick Pitarra!
megan ♡

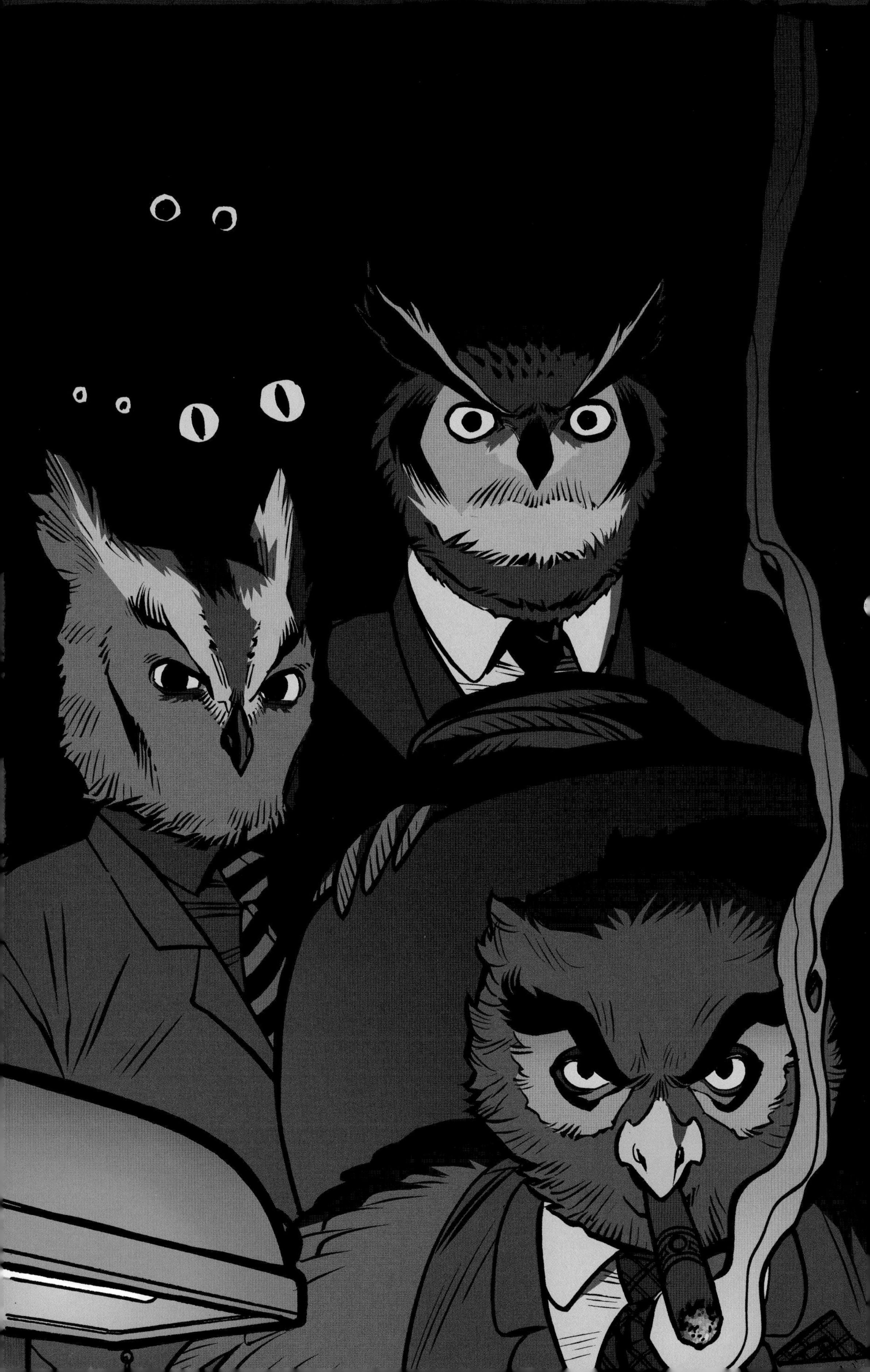

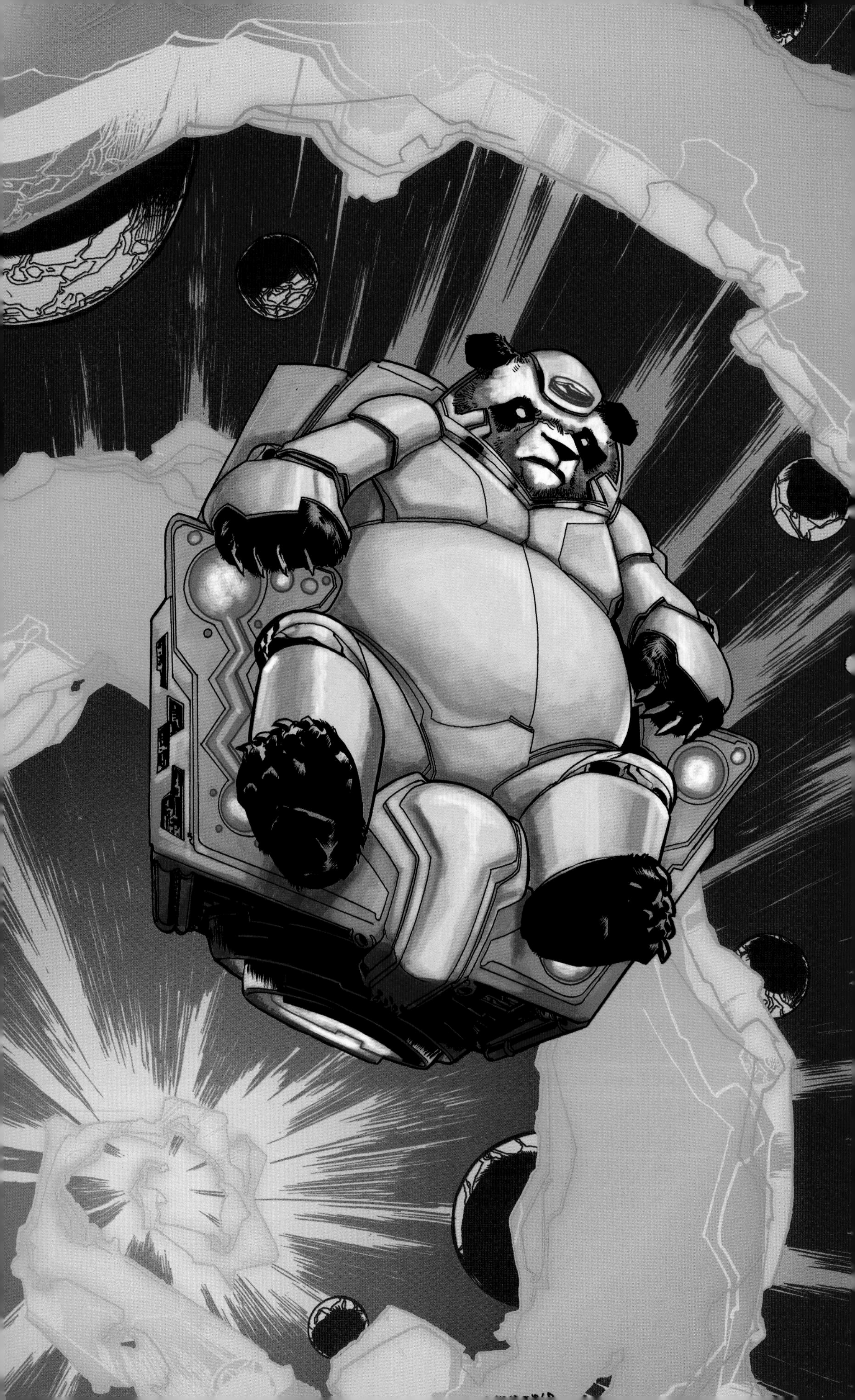

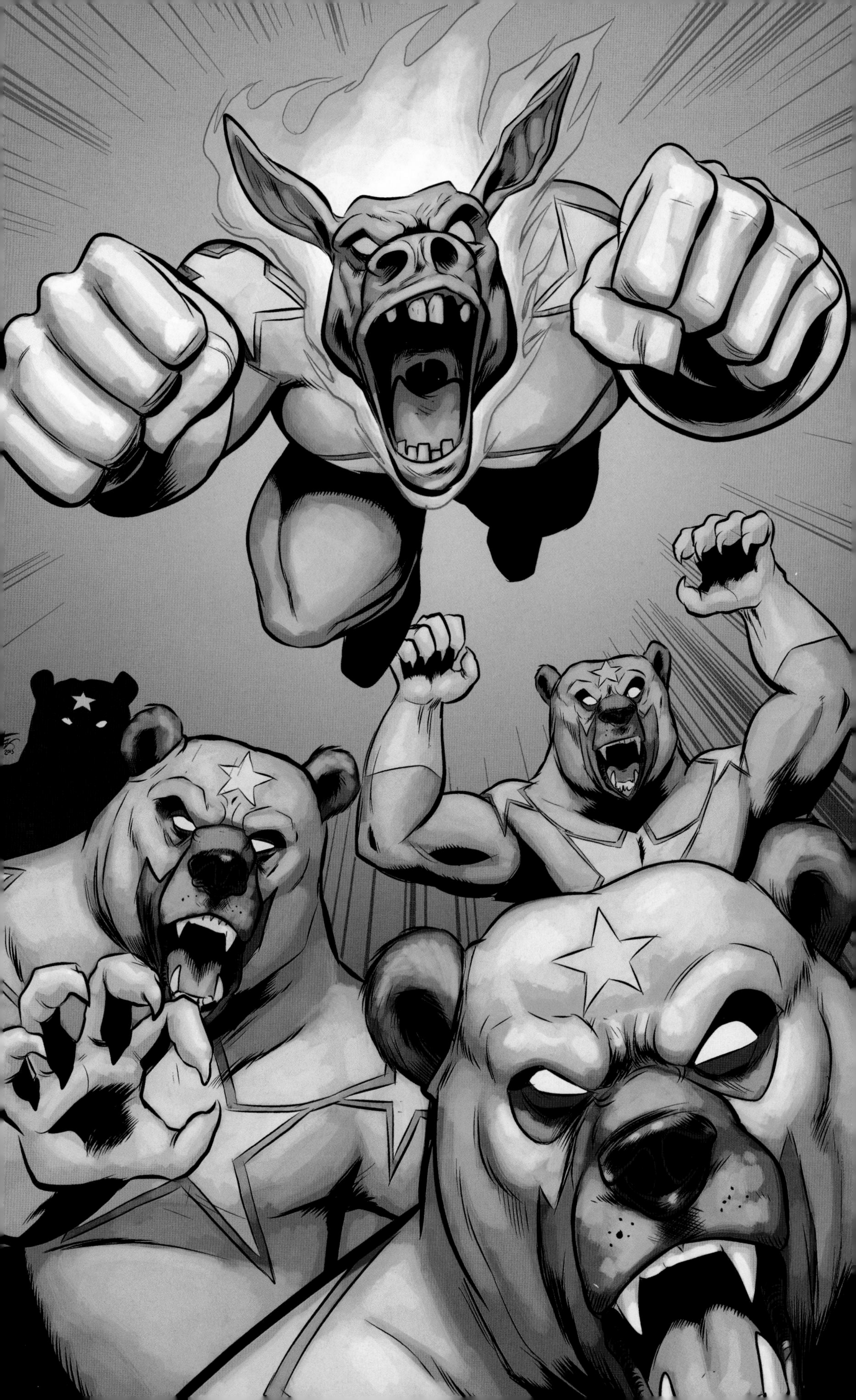

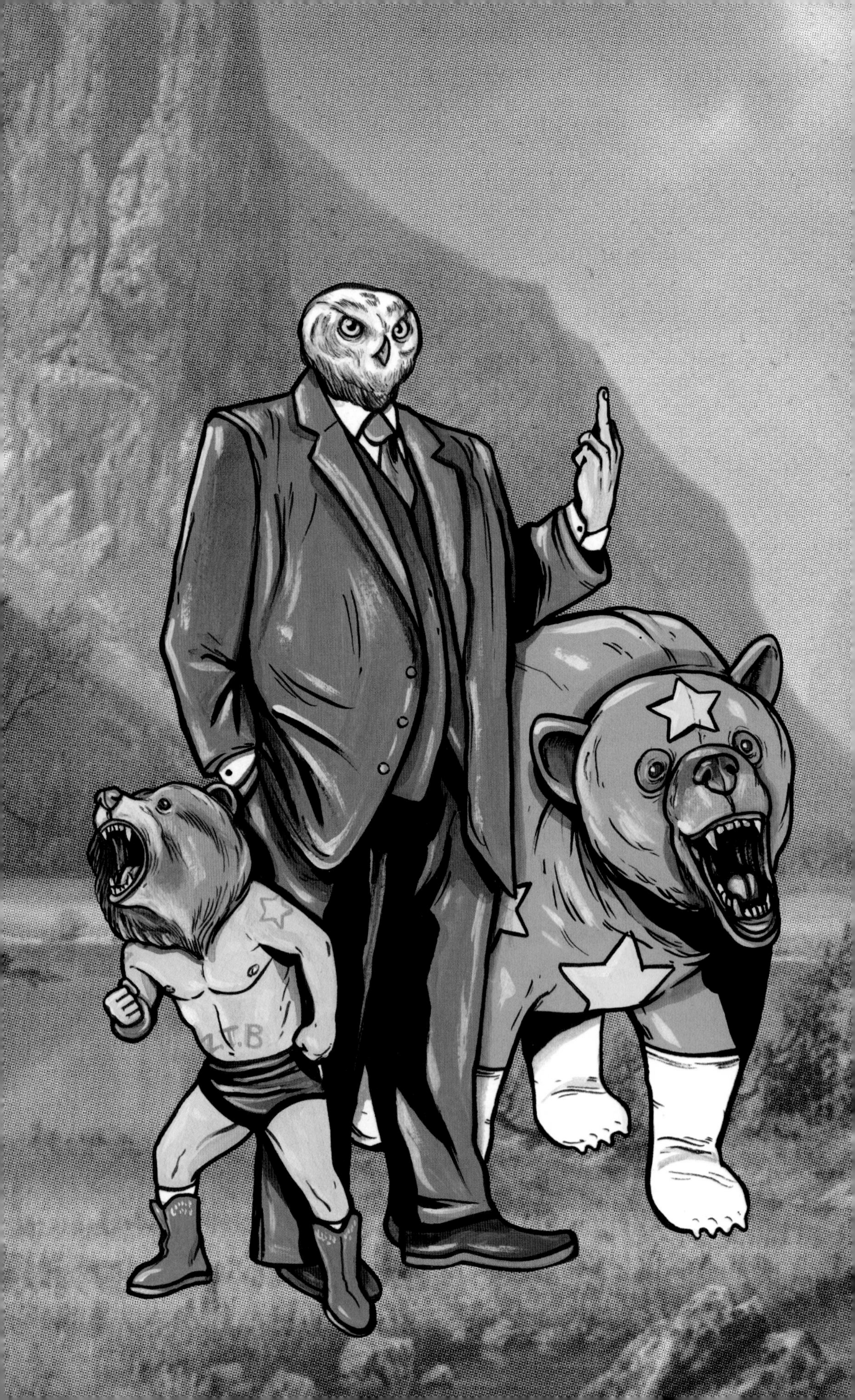

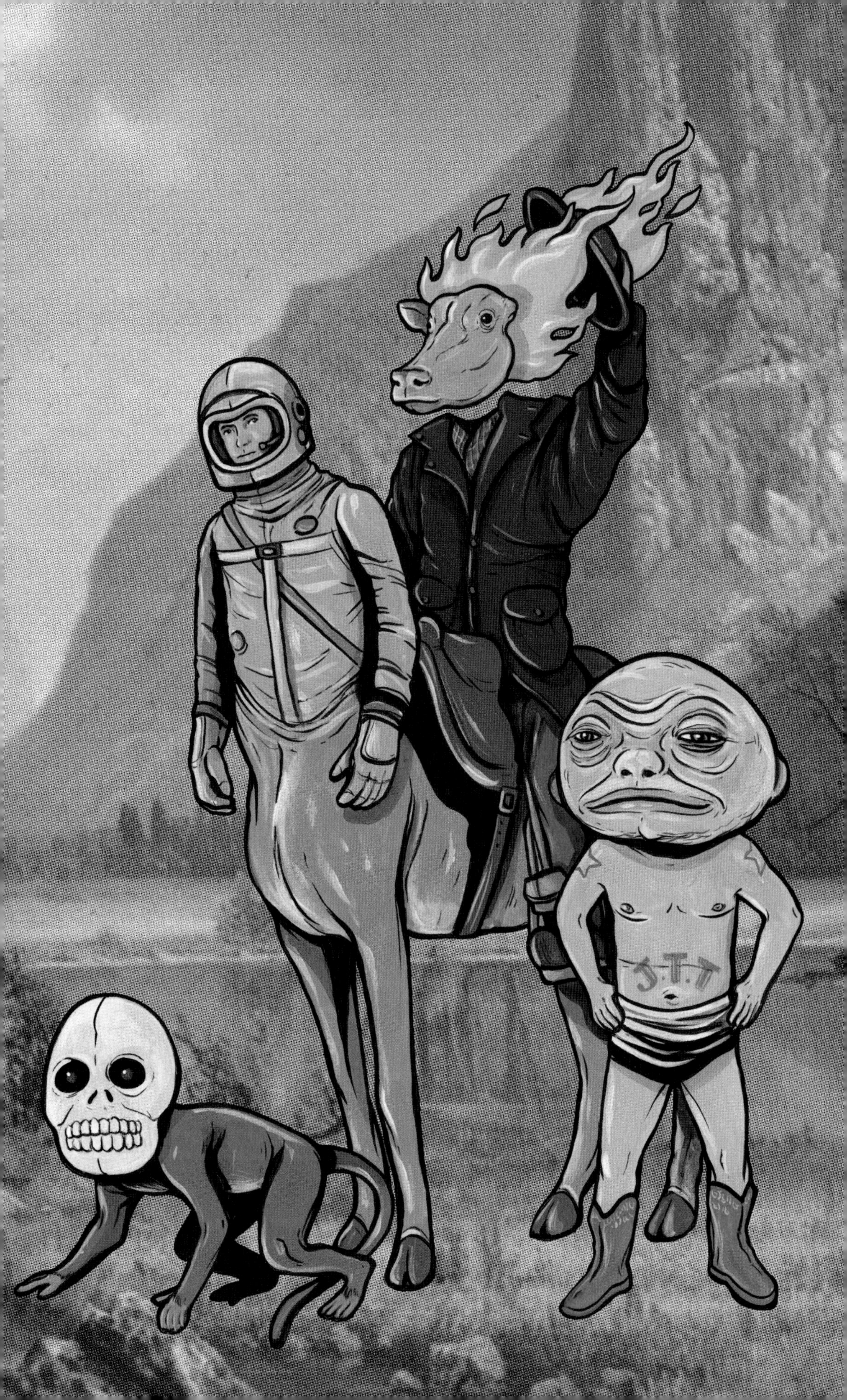

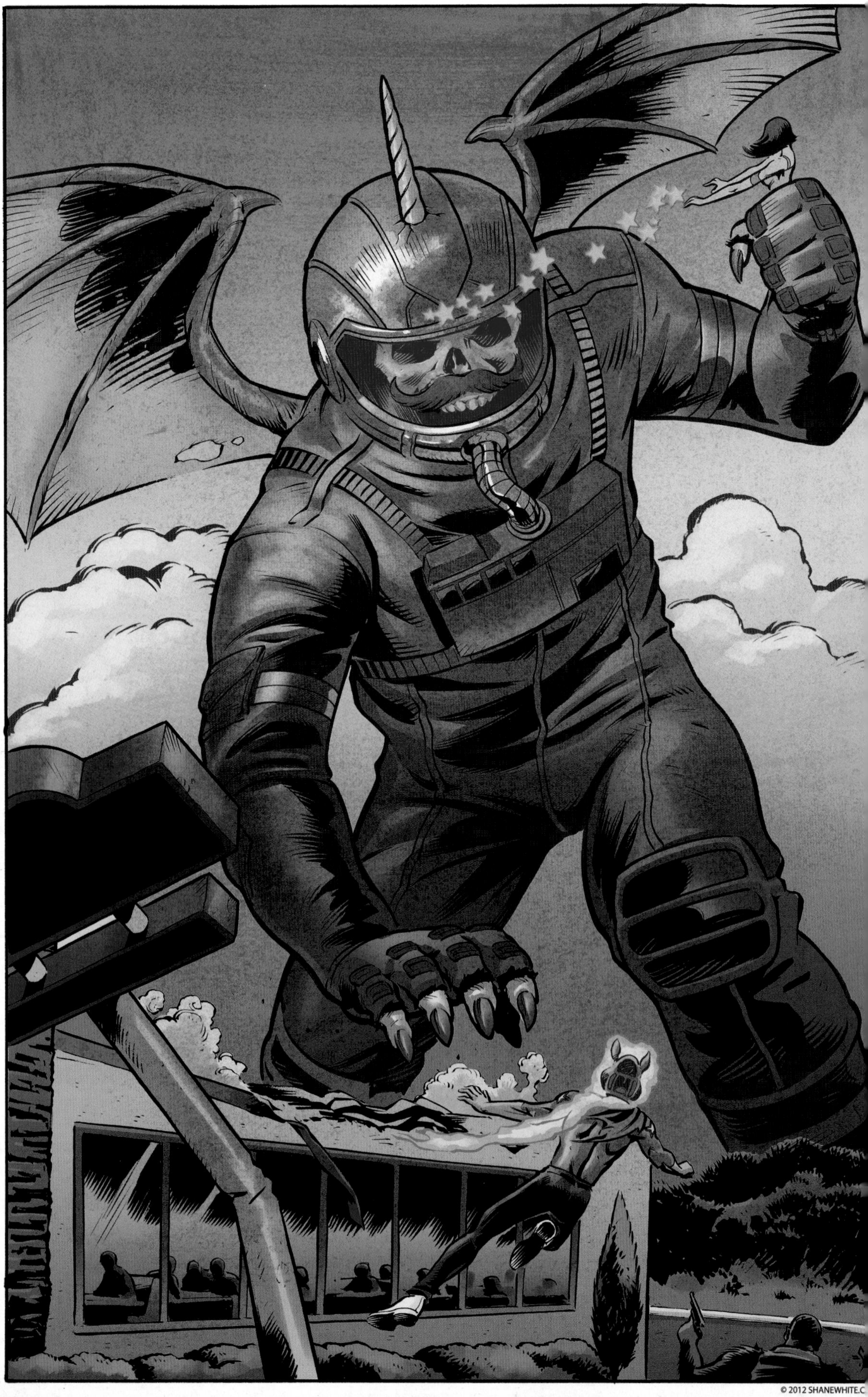

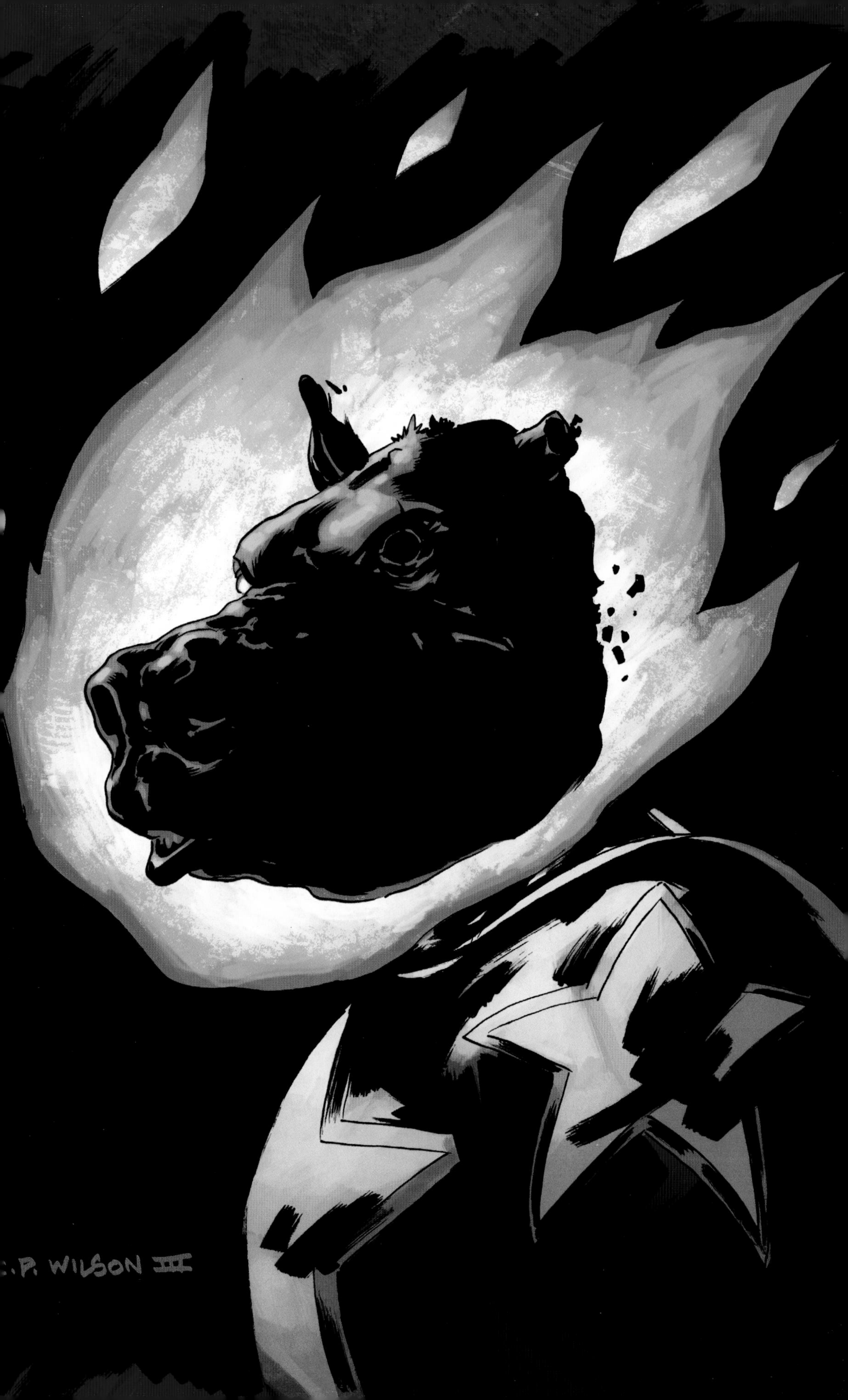
P. WILSON III

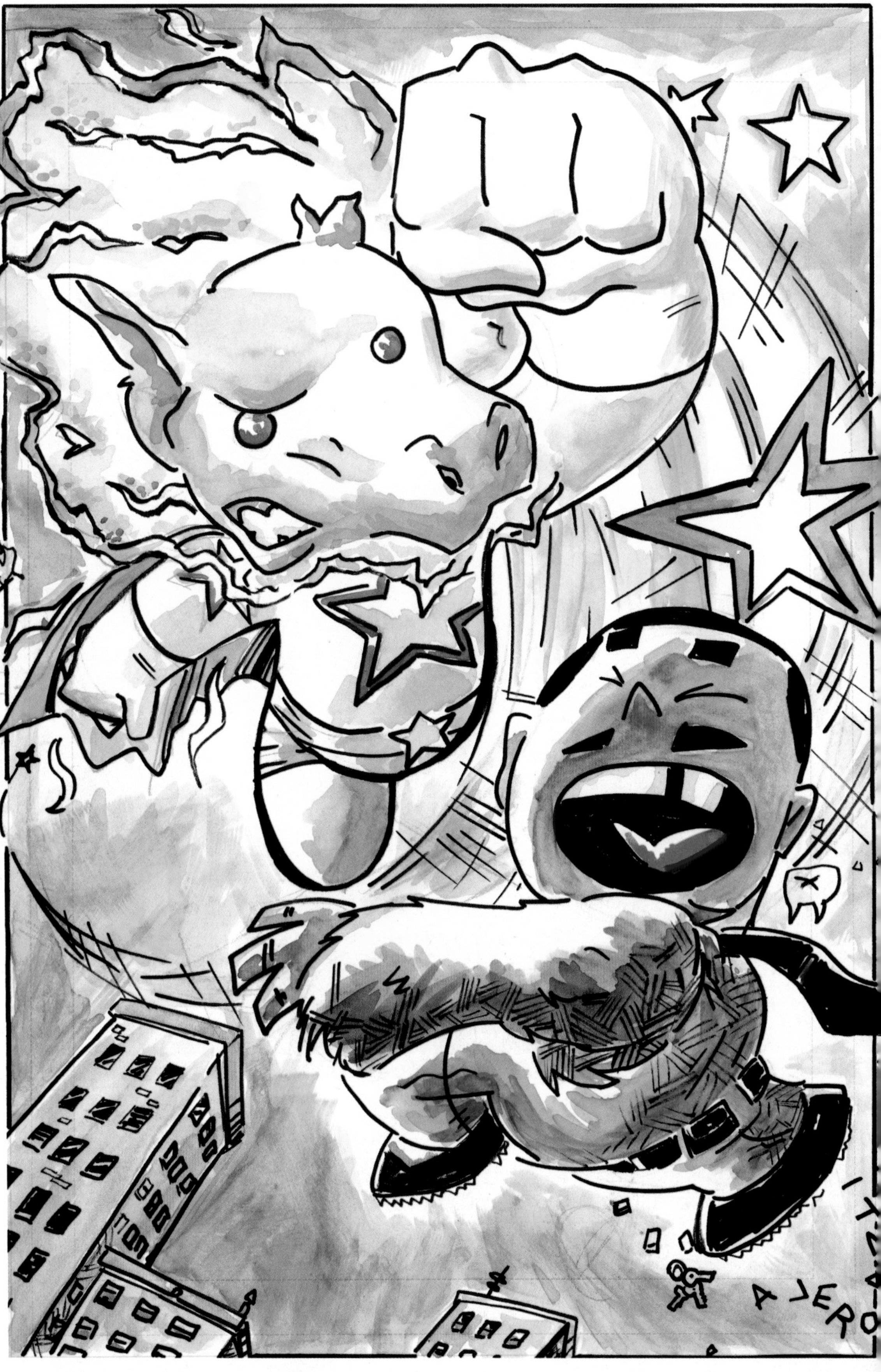
AJERO

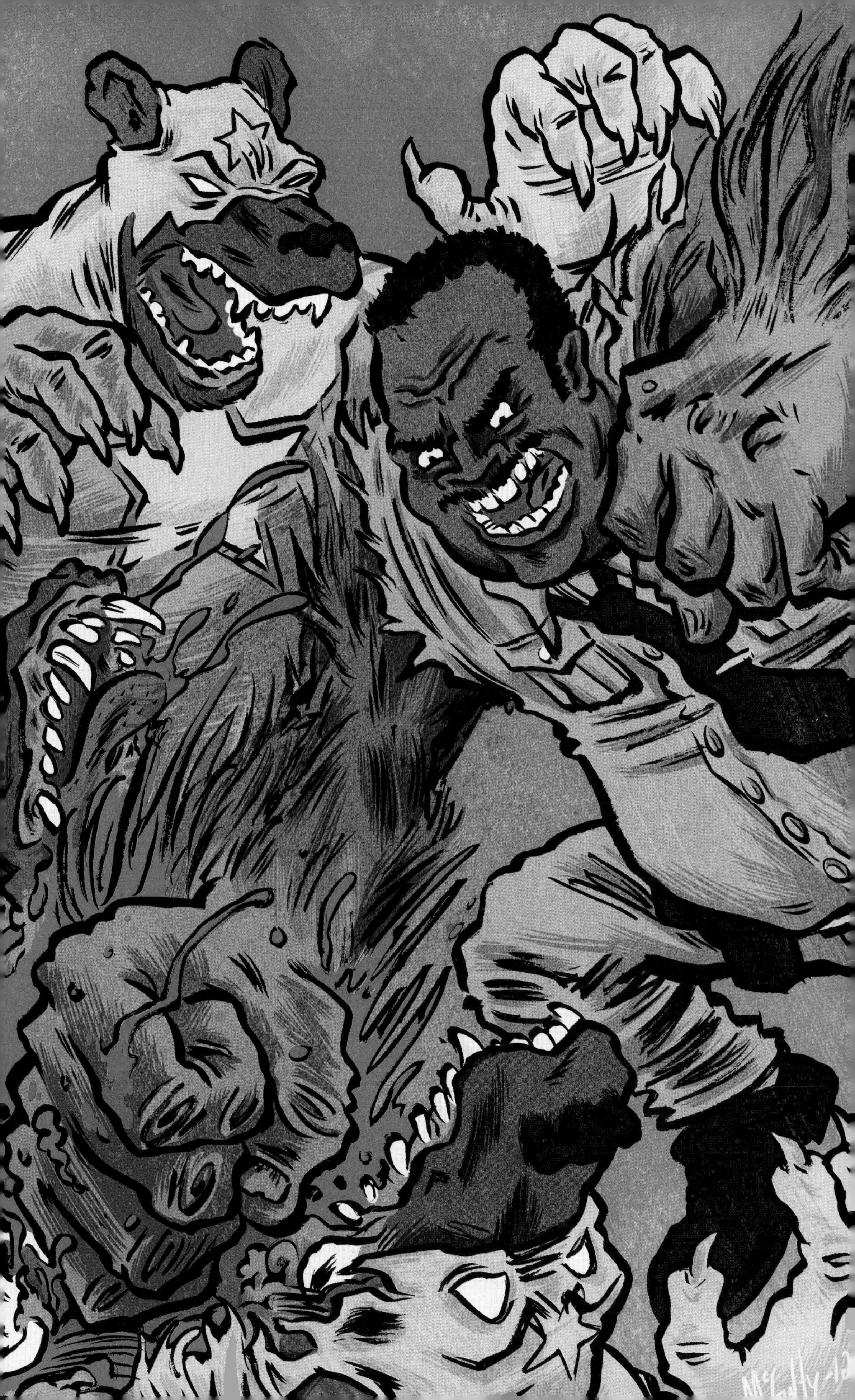

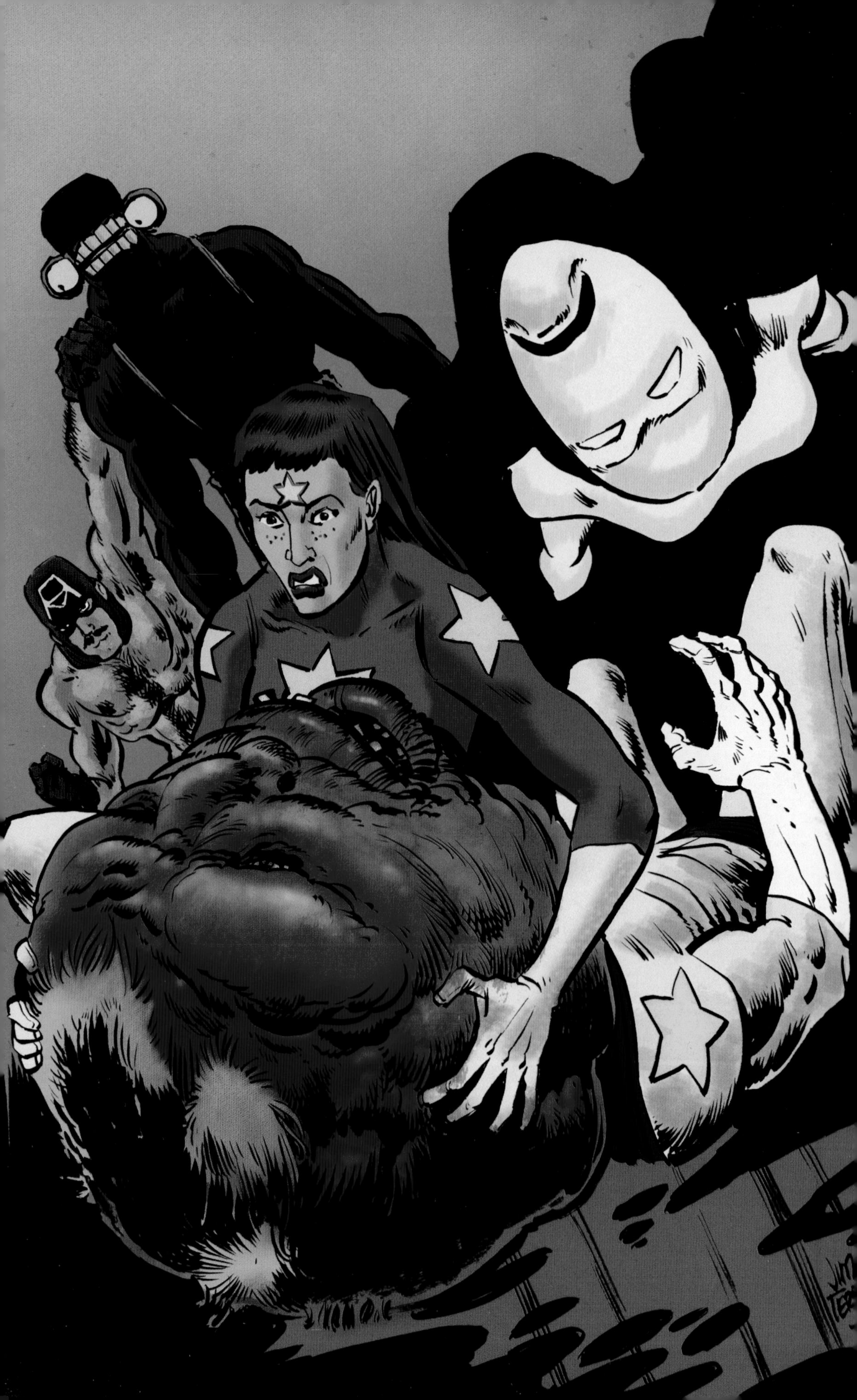

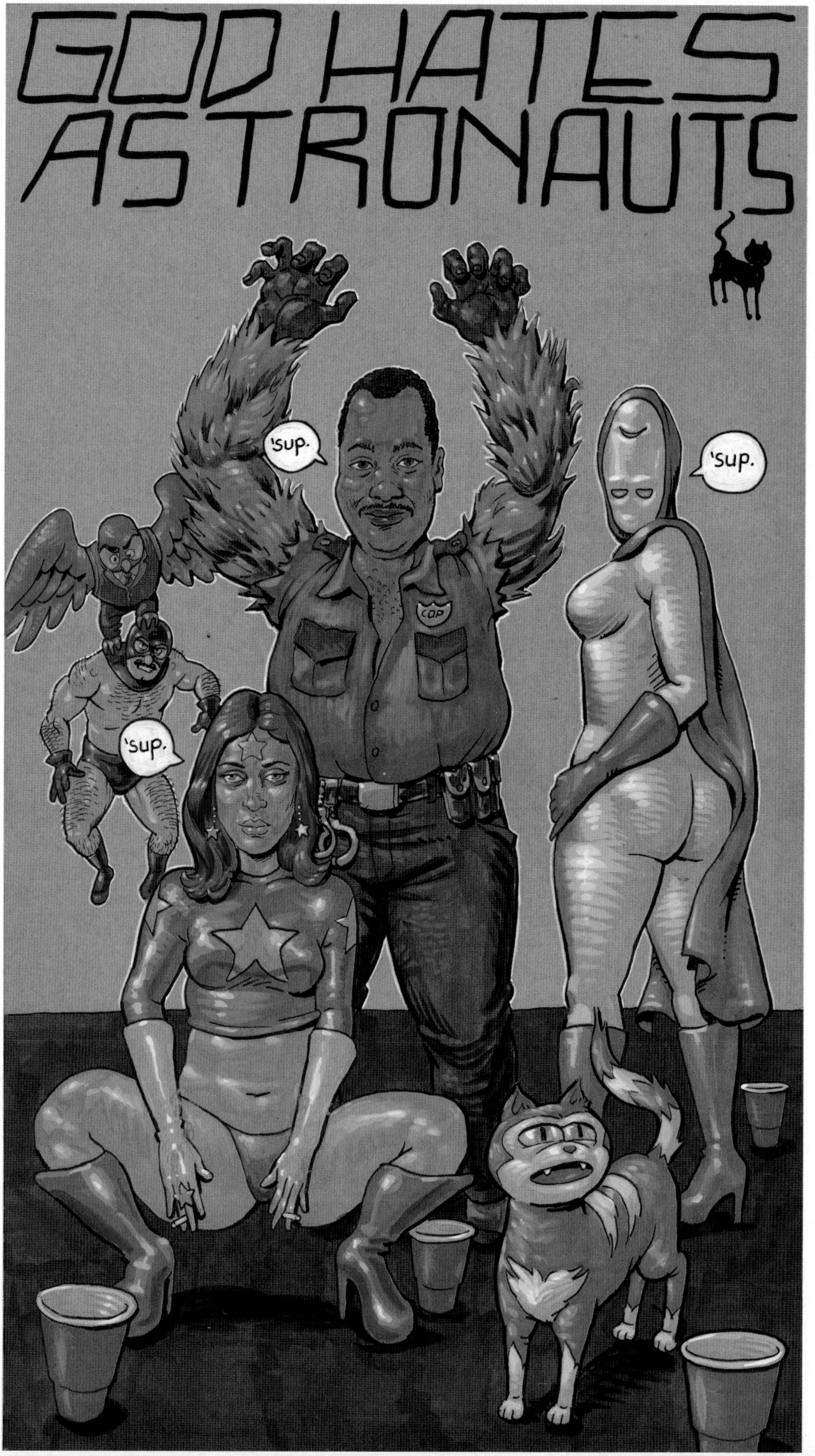
GOD HATES ASTRONAUTS
'sup.
'sup.
'sup.
COP

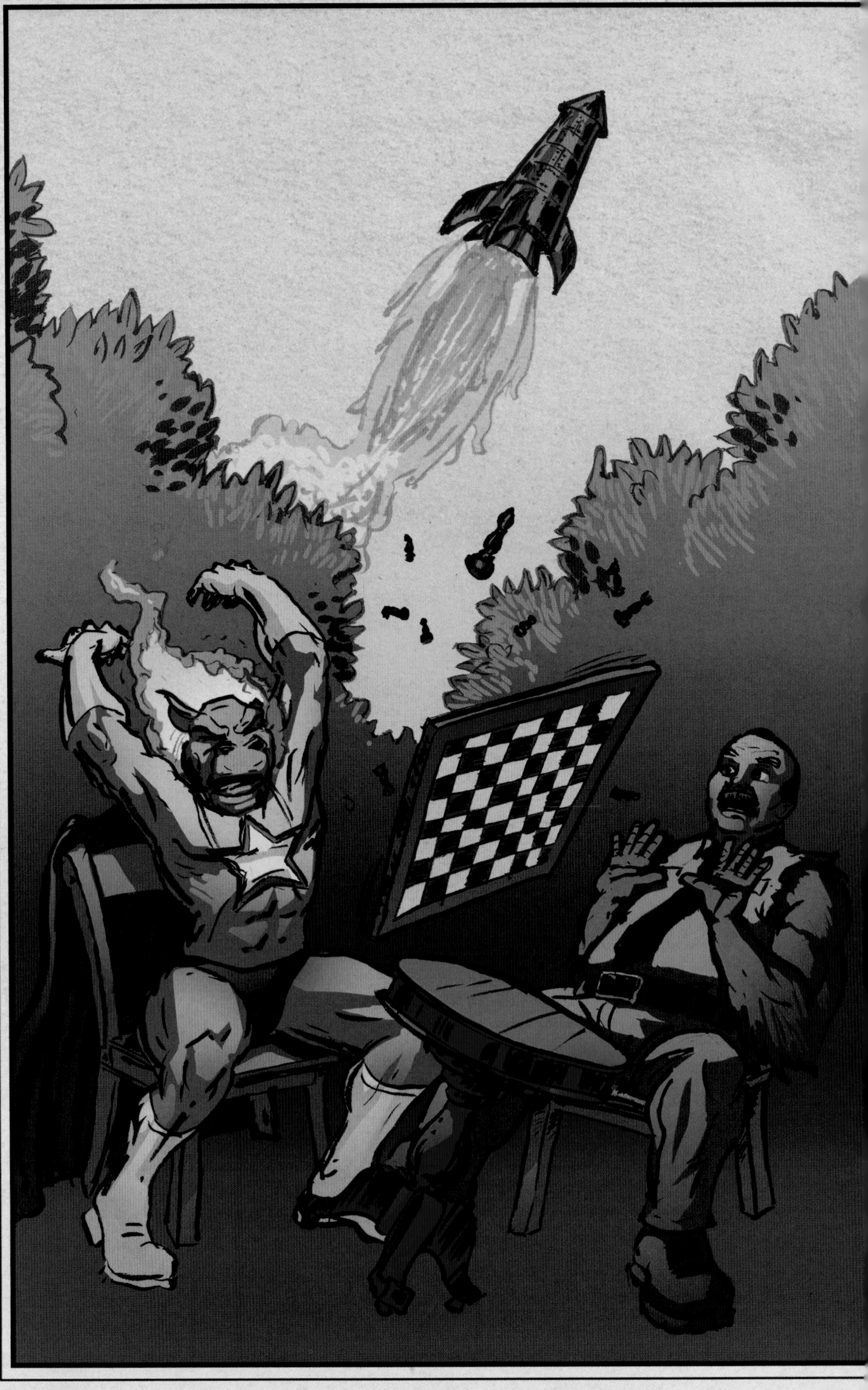

Sunday in the Park with Gnarled

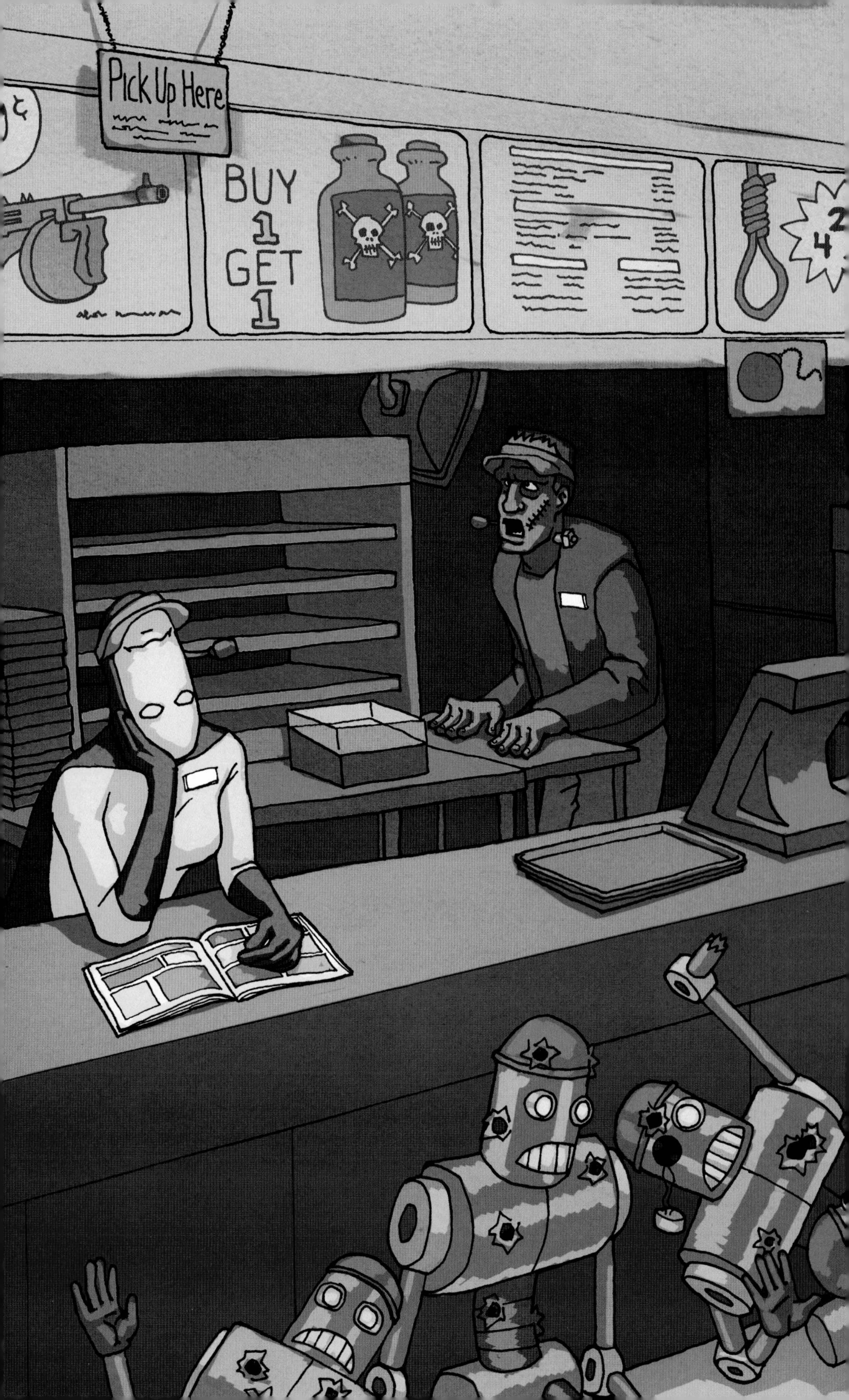
Pick Up Here
BUY
1
GET
1

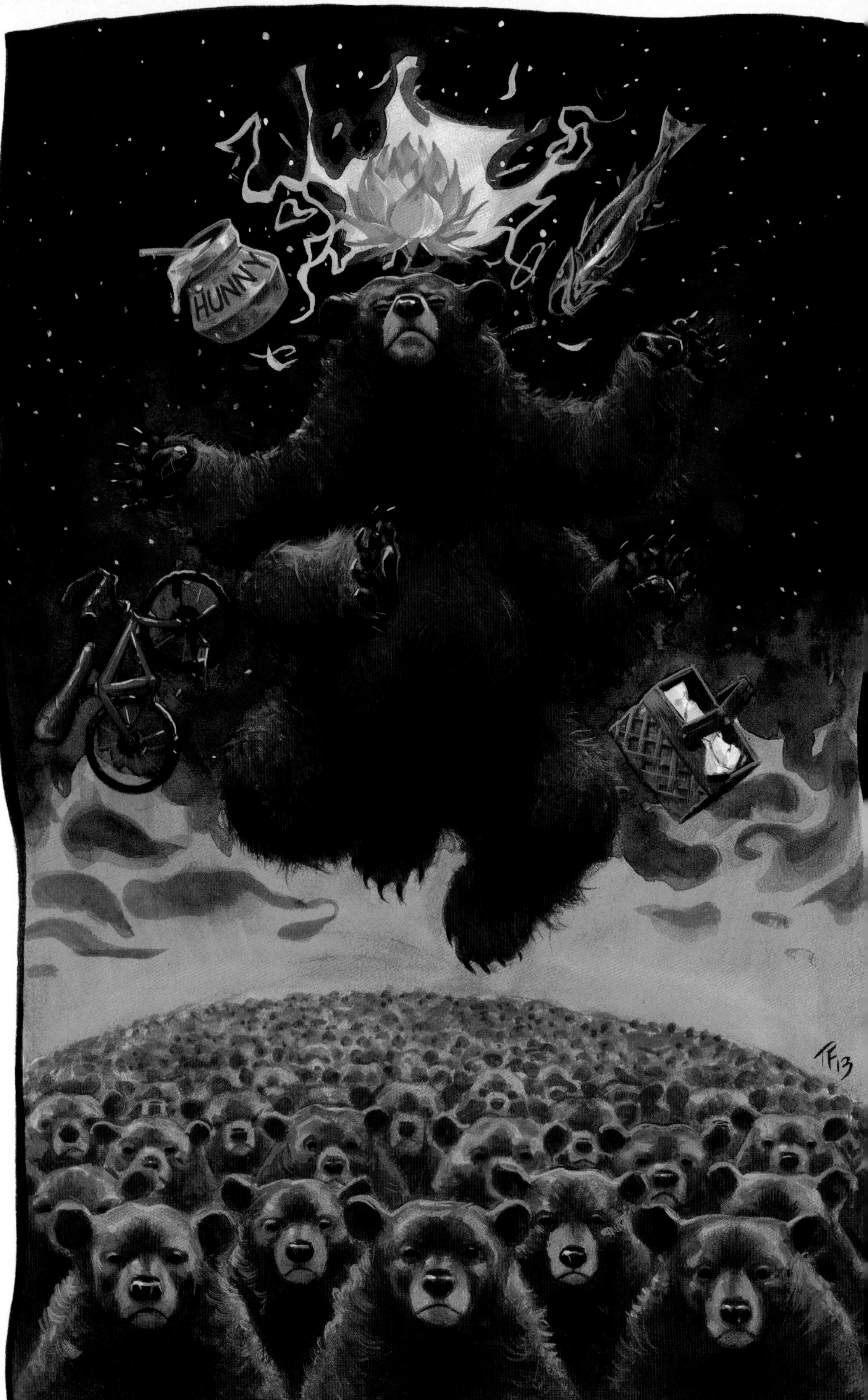
HUNNY
TF13

· BHEARGAVAD GITA ·

THE 24-HOUR COMICS

The following section presents two 24-page, 24-hour comics that take place within the God Hates Astronauts Universe. The 24-hour comic is a challenge created by Scott McCloud to create an entire 24-page comic, a page an hour for 24 hours straight with no pre-planning, breaks or preparation. You just start the clock and you don't stop until you are finished... which is hopefully 24 hours later. A year ago I actually took the principle to make my improv comic *"Blast Furnace: Recreational Thief"* which I created a page a day, five days a week for six months.

The first comic you will see served as a rough draft for what would become God Hates Astronauts. While the art is super rough, I still think it's fun to see the way the story originally started off. There are some fun characters who hit the cutting room floor like "Benda-Girl" and "Steven The Wretched". Also note that "The Impossible" was originally a dude and was named "Mister Improbable".

The second 24-hour comic is one that I did while working on GHA issue two. It explores the owl crime syndicate and introduces a few new characters including "The Shootist." While it doesn't appear in any issues up until now, I've always considered it to be canon within the GHA Universe and I think it serves as an issue zero for the series.

I hope you enjoy and I apologize for making you turn the book sideways to read them. THANKS!

TURN BOOK SIDEWAYS NOW!

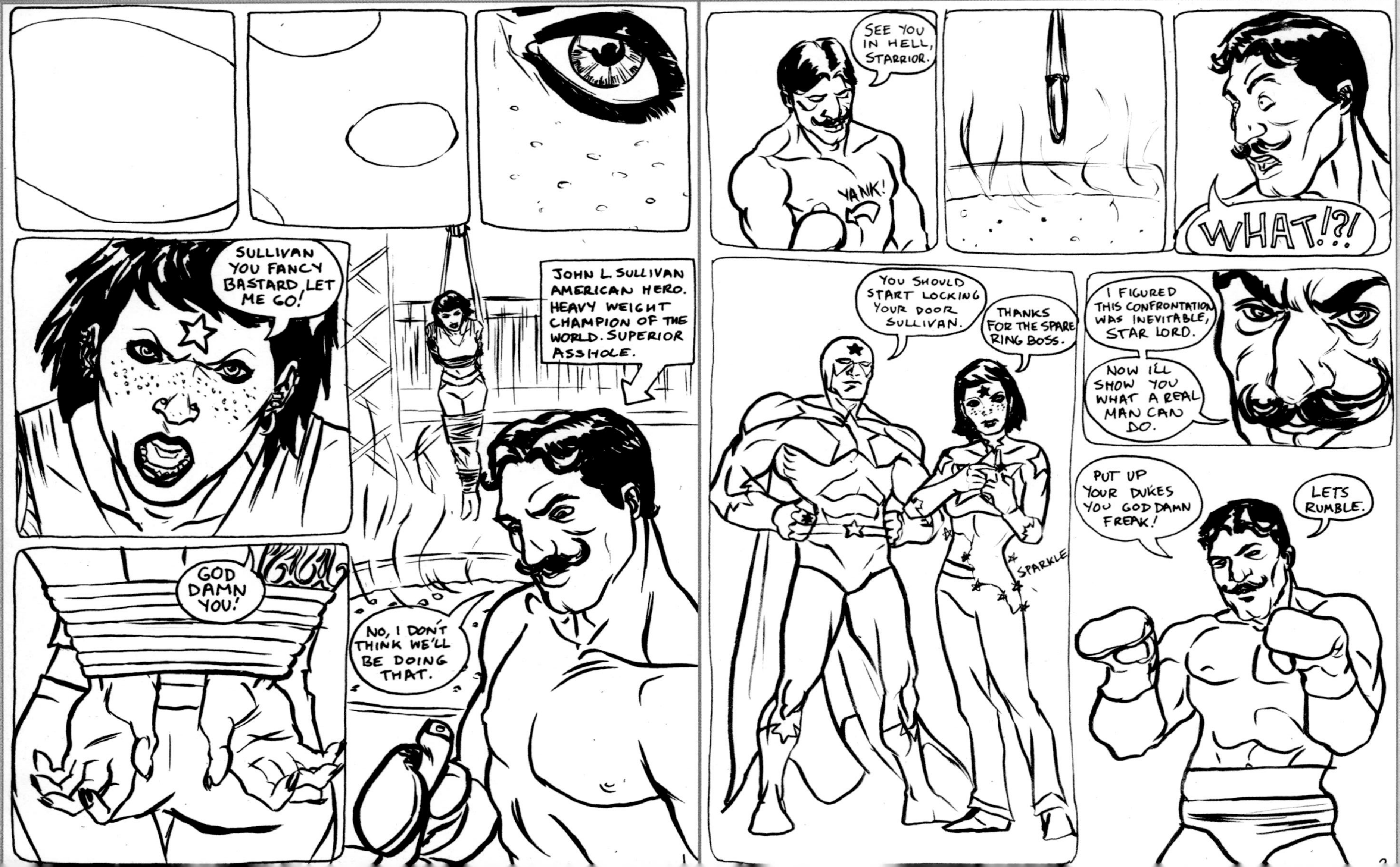
SULLIVAN YOU FANCY BASTARD, LET ME GO!
JOHN L. SULLIVAN AMERICAN HERO. HEAVY WEIGHT CHAMPION OF THE WORLD. SUPERIOR ASSHOLE.
GOD DAMN YOU!
NO, I DON'T THINK WE'LL BE DOING THAT.
1
SEE YOU IN HELL, STARRIOR.
YANK!
WHAT!?!
YOU SHOULD START LOCKING YOUR DOOR SULLIVAN.
THANKS FOR THE SPARE RING BOSS.
SPARKLE
I FIGURED THIS CONFRONTATION WAS INEVITABLE, STAR LORD.
NOW I'LL SHOW YOU WHAT A REAL MAN CAN DO.
PUT UP YOUR DUKES YOU GOD DAMN FREAK!
LETS RUMBLE.
2

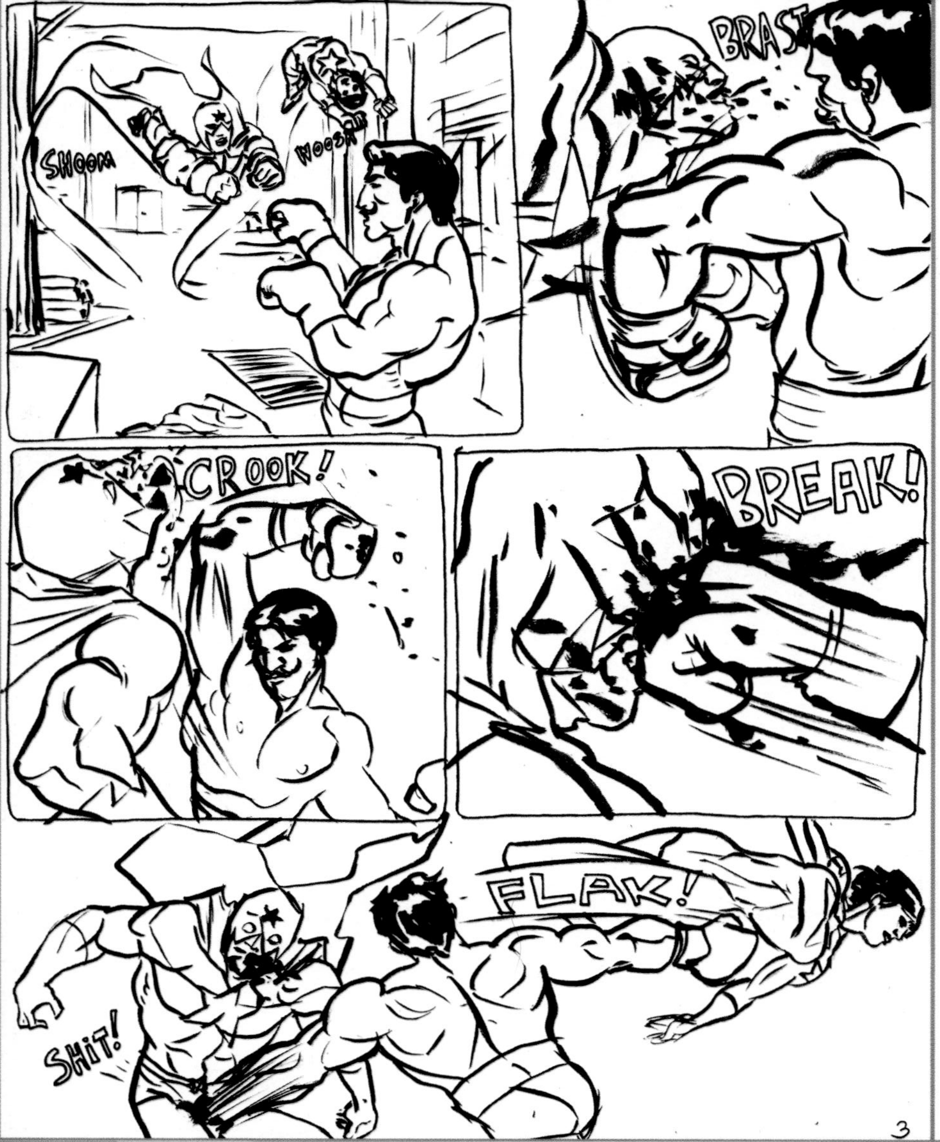
SHOOM
WOOSH
BRAST
CROOK!
BREAK!
FLAK!
SHIT!

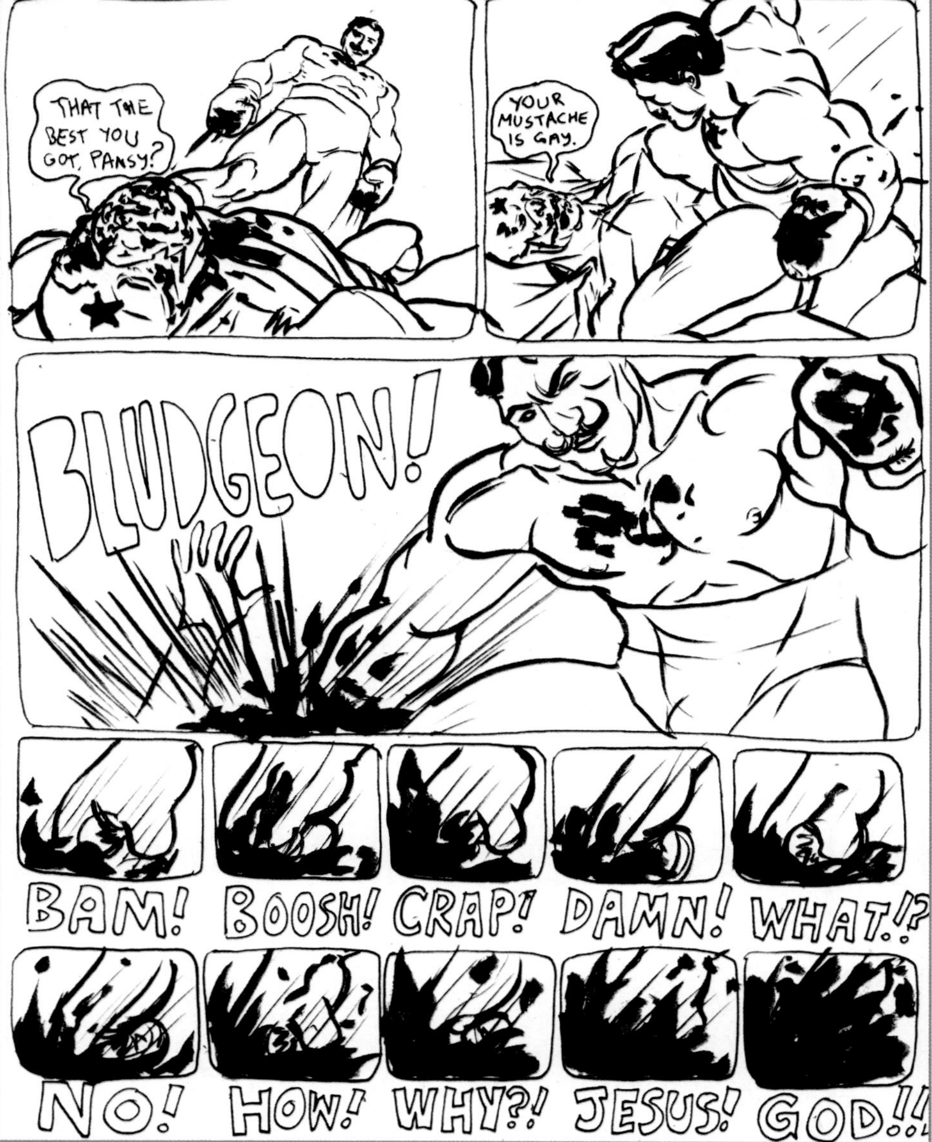
THAT THE BEST YOU GOT, PANSY?
YOUR MUSTACHE IS GAY.
BLUDGEON!
BAM!
BOOSH!
CRAP!
DAMN!
WHAT!?
NO!
HOW!
WHY?!
JESUS!
GOD!!

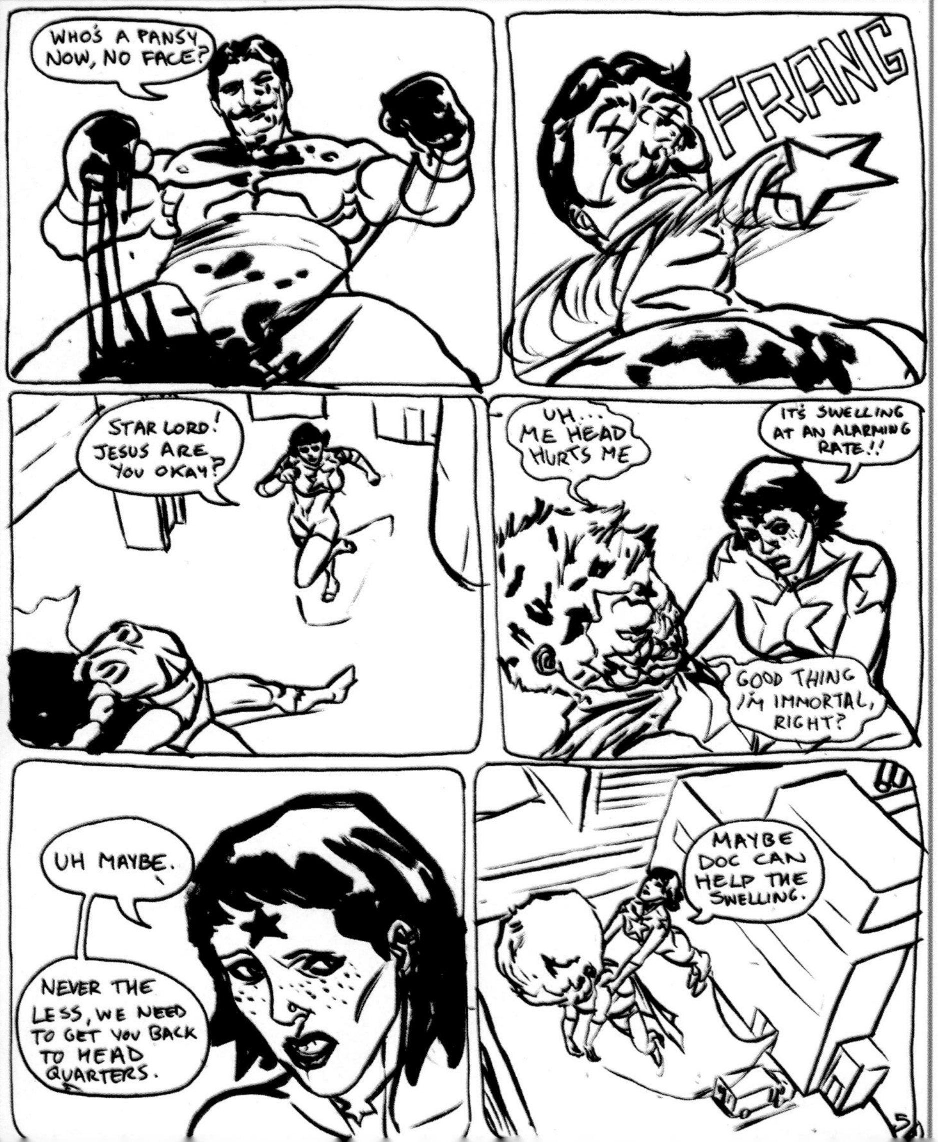
WHO'S A PANSY NOW, NO FACE?
FRANG
STAR LORD! JESUS ARE YOU OKAY?
UH... ME HEAD HURTS ME
IT'S SWELLING AT AN ALARMING RATE!!
GOOD THING I'M IMMORTAL, RIGHT?
UH MAYBE.
NEVER THE LESS, WE NEED TO GET YOU BACK TO HEAD QUARTERS.
MAYBE DOC CAN HELP THE SWELLING.

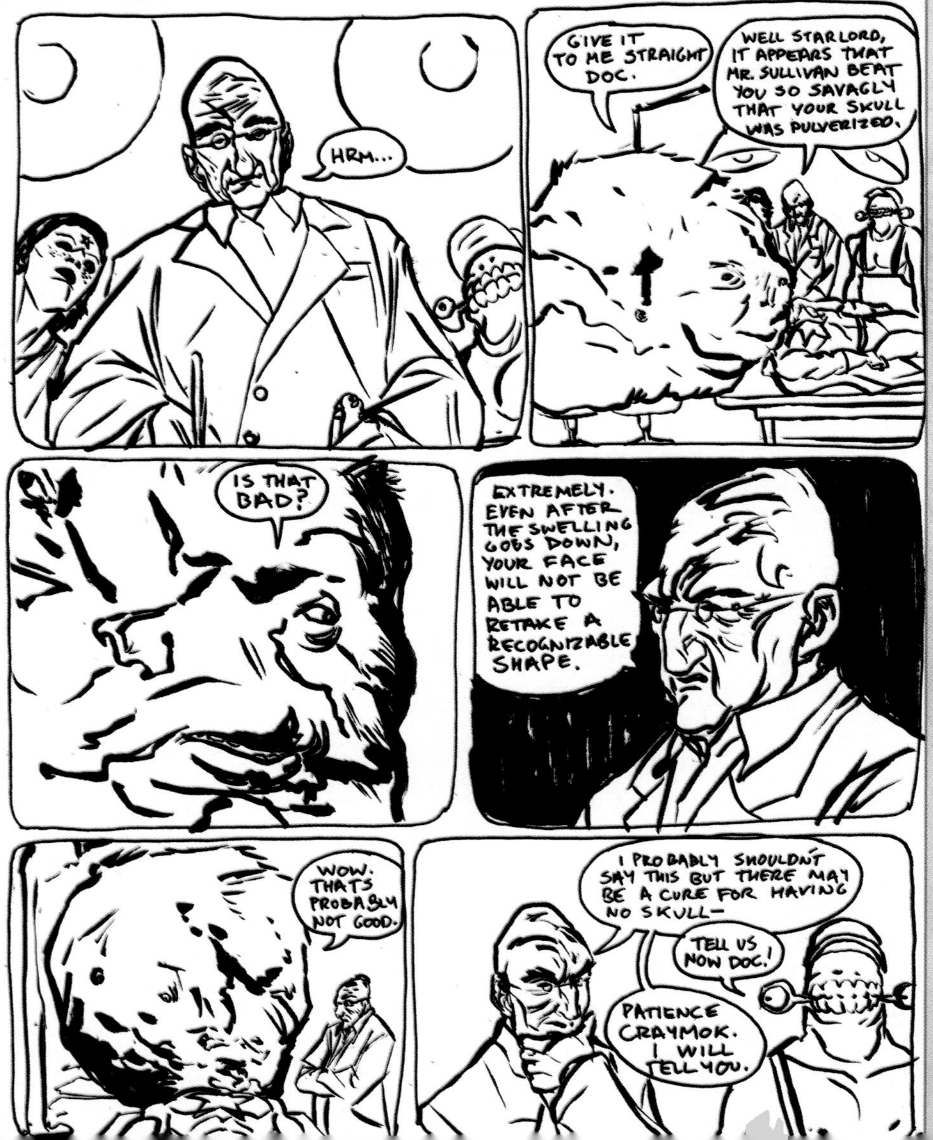
HRM...
GIVE IT TO ME STRAIGHT DOC.
WELL STARLORD, IT APPEARS THAT MR. SULLIVAN BEAT YOU SO SAVAGLY THAT YOUR SKULL WAS PULVERIZED.
IS THAT BAD?
EXTREMELY. EVEN AFTER THE SWELLING GOES DOWN, YOUR FACE WILL NOT BE ABLE TO RETAKE A RECOGNIZABLE SHAPE.
WOW. THATS PROBABLY NOT GOOD.
I PROBABLY SHOULDN'T SAY THIS BUT THERE MAY BE A CURE FOR HAVING NO SKULL—
TELL US NOW DOC.!
PATIENCE CRAYMOK. I WILL TELL YOU.

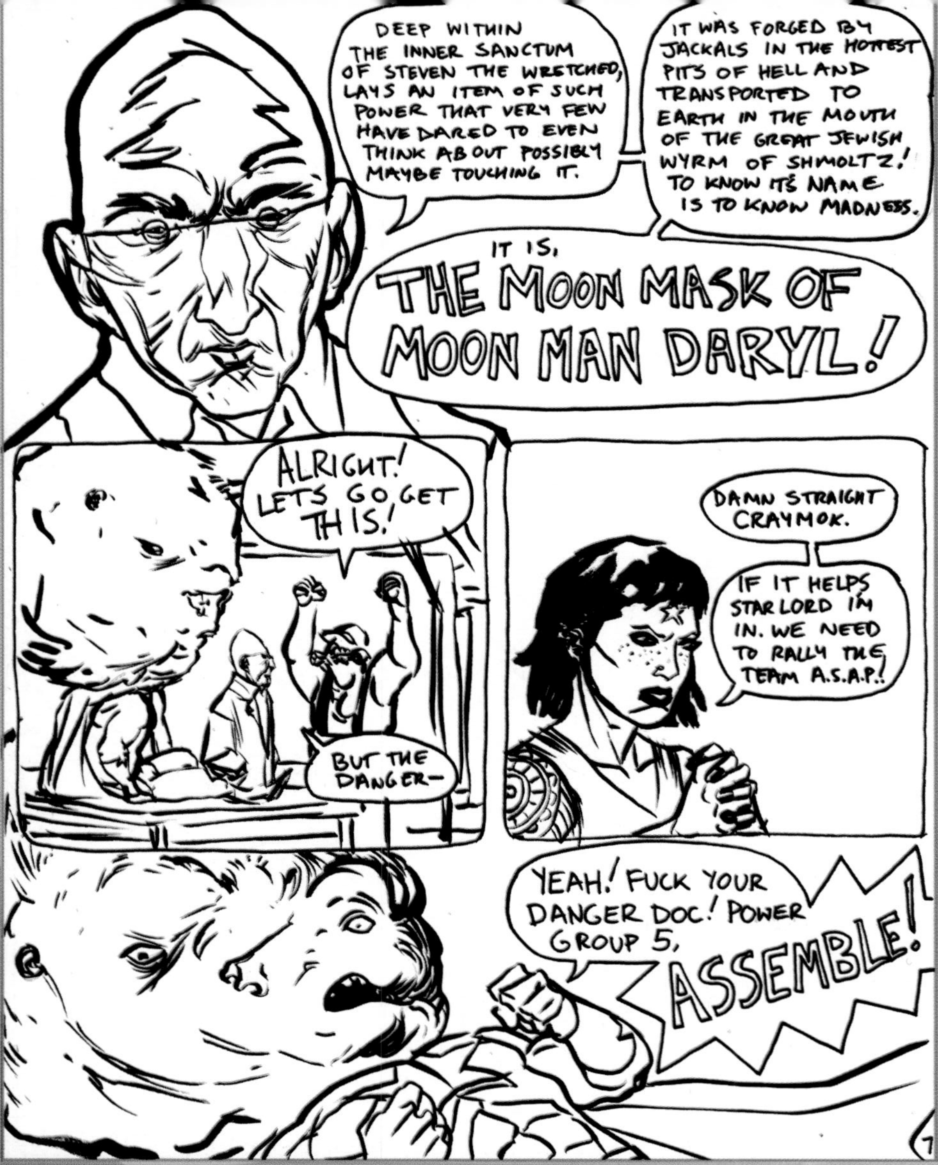
DEEP WITHIN THE INNER SANCTUM OF STEVEN THE WRETCHED, LAYS AN ITEM OF SUCH POWER THAT VERY FEW HAVE DARED TO EVEN THINK ABOUT POSSIBLY MAYBE TOUCHING IT.
IT WAS FORGED BY JACKALS IN THE HOTTEST PITS OF HELL AND TRANSPORTED TO EARTH IN THE MOUTH OF THE GREAT JEWISH WYRM OF SHMOLTZ! TO KNOW ITS NAME IS TO KNOW MADNESS.
IT IS, THE MOON MASK OF MOON MAN DARYL!
ALRIGHT! LETS GO GET THIS!
BUT THE DANGER–
DAMN STRAIGHT CRAYMOK.
IF IT HELPS STARLORD IM IN. WE NEED TO RALLY THE TEAM A.S.A.P.!
YEAH! FUCK YOUR DANGER DOC! POWER GROUP 5, ASSEMBLE!

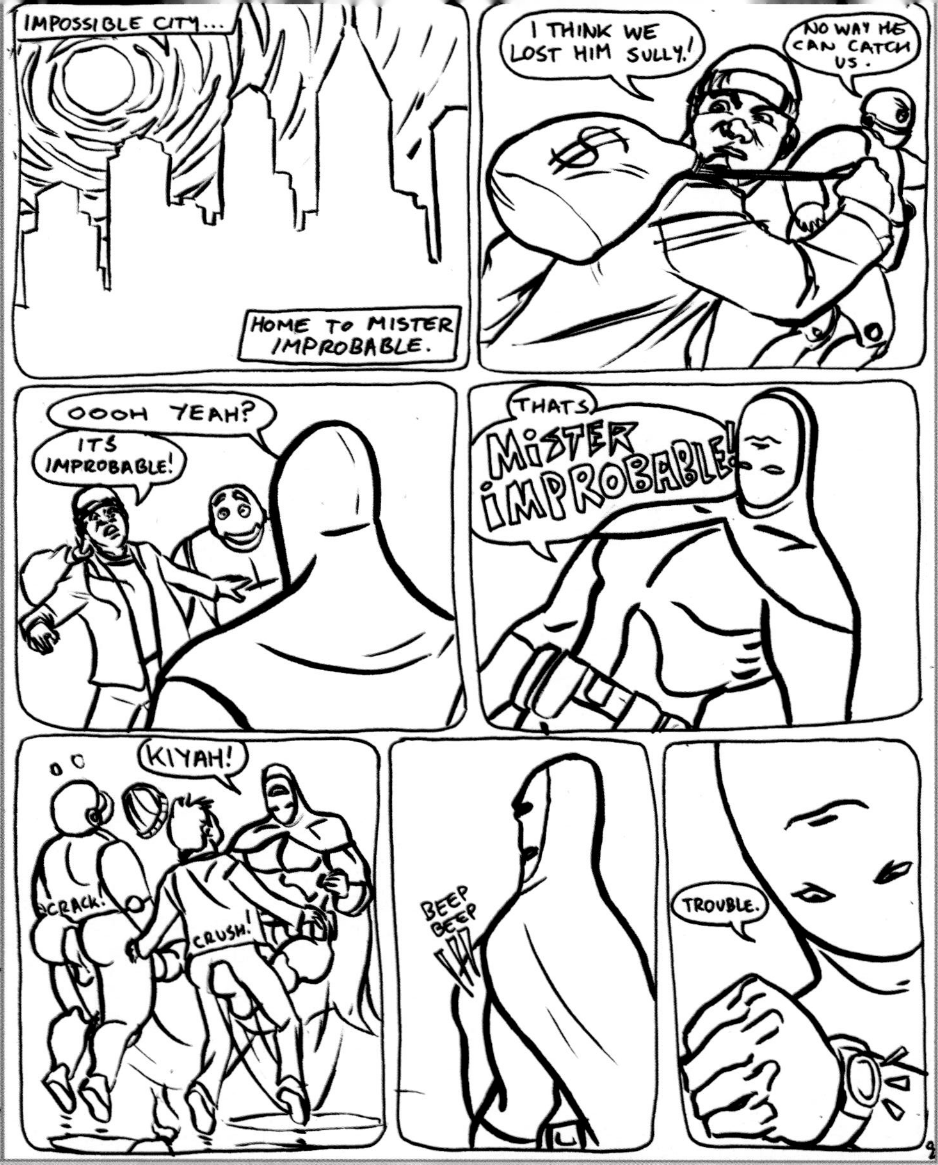
IMPOSSIBLE CITY...
HOME TO MISTER IMPROBABLE.
I THINK WE LOST HIM SULLY!
NO WAY HE CAN CATCH US.
OOOH YEAH?
ITS IMPROBABLE!
THATS MISTER IMPROBABLE!
KIYAH!
CRACK!
CRUSH!
BEEP BEEP
TROUBLE.

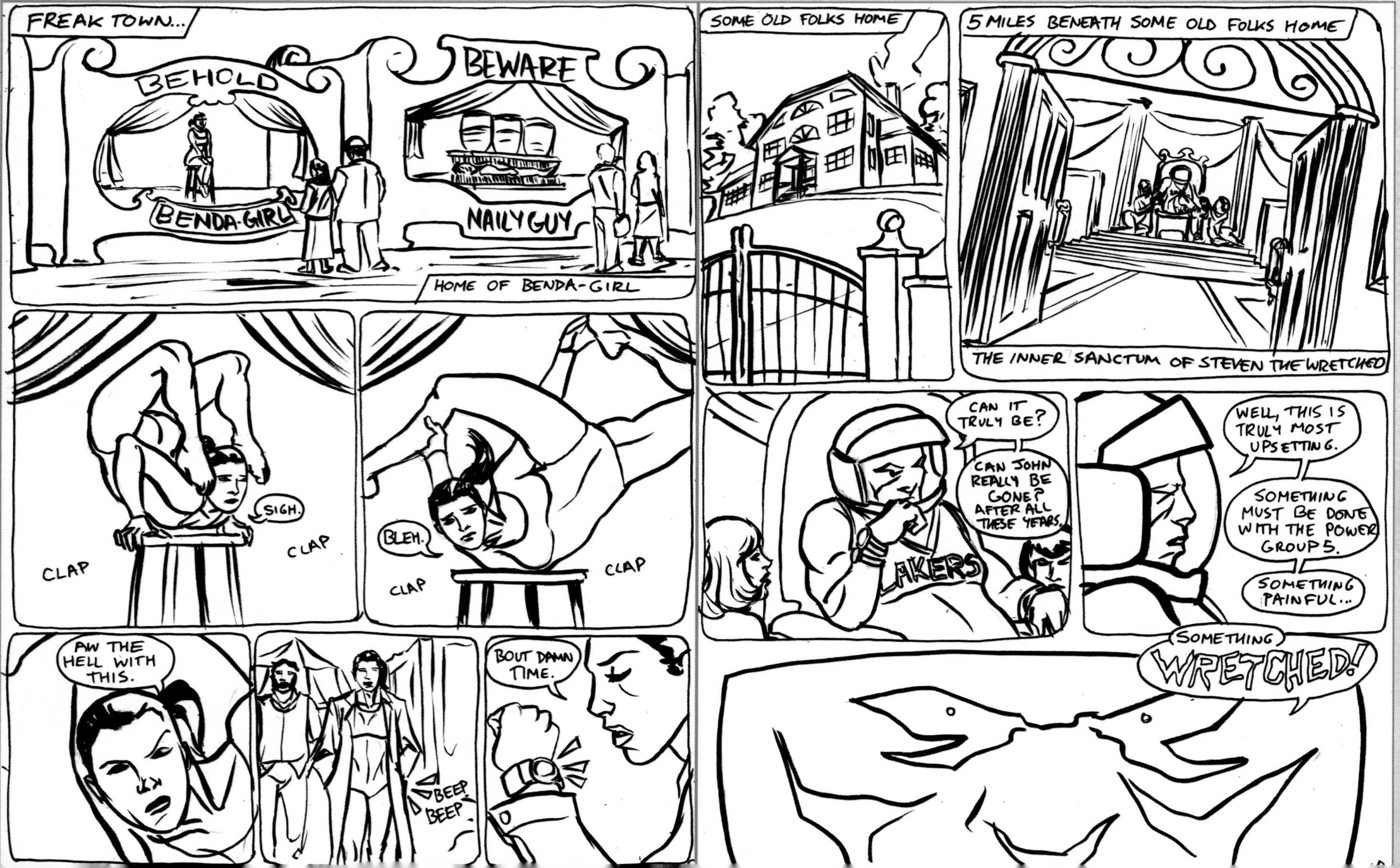
FREAK TOWN...
BEHOLD
BENDA-GIRL
BEWARE
NAILYGUY
HOME OF BENDA-GIRL
SIGH.
CLAP
CLAP
BLEH.
CLAP
CLAP
AW THE HELL WITH THIS.
BEEP. BEEP.
BOUT DAMN TIME.
SOME OLD FOLKS HOME
5 MILES BENEATH SOME OLD FOLKS HOME
THE INNER SANCTUM OF STEVEN THE WRETCHED
CAN IT TRULY BE?
CAN JOHN REALLY BE GONE? AFTER ALL THESE YEARS.
LAKERS
WELL, THIS IS TRULY MOST UPSETTING.
SOMETHING MUST BE DONE WITH THE POWER GROUP 5.
SOMETHING PAINFUL...
SOMETHING
WRETCHED!

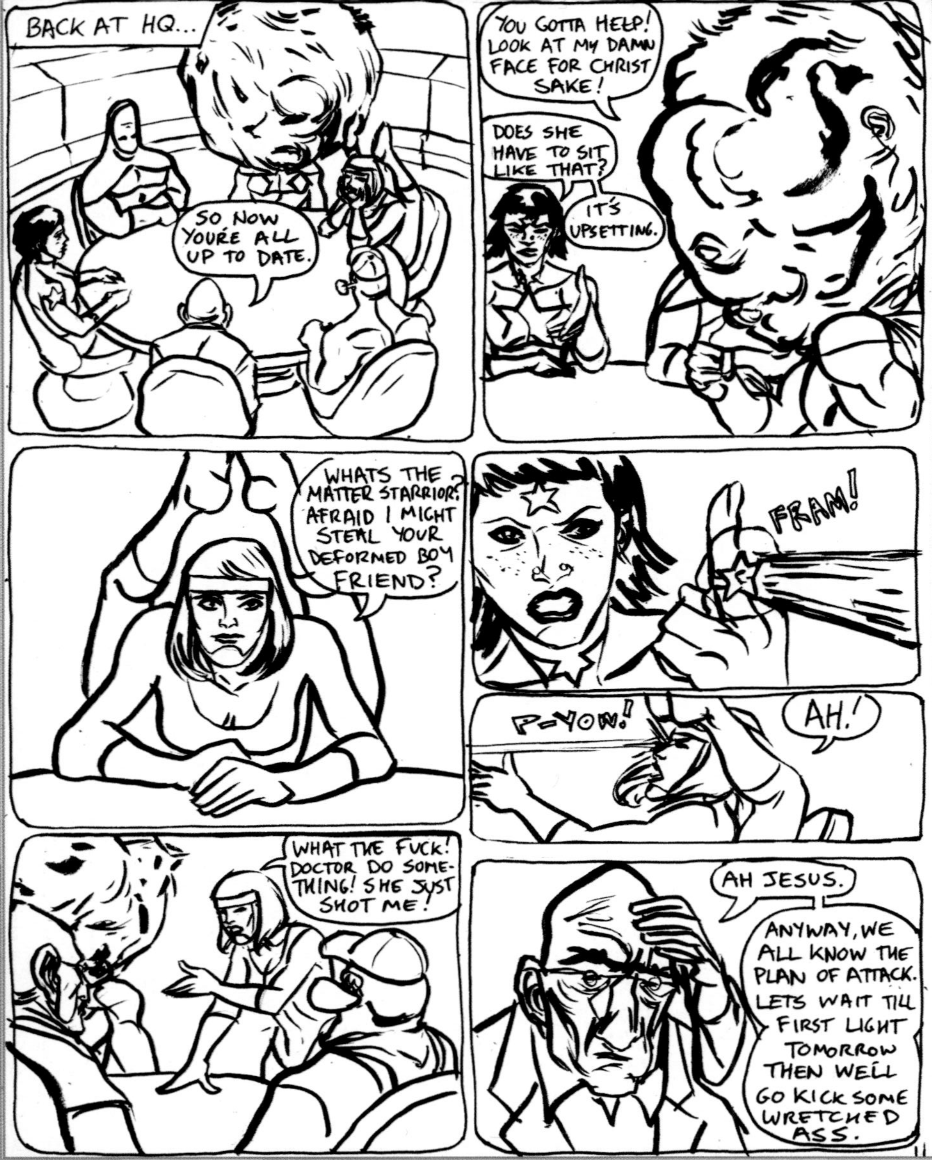

BACK AT HQ...
SO NOW YOU'RE ALL UP TO DATE.
YOU GOTTA HELP! LOOK AT MY DAMN FACE FOR CHRIST SAKE!
DOES SHE HAVE TO SIT LIKE THAT?
IT'S UPSETTING.
WHATS THE MATTER STARRIOR? AFRAID I MIGHT STEAL YOUR DEFORMED BOY FRIEND?
FRAM!
P-YOW!
AH!
WHAT THE FUCK! DOCTOR DO SOME-THING! SHE JUST SHOT ME!
AH JESUS.
ANYWAY, WE ALL KNOW THE PLAN OF ATTACK. LETS WAIT TILL FIRST LIGHT TOMORROW THEN WE'LL GO KICK SOME WRETCHED ASS.
11

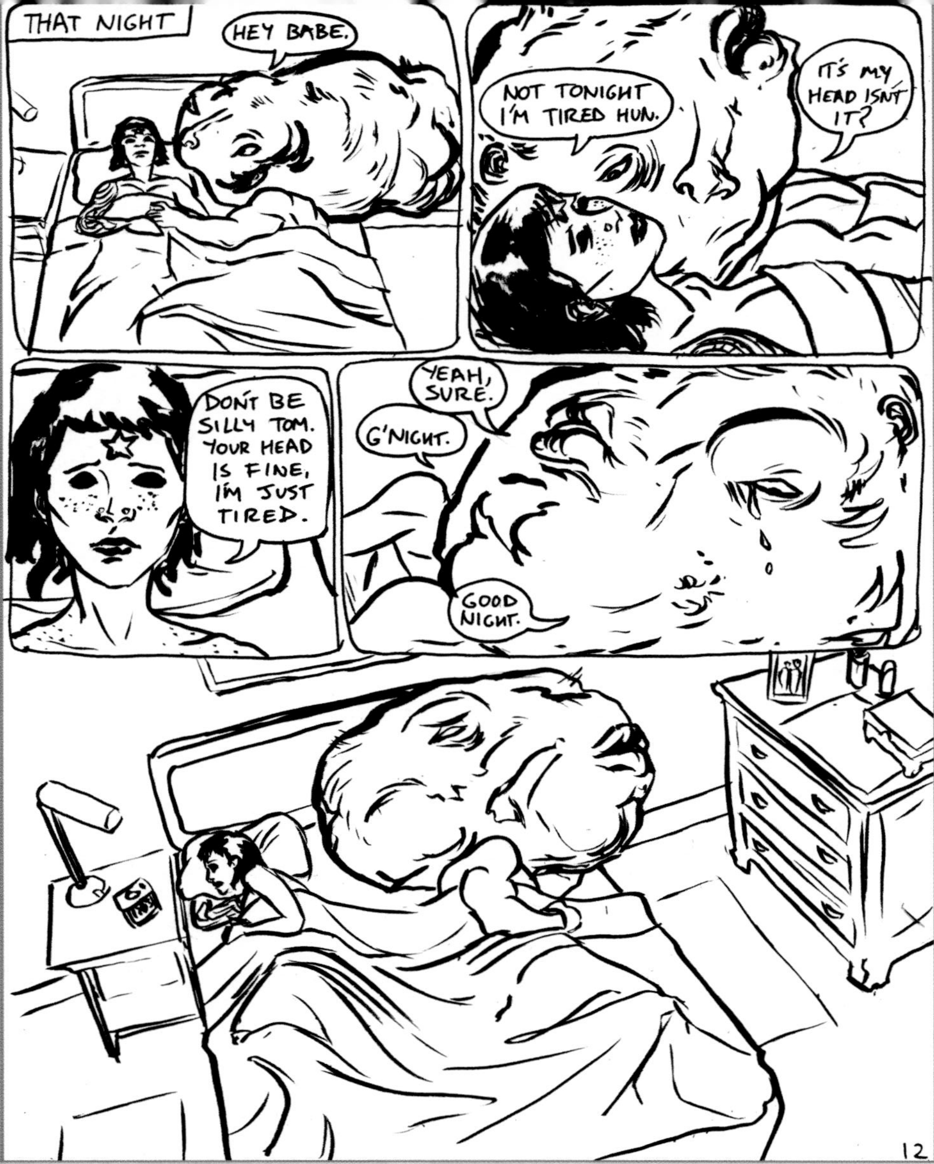

THAT NIGHT
HEY BABE.
NOT TONIGHT I'M TIRED HUN.
IT'S MY HEAD ISN'T IT?
DON'T BE SILLY TOM. YOUR HEAD IS FINE, I'M JUST TIRED.
YEAH, SURE.
G'NIGHT.
GOOD NIGHT.

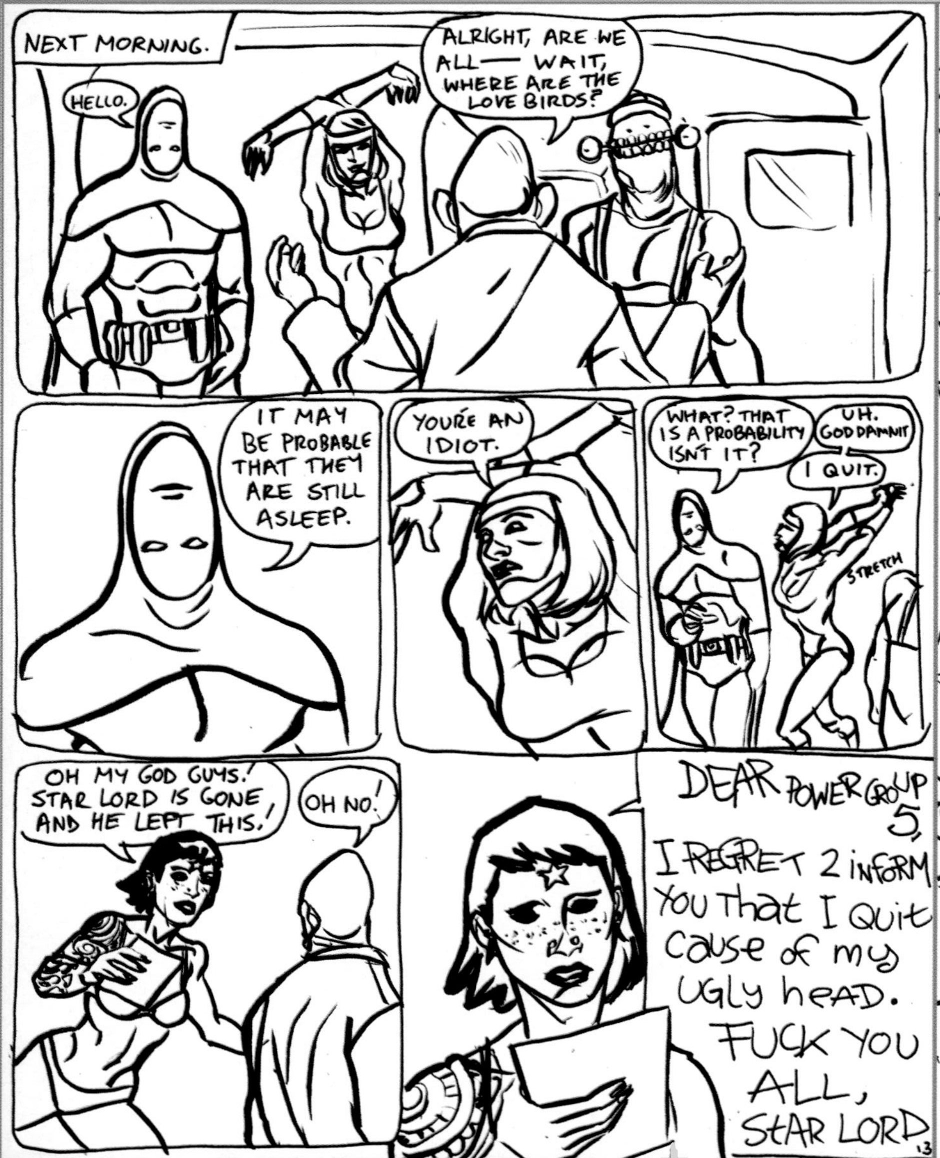
NEXT MORNING.
HELLO.
ALRIGHT, ARE WE ALL— WAIT, WHERE ARE THE LOVE BIRDS?
IT MAY BE PROBABLE THAT THEY ARE STILL ASLEEP.
YOU'RE AN IDIOT.
WHAT? THAT IS A PROBABILITY ISN'T IT?
UH. GODDAMNIT
I QUIT.
STRETCH
OH MY GOD GUYS! STAR LORD IS GONE AND HE LEFT THIS!
OH NO!
DEAR POWER GROUP 5,
I REGRET 2 INFORM YOU THAT I QUIT CAUSE OF MY UGLY HEAD.
FUCK YOU ALL,
STAR LORD

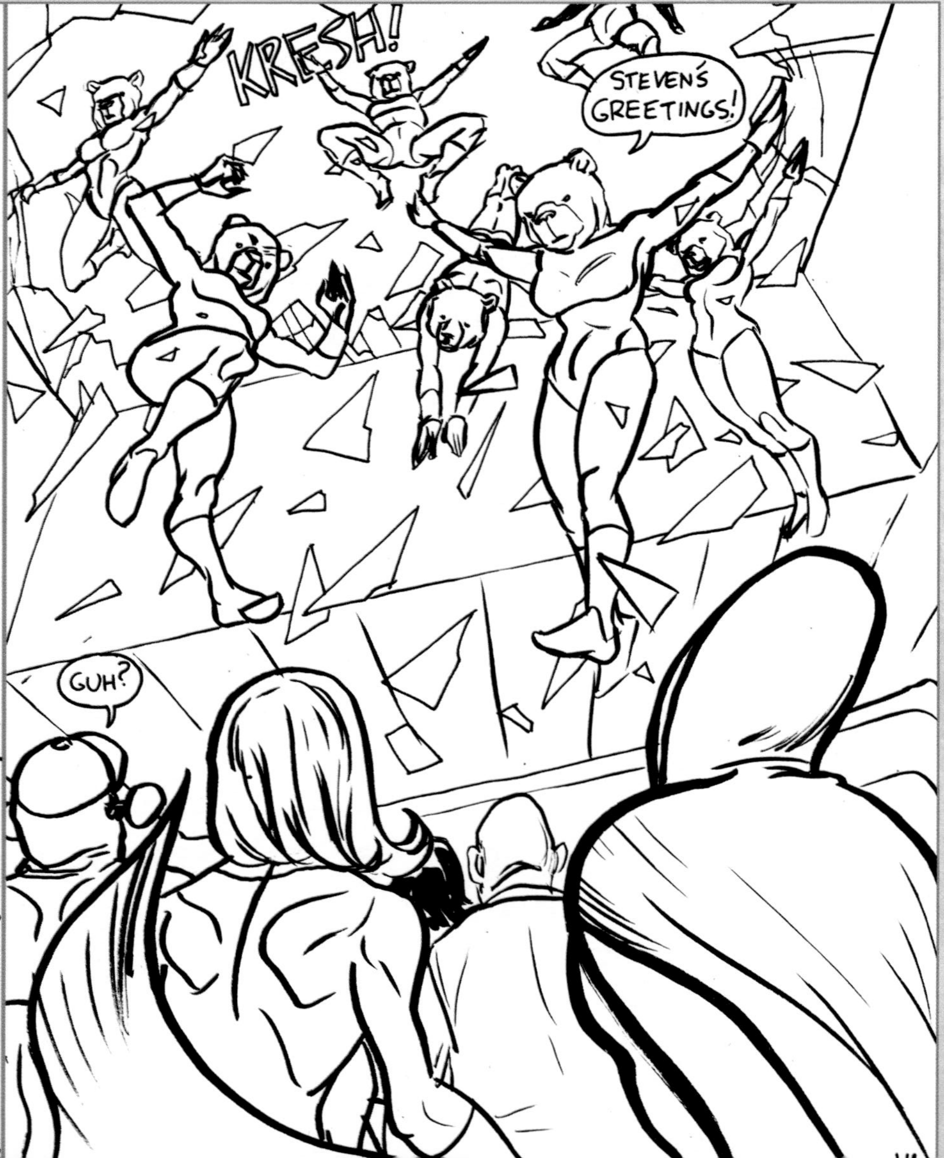
KRESH!
STEVEN'S GREETINGS!
GUH?

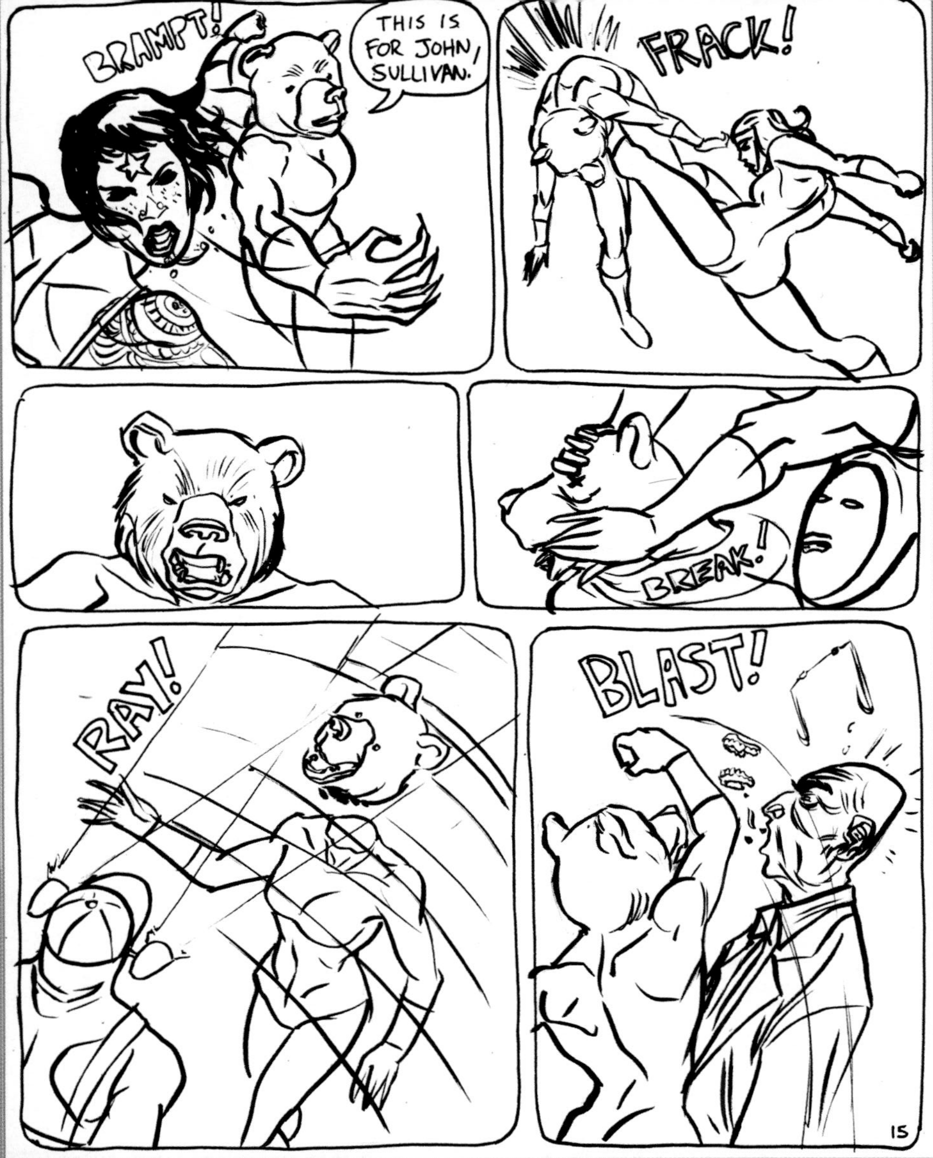
BRAMPT!
THIS IS FOR JOHN SULLIVAN.
FRACK!
BREAK!
RAY!
BLAST!

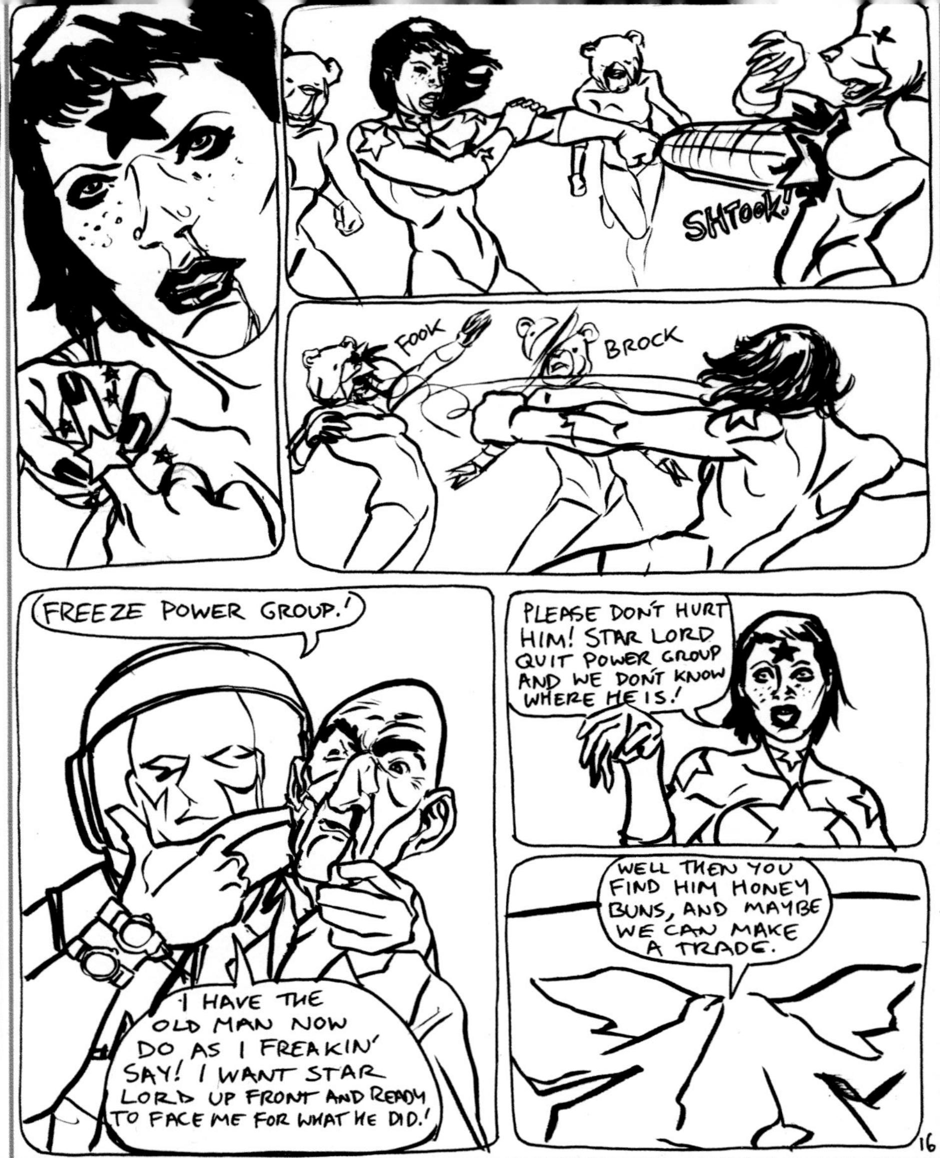
SHTOOK!
FOOK
BROCK
FREEZE POWER GROUP.!
I HAVE THE OLD MAN NOW DO AS I FREAKIN' SAY! I WANT STAR LORD UP FRONT AND READY TO FACE ME FOR WHAT HE DID.!
PLEASE DON'T HURT HIM! STAR LORD QUIT POWER GROUP AND WE DON'T KNOW WHERE HE IS!
WELL THEN YOU FIND HIM HONEY BUNS, AND MAYBE WE CAN MAKE A TRADE.

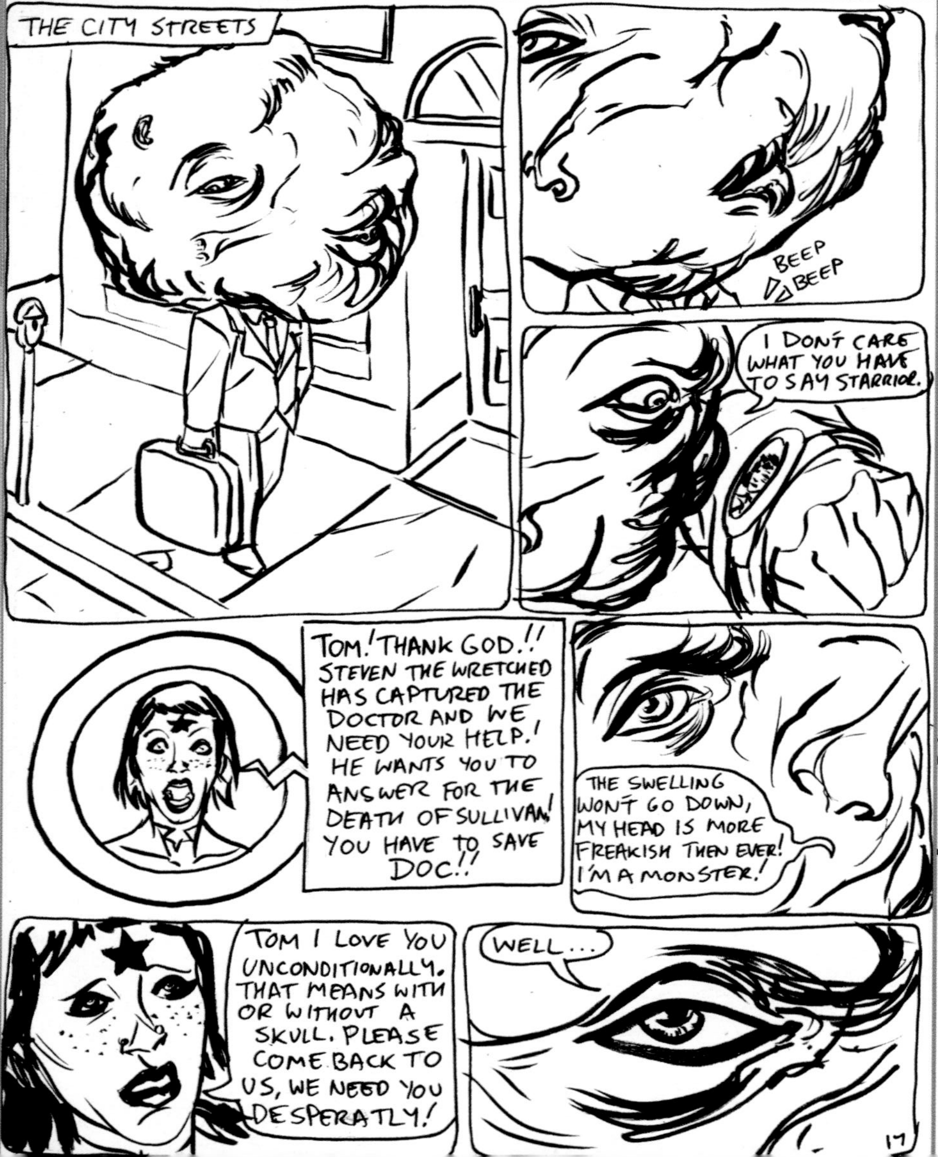
THE CITY STREETS
BEEP BEEP
I DON'T CARE WHAT YOU HAVE TO SAY STARRIOR.
TOM! THANK GOD.!! STEVEN THE WRETCHED HAS CAPTURED THE DOCTOR AND WE NEED YOUR HELP.! HE WANTS YOU TO ANSWER FOR THE DEATH OF SULLIVAN! YOU HAVE TO SAVE DOC.!!
THE SWELLING WON'T GO DOWN, MY HEAD IS MORE FREAKISH THEN EVER! I'M A MONSTER!
TOM I LOVE YOU UNCONDITIONALLY. THAT MEANS WITH OR WITHOUT A SKULL. PLEASE COME BACK TO US, WE NEED YOU DESPERATLY!
WELL...

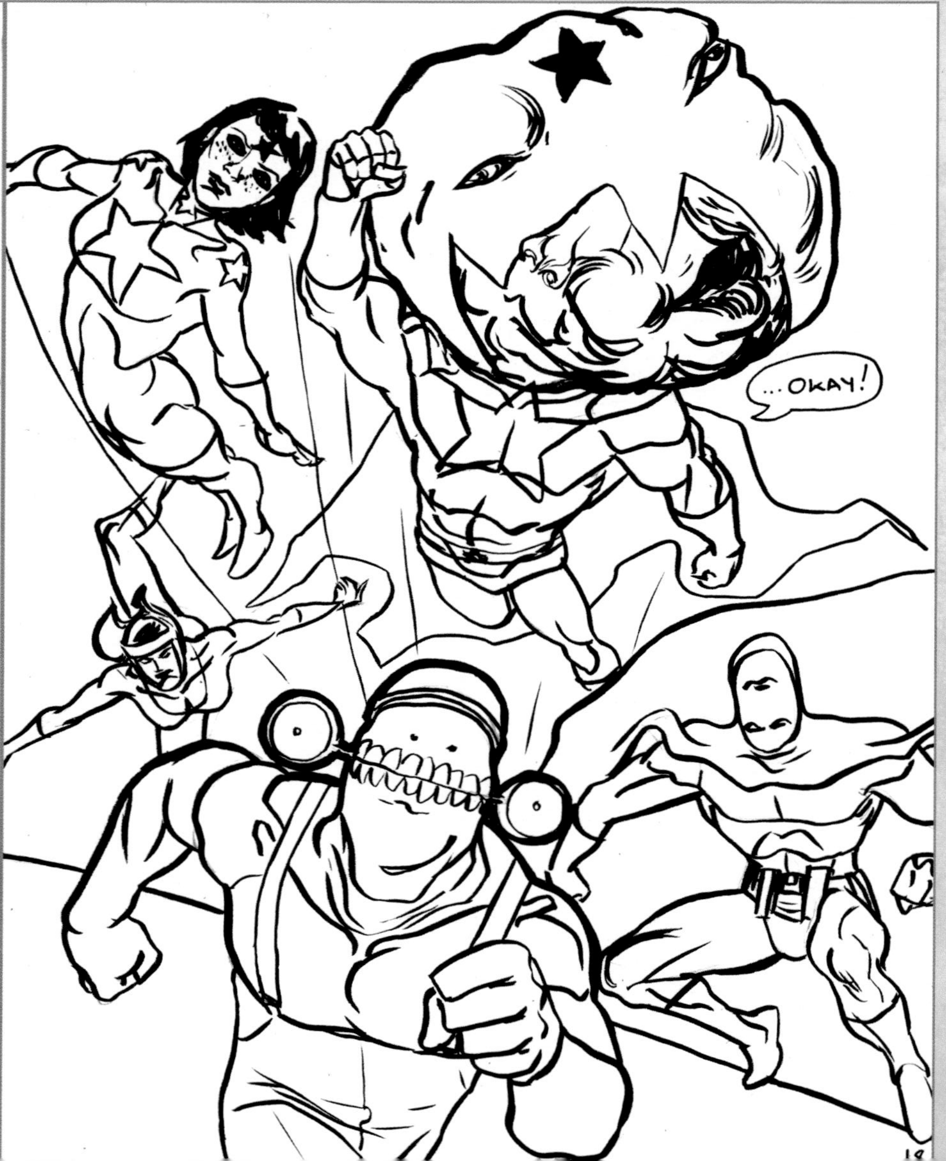
...OKAY!

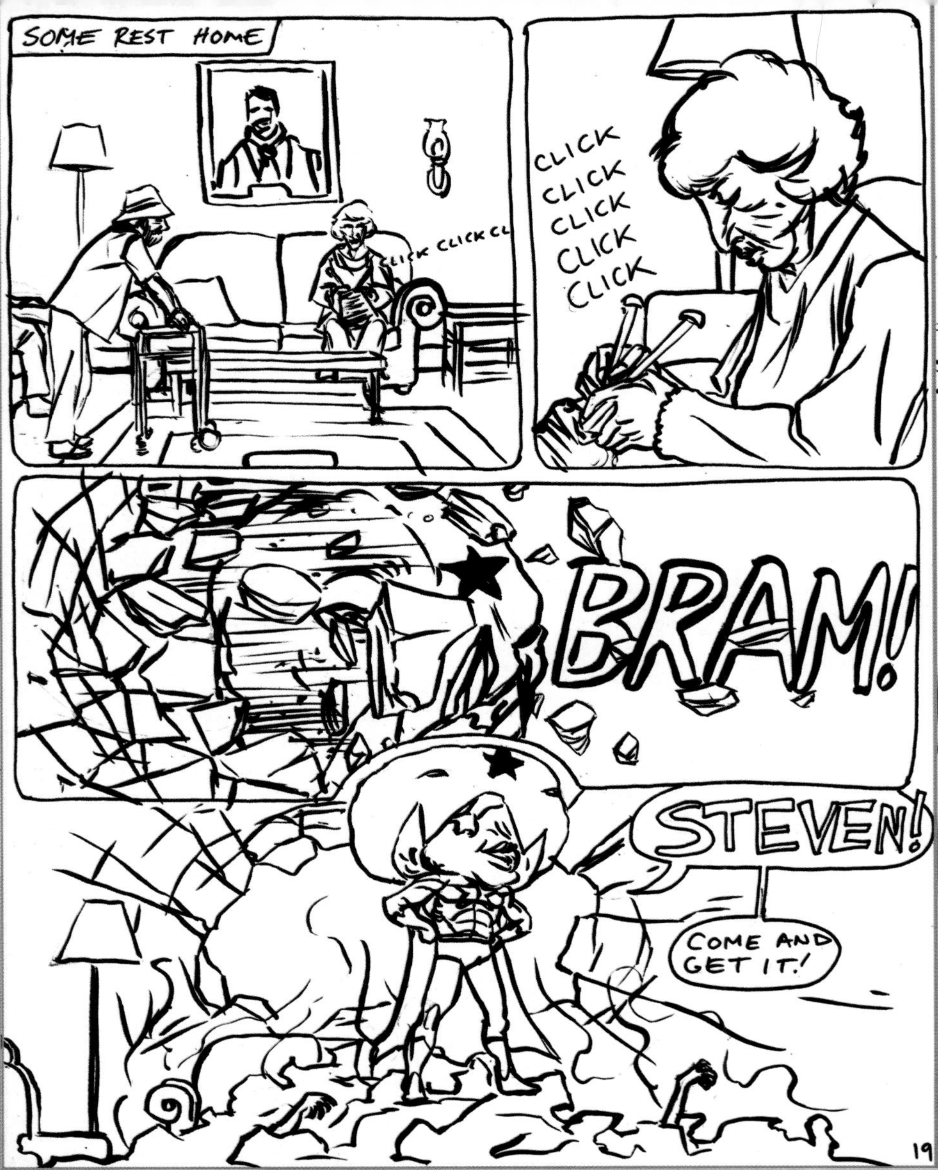
SOME REST HOME
CLICK CLICK CL
CLICK
CLICK
CLICK
CLICK
CLICK
BRAM!
STEVEN!
COME AND GET IT!

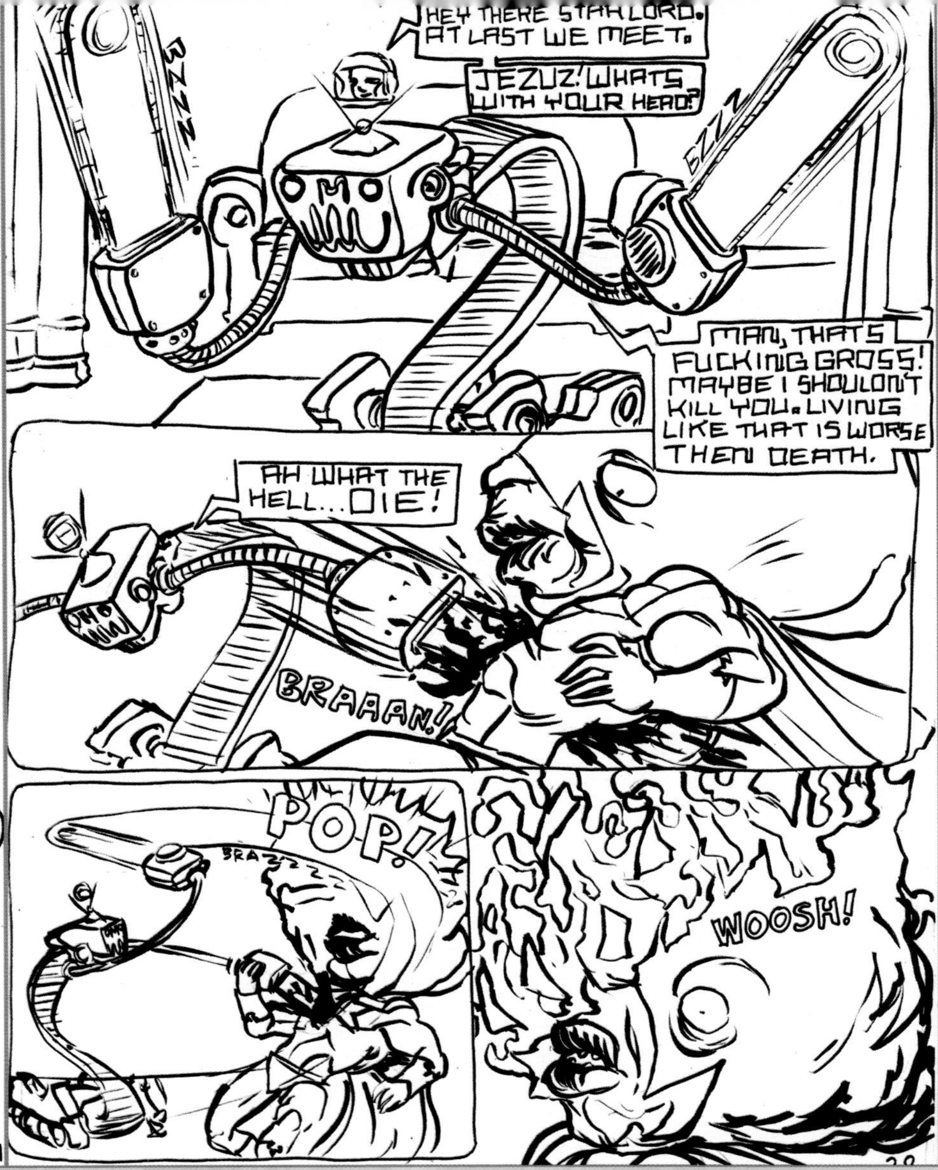
BZZZ
HEY THERE STAR LORD. AT LAST WE MEET.
JEZUZ! WHATS WITH YOUR HEAD?
BZZZ
MAN, THATS FUCKING GROSS! MAYBE I SHOULDN'T KILL YOU. LIVING LIKE THAT IS WORSE THEN DEATH.
AH WHAT THE HELL...DIE!
BRAAAN!
POP!
BRAZZZ
WOOSH!

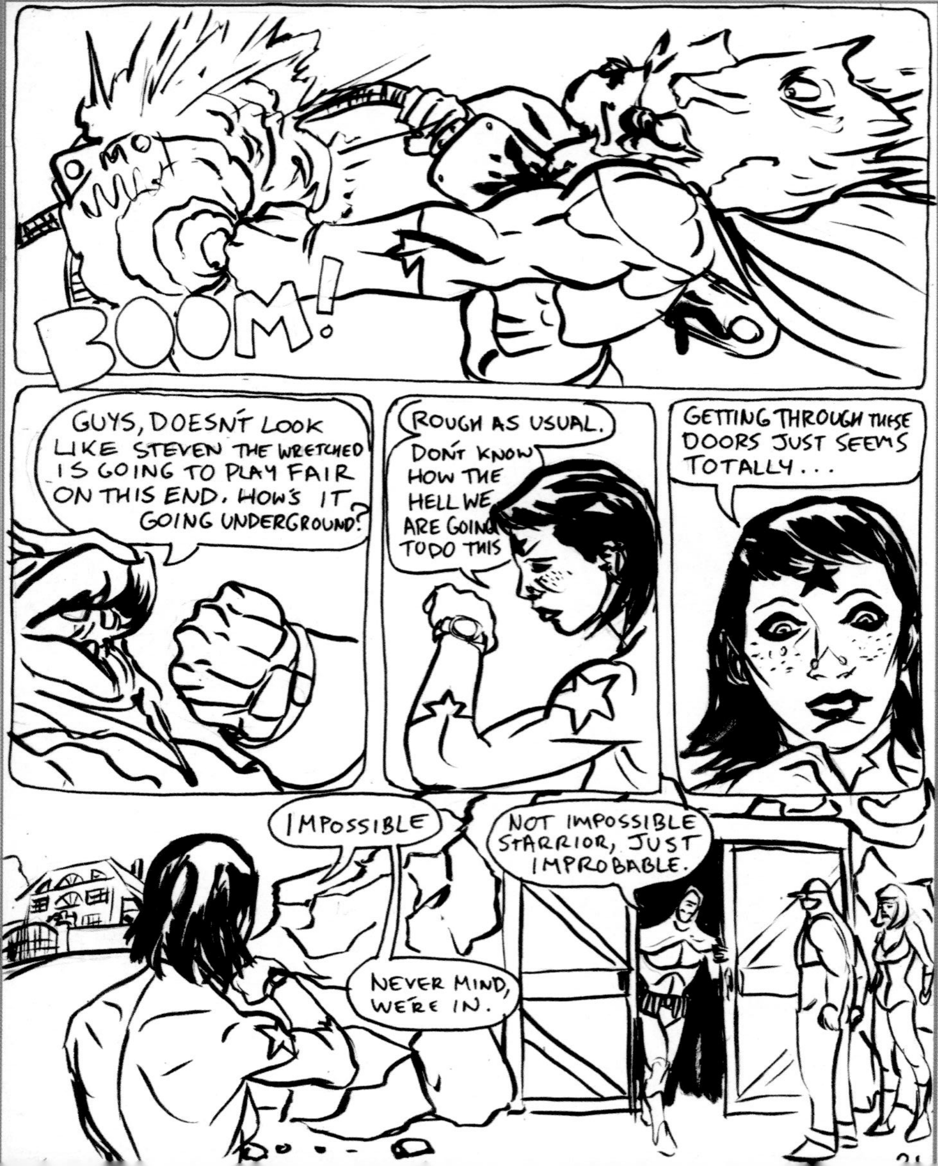
BOOM!
GUYS, DOESN'T LOOK LIKE STEVEN THE WRETCHED IS GOING TO PLAY FAIR ON THIS END. HOW'S IT GOING UNDERGROUND?
ROUGH AS USUAL.
DON'T KNOW HOW THE HELL WE ARE GOING TO DO THIS
GETTING THROUGH THESE DOORS JUST SEEMS TOTALLY...
IMPOSSIBLE
NOT IMPOSSIBLE STARRIOR, JUST IMPROBABLE.
NEVER MIND, WE'RE IN.

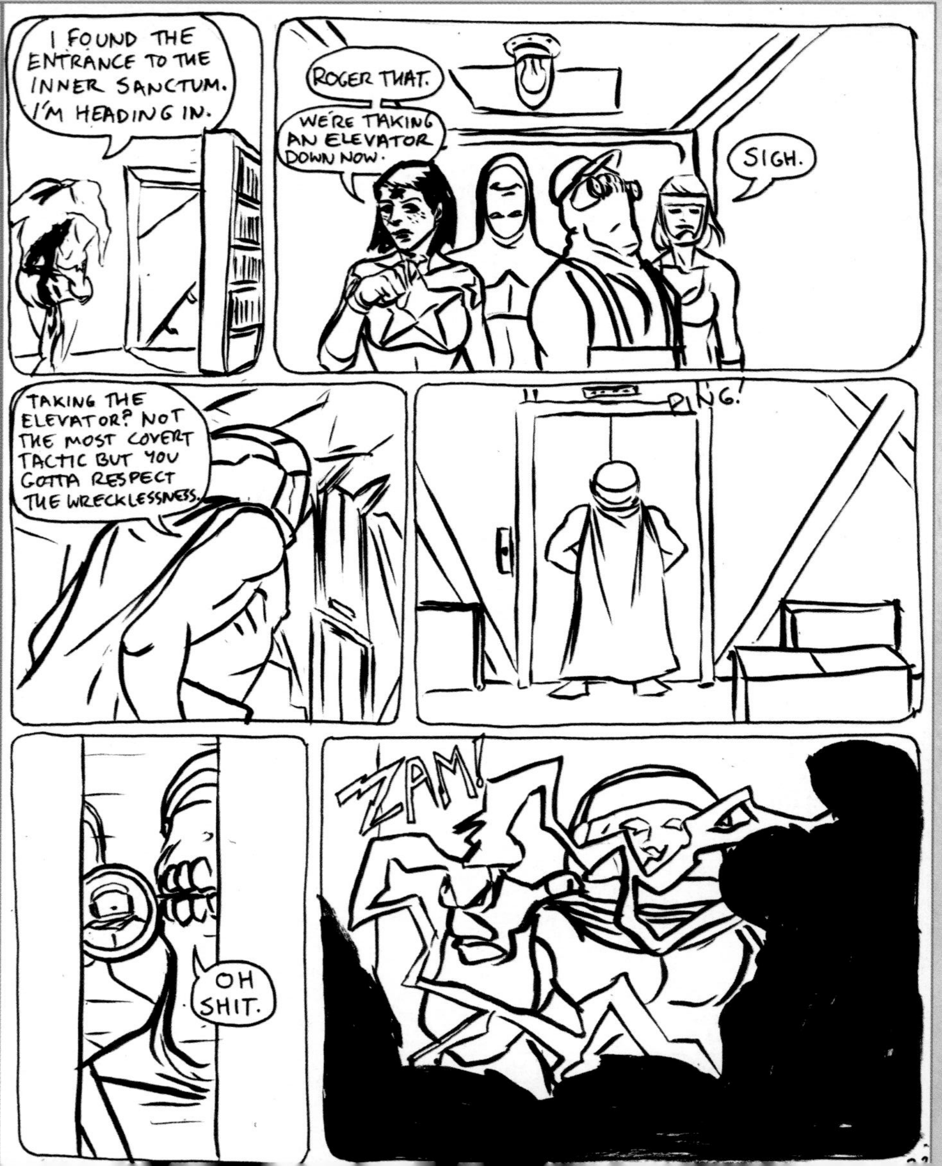
I FOUND THE ENTRANCE TO THE INNER SANCTUM. I'M HEADING IN.
ROGER THAT.
WE'RE TAKING AN ELEVATOR DOWN NOW.
SIGH.
TAKING THE ELEVATOR? NOT THE MOST COVERT TACTIC BUT YOU GOTTA RESPECT THE WRECKLESSNESS.
PING!
OH SHIT.
ZAM!

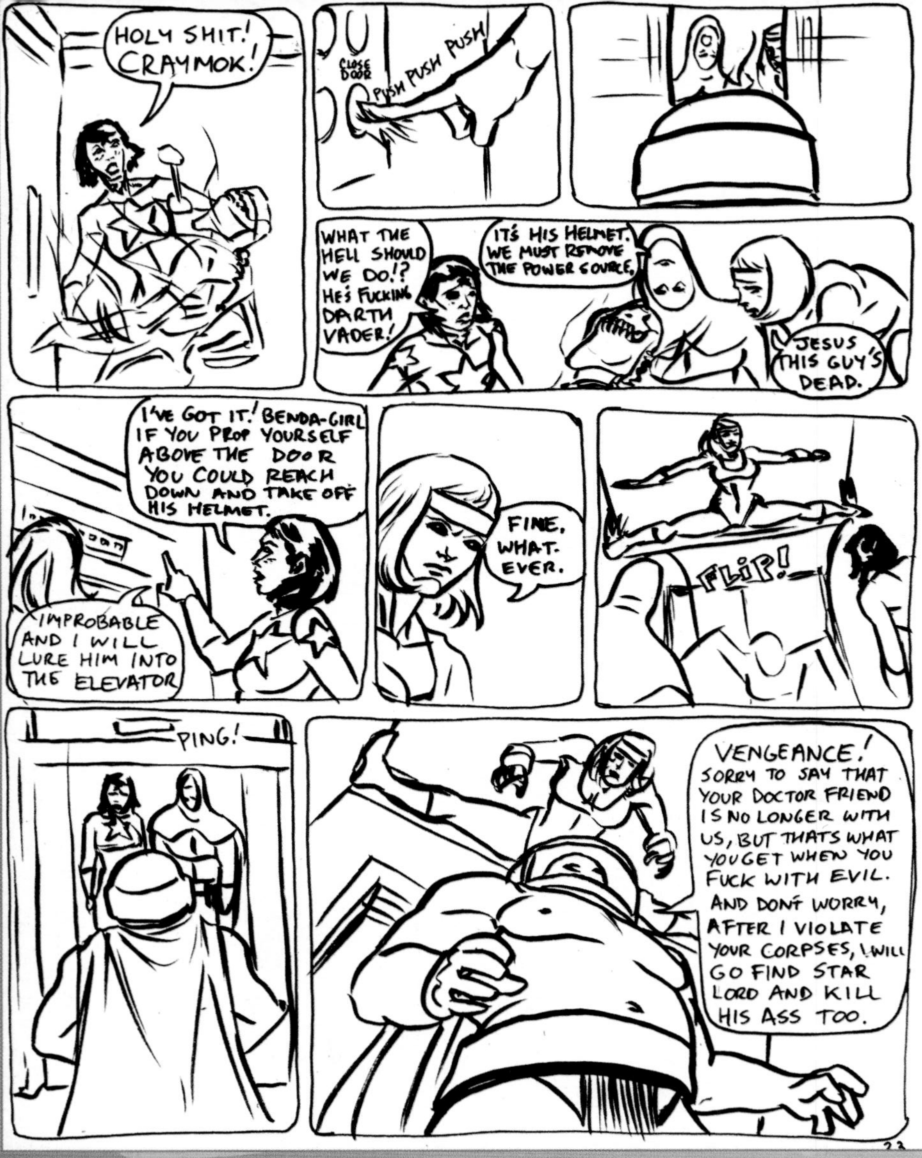
HOLY SHIT! CRAYMOK!
CLOSE DOOR
PUSH PUSH PUSH
WHAT THE HELL SHOULD WE DO!? HE'S FUCKING DARTH VADER!
IT'S HIS HELMET. WE MUST REMOVE THE POWER SOURCE.
JESUS THIS GUY'S DEAD.
I'VE GOT IT! BENDA-GIRL IF YOU PROP YOURSELF ABOVE THE DOOR YOU COULD REACH DOWN AND TAKE OFF HIS HELMET.
IMPROBABLE AND I WILL LURE HIM INTO THE ELEVATOR
FINE. WHAT-EVER.
FLIP!
PING!
VENGEANCE! SORRY TO SAY THAT YOUR DOCTOR FRIEND IS NO LONGER WITH US, BUT THATS WHAT YOU GET WHEN YOU FUCK WITH EVIL. AND DON'T WORRY, AFTER I VIOLATE YOUR CORPSES, I WILL GO FIND STAR LORD AND KILL HIS ASS TOO.
23

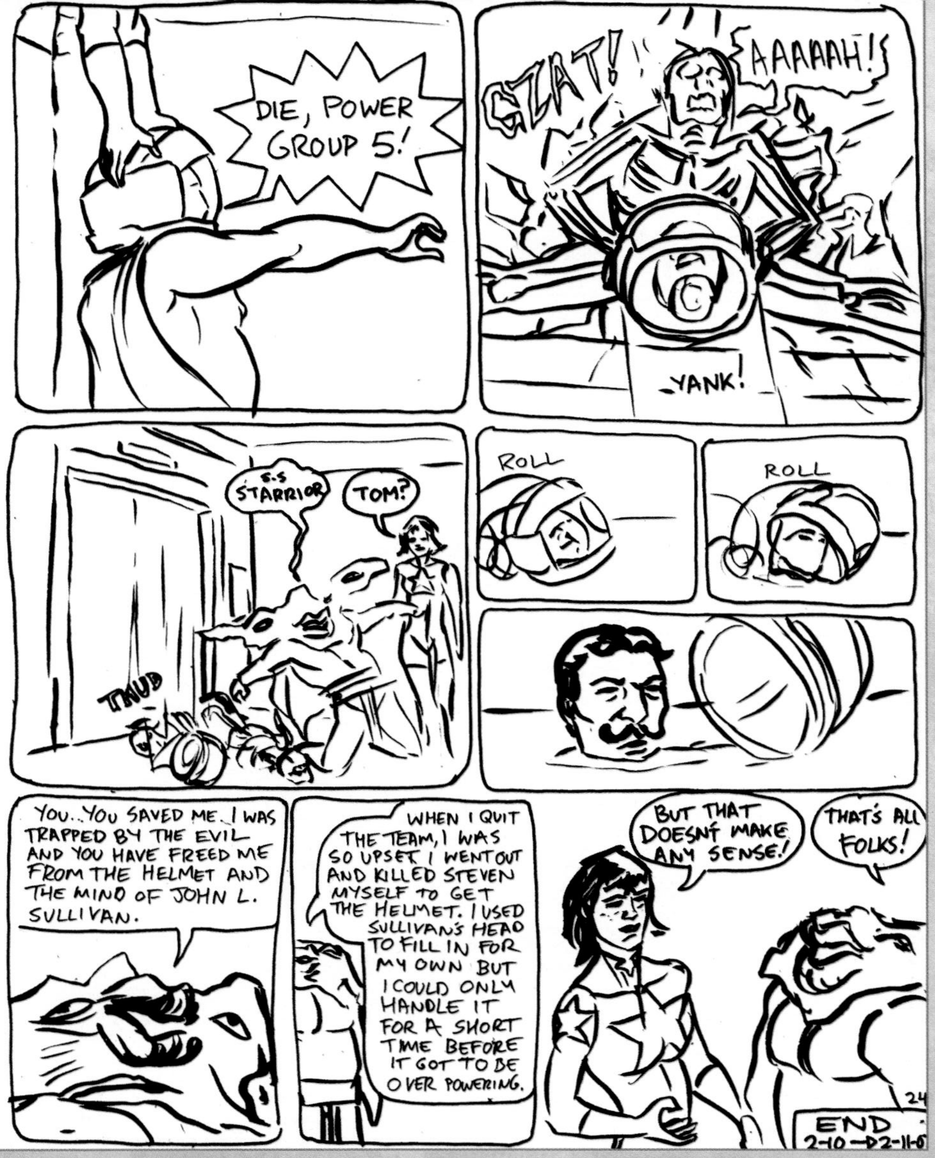
DIE, POWER GROUP 5!
GZZAT!
AAAAAH!
YANK!
S.S STARRIOR
TOM?
THUD
ROLL
ROLL
YOU.. YOU SAVED ME. I WAS TRAPPED BY THE EVIL AND YOU HAVE FREED ME FROM THE HELMET AND THE MIND OF JOHN L. SULLIVAN.
WHEN I QUIT THE TEAM, I WAS SO UPSET I WENT OUT AND KILLED STEVEN MYSELF TO GET THE HELMET. I USED SULLIVAN'S HEAD TO FILL IN FOR MY OWN BUT I COULD ONLY HANDLE IT FOR A SHORT TIME BEFORE IT GOT TO BE OVER POWERING.
BUT THAT DOESN'T MAKE ANY SENSE!
THAT'S ALL FOLKS!
24
END

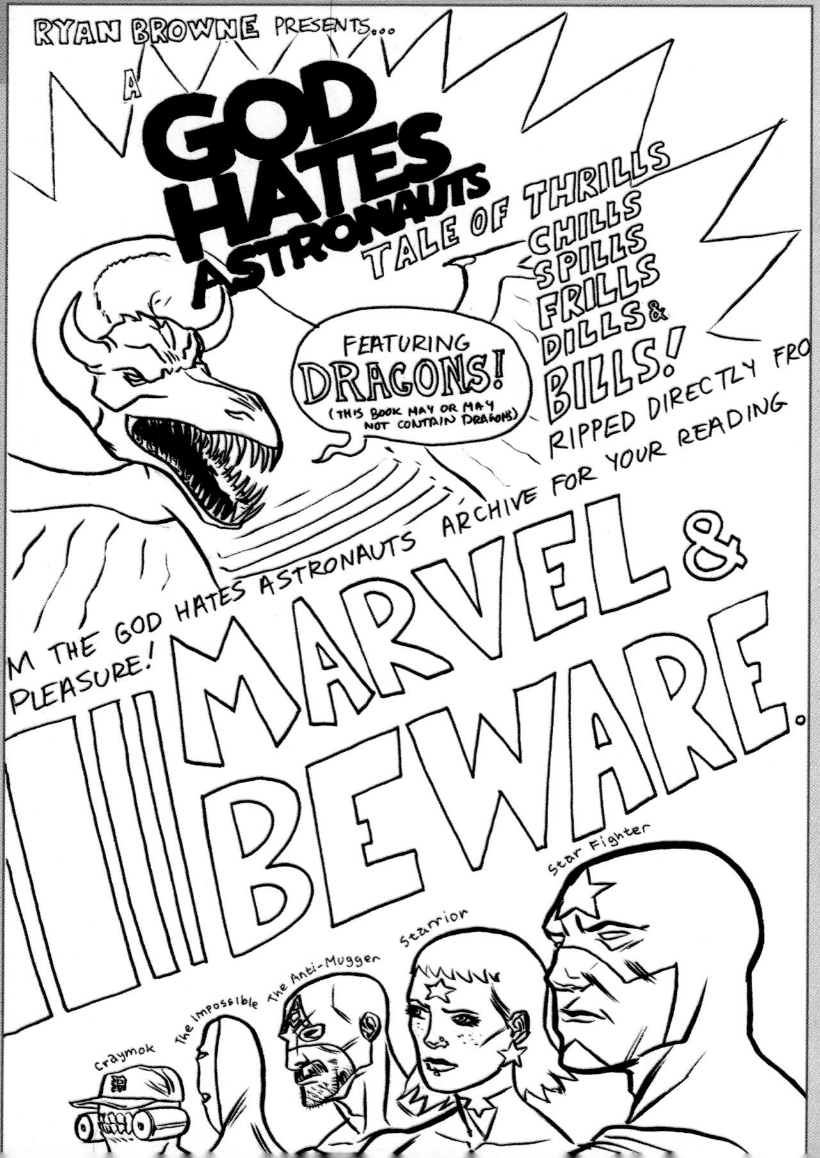
RYAN BROWNE PRESENTS...
A GOD HATES ASTRONAUTS TALE OF THRILLS CHILLS SPILLS FRILLS DILLS & BILLS!
FEATURING DRAGONS!
(THIS BOOK MAY OR MAY NOT CONTAIN DRAGONS)
RIPPED DIRECTLY FRO
M THE GOD HATES ASTRONAUTS ARCHIVE FOR YOUR READING PLEASURE!
MARVEL & BEWARE.
Star Fighter
Starrion
The Anti-Mugger
The Impossible
Craymok

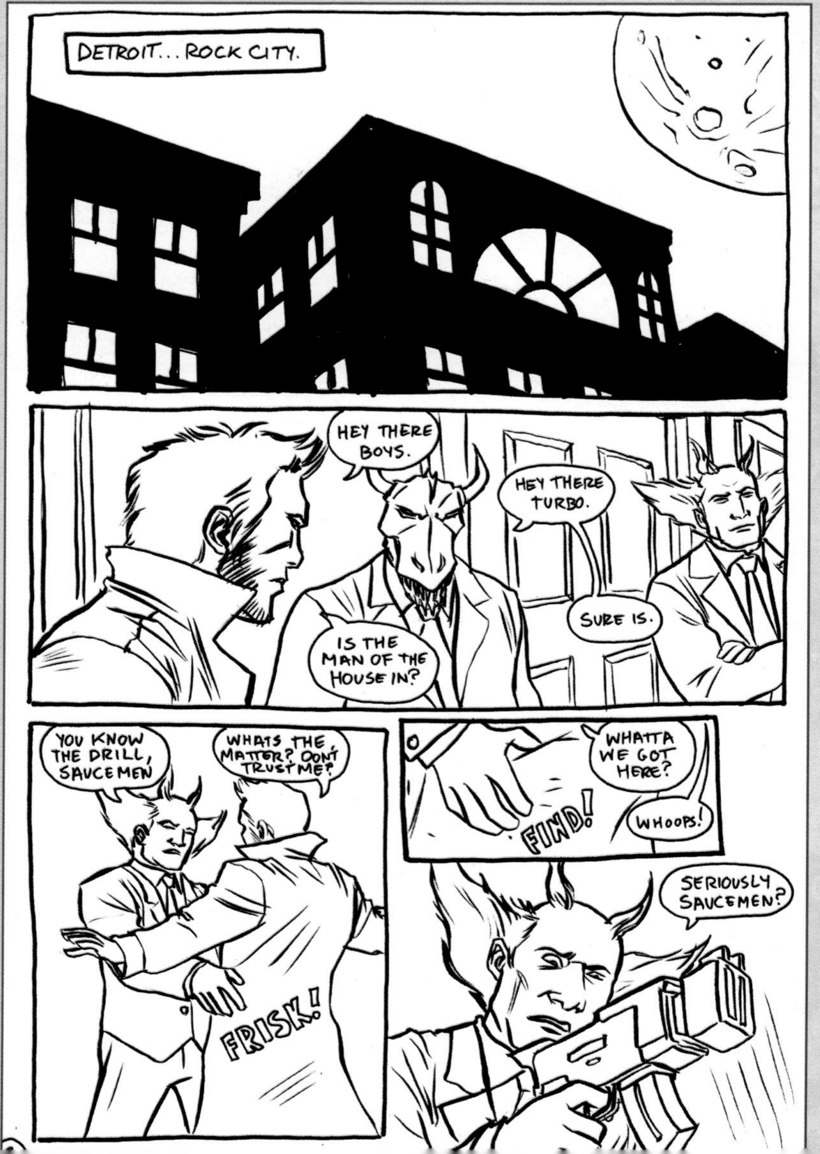
DETROIT... ROCK CITY.
HEY THERE BOYS.
HEY THERE TURBO.
IS THE MAN OF THE HOUSE IN?
SURE IS.
YOU KNOW THE DRILL, SAUCEMEN
WHATS THE MATTER? DONT TRUST ME?
FRISK!
WHATTA WE GOT HERE?
FIND!
WHOOPS!
SERIOUSLY SAUCEMEN?

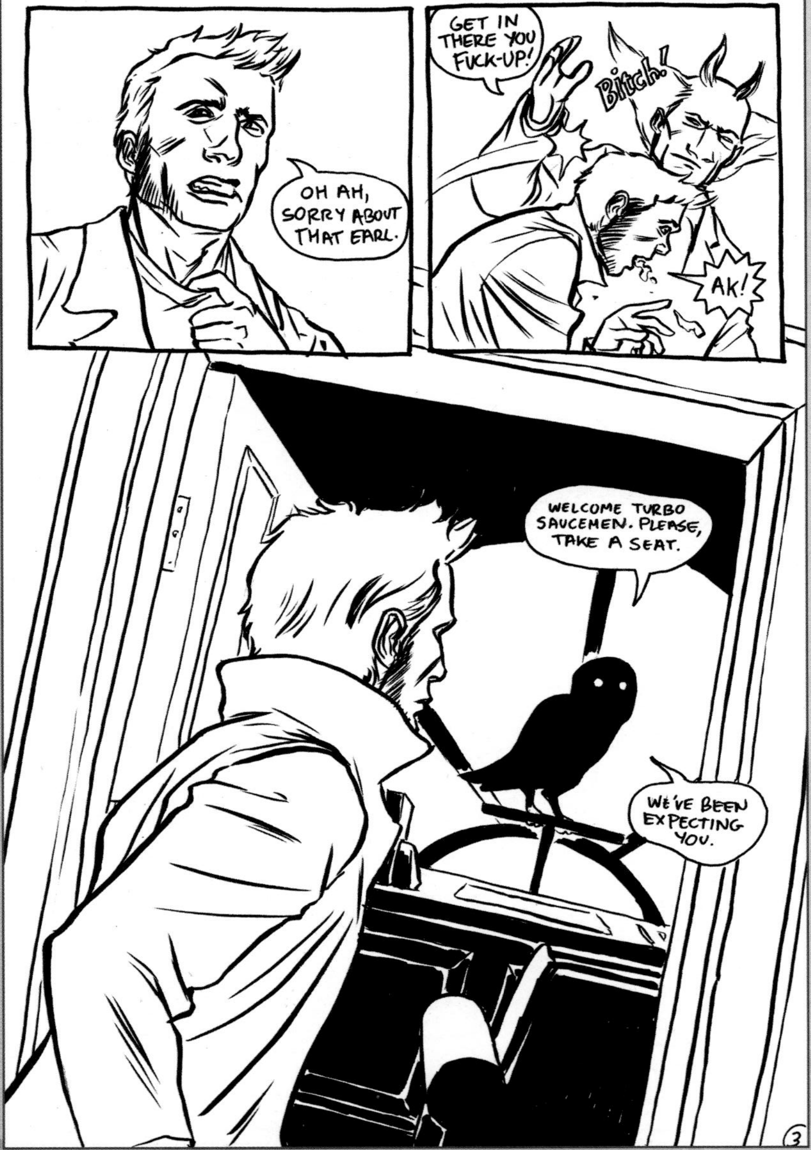
OH AH, SORRY ABOUT THAT EARL.
GET IN THERE YOU FUCK-UP!
Bitch!
AK!
WELCOME TURBO SAUCEMEN. PLEASE, TAKE A SEAT.
WE'VE BEEN EXPECTING YOU.

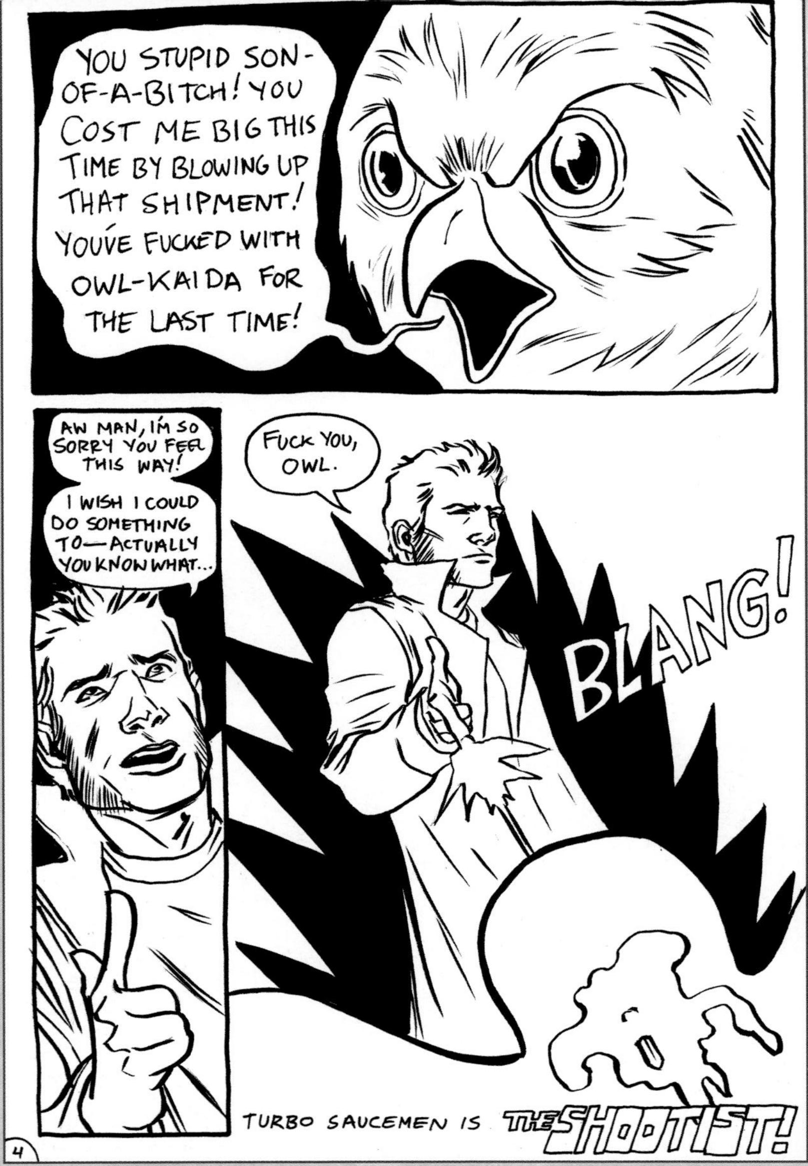
YOU STUPID SON-OF-A-BITCH! YOU COST ME BIG THIS TIME BY BLOWING UP THAT SHIPMENT! YOU'VE FUCKED WITH OWL-KAIDA FOR THE LAST TIME!
AW MAN, I'M SO SORRY YOU FEEL THIS WAY!
I WISH I COULD DO SOMETHING TO—ACTUALLY YOU KNOW WHAT...
FUCK YOU, OWL.
BLANG!
TURBO SAUCEMEN IS THE SHOOTIST!

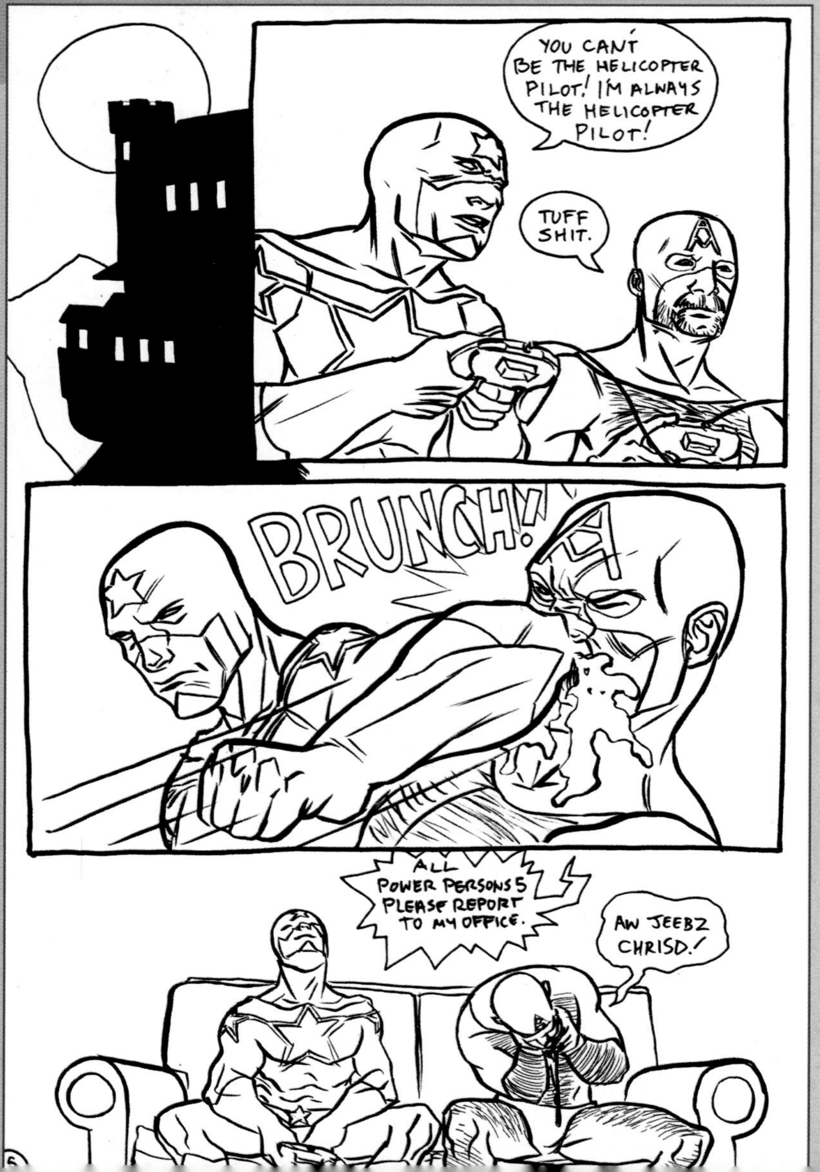
YOU CAN'T BE THE HELICOPTER PILOT! I'M ALWAYS THE HELICOPTER PILOT!
TUFF SHIT.
BRUNCH!
ALL POWER PERSONS 5 PLEASE REPORT TO MY OFFICE.
AW JEEBZ CHRISD.!
5

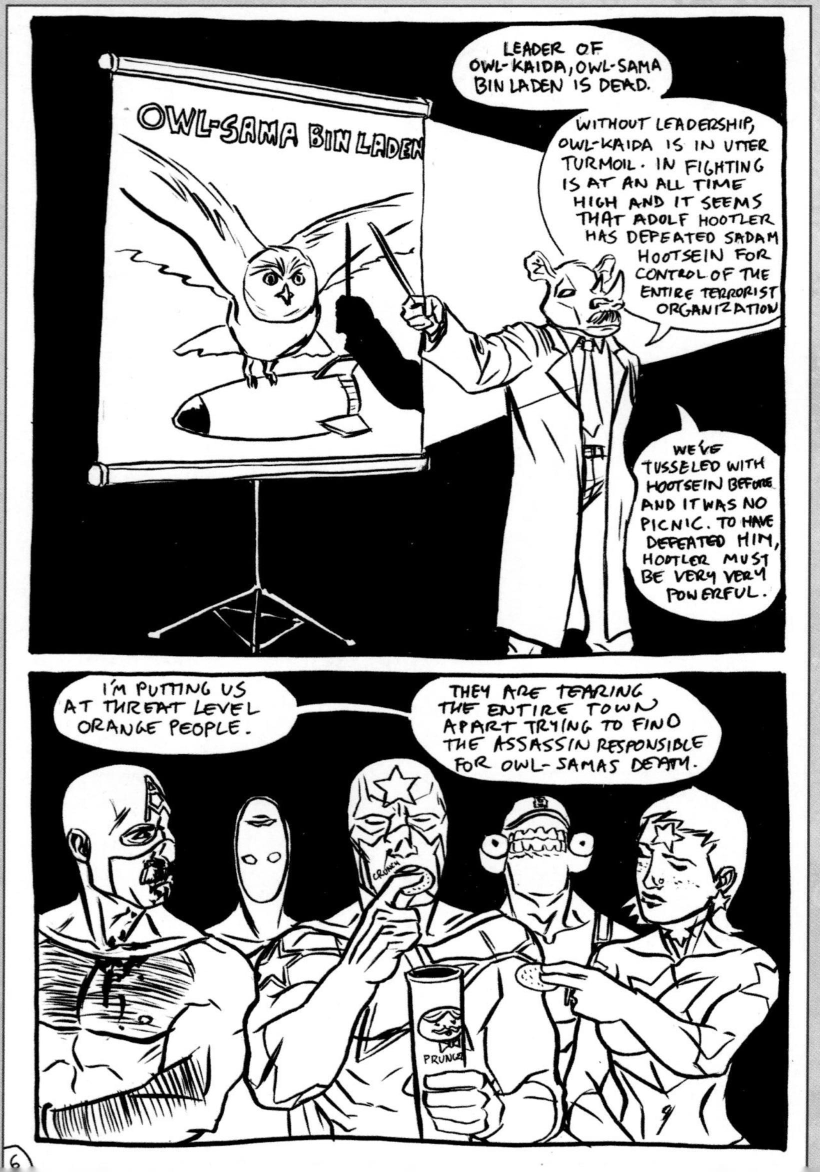
OWL-SAMA BIN LADEN
LEADER OF OWL-KAIDA, OWL-SAMA BIN LADEN IS DEAD.
WITHOUT LEADERSHIP, OWL-KAIDA IS IN UTTER TURMOIL. IN FIGHTING IS AT AN ALL TIME HIGH AND IT SEEMS THAT ADOLF HOOTLER HAS DEFEATED SADAM HOOTSEIN FOR CONTROL OF THE ENTIRE TERRORIST ORGANIZATION
WE'VE TUSSELED WITH HOOTSEIN BEFORE AND IT WAS NO PICNIC. TO HAVE DEFEATED HIM, HOOTLER MUST BE VERY VERY POWERFUL.
I'M PUTTING US AT THREAT LEVEL ORANGE PEOPLE.
THEY ARE TEARING THE ENTIRE TOWN APART TRYING TO FIND THE ASSASSIN RESPONSIBLE FOR OWL-SAMAS DEATH.
CRUNCH
PRUNGS
6

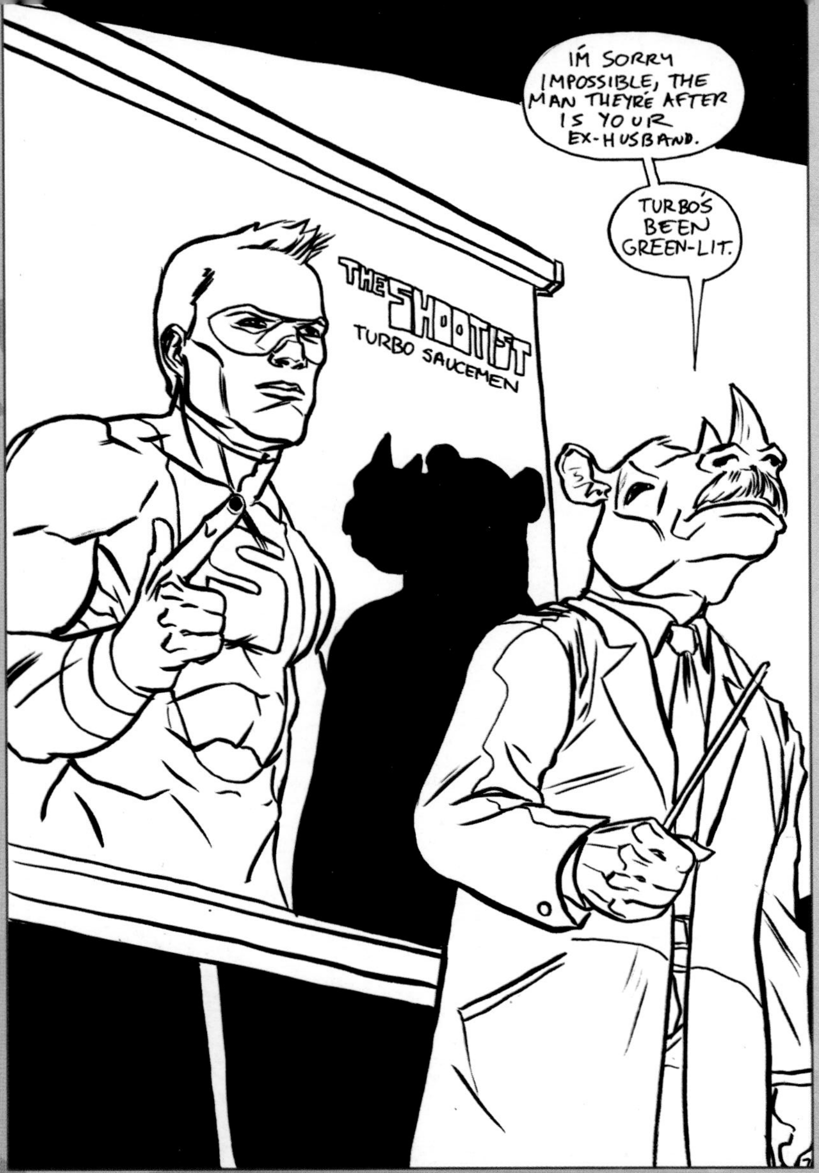
THE SHOOTIST
TURBO SAUCEMEN
I'M SORRY IMPOSSIBLE, THE MAN THEY'RE AFTER IS YOUR EX-HUSBAND.
TURBO'S BEEN GREEN-LIT.

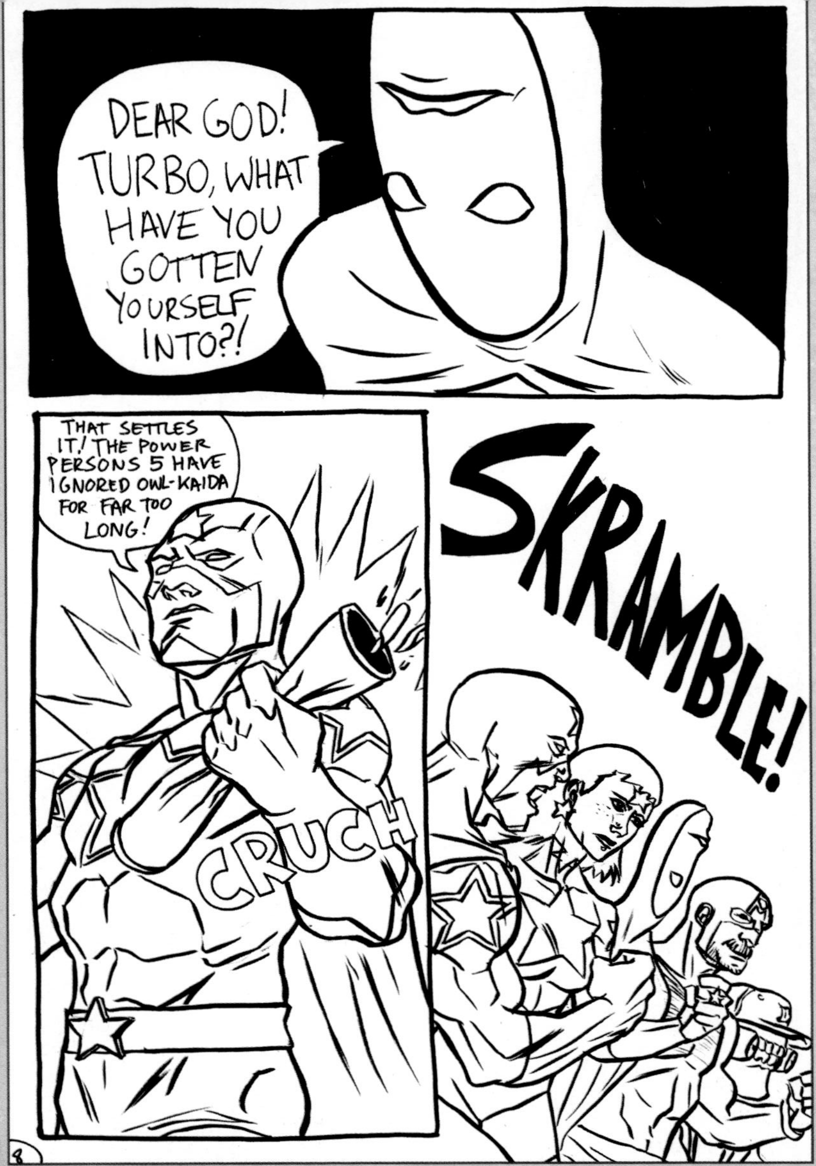
DEAR GOD! TURBO, WHAT HAVE YOU GOTTEN YOURSELF INTO?!
THAT SETTLES IT! THE POWER PERSONS 5 HAVE IGNORED OWL-KAIDA FOR FAR TOO LONG!
CRUCH
SKRAMBLE!

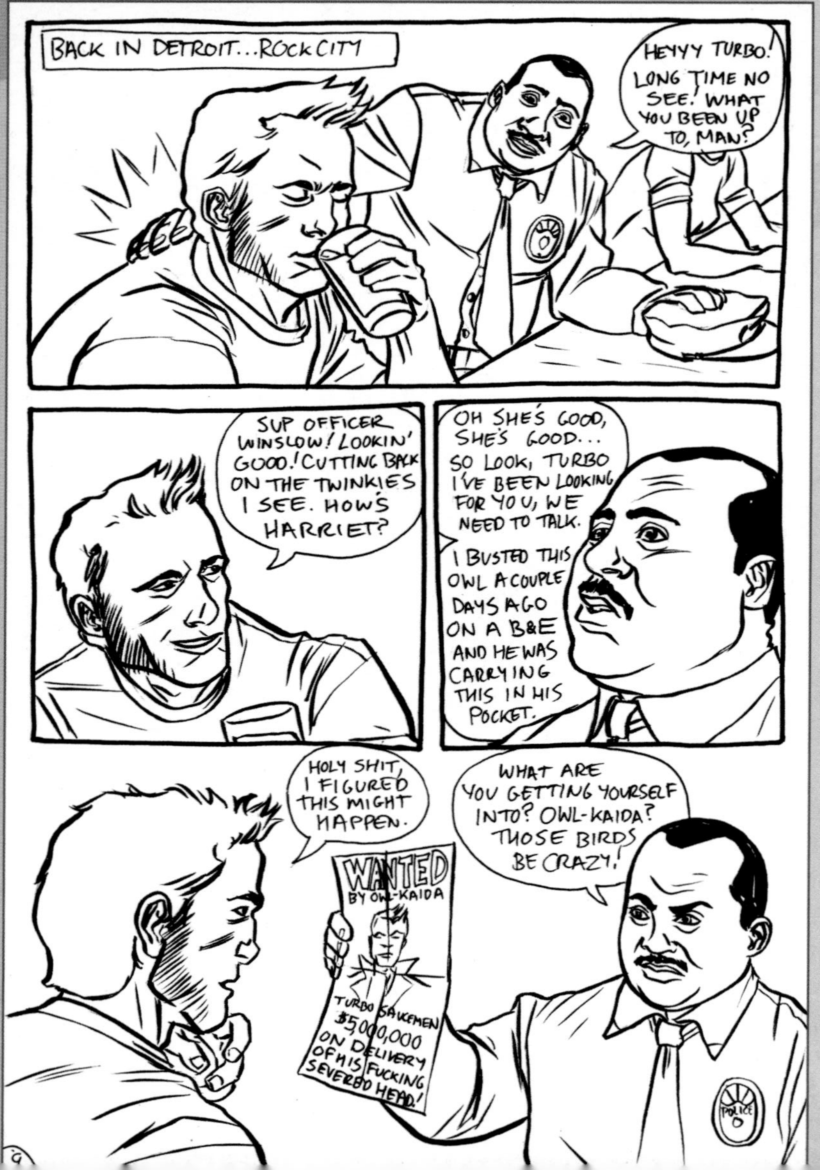
BACK IN DETROIT...ROCK CITY
HEYYY TURBO! LONG TIME NO SEE! WHAT YOU BEEN UP TO, MAN?
SUP OFFICER WINSLOW! LOOKIN' GOOD! CUTTING BACK ON THE TWINKIES I SEE. HOW'S HARRIET?
OH SHE'S GOOD, SHE'S GOOD... SO LOOK, TURBO I'VE BEEN LOOKING FOR YOU, WE NEED TO TALK.
I BUSTED THIS OWL A COUPLE DAYS AGO ON A B&E AND HE WAS CARRYING THIS IN HIS POCKET.
HOLY SHIT, I FIGURED THIS MIGHT HAPPEN.
WHAT ARE YOU GETTING YOURSELF INTO? OWL-KAIDA? THOSE BIRDS BE CRAZY!
WANTED
BY OWL-KAIDA
TURBO SAKEMEN
$5,000,000
ON DELIVERY OF HIS FUCKING SEVERED HEAD!
POLICE

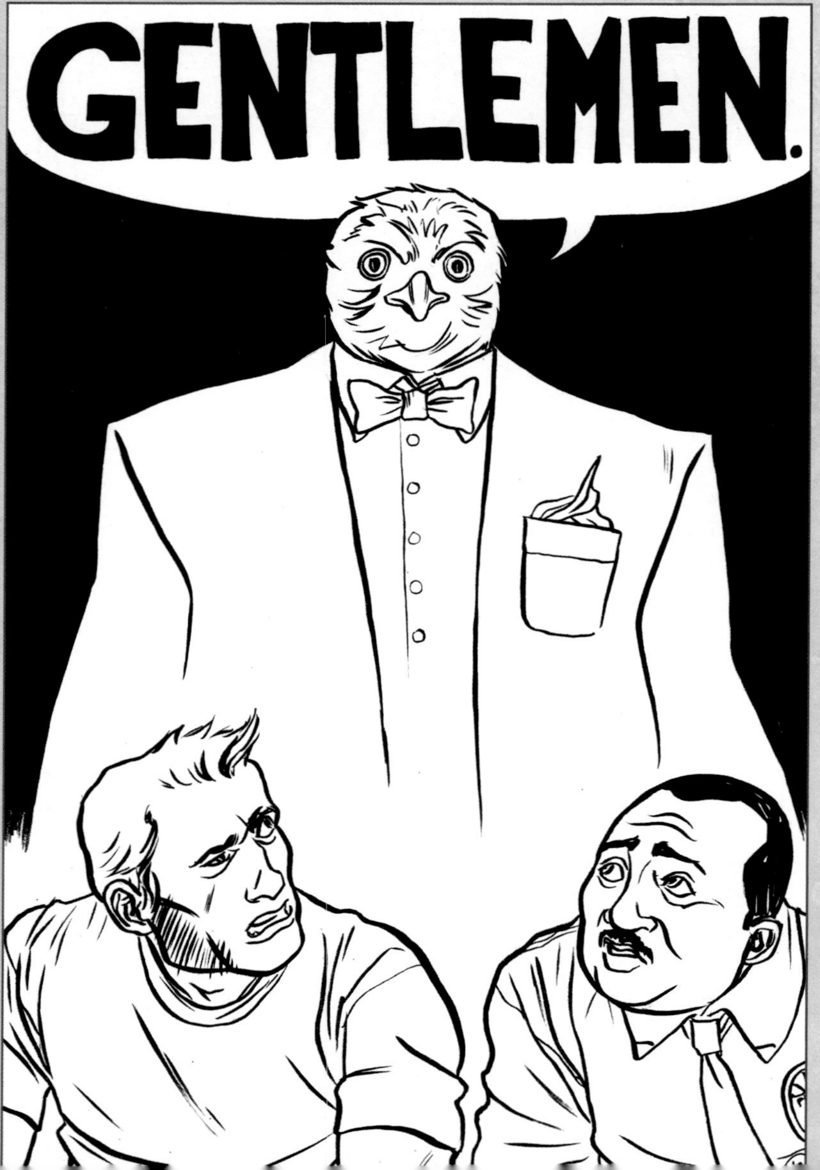
GENTLEMEN.

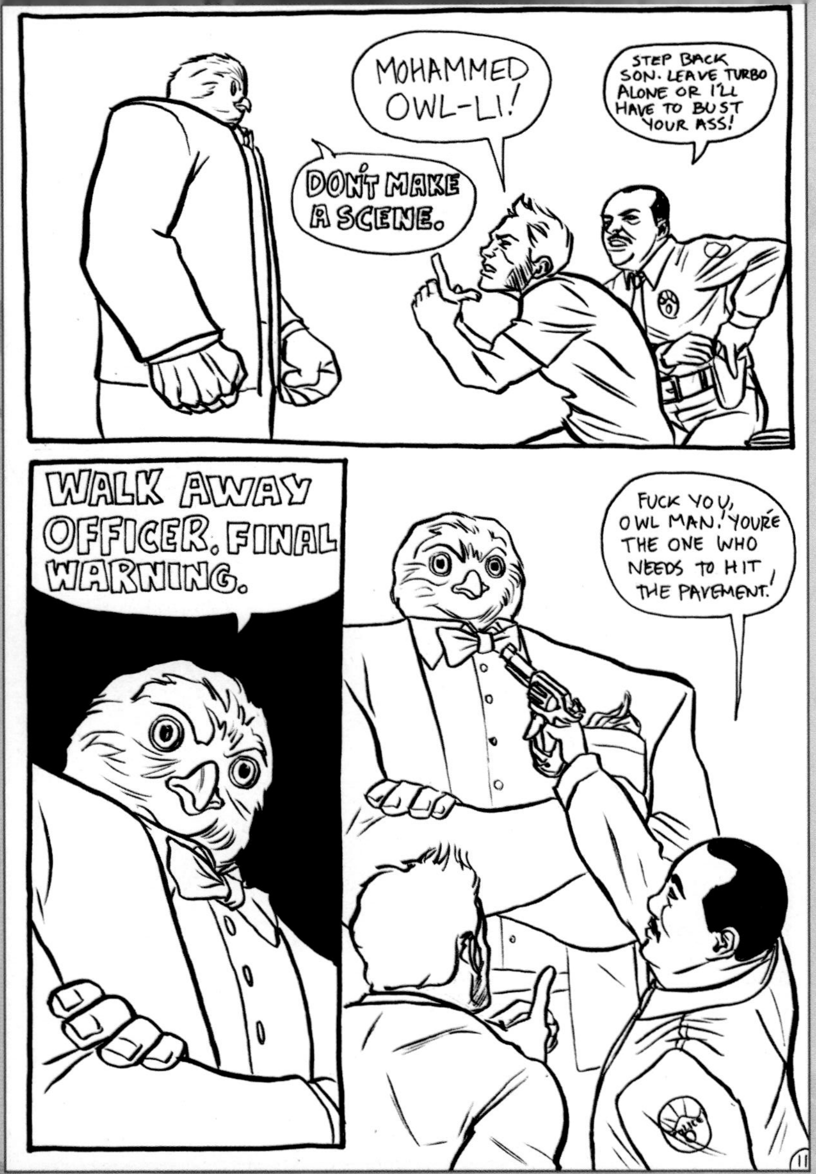
MOHAMMED OWL-LI!
DON'T MAKE A SCENE.
STEP BACK SON. LEAVE TURBO ALONE OR I'LL HAVE TO BUST YOUR ASS!
WALK AWAY OFFICER. FINAL WARNING.
FUCK YOU, OWL MAN! YOU'RE THE ONE WHO NEEDS TO HIT THE PAVEMENT!
11

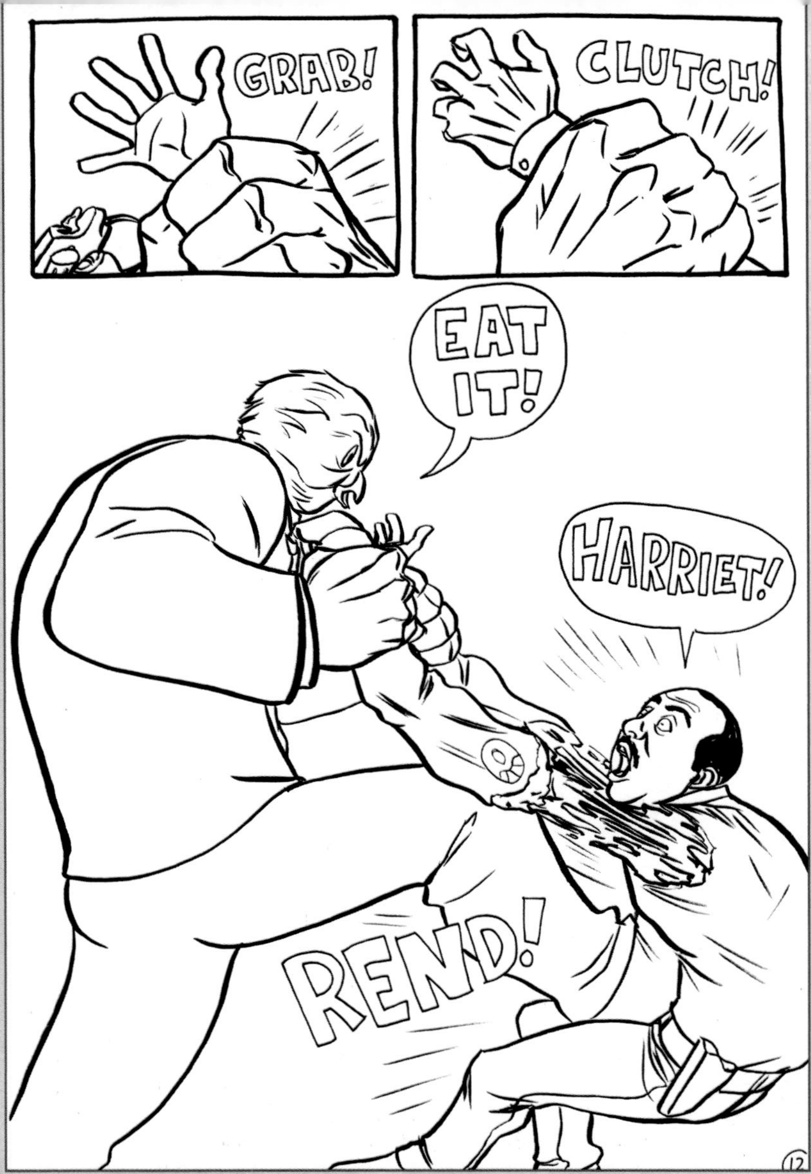
GRAB!
CLUTCH!
EAT IT!
HARRIET!
REND!
12

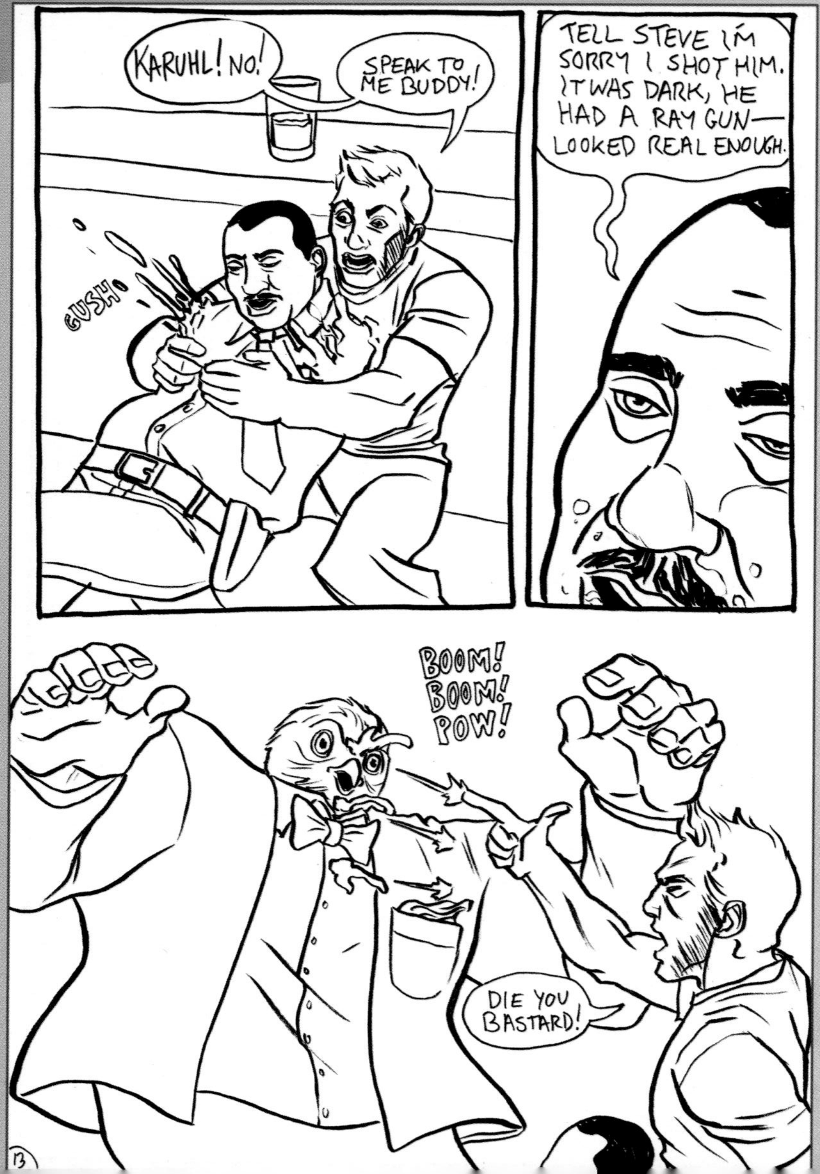
KARUHL! NO!
SPEAK TO ME BUDDY!
GUSH
TELL STEVE I'M SORRY I SHOT HIM. IT WAS DARK, HE HAD A RAY GUN— LOOKED REAL ENOUGH.
BOOM! BOOM! POW!
DIE YOU BASTARD!
13

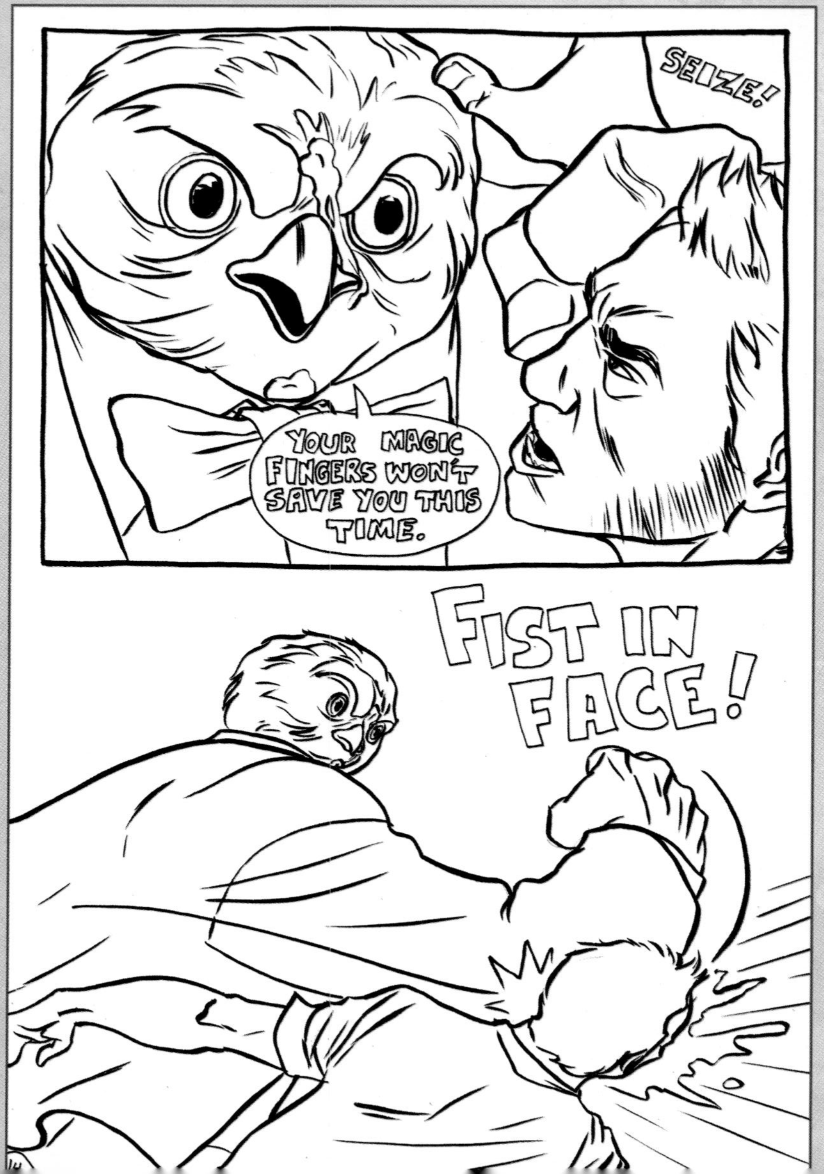
SEIZE!
YOUR MAGIC FINGERS WON'T SAVE YOU THIS TIME.
FIST IN FACE!
14

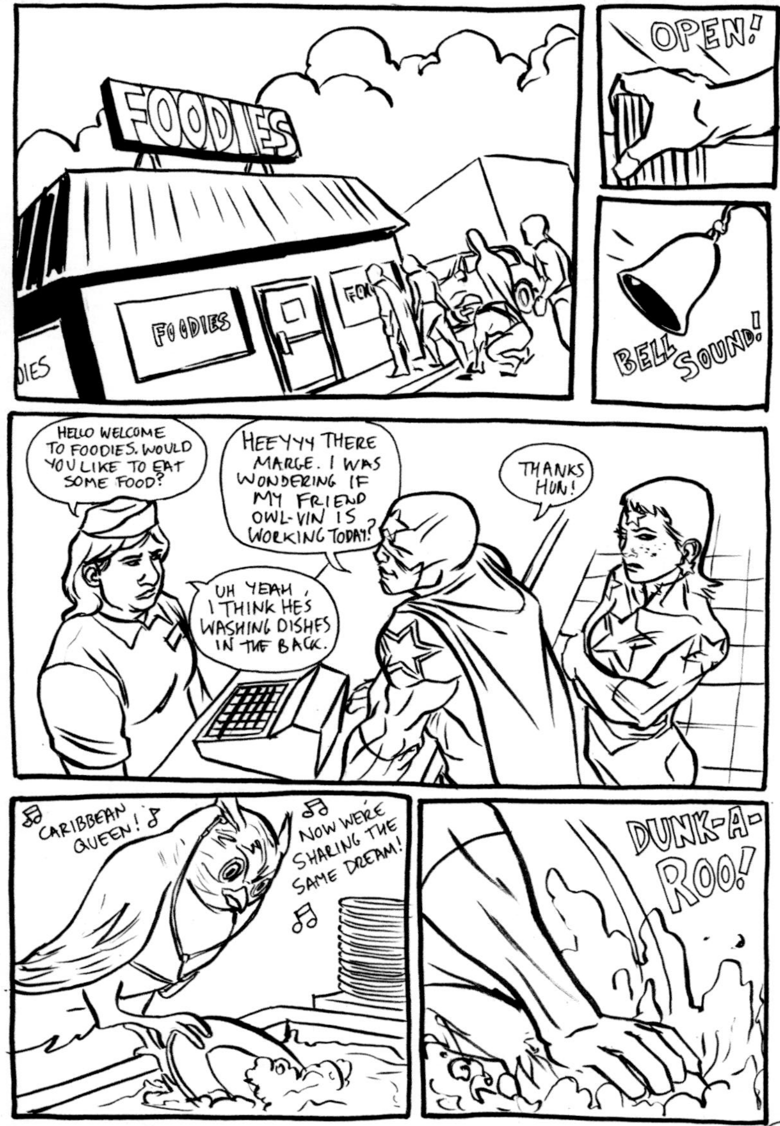
FOODIES
FOODIES
OPEN!
BELL SOUND!
HELLO WELCOME TO FOODIES. WOULD YOU LIKE TO EAT SOME FOOD?
HEEYYY THERE MARGE. I WAS WONDERING IF MY FRIEND OWL-VIN IS WORKING TODAY?
UH YEAH, I THINK HE'S WASHING DISHES IN THE BACK.
THANKS HUN!
♫ CARIBBEAN QUEEN! ♪
♫ NOW WE'RE SHARING THE SAME DREAM! ♫
DUNK-A-ROO!

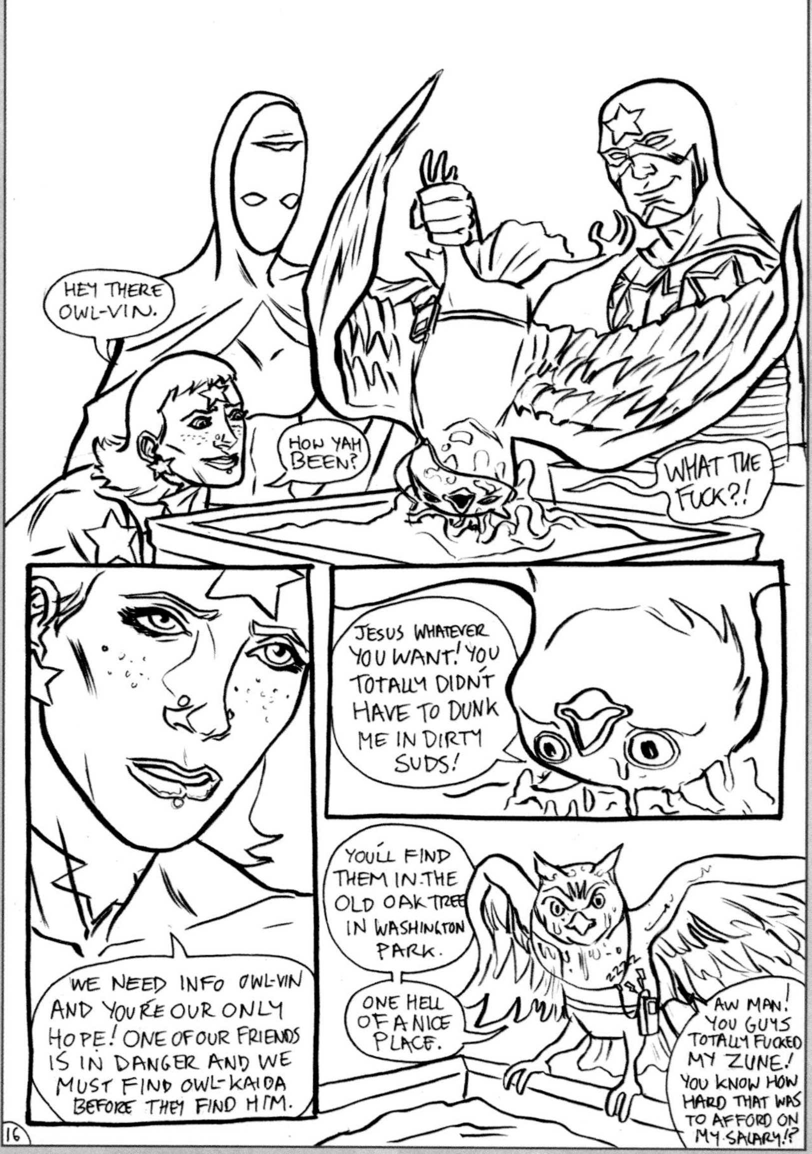
HEY THERE OWL-VIN.
HOW YAH BEEN?
WHAT THE FUCK?!
WE NEED INFO OWL-VIN AND YOU'RE OUR ONLY HOPE! ONE OF OUR FRIENDS IS IN DANGER AND WE MUST FIND OWL-KAIDA BEFORE THEY FIND HIM.
JESUS WHATEVER YOU WANT! YOU TOTALLY DIDN'T HAVE TO DUNK ME IN DIRTY SUDS!
YOU'LL FIND THEM IN THE OLD OAK TREE IN WASHINGTON PARK.
ONE HELL OF A NICE PLACE.
AW MAN! YOU GUYS TOTALLY FUCKED MY ZUNE! YOU KNOW HOW HARD THAT WAS TO AFFORD ON MY SALARY!?

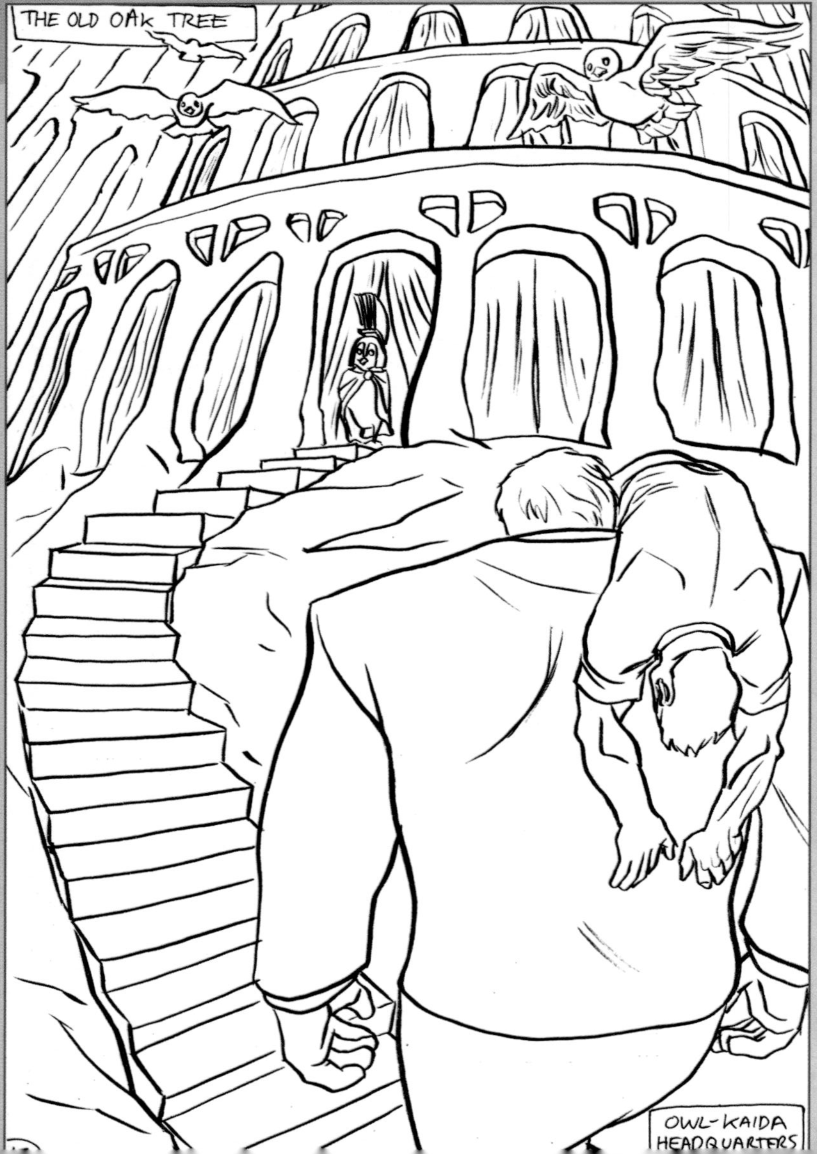
THE OLD OAK TREE
OWL-KAIDA HEADQUARTERS

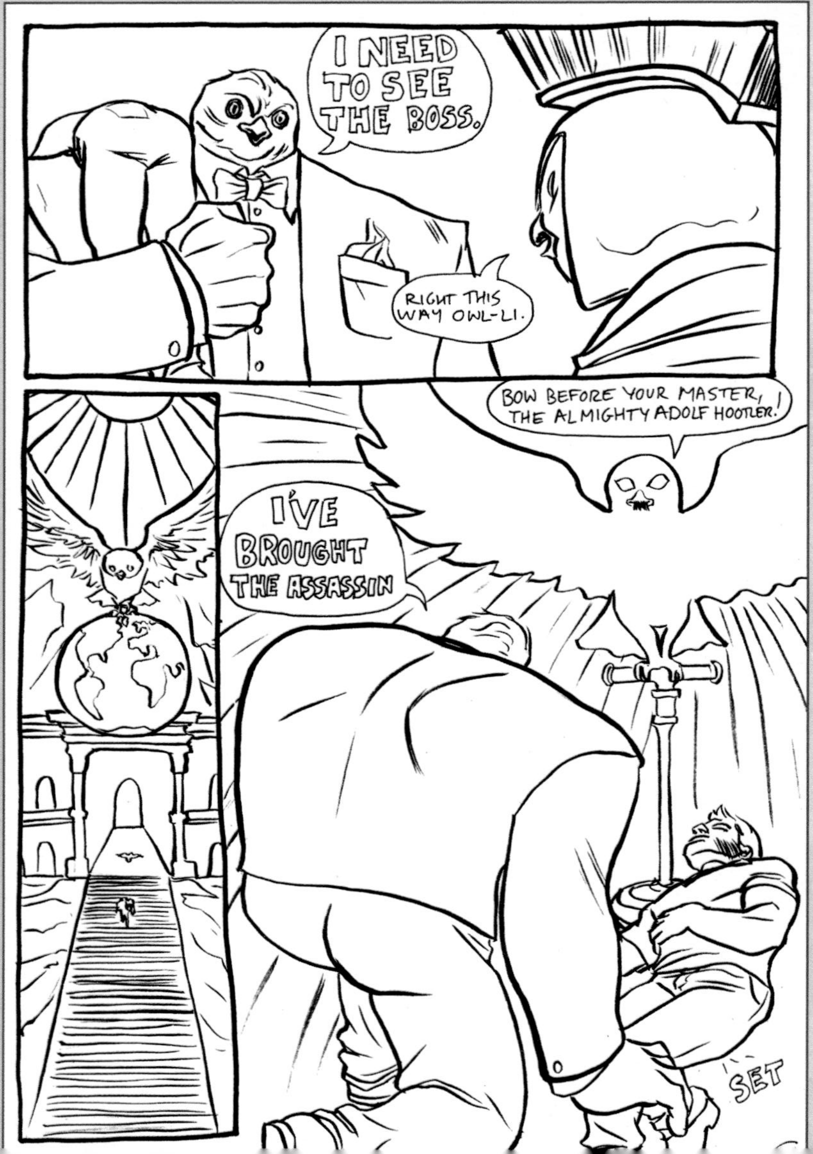
I NEED TO SEE THE BOSS.
RIGHT THIS WAY OWL-LI.
BOW BEFORE YOUR MASTER, THE ALMIGHTY ADOLF HOOTLER!
I'VE BROUGHT THE ASSASSIN
SET

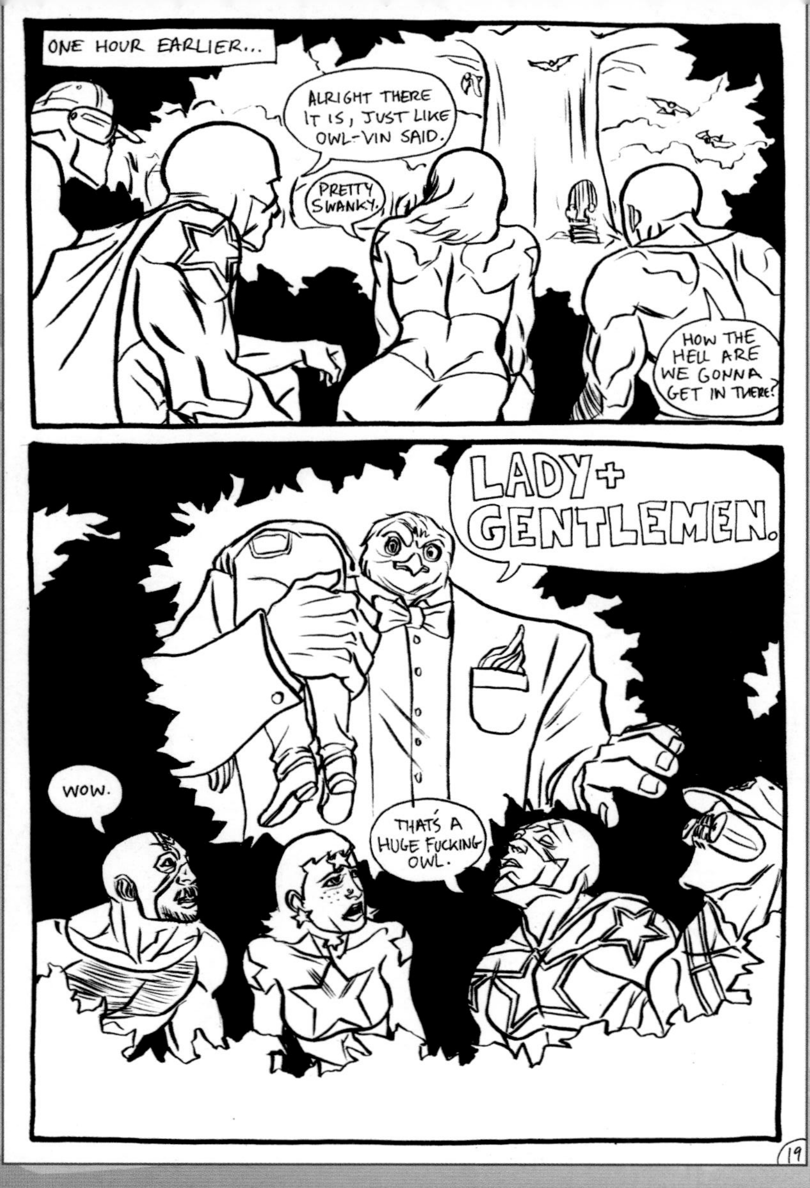
ONE HOUR EARLIER...
ALRIGHT THERE IT IS, JUST LIKE OWL-VIN SAID.
PRETTY SWANKY.
HOW THE HELL ARE WE GONNA GET IN THERE?
LADY + GENTLEMEN.
WOW.
THAT'S A HUGE FUCKING OWL.
19

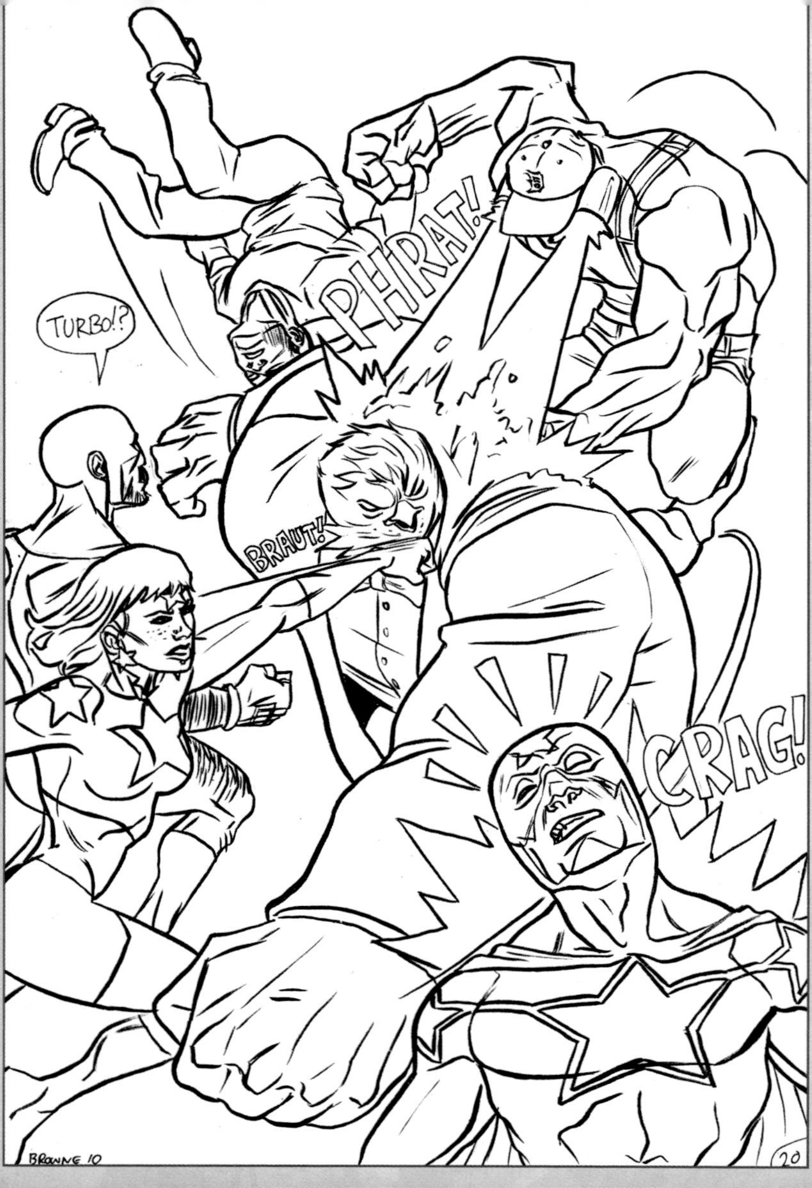
TURBO!?
PHRAT!
BRAUT!
CRAG!
BROWNE 10
20

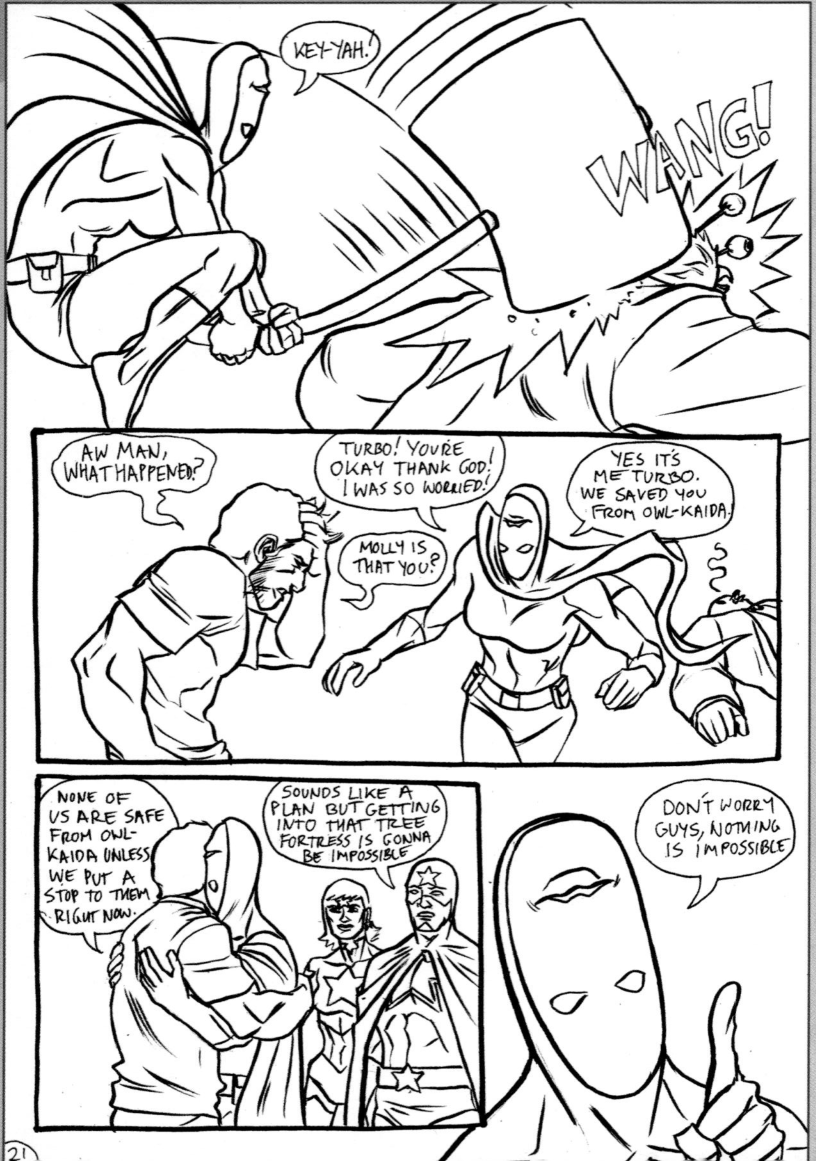
KEY-YAH!
WANG!
AW MAN, WHAT HAPPENED?
TURBO! YOU'RE OKAY THANK GOD! I WAS SO WORRIED!
MOLLY IS THAT YOU?
YES IT'S ME TURBO. WE SAVED YOU FROM OWL-KAIDA.
NONE OF US ARE SAFE FROM OWL-KAIDA UNLESS WE PUT A STOP TO THEM RIGHT NOW.
SOUNDS LIKE A PLAN BUT GETTING INTO THAT TREE FORTRESS IS GONNA BE IMPOSSIBLE
DON'T WORRY GUYS, NOTHING IS IMPOSSIBLE

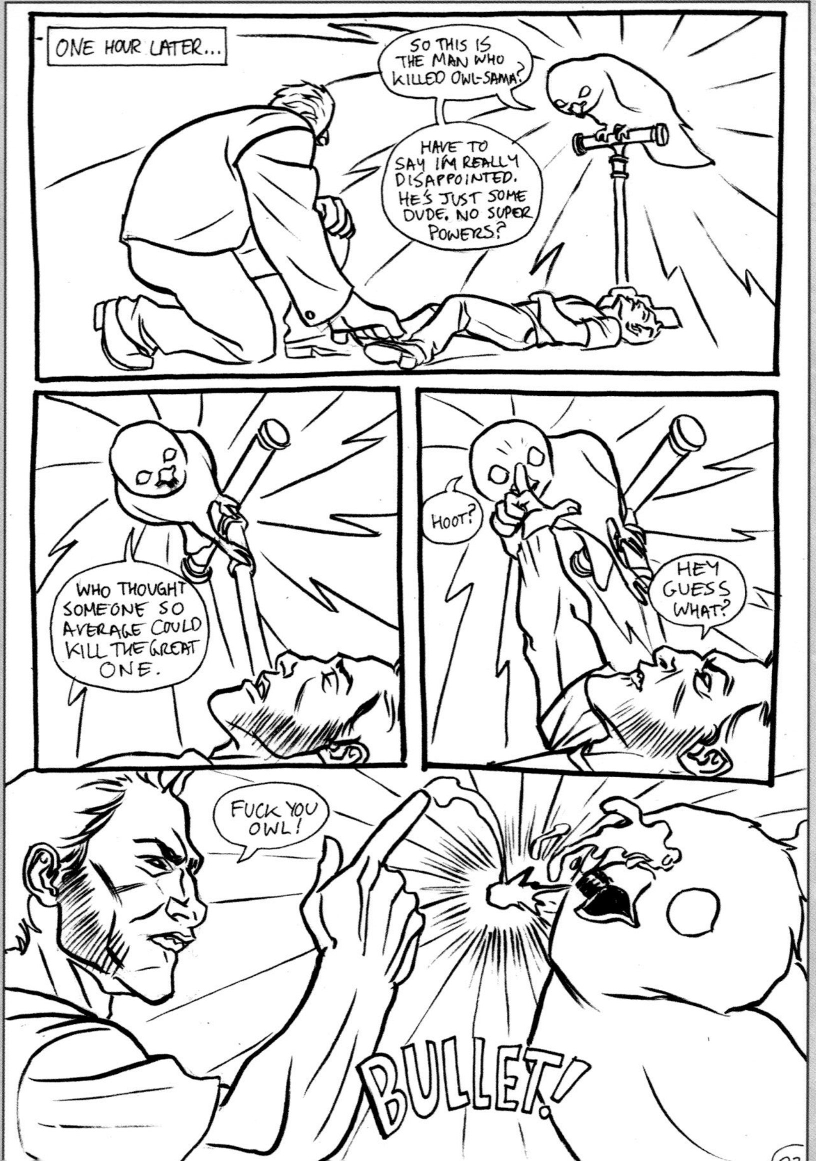
ONE HOUR LATER...
SO THIS IS THE MAN WHO KILLED OWL-SAMA?
HAVE TO SAY I'M REALLY DISAPPOINTED. HE'S JUST SOME DUDE. NO SUPER POWERS?
WHO THOUGHT SOMEONE SO AVERAGE COULD KILL THE GREAT ONE.
HOOT?
HEY GUESS WHAT?
FUCK YOU OWL!
BULLET!

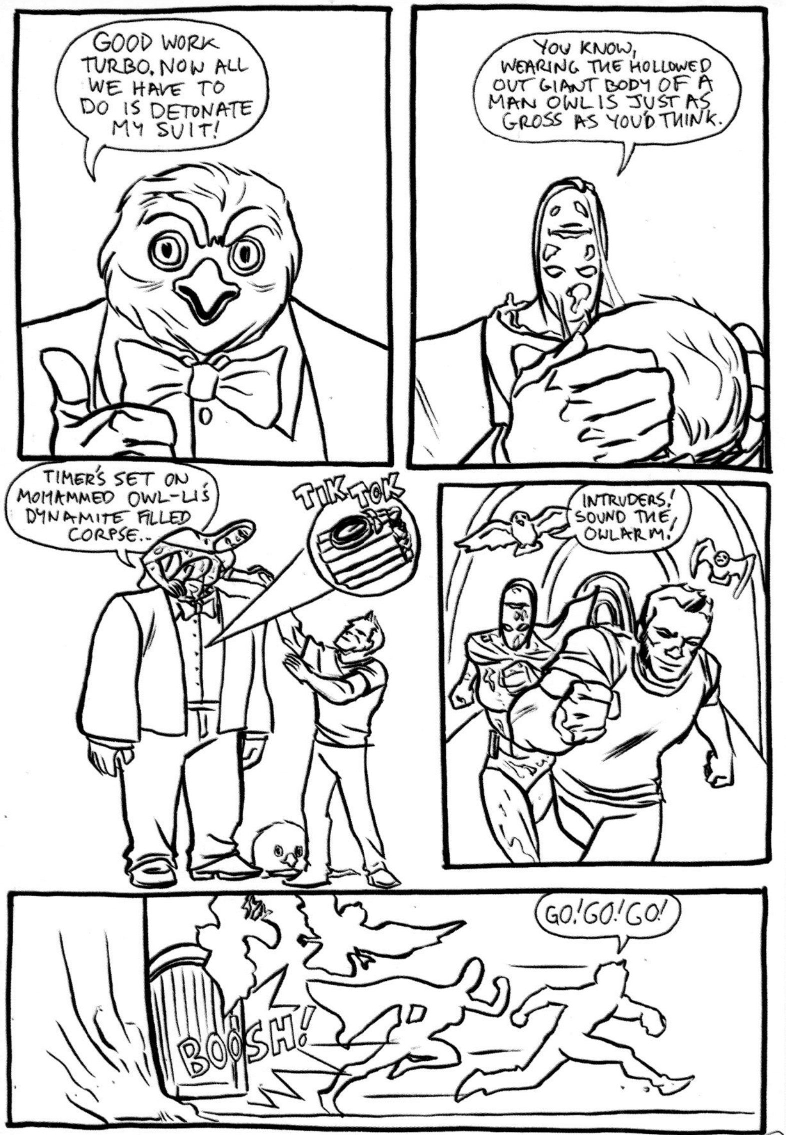
GOOD WORK TURBO. NOW ALL WE HAVE TO DO IS DETONATE MY SUIT!
YOU KNOW, WEARING THE HOLLOWED OUT GIANT BODY OF A MAN OWL IS JUST AS GROSS AS YOU'D THINK.
TIMER'S SET ON MOHAMMED OWL-LI'S DYNAMITE FILLED CORPSE..
TIK TOK
INTRUDERS! SOUND THE OWLARM!
GO! GO! GO!
BOOSH!
23

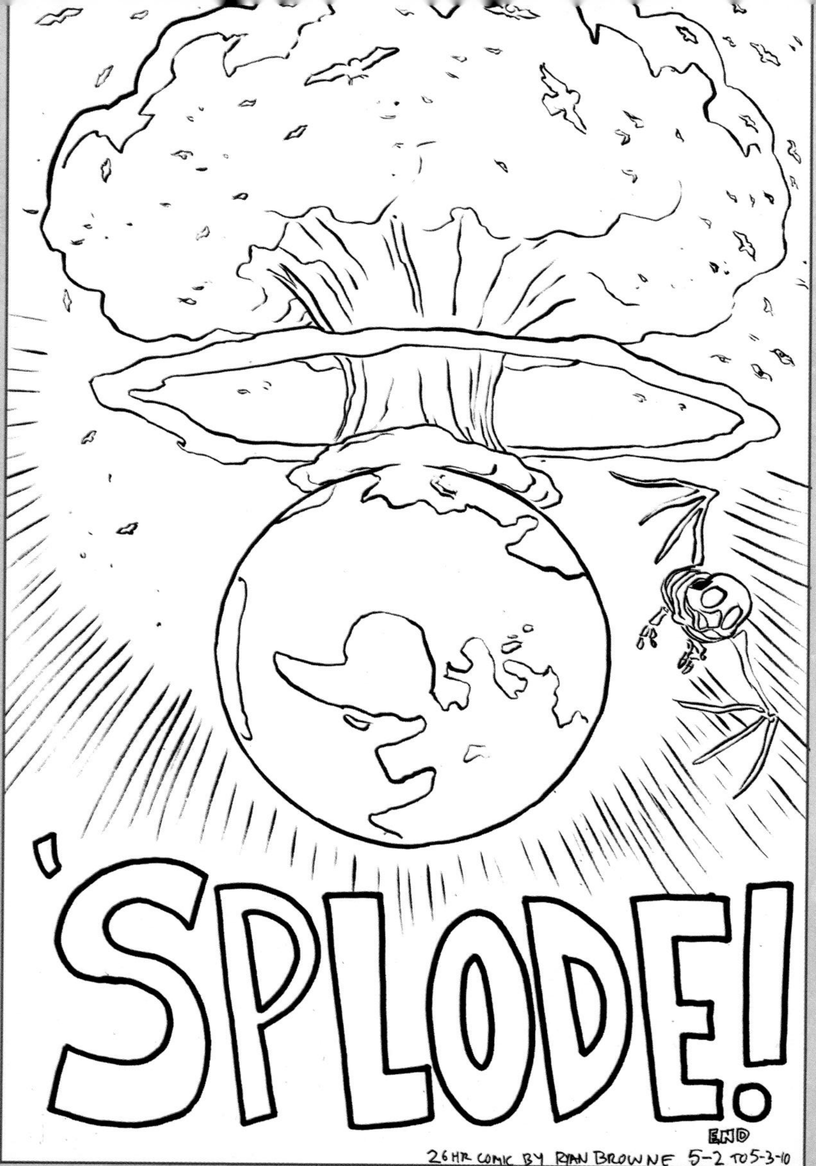
'SPLODE!
END
26HR COMIC BY RYAN BROWNE 5-2 TO 5-3-10

THE GOD HATES ASTRONAUTS REFERENCE GUIDE

Believe it or not, God Hates Astronauts is crammed with shockingly stupid references that are largely for my own personal enjoyment. Here is a handy guide to a few of the references to RoboCop, Die Hard and other crap.

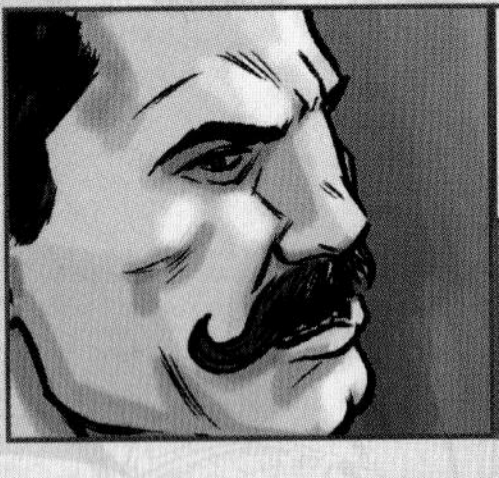

JOHN L. SULLIVAN. The use of John L. Sullivan was inspired entirely by a viewing of Ken Burns' documentary about Jack Johnson entitled "Unforgivable Blackness."

THE HEAD THAT WOULDN'T DIE is a reference to the film "The Thing That Wouldn't Die" which lists this as the incorrect title at the top of the end credits.

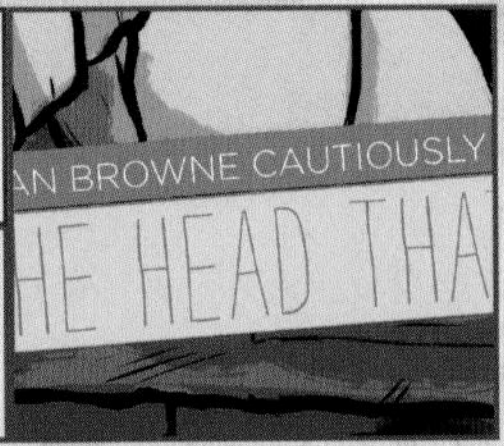
AN BROWNE CAUTIOUSLY
HE HEAD THA

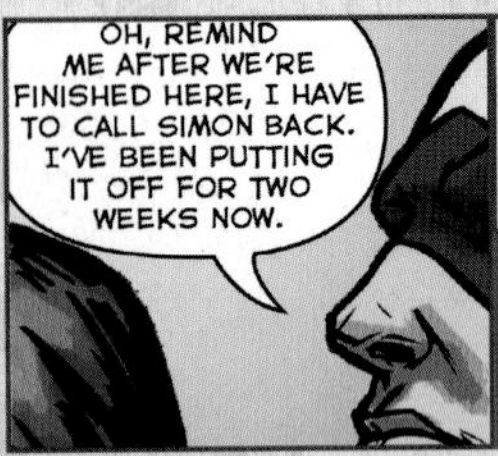
OH, REMIND ME AFTER WE'RE FINISHED HERE, I HAVE TO CALL SIMON BACK. I'VE BEEN PUTTING IT OFF FOR TWO WEEKS NOW.

SIMON is the name of my cat who appears as the cat lawyer in issue three. Originally this character was going to be private investigator.

STAR FIGHTER is inspired by John C. Reilly's character in "Boogie Nights." His original name was "Star Lord" but needed to change for copyright reasons.

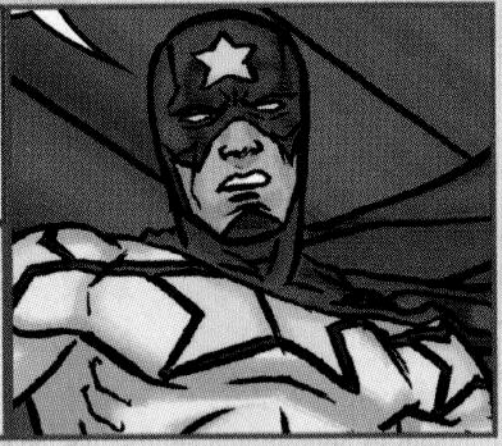

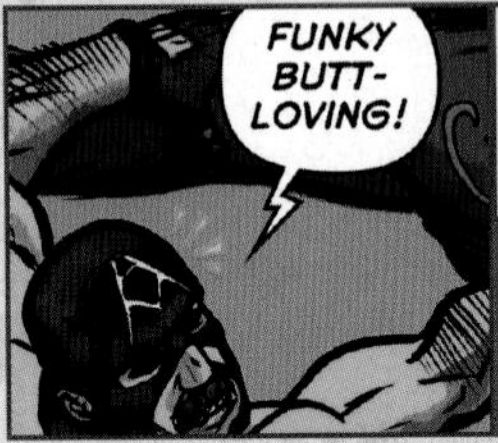
FUNKY BUTT-LOVING!

FUNKY BUTT-LOVING is a quote from the immortal classic "Rookie of the Year." Possibly the most graphic thing ever said in a children's film.

HE CAN FIX ANYTHING is RoboCop reference number one. It refers to Murphy telling Lewis that OCP will be able to repair her wounds at the end of the film.

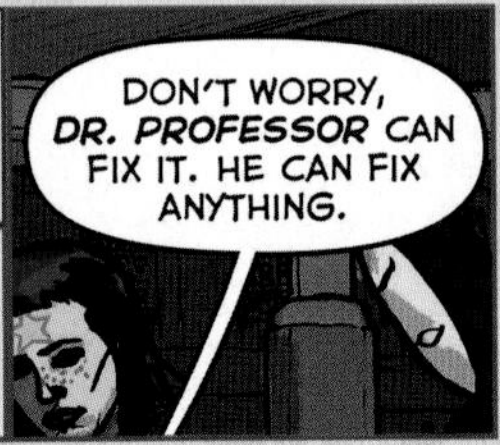
DON'T WORRY, DR. PROFESSOR CAN FIX IT. HE CAN FIX ANYTHING.

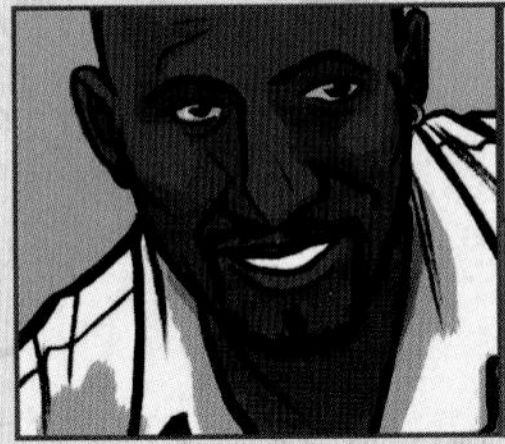

MONTEL WILLIUMS is a reference to my own appearance as a guest on "The Montel Williams Show" in the episode entitled "Terror Caught On Tape." True story.

ASTRONAUT FARMERS were intended as a one-off joke which I think is sadly obvious. The astronaut stuff comes from my love of The Upright Citizens Brigade.

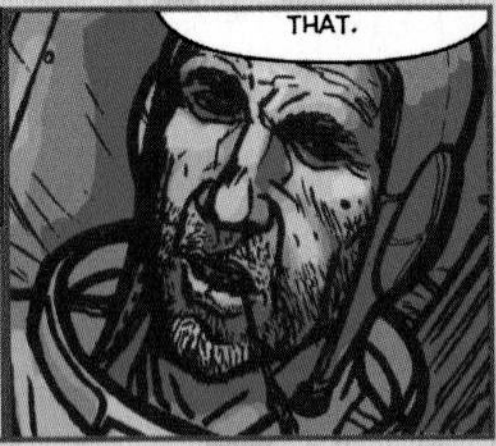
THAT.

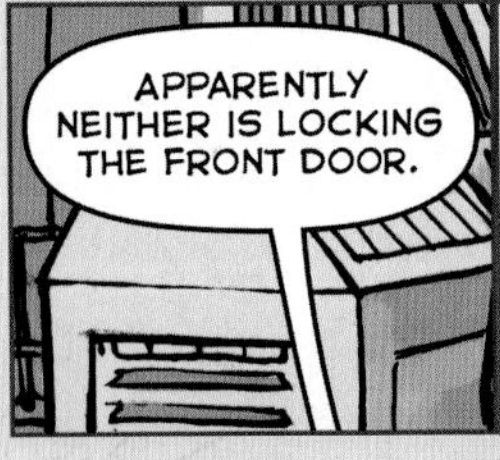
APPARENTLY NEITHER IS LOCKING THE FRONT DOOR.

NEVER LOCKING THE FRONT DOOR is a reference to Nick Frost's character "Ed" in "Shaun of the Dead" that never locks the front door.

THE NUDE FIGHT has censored naughty bits at a recommendation from Mike Costa who saw something similar in the comic "Trencher." I originally drew them nude.

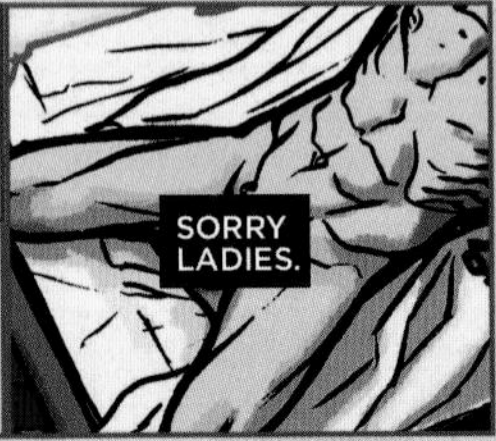
SORRY LADIES.

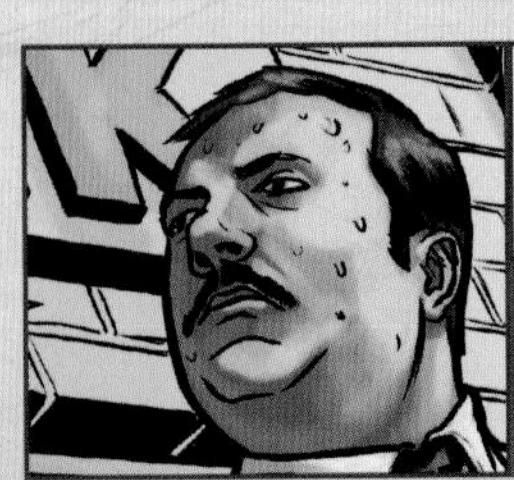

PAUL BLORT, BANK COP. Have you seen "Paul Blart: Mall Cop"? It's so confusingly unfunny and depressing. One of my favorite horrible films of all time.

OWL CAPONE enters the bank with a direct quote from "Pulp Fiction." I have so many more owl puns to use including "Sgt. Owl Powell" from Die Hard. One day...

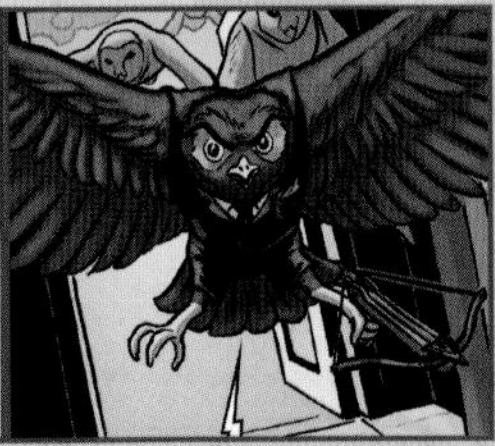

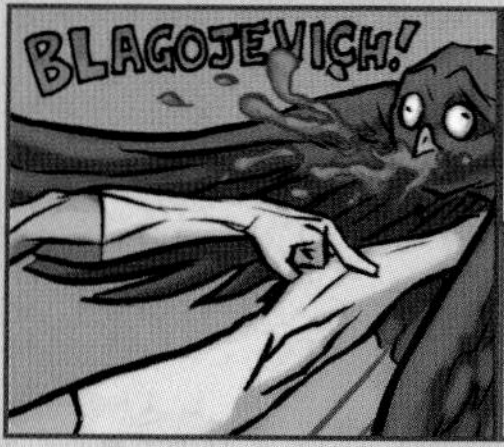
BLAGOJEVICH!

BLAGOJEVICH is the only reference I'll ever make to politics in my work and it's already horribly dated at the time of publication. Whoops?

DIE, OWL, DIE is a classic "The Simpsons" reference from the Sideshow Bob episode, "Cape Feare."

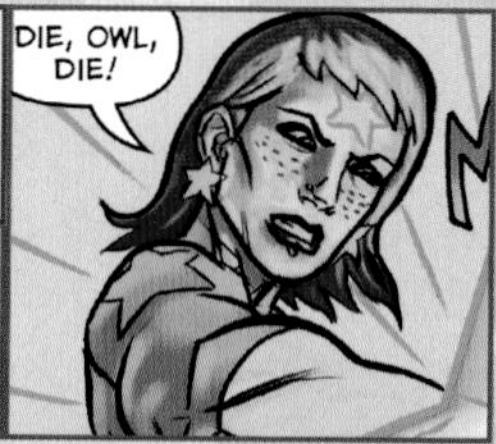
DIE, OWL, DIE!

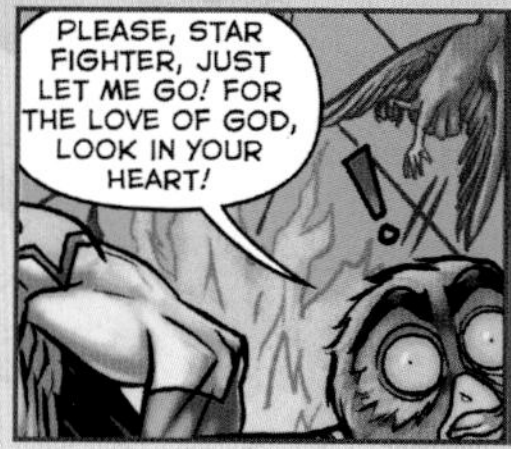
PLEASE, STAR FIGHTER, JUST LET ME GO! FOR THE LOVE OF GOD, LOOK IN YOUR HEART!

LOOK IN YOUR HEART is a reference to one of my all time favorite films, "Miller's Crossing."

BORN AGAIN is a reference to "Daredevil: Born Again" by Frank Miller and David Mazzucchelli where a broken Matt Murdock is sleeping in an alley to start an issue.

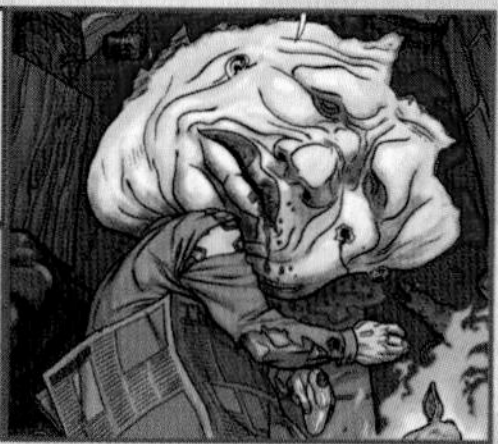

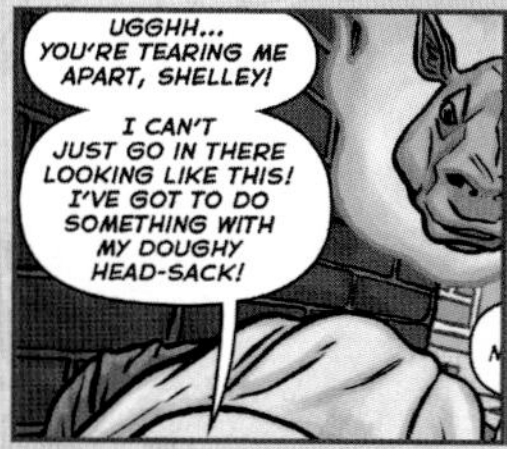
UGGHH... YOU'RE TEARING ME APART, SHELLEY!
I CAN'T JUST GO IN THERE LOOKING LIKE THIS! I'VE GOT TO DO SOMETHING WITH MY DOUGHY HEAD-SACK!

YOU'RE TEARING ME APART is a reference to the film, "The Room" which I consider to be the all-time best bad film ever made.

STAR FIGHTER QUITS is a reference to the "Spider-Man Quits" panel from "The Amazing Spider-Man" #50.

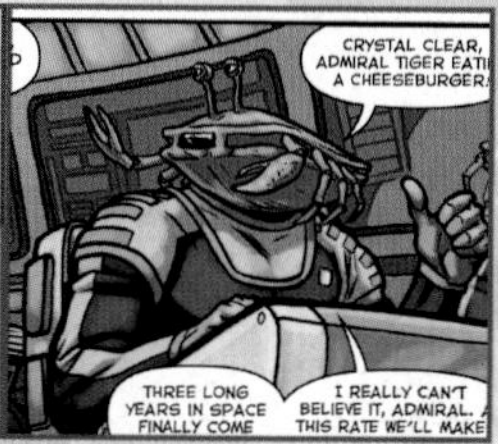
CRYSTAL CLEAR, ADMIRAL TIGER EATI A CHEESEBURGER!
THREE LONG YEARS IN SPACE FINALLY COME
I REALLY CAN'T BELIEVE IT, ADMIRAL. THIS RATE WE'LL MAKE

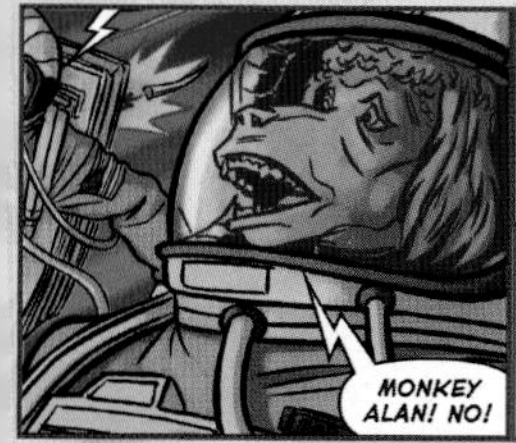
MONKEY ALAN! NO!

MONKEY ALLEN is a character referenced in the British version of "The Office" but never seen on screen. I assume that "Monkey Allen" must be an astronaut monkey.

FAMILY MATTERS references are common in my work, but really the love is for Reginald VelJohnson. He manages to appear in almost everything I create.

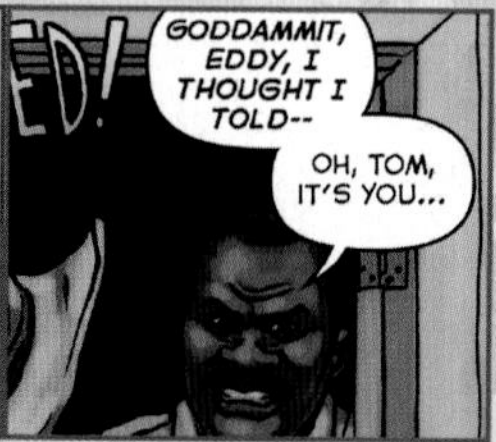
GODDAMMIT, EDDY, I THOUGHT I TOLD--
OH, TOM, IT'S YOU...

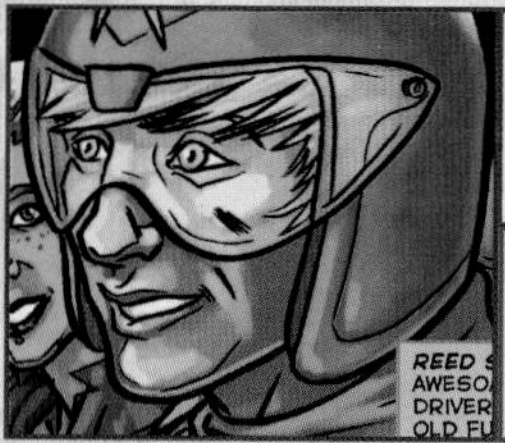

REED SPACER is probably the stupidest joke in the entire book. Originally he was supposed to die in the coming battle, but I just ran out of room in the issue.

THE IMPOSSIBLE'S FACE is a really dumb obvious reference from "The Empire Strikes Back." but part of me loves how over the top and nonsensical it is.

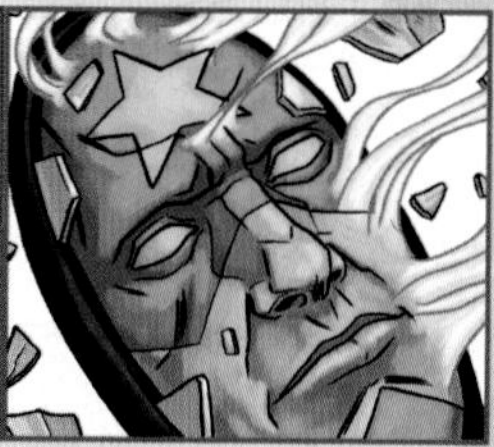

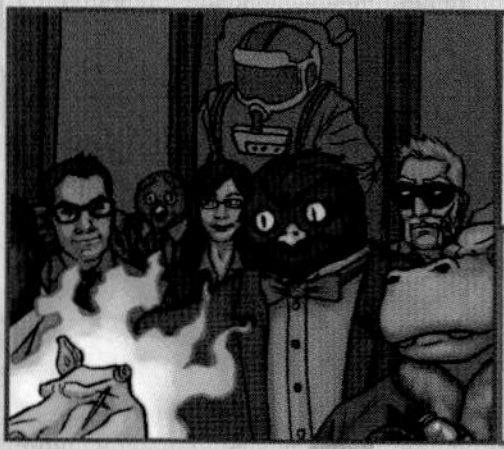

COURTROOM CAMEOS include Mohammed Owli, Owlvin, Montel Williums, The Shootist, Blast Furnace, the owners of Challengers Comics, Chris Burnham, my wife Carrie and I.

DEATH BLOW is a reference to the fantastic fake movie titles they use in "Seinfeld."

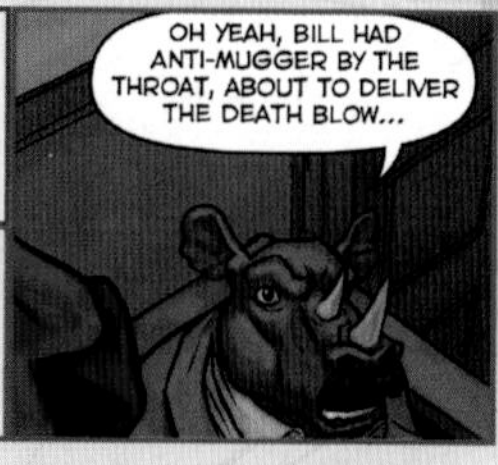
OH YEAH, BILL HAD ANTI-MUGGER BY THE THROAT, ABOUT TO DELIVER THE DEATH BLOW...

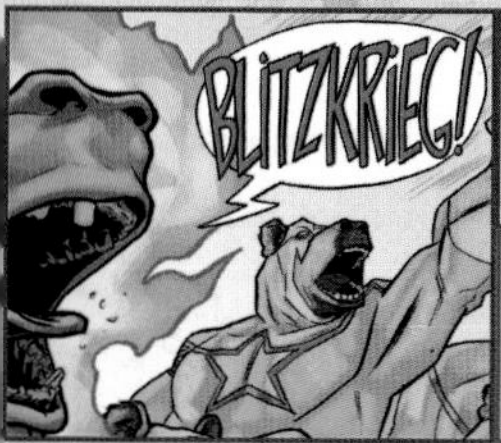
BLITZKRIEG!

THE THIRD AND FINAL BLITZKRIEG is a continuing call back reference to the first issue and is a nice role reversal because this time our hero plays the aggressor.

COSMIC ZAP is a reference to the greatest board game of all time, "Cosmic Encounters."

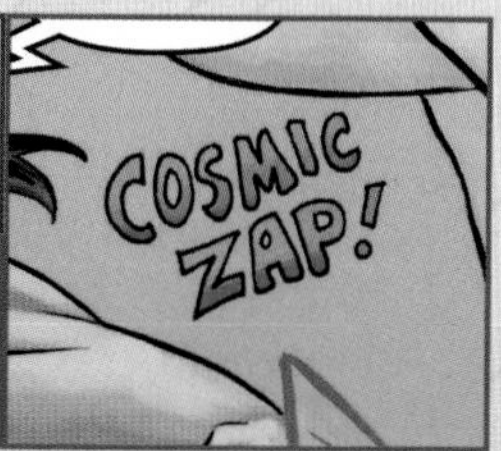
COSMIC ZAP!

PURPLE...

MONKEY...

DISH-WASHER...

PURPLE MONKEY DISHWASHER is another quote from "The Simpsons"—a show that is about 90 percent responsible for my sense of humor.

THE DEATH OF CRAZY TRAIN composition is a direct reference to the cover of the first issue of Miller and Mazzucchelli's "Batman: Year One" story arc.

TO BEAR ARMS!

YOUR MOTHER!

THE RIGHT TO BEAR ARMS JOKE isn't a particular reference to anything, it was just a dumb joke that I thought of while making the first issue and I sat on it for four years.

"YOUR MOTHER" is a reference to an insult shouted by Egon in the first "Ghostbusters" film—which, by the way, features a command performance from Reginald VelJohnson.

YOU'RE FIRED!

VALUE EAL?

FRENCH FRIED POTATERS.

THE

THE "YOU'RE FIRED" SCENE is a page long reference to the ending of RoboCop. Will we ever really know what happened to end the skirmish at HQ? I sure don't.

FRENCH FRIED POTATERS is a not so subtle reference to the film "Sling Blade." Billy Bob later became a Hollywood legend with his performance in "The Astronaut Farmer."

SIMON THE CAT LAWYER WITH A JET PACK is actually my cat Simon. And yes, my cat does actually have a jet pack and regularly practices law. Thanks for asking.

THE BEDROOM RETURNS in a truly horrific sex scene! I almost couldn't bring myself to draw this scene though it is fun to see how my art changed over five years.

MAYBE W SEE A C OR THER SOME

"BLAST FURNACE: RECREATIONAL THIEF" (my other graphic novel) is sitting on the nightstand in the bedroom flashback.

SUPER SULLIVAN is a reference to "Super Shredder" in "TMNT 2: Secret of the Ooze." NINJA RAP!!!

GIVE ME BACK MY WIFE!!!

"GIVE ME BACK MY WIFE!!!" is a reference to the trailer for the Ron Howard film "Ransom" which featured Mel Gibson screaming "Give me back my son!" at full intensity.

GNARLED WINSLOW'S SHOT HEARD ROUND THE WORLD finds a certain similarity to the amazing shot that saved the life of John McClane at the end of Die Hard.

Well I think that covers most of the big ones. There are a ton of little references here and there, but I will leave those as secrets only to be shared as a bargaining chip if my life is ever on the line. You never know... INFORMATION IS POWER!!!!

THE STORY OF GOD HATES ASTRONAUTS

So that was God Hates Astronauts... so far. There are a lot of factors that will go into my decision to continue the story, none of which are a lack of interest. For now we will call it done, and my six-year journey with writing, drawing, publishing and marketing my own comic is complete.

Over the duration of the book, I was frequently asked, "What is God Hates Astronauts all about?" I have always struggled to come up with a single quick "elevator pitch" to encapsulate what this book is actually trying to accomplish. In all honesty, I think God Hates Astronauts is about letting myself make a comic book that I would love to read. Something that's reckless, bizarre, offensive, referential, silly and colorful. One day I will be exposed as being a one-trick pony—funny sound effects surrounding extreme violence and a bunch of swearing—but for now I think it's working for me.

Six years ago I sat down with a friend to create an improvised 24-hour comic. We both produced our own 24 pages of story in 24 consecutive hours. My 24-hour comic (which I have included in this collection) became the rough draft for what would be GHA. Five months later, after many story tweaks and alterations, I had my first issue written, drawn, colored and lettered. It represented the first finished comic product of my career. I had previously drawn two issues of the ill-fated comic "Amazing Adventures of Science Fact"—a GHA-esque book that featured very little adventure and almost no scientific fact. My fear of actually constructing a story entirely by myself led me to bring in writer Mike Costa to script the book that I was drawing. In the end, the inability to get the book picked up by a publisher resulted in two unfinished issues. One day the book might reach the light of day, but for now it will stand as a GHA prequel that never was.

The first printing of God Hates Astronauts was 50 copies, only half colored and released under the pen name of "Michigan Browne" for some reason. It featured a bizarre cover with a bunch of lasers and Star Fighter's huge gross face. It was produced entirely to give out to publishers and I'm almost certain that none of the copies still exist. The second printing of GHA was 75 fully colored copies and featured a new blue cover with the Power Persons Five standing triumphantly. A few of these still exist here and there but they are pretty rare. This edition was met by the same disinterest and non-replies from publishers as the first edition. After two fruitless printings and a handful of wasted dollars, the book became effectively dead.

This is the reason for the quality jump in the art between the first two issues. After I quit the book, I went on to do many different things, working as an illustrator, a designer, a penciler for Devil's Due Publishing and artist on a canceled project from Archaia.

About three years after making GHA number one, I met artist Darick Robertson at a con and gave him a copy of the book. His response to the book was extremely positive and he urged me to continue the book. With his help I decided to try again with a third printing of God Hates Astronauts. Three years after the initial release, GHA got an upgrade to the digitally painted cover that is featured in this collection and sported a supremely awesome pull quote from Darick. I also started working on GHA issue two and produced the second 24-hour comic within this collection. Now, with a little bit of self-confidence, I once again began to regularly attend comic shows and forced the book into the hands of creators. Two of those creators were Chris Burnham and Zander Cannon.

Chris really pushed me to get this book out to the world and Zander exposed me to the idea of GHA becoming a web-comic. I enlisted a friend to help me build a web-comic site and took to social media to get the word out to the masses. With gentle nudging from Burnham, the online fan base started to grow. However as I was creating and posting the second issue the frustrations of creating a comic book in my spare time became too much. I decided to put the book on hiatus again and for ten months I worked on paying comic jobs such as *"Smoke and Mirrors"* for IDW.

To keep some of my web-comic fan base happy (and as a seriously crazy experiment) I decided to produce a daily web-comic. Thus the black and white comic *"Blast Furnace: Recreational Thief"* was produced a page a day, five days a week for six months. While it proved to be a satisfying and fun experiment, it wasn't a financial success. The small print run of mini-comics didn't sell and the book failed to attract the following of GHA. In an effort to get more exposure for the finished book, I ran a Kickstarter campaign to fund the printing of the collected edition. It was a shocking success to say the least and taught me the power of crowd sourced funding. At this date, the fate of *"Blast Furnace Volume Two: The Search For More Money"* remains undecided.

After completing *"Smoke and Mirrors"* and *"Blast Furnace,"* I once again set my sights on GHA and completed issue three. Finally, six years after it started, the story of Star Fighter and Starrior was finally finished. Now using the friends and fans that I have made over the six year journey of GHA, I made this book. It features basically everything worth showing and I feel it is the best thing I have ever made. I wish that 25-year-old Ryan could somehow see where the goofy 24-hour comic has ended up, but maybe that would just ruin the surprise of it all.

Then came the Kickstarter campaign... and the world voted with their wallets! After all the years of stuggling to find an audience for the book I finally was able to find a community where GHA could be at home. With the Kickstarter campaign, I funded the hardcover version of the edition you now hold in your hands. The visibility and success of the campaign convinced Image to take a chance on this stupid old book of mine and I hope they never look back!

Thanks to everyone for all the continued support over the years. I don't know what will happen next, but I sure hope to see you at some point in the future for *"God Hates Astronauts Volume Two: A Star is Born!"*

RYAN "MICHIGAN" BROWNE
FEBRUARY 11 / AUGUST 26, 2013 CHICAGO, ILLINOIS

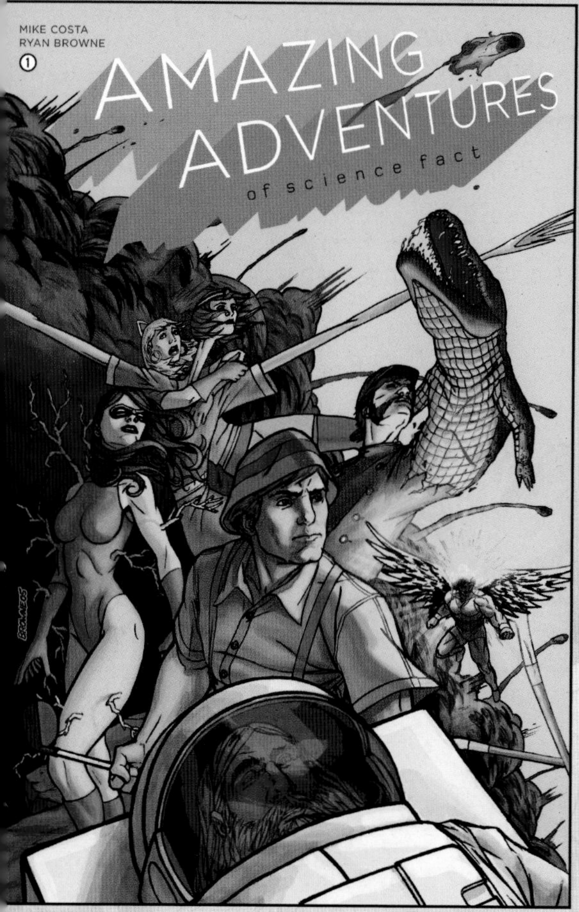
MIKE COSTA
RYAN BROWNE
1
AMAZING ADVENTURES
of science fact

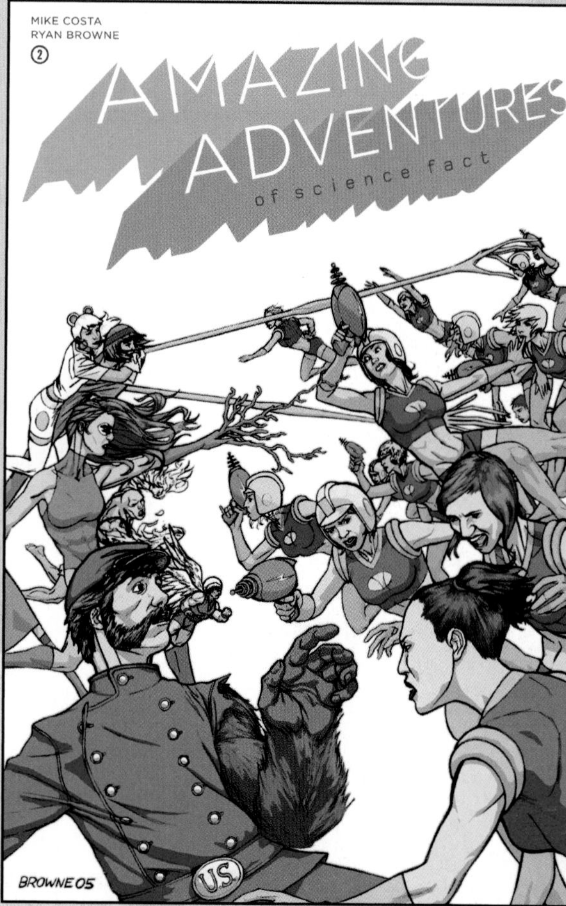
MIKE COSTA
RYAN BROWNE
2
AMAZING ADVENTURES
of science fact
U.S.
BROWNE 05

COVERS FROM "AMAZING ADVENTURES OF SCIENCE FACT"

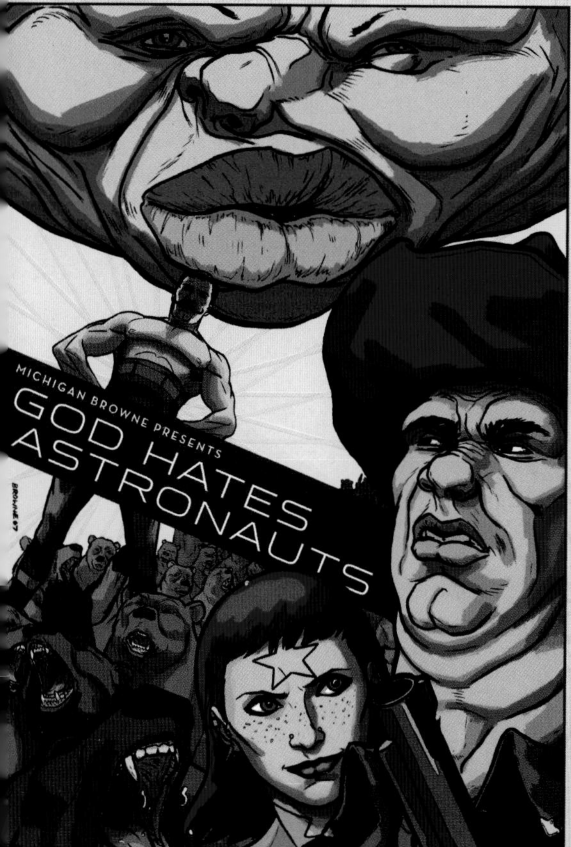
MICHIGAN BROWNE PRESENTS
GOD HATES ASTRONAUTS
ISSUE ONE

FIRST PRINTING COVER

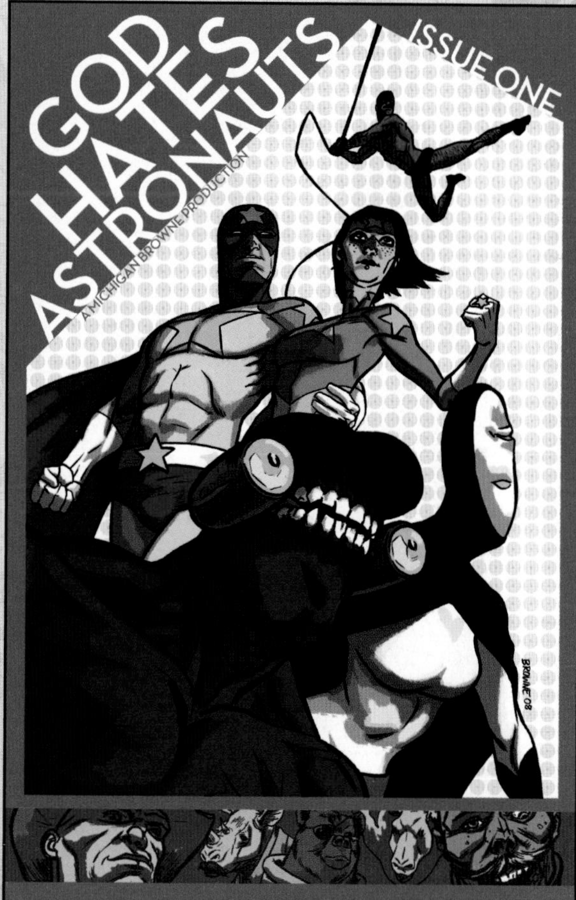
GOD HATES ASTRONAUTS
ISSUE ONE
A MICHIGAN BROWNE PRODUCTION
BROWNE 08

SECOND PRINTING COVER

I DREW THIS SOMETIME AFTER COMPLETING ISSUE ONE. I DON'T REMEMBER IF THIS WAS SUPPOSED TO HAVE ANYTHING TO DO WITH WHAT WOULD HAPPEN IN ISSUE TWO, BUT I THOUGHT COLORING IT NOW WOULD BE A NICE END CAP.

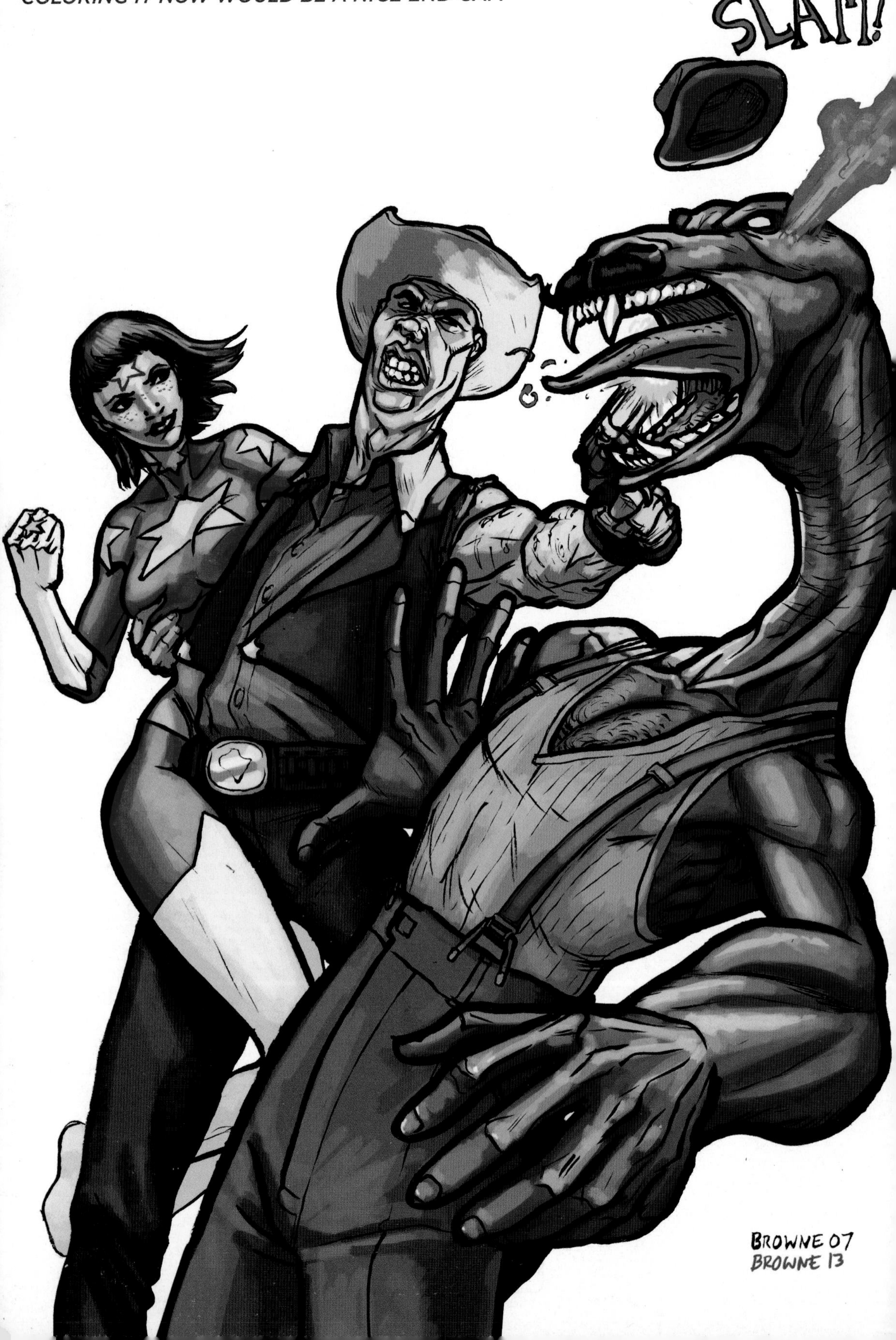
SLAM!
BROWNE 07
BROWNE 13